Genocide and Retribution

Holocaust Studies Series

Randolph L. Braham, Editor
The Institute for Holocaust Studies
The Graduate School and University Center
The City University of New York

Previously published books in the Series:
  Perspectives on the Holocaust, 1982
  Contemporary Views on the Holocaust, 1983

The Holocaust Studies Series is published in cooperation with the Institute for Holocaust Studies. These books are outgrowths of lectures, conferences, and research projects sponsored by the Institute. It is the purpose of the series to subject the events and circumstances of the Holocaust to scrutiny by a variety of academics who bring different scholarly disciplines to the study.

Genocide and Retribution:

The Holocaust in Hungarian-Ruled Northern Transylvania

Randolph L. Braham

Kluwer•Nijhoff Publishing
a member of the Kluwer Academic Publishers Group
Boston-The Hague-Dordrecht-Lancaster

Distributors for North America:
Kluwer Boston, Inc.
190 Old Derby Street
Hingham, MA 02043, U.S.A.

Distributors Outside North America:
Kluwer Academic Publishers Group
Distribution Centre
P. O. Box 322
3300AH Dordrecht, The Netherlands

Library of Congress Cataloging in Publication Data
Main entry under title:

Genocide and retribution.

  (Holocaust studies series)
  Bibliography: p.
  Includes index.
  1. Jews—Romania—Transylvania—Persecutions.
2. Holocaust, Jewish (1939–1945)—Romania—Transylvania.
3. War crimes trials—Romania. 4. Transylvania (Romania)
—Ethnic relations. I. Braham, Randolph L. II. Series.
DS135.R72T74 1983   940.53′15′0392404984   83-6104
ISBN 0-89838-146-0

Copyright © 1983 by Kluwer•Nijhoff Publishing

No part of this book may be reproduced in any form by print,
photoprint, microfilm, or any other means without written
permission of the publisher.

Printed in the United States of America

To the memory of

MARTIN and ROZÁLIA MEISTER
and
FÁBIÁN and ESZTER WEISS
the parents of
Sam and Olga Meister of Toronto, Canada,

FERENC and AURÉLIA ORDENTLICH
and
SÁMUEL and HELÉN ADLER
the parents of
Ted and Hedy Orden of Beverly Hills, California,

JÓZSEF and TERÉZIA ZÉLIG
and
IGNÁC and FÁNI SALAMON
the parents of
Ernest and Elizabeth Zelig of Manhasset, New York

Contents

Preface ix

I
Introductory Essay 1
The Jews of Transylvania: A Historical Overview 3
The Post–World War I Era 5
Northern Transylvania under Hungarian Rule 10
The German Occupation and the Final Solution 16
The Ghettoization in Northern Transylvania: An Overview 42
Notes 43

II
Judgment of the People's Tribunal of Cluj (Kolozsvár); 31 May 1946, Judgment Number 8 53
The Nagyvárad Ghetto 79
The Ghetto of Szatmárnémeti 101
The Ghetto of Kolozsvár 123
The Ghettos in the Székely Land 141
The Ghetto of Marosvásárhely 143
The Ghetto of Szászrégen 150
The Ghetto of Sepsiszentgyörgy 155
The Ghetto of Máramarossziget 157
The Ghetto of Szilágysomlyó 162
The Ghetto of Dés 178
The Beszterce Ghetto 187
The Sentences 201
Notes 224

III
Appendixes 227
  1. Reference List of Selected Geographic Name Changes 229
  2. Number of Jews Deported from the Major Entrainment Centers in Northern Transylvania by Transport and Date of Entrainment; 233

3. Law No. 312 of the Romanian Ministry of Justice, dated 21 April 1945 — 234
4. Statement of László Endre of 17 December, 1945 — 241
5. Statement of László Baky of 18 December, 1945 — 246

Selected Bibliography — 250
Index — 252

Preface

During the dark years of the Holocaust, many of the millions of labor and concentration camp victims were sustained in their struggle for survival by the hope that their tormentors would not escape retribution. This expectation was reinforced by the warnings issued by the statesmen of the anti-Axis coalition and the declarations of the United States, Great Britain, and the USSR.

Shortly after the cessation of hostilities, war crimes trials were indeed initiated in all parts of liberated Europe. Many of the accused were indicted, among other things, for crimes committed against Jews. People's tribunals for the prosecution of war crimes and crimes against humanity were also established in Romania, a country that extricated itself from the Axis Alliance on 23 August 1944.

The Romanian people's tribunals were set up and operated under the provisions of Law No. 312, issued by the Ministry of Justice on 21 April 1945. One of these tribunals was established in Cluj (Kolozsvár) and entrusted primarily with the prosecution of those involved in the violation of the rights of people living in Northern Transylvania, the part of the province that was transferred to Hungary under the terms of the Second Vienna Award (August 1940) and which remained under Hungarian rule from early September 1940 until its liberation by Soviet-Romanian forces in the fall of 1944. The crimes committed against the citizens of Northern Transylvania both within and outside the province were the subject of two major trials. In the first of these, 63 individuals were accused of crimes against Romanians and certain Jews during the occupation of Northern Transylvania by Hungarian troops in September 1940. The destruction of the Jews of Northern Transylvania was the subject of the second mass trial, involving 185 individuals. Of these, only 51 were in custody; the others were tried in absentia. Among the 185 individuals tried for war crimes and crimes against humanity were the government, military, police, and gendarmerie officers and officials of the counties and cities that served as concentration and entrainment centers in Hungarian-ruled Northern Transylvania. The trial was held in the spring of 1946, Justice Nicolae Matei presiding.

The trial ended in late May 1946 when the People's Tribunal announced its Judgment. The sentences were harsh: Thirty of the accused were condemned to death; the others received prison terms totaling 1,204 years. However, all those condemned to death were among those tried in absentia, having fled with the withdrawing Nazi forces. The percentage of absentees was high among those who were condemned to life imprisonment. Among those under arrest, three were condemned to life imprisonment, six were freed after having been found innocent of the charges brought against them, and the remainder were sentenced to various types of imprisonment, ranging from three to 25 years. The harshest penalties were meted out to those who were especially cruel in the ghettos.

The survivors had no reason to rejoice, however. Aside from the frustrations encountered in their endeavor to reacquire the apartments and property the Nazi and the Hungarian quisling authorities had confiscated from them, they were also shocked to see many of their tormentors freed within a few years as "socially rehabilitated" individuals. As was the case in all the People's Democracies of Eastern Europe during the Stalinist era, in Romania too the regime found it necessary to adopt a new social policy that embraced some of those convicted in 1946. Under a decree adopted early in 1950, the inmates who "demonstrated good behavior, performed their tasks conscientiously, and proved that they became fit for social cohabitation during their imprisonment" were made eligible for immediate release irrespective of the severity of their original sentence.

The pursuit of new political and ideological objectives in the Soviet bloc, as elsewhere in postwar Europe, led to a reneging on wartime commitments relating to retribution. The partners in the anti-Axis coalition, eager to appease public opinion and to hasten political evolution in the areas under their control or influence, became in the course of time not only more reluctant to initiate legal proceedings against Nazis suspected of war crimes, but also progressively more lenient toward those already convicted. Clearly, expediency both East and West triumphed over morality and justice.

Regardless of how fully the convicted criminals paid for their crimes, to the Holocaust survivors of Northern Transylvania the Judgment of the People's Tribunal will forever remain an important record of the catastrophe that befell them and their loved ones during the Hungarian era and especially in 1944–45. The desire to preserve this record and make it available to the world at large led to the publication of this work. The Judgment is reproduced in full. In my translation I strove to reproduce the document as faithfully as possible, with only minor changes required for accuracy and consistency. These changes

PREFACE

apply to names of the defendants and to geographic names. Since many of the Hungarian names in the original text are either misspelled or in their Romanianized version, the defendants are identified in this work by their original names. The spelling used is that in the 3 June 1946 issue of *Igazság* (Truth), the Hungarian-language daily of Cluj that published the summary of the People's Tribunal's decision. The index to this volume records all the names by which a particular defendant is identified. Geographic names are rendered in their Hungarian version, reflecting the need for consistency and to assure the authenticity of the documents rather than national preference. Their Romanian equivalents are shown in Appendix 1, Reference List of Selected Geographic Name Changes.

The text of the Judgment is preceded by a historical overview of the Jews of Transylvania. In this essay I have emphasized the Holocaust period in the Hungarian-held parts of the province—the focus of the Judgment. Related topics such as the wartime history of the Jews in the Romanian-held southern part of Transylvania, the help received by Hungarian-Jewish refugees in Romania, the massacre at Sármás (September 1944), and the post–deportation fate of the Northern Transylvanian Jews have been adequately treated elsewhere.

This volume could not have been published without the generous support of several institutions. I am especially grateful for the grants received from the Memorial Foundation for Jewish Culture and the Research Foundation of The City University of New York, making possible the investigation of several archival holdings in Israel and Romania. The support of the Holocaust Survivors Memorial Foundation and of the Graduate School and University Center of The City University of New York has been invaluable. I want to acknowledge especially the encouragement and support offered by President Harold M. Proshansky, Provost Stanley Waren, and Dean Solomon Goldstein. I am also thankful for the wholehearted cooperation of "Asociaţia România" of Bucharest for making the Judgment and many other related documents available. I particularly want to express my gratitude to Dr. Virgil Cândea, Radu Bănică and Gheorghe Oancea for their courtesy and understanding.

The principal financial support for the publication of this volume was provided by survivors from Northern Transylvania in memory of their parents who perished in the Holocaust. Their generosity is recognized on a special memorial page. I am happy to acknowledge the professional advice and editorial assistance received from Philip D. Jones and Bernadine Richey of Kluwer •Nijhoff Publishing. Thanks are also due to my wife Elizabeth and my sons Steven and Robert for their consistent support and for sharing many of the burdens entailed by the preparation of this volume.

Randolph L. Braham
January 1983

I INTRODUCTORY ESSAY

The Jews of Transylvania: A Historical Overview

The origins of the Jews of Transylvania,[1] currently a province of Romania, are mired in historical controversy. Some historians and archeologists, without providing any acceptable evidence, trace their earliest settlements to the first and second centuries A.D., when the territory was part of Roman Dacia. The earliest recorded Jewish settlements were established during the 1571–1687 period, when the province and some of its bordering territories constituted an independent principality ruled almost continuously by Hungarian-Transylvanian princes. The earliest Jews, following the trade routes to the north of the province, reportedly arrived from the Balkan territories, which were then part of the Ottoman Empire. The first organized Jewish community, composed primarily of Turkish Sephardi Jews, was established in Gyulafehérvár, the seat of the prince. The Jews' legal residence was restricted to this town only. However, they managed in the course of time to settle in the neighboring communities as well, and their ranks were soon swelled by Ashkenazi Jews who came from the adjacent territories north and west of the province.

The fortunes of the small Jewish community varied with the attitude of the particular princes. They fared quite well under Gábor Bethlen, the Protestant prince who was relatively tolerant toward all religions. It was during his rule

(1613–1629) that the Jews obtained a letter of protection (1623) under which they acquired considerable rights.[2] Under his predecessors, however, the lot of the Jews was quite insecure, for the General Assemblies of the Classes were eager to restrict their number. A decision to this effect was in fact passed in 1578.

The status of the Jews changed considerably after the defeat of the Turkish forces near Vienna in the early 1680s, when after a valiant but futile attempt to establish an independent Transylvania, the province came under Austrian rule. The Jews thereafter began to settle on the estates of noblemen, who were not bound by the residence restrictions. They were, however, still prohibited from settling in the towns. Although this prohibition was theoretically eliminated during the revolution of 1848–49, in practice it remained in effect, with a few exceptions, in most towns until late in the second half of the nineteenth century.

The Jewish population of the province increased gradually, from an estimated 2,000 in 1766 to 5,175 in 1825 and 15,600 in 1850. Between 1754 and 1879, the Jews of Transylvania were organizationally under the jurisdiction of a chief rabbi seated in Gyulafehérvár. An attempt to establish a more democratic, unified communal organization was made in 1866, when representatives of the various Jewish communities met in Kolozsvár. This plan came to naught, however, because shortly thereafter, under the terms of the *Ausgleich* (Settlement) establishing the Austro-Hungarian Empire, Transylvania was attached to the Hungarian Kingdom.[3]

With the establishment of greater Hungary, the fate of Transylvanian Jewry became, to a large extent, intertwined with that of Hungarian Jewry as a whole. During the so-called "Golden Era" in the history of the Jews of Hungary,[4] a period extending from their emancipation in 1867 to World War I, the Transylvanian Jews eagerly embraced the Magyar cause. Like their brethren in other parts of the kingdom, they adopted the Hungarian language and culture with a "spontaneous eagerness" that was obviously not always appreciated by the other cohabiting minorities. They played a singularly important role in the Magyarization of the province, grateful for the economic and professional opportunities and for the protection they received after the emancipation. They were in the forefront of the modernization process, playing a leading role in the commercial and industrial progress of the region. They also played a dominant role in the professions and in the arts and letters. A great proportion of the Jews, however, remained quite poor, hardly able to eke out a living as unskilled laborers, artisans, small shop- and innkeepers, and traders and peddlers. This was especially the case in the northwestern parts of the province, which were inhabited by a large number of pious, Yiddish-speaking Orthodox Jews who resisted the pressures of modernization.

Partially because of the general prosperity enjoyed during this period, the Jewish population in the region increased significantly. While in 1880 the number of Jews was still only about 30,000, by 1900 their number increased to over 53,000 and by 1910 to almost 65,000. Organizationally, the Transylvanian Jews reflected the schism that affected Hungarian Jewry as a whole. Because of the failure of the 1868–69 congress,[5] the Jewish communities could not achieve unity. As elsewhere in the country, the communities were organized along the lines determined by their particular spiritual and lay leaders. The overwhelming majority of communities organized themselves along Orthodox lines, remaining predominantly under the guidance and leadership of their rabbis. A smaller number, especially in the larger and more enlightened cities, established themselves as Neolog, i.e., modern-conservative congregations. Still others identified themselves as Status Quo Ante congregations.

The "Golden Era" came to an end with the defeat of the Central Powers in 1918. The Hungarian Kingdom disintegrated, and the *Interessengemeinschaft* (commonality of interests) between the Magyars and the Jews all but evaporated. The era of progress and tranquillity was followed by a period of revolutions, first by the Left, then by the Right. The latter was accompanied by a "White Terror" that claimed many Jews as its victims.

The Post–World War I Era

The Political and Socioeconomic Status of Transylvanian Jewry

Following the end of World War I, Transylvania was acquired by Romania. The enlarged province, including the areas identified by the Romanians as Crişana and the Banat, contained a Jewish population of over 181,000 (1920) —close to 3.6 percent of the total population. During the interwar period, the Transylvanian Jews were organized into 110 congregations—80 Orthodox, 23 Neolog, and the remainder Status Quo Ante.

The Jews of Transylvania experienced no fundamental change in their socioeconomic status as a result of the political-territorial changes that affected the region after 1918. The historical and cultural heritage binding the Transylvanian Jews to Hungary and the socioeconomic and political realities that bound them to Romania were the source of many conflicts during the interwar period. To a considerable extent the Jews of Transylvania were victims of the milieu in which they lived. The Romanians resented them because of their proclivity to Hungarian culture and, by implication, to Hungarian revisionism and irredentism; the Hungarians, and especially the Right radicals, accused them of being "renegades" in the service of the Left.

The socioeconomic structure of Transylvanian Jewry was similar to that of the Jews in the neighboring provinces. Many were engaged in business or trade, and their percentage in the free professions and white-collar fields outside of government was relatively high. Only a handful of Jews were associated with mining and heavy industry and even fewer with the military. While no data on income distribution are available, the many studies on Transylvania reveal that a considerable proportion of Jews could barely eke out a living; many depended for their survival on the generosity of their relatives or the community.

The political posture of the Jews of Transylvania was rather passive. During the interwar period, the Jews of the region were considerably less active in the major parties of Romania than their brethren of Wallachia and Moldavia. The political culture of the Transylvanian Jews was forged by their earlier experiences in the Hungarian Kingdom. The Romanian parties, in turn, exerted practically no effort to solicit the support of the Transylvanian Jewish vote. The politically active elements of the Jewish intelligentsia and middle classes tended to support either the Jewish party *(Partidul Evreesc)* or the Hungarian Party *(Magyar Párt)*. The Zionist movement was relatively strong, with the Jewish national political consciousness having been fostered by the activities of the Transylvanian Jewish National League *(Erdélyi Zsidó Nemzeti Szövetség)*. Established in November 1918 as a result of the dedicated though not always harmonious efforts of the existing Zionist organizations, the league operated on guidelines clearly based on Zionist principles. A number of politically active leaders of Transylvanian Jewry, including Tivadar Fischer, József Fischer, and Ernő Marton, were elected during the 1930s to serve in the Romanian Parliament.[6]

In the wake of the many anti-Semitic excesses during the Goga-Cuza era (1937–38) and the general upswing of the Romanian brand of fascism spearheaded by the Iron Guard *(Garda de Fier),* a number of Jews came to the conclusion that the class-based program of the Marxists offered a swifter and more realistic solution to the problem of anti-Semitism than what they perceived to be the nationalist-exclusivist program of the Zionists. Some Jewish Marxists acquired leadership positions in the illegal Communist party organizations, both at the local and central levels.

The situation of the Jews worsened considerably following the Soviet incorporation of Bessarabia and Northern Bukovina. The legal and administrative measures adopted during the Goga-Cuza era laid the groundwork for the physical violence that was directed against the Jews after June 1940.

Toward the Second Vienna Award

During the interwar period, Hungary's revisionist ambitions were intertwined with those of the Third Reich, which was also striving to undo the perceived injustices of the Versailles Treaty. The first results of the pro-Axis policies were achieved in November 1938 when, under the terms of the First Vienna Award, Hungary acquired the Upper Province *(Felvidék)* from Czechoslovakia. A few months later, concurrently with the establishment of the "independent" Slovak state (March 1939), Hungary also acquired Carpatho-Ruthenia *(Kárpátalja)*. The attention of the Hungarians was subsequently directed toward the settlement of their historical dispute with the Romanians over the issue of Transylvania. The strategy of the Hungarians was to synchronize their claims against the Romanians with the expected advancement of Soviet demands for the reacquisition of Bessarabia—the territory the Russians lost in 1919. Almost immediately after the Soviet press took up the issue of Bessarabia in November 1939, General Henrik Werth, the Germanophile Hungarian chief of staff, advised the Hungarian government that in case of a Soviet attack on Romania Hungary should also get involved for the recovery of "the whole of Transylvania."[7]

The Soviet leaders, on 23 June 1940, informed the Germans of their intentions to acquire from Romania not only Bessarabia but also a part of Bukovina. Three days later they sent an ultimatum to the Romanians, who had no alternative but to yield since France—their traditional ally—had just been defeated and the Axis partners supported the Soviet claims. The Hungarians lost no time in pressing their own demands against Romania, which the Russians reportedly also found quite legitimate at the time.[8] On 10 July Prime Minister Pál Teleki, accompanied by István Csáky, the Hungarian foreign minister, met Hitler in Munich to impress upon him the need for the settlement of the issue of Transylvania. The Hungarian statesmen were somewhat disappointed by the position of their erstwhile ally. Germany was eager to acquire Romania's friendship, not only to enhance its effectiveness as a prospective partner in the Axis military alliance, but also to secure a reliable source of petroleum. The Führer warned the Hungarians that they could expect no help from either Germany or Italy if they proceeded with their planned attack on Romania. Hitler's position on this issue had been crystallized earlier in the month when Admiral Miklós Horthy, the Regent of Hungary, had contacted him with the same request. He remained adamant in spite of Horthy's arguments that, in view of the inevitable future conflict with the USSR, German interests themselves required that Transylvania, Europe's only natural fortress, be in the possession of their trusted friends. Horthy tried to influence the Führer not only with his evaluation of the Romanians as "morally rotten" and unreliable allies, but also with arguments based on his deep-rooted anti-Semitism. He informed Hitler that the reason the Jews of Transylvania were satisfied with Romanian rule was the corruption and venality in the country. He also felt it necessary to note that the Jews caused much mischief in Hungary, emphasizing that while "every decent man was at the front, the Jews had organized revolution and established Bolshevism."[9]

Since Hitler was already involved in the planning of "Operation Barbarossa"—the code name for the campaign against the USSR, which stipulated both Hungarian and Romanian participation—he offered his good offices. His mediation efforts led to the Hungarian-Romanian negotiations that began in Turnu-Severin, Romania, on 10 August. The position of the negotiators was expectedly contradictory; after about ten days of futile wrangling, German Foreign Minister Joachim von Ribbentrop, fearing a possible Russian move against Romania, decided with his Italian counterpart, Count Galeazzo Ciano, to invite the Hungarians and the Romanians to Vienna for some "friendly advice." The meeting began on 28 August, and two days later the Hungarians and the Romanians were informed of the details of the arbitration terms.

Under the terms of the Second Vienna Award, as the Axis-imposed settlement came to be known, the Hungarians received an area of 43,591 square kilometers (see figure 1) with a population of approximately 2.5 million. The area ceded to Hungary included the northern half of Transylvania, encompassing all of Szilágy, Beszterce-Naszód, Csík, and Szolnok-Doboka counties, most of Háromszék and Maros-Torda counties, and parts of Kolozs County.

The Romanians had to vacate the ceded territory within two weeks. The re-entry of the Hungarians began on 5 September 1940 and was completed by the 13th. A civilian administration replaced the military one shortly after the Hungarian Parliament enacted a law on 2 October that provided for the incorporation of Northern Transylvania into Hungary.[10]

Partly because of the anti-Semitic excesses that took place in Romania after the Soviet annexation of Bessarabia and Northern Bukovina, many Transylvanian Jews received the news of the Second Vienna Award with considerable satisfaction. This feeling was reinforced by the older Jews, who still remembered the "Golden Era" of pre–World War I Hungary, and by the Jewish ignorance of the realities of the anti-Semitic policies of the Horthy regime. In fact, shortly after the annexation of Northern Transylvania, a number of Hungarian-Jewish patriots felt it necessary to emphasize that they had remained loyal to the Magyar cause, opposing both the Romanian and the Zionist "pressures."[11] It is one of the ironies and tragedies of history that after the division of Transylvania in 1940, the Transylvanian Jews fared far worse in the part allotted to Hungary—the country with which they maintained so

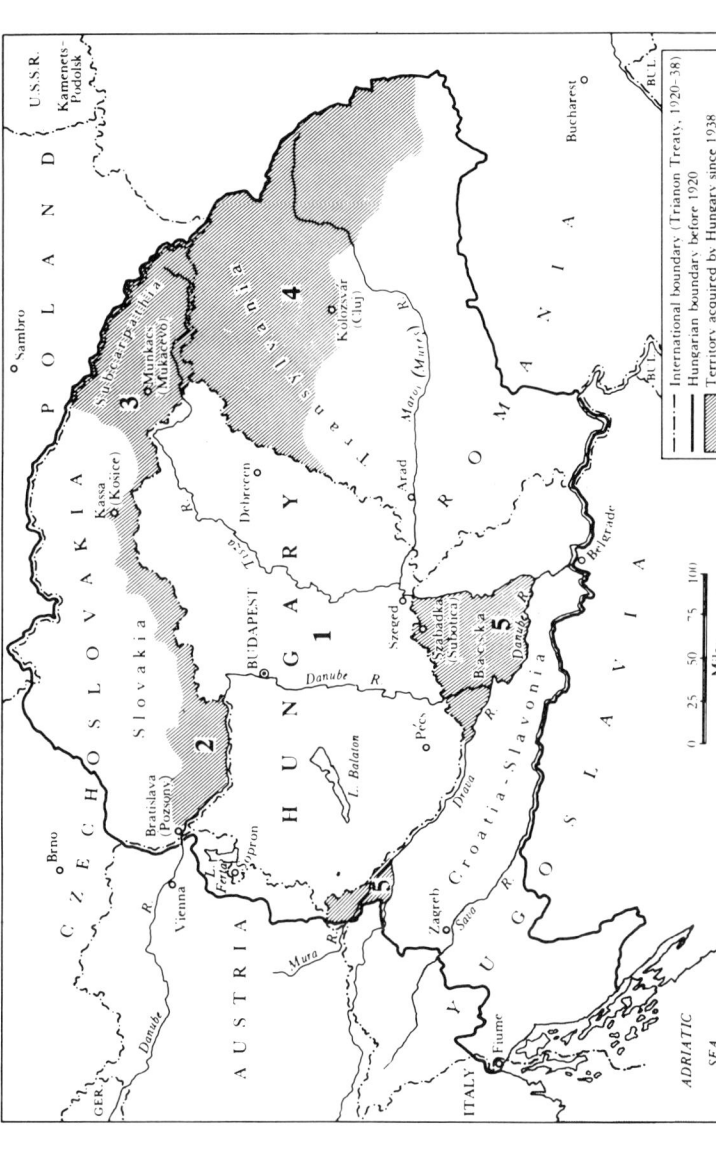

Figure 1. Hungary, 1919–1945. 1. Trianon Hungary; 2. Upper Province *(Felvidék)*, 4,630 sq. m., acquired from Czechoslovakia in November 1938; 3. Carpatho-Ruthenia or Subcarpathia, 4,257 sq. m., acquired from Czechoslovakia in March 1939; 4. Northern Transylvania, 43,494 sq. m., acquired from Romania in August 1940; 5. The Bačka (Bácska), the Baranya Triangle, the Prekomurje *(Muravidék)*, and the Medjumurje *(Muraköz)*, 4,488 sq. m., acquired from Yugoslavia in April 1941.

many cultural and emotional ties—than in the part left with Romania—the state so frequently identified with anti-Semitic excesses in the course of its history.

Northern Transylvania under Hungarian Rule

The Jewish Population of Northern Transylvania

The population of the ceded territory is shown in table 1.[12] The census figures are dubious, for both the Romanians and the Hungarians used them in their struggle to justify their respective claims to Transylvania. This was particularly true of the statistical treatment of the Jewish minority.

Before the partition the total Jewish population of Transylvania was about 200,000. Of these 164,052, or four-fifths, lived in the territories ceded to Hungary. The more important Jewish population centers and settlements of Northern Transylvania as reflected by the 1941 census are shown in table 2.[13] The 50 localities listed under the 11 Northern Transylvanian counties contained a total Jewish population of 111,334, or 67.9 percent of the territory's Jews. During the interwar period, when all of Transylvania was under Romanian rule, many of the region's Jews gravitated toward the western and northwestern parts of the country, the areas adjacent to the large Jewish centers of northeastern Hungary and Carpatho-Ruthenia. Many of them settled in the larger cities, including Kolozsvár, Máramarossziget, Marosvásárhely, Nagykároly, Nagyvárad, and Szatmárnémeti, giving these cities a

Table 1. Population of Ceded Portion of Transylvania

	Census of 1910 (Hungarian, by mother-tongue)		Census of 1930 (Romanian, by nationality)		Census of 1941 (Hungarian)
Magyar	1,125,732			911,550	1,347,012
Romanian	926,268			1,176,433	1,066,353
German	90,195	German	68,694	German	47,501
Yiddish		Jews	138,885	Yiddish	45,593
Ruthene	16,284			Ruthene	20,609
Slovak	12,807	Others	99,585	Slovak	20,908
				Romany	24,729
Other	22,968			Others	4,586
Total	2,194,254		2,395,147		2,577,291

INTRODUCTORY ESSAY   11

somewhat Jewish character. As a result of the demographic changes brought about during the 1910–1941 period by immigration, internal mobility, and other factors, the percentage of Jews in these counties and cities exceeded the national (4.2 percent) as well as the Transylvanian (3.4 percent) average. This

Table 2. Important Jewish Population Centers of Northern Transylvania

Locality	Jewish Population	Percent of Local Population	Locality	Jewish Population	Percent of Local Population
Beszterce-Naszód County			Máramaros *(con't.)*		
Beszterce	2,370	14.5	Alsóvisó	514	10.9
Naszód	417	13.0	Petrova	584	12.3
Óradna	295	6.7	Bárdfalva	508	20.5
Magyarnemecse	248	14.7	Barcánfalva	393	9.7
Bihar County			Felsőszelistye	357	8.7
Nagyvárad	21,133	22.7	Jód	217	7.2
Margitta	1,725	26.1	Maros-Torda County		
Érmihályfalva	1,662	18.2	Marosvásárhely	5,693	12.7
Székelyhid	605	10.2	Szászrégen	1,635	16.1
Nagyszalonta	593	3.9	Erdőszentgyörgy	239	6.8
Csík County			Szatmár County		
Gyergyószentmiklós	559	5.1	Szatmárnémeti	12,960	24.9
Csikszereda	299	4.3	Nagybánya	3,623	16.9
Gyergyótölgyes	198	4.4	Nagykároly	2,255	14.2
Háromszék County			Nagysomkút	897	27.9
Sepsiszentgyörgy	400	2.8	Szinérváralja	712	12.6
Kolozs County			Aranyosmeggyes	316	7.1
Kolozsvár	16,763	15.1	Sárközujlak	179	4.5
Bánffyhunyad	960	18.7	Szilágy County		
Hidalmás	301	15.3	Szilágysomlyó	1,496	16.5
Máramaros County			Tasnád	752	13.6
Máramarossziget	10,144	39.1	Szilágycseh	531	15.2
Felsővisó	4,269	34.7	Zilah	394	4.6
Visóoroszi	1,084	29.8	Szolnok-Doboka County		
Borsa	2,409	19.6	Dés	3,719	19.3
Majszin	1,067	19.0	Szamosujvár	847	13.4
Szaplonca	920	23.3	Magyarlápos	717	29.7
Tiszakarácsonyfalva	911	46.0	Bethlen	714	20.8
Rozália	737	21.2	Udvarhely County		
Dragomérfalva	684	20.5	Székelyudvarhely	329	2.7

is most dramatically illustrated with the demographic changes in the larger cities, as shown in table 3.[14]

The expanded Jewish population in these cities also reflected an increase in the percentage of Jews in the respective counties. Thus the percentage of Jews in Bihar County, which includes Nagyvárad, increased from 2.5 in 1910 to 6.1 in 1941. Kolozs County, containing the city of Kolozsvár, and Szatmár County, containing Szatmárnémeti, increased in Jewish population during the corresponding period from 4.4 and 7.4 to 7.1 and 8.1 percent, respectively.[15]

The ratio of Jews along the eastern and southern slopes of the Carpathians, especially in the so-called Székely Land, and in the Banat was always relatively low. The decline in the percentage of Jews in these areas was accompanied during the 1910–1941 period by a considerable decrease in the percentage of Jews in some of the counties of central Transylvania as well. This is reflected by the figures shown in table 4.[16]

The Introduction of Anti-Jewish Measures

The illusions cherished by many Transylvanian Jews regarding the Hungarians' replacing the Romanians soon gave way to disbelief and despair. Some of the anti-Jewish measures in effect in Hungary were introduced in Northern Transylvania by the military authorities shortly after the completion of the region's occupation on 13 September 1940. The major anti-Jewish laws were introduced by the civilian authorities early in 1941.[17] The Jewish newspapers, including the *Uj Kelet* (New East) of Kolozsvár, were suppressed, as were all nondenominational clubs and associations.[18]

The Hungarian and Romanian democratic, or moderate, press fared no better. The local journals and periodicals were soon transformed into mouthpieces of the Right, and the liberal journalists were silenced. Periodicals such

Table 3. Population Increase from 1910 to 1941

	Jewish Population		Increase (Percent)
	1910	1941	
Kolozsvár	7,046	16,763	138.0
Marosvásárhely	2,755	5,693	106.6
Nagyvárad	15,155	21,333	40.8
Szatmárnémeti	7,194	12,960	81.6

Table 4. Percent of Jews According to County

County	Percent of Jews	
	1910	1941
Beszterce-Naszód	5.7	4.3
Csík	1.6	0.2
Háromszék	0.8	0.6
Szilágy	4.3	2.9
Szolnok-Doboka	5.1	4.3
Udvarhely	1.1	0.7

as *Hitel* (Credit), *Pásztortüz* (Shepherd's Fire), and *Katolikus Status* (Catholic Status) of Kolozsvár, as well as their contributors (many of whom had earlier been known as moderate) became the spokesmen for fascism. The organs of the major communities, including the *Ellenzék* (Opposition) of Kolozsvár, edited by Gyula Zathureczky, the *Székely Nép* (Székely People) of Sepsiszentgyörgy, edited by Ferenc Koréh, and the *Szamosvölgye* (Szamos Valley) of Dés, edited by László Sztojka, emerged as effective purveyors of the new pro-Axis and anti-Semitic order in the region. A similar anti-Semitic posture was also adopted by the other local papers, including the *Székely Szó* (Székely Word) of Marosvásárhely and the weekly *Gyergyói Lapok* (Gyergyó Papers) of Gyergyószentmiklós. The major organ inciting the local German-speaking Swabian and Saxon population against the Jews was the *Siebenbürgische Deutsche Zeitung* (German Newspaper of Transylvania).

The swing to the Right was also joined by the various economic and social associations, including the Baross Association, the Hangya Cooperative, and the Wesselényi Rifle Club. The *Erdélyi Helikon* (Transylvanian Helicon), one of the leading cultural institutions in the region, came under the influence of writers like József Nyirő, one of the foremost literary representatives of the extreme Right.

The discriminatory measures affected the Jews particularly harshly in their economic and educational pursuits. While those in business and the professions managed to make ends meet by circumventing the laws and taking advantage of loopholes, practically all civil servants were dismissed and the unskilled workers could hardly survive. The drive for the "spiritual purification" of the country hit especially hard at Jewish students: They were almost totally excluded from secondary schools and institutions of higher learning. The exclusionary *Numerus Clausus* provisions of the laws (specifying the allowed percentage of Jews) were so applied as to assure in practice a *Numerus*

Nullus in all state educational institutions.[19] Whereas the Jewish leadership of Northern Transylvania solved the educational needs of secondary-school Jewish youth by establishing Jewish denominational secondary schools in Kolozsvár and Nagyvárad, the status of Jewish students in higher education remained deplorable. During the 1940–41 academic year, for example, the University of Kolozsvár admitted only ten Jewish students, whose parents had some special connections with the authorities. But even these students were hardly able to attend classes because of Jew-baiting by their Christian colleagues.

The heavy hand of the military and civilian authorities was felt particularly in the four counties of the Székely area, which the Hungarians considered "holy." The Jews of the area were subjected to a review of their citizenship; as a result many found themselves in custody because of their "doubtful" status.

The drive against "alien" Jews was intensified in the summer of 1941, when the KEOKH (*Külföldieket Ellenőrző Országos Központi Hatóság;* National Central Alien Control Office), the agency entrusted with jurisdiction over foreign nationals living in Hungary, began a roundup of Jews who could not prove their Hungarian citizenship. The drive affected especially the northeastern parts of Hungary, including the Orthodox centers in Northern Transylvania. According to the plan worked out by the authorities, the "alien" Jews were to be resettled in the Hungarian-occupied parts of Galicia. The rationale for the resettlement was provided by Dr. Gábor Ajtay, the deputy prefect of Máramaros County, on 8 July 1941:[20]

> Law No. IV of 1939 Concerning the Restriction of the Participation of Jews in Public and Economic Life, the measures adopted for its implementation, and the Third Anti-Jewish Law now being prepared compel and will compel the Jews living in the country to yield to the Hungarians their position in public and economic life, just as they were compelled to yield their positions in the civil service. In Máramaros County, where the anti-Jewish laws and the license revisions, among other things, were not yet implemented, there live more than 45,000 Jews, who or whose elders infiltrated into the county from Galicia, Bukovina, and Poland. In the city of Máramarossziget alone the number of Jews is over 10,000. The implementation of the anti-Jewish measures, which will begin with the greatest severity in the near future, will affect local Jews at their economic foundation. In view of the fact that a large part of Galicia has been occupied by *Honvéd* troops and in order to bring about an equitable solution of this problem before the implementation of the anti-Jewish measures, I appeal to the Jews living in the county's territory and especially to those who desire to resettle in Galicia to apply within eight days to file the appropriate forms with the designated authorities, namely the mayor of the city of Máramarossziget or the agents specified by him and the rural authorities in the villages. I would like to draw the attention of those interested in the idea that the resettlement will be organized and carried out on a centralized basis, which is

facilitated by the fact that the bulk of the population in the occupied territories either retreated with or were removed by the Russians and for this reason no major difficulty is expected in the settlement of the Jews and the starting of a new life. It will serve the interests of the Jews if they liquidate their uncertain situation in the county by yielding their position and begin a new life on the soil of Galicia with the aid of the authorities.

The KEOKH campaign resulted in the roundup of close to 18,000 "alien" Jews. In August, soon after deportation to the Kamenets-Podolsk area, approximately 16,000 of their number, together with approximately 7,000 indigenous Jews, were massacred. This was the first five-figure massacre in the Nazis' Final Solution program.[21]

Another major Hungarian anti-Jewish policy, which extended to Northern Transylvania shortly after its annexation, pertained to the treatment of Jewish males of military age (20 to 48).[22] No longer trusted to bear arms, the Jews were conscripted into special labor service companies. The affected Jewish men were conscripted into various types of labor service companies that were subsequently assigned to a variety of public works and military-related projects within Hungary and along the Ukrainian front. The treatment of the labor servicemen varied from company to company, depending on the attitude of the commanding officers and the guards. The fate of the companies serving with the Second Hungarian Army in the Ukraine and of those transferred to Bor, Serbia, to work in the copper mines operated by the Todt Organization was particularly harsh. Many of these companies, both regular and punitive, were manned by Jews from Northern Transylvania. As in many other parts of Hungary, a considerable number of these Jews were mobilized into labor service by the local authorities on the advice of Right radical elements who were pursuing their own economic and political interests: By ensuring the mobilization of the richer Jews involved in industry, business, and the professions, the Right radicals could advance their own private interests as well as contribute to the solution of the Jewish question. Ironically, after the German occupation on 19 March 1944, the labor service system, which remained under the exclusive jurisdiction of the Hungarian Ministry of Defense, emerged as a source of refuge for many Jewish men of military age. In Northern Transylvania, many Jews owed their survival to the humanitarian activities of the commander of the recruitment center in Nagybánya, Colonel Imre Reviczky, who was honored as a "Righteous Gentile" after the war.[23] Although the Jews of Northern Transylvania, like those of Hungary as a whole, were subjected to harsh legal and economic measures and thousands of them were killed at Kamenets-Podolsk and in the Ukraine, they were relatively well off, especially in comparison with the fate that befell the Jewish communities in the neighboring countries. But when catastrophe struck with the German occupation, the

Jews of Northern Transylvania were subjected, along with almost all the other Jews of Hungary, to the most ruthless and concentrated process of destruction of the war.

The German Occupation and the Final Solution

The details for the systematic implementation of the Final Solution in German-dominated Europe were discussed at the Wannsee Conference of 20 January 1942.[24] Shortly thereafter the deportations began from Slovakia, the Third Reich, and the German-occupied areas. The campaign for the solution of the Jewish question was also extended to Hungary, but the government of Miklós Kállay, while adopting a series of appeasement measures at home, consistently rejected all German attempts to deport the Jews. The safety the Hungarian Jews enjoyed during the first four and a half years of the war came to an end on 19 March 1944, when the Germans, alarmed by the attempts of the Hungarians to find an honorable way out of the war, occupied the country.[25] This measure by the Third Reich, designed primarily to safeguard its military and security interests, also provided the Nazis with the opportunity to enforce their own racial-ideological objectives. Toward this end they obtained the wholehearted support of the new Döme Sztójay government, which Admiral Horthy appointed shortly after the occupation.[26] The *Sonderkommando* (Special Commando) of Adolf Eichmann, which arrived in Budapest with contingency plans for the possible solution of the Jewish question, was impressed with the eagerness and radicalism with which the Hungarian pro-Nazi elements—including László Baky, László Endre, and Andor Jaross—wanted to bring about the liquidation of Hungarian Jewry.

The drive against the Jews began with the establishment of a Central Jewish Council *(Központi Zsidó Tanács)* in Budapest under the command of the Eichmann-*Sonderkommando*. Composed of the traditional leaders of Hungarian Jewry, the council, abandoned by the Hungarian authorities, had to comply with the German demands while doing its best to protect the interests of the community as it perceived them.[27] Very shortly, the Sztójay government started releasing an avalanche of anti-Jewish decrees, including those pertaining to the expropriation of the Jews and to their compulsory wearing of the telltale Yellow Star of David. The details for the ghettoization of the Jews, worked out in the Ministry of the Interior on 4 April 1944, were incorporated in Decree No. 6163/1944 of 7 April, which was issued secretly under the signature of Baky to all the appropriate representatives of the local organs of state power. Although the formal decree on the ghettoization of the Jews wasn't adopted by the Council of Ministers until 26 April, the quisling authorities had already begun their drive in Carpatho-Ruthenia on 16 April. The military rationale for the operation was provided on 12 April, when the government declared Carpatho-Ruthenia and Northern Transylvania to have become military operational zones as of 1 April. Shortly thereafter Sztójay appointed Béla Ricsóy-Uhlarik to serve as government commissioner for the military operational zone in Northern Transylvania.[28]

The master plan for the concentration and deportation of the Jews was worked out by a dejewification unit, which acted under the guidance of the Baky-Endre group in the Ministry of the Interior and in close cooperation with the Eichmann-*Sonderkommando.* This unit was headed by Lieutenant Colonel László Ferenczy in his capacity as liaison officer of the Hungarian Gendarmerie to the German Security Police.[29] The master plan called for the implementation of the ghettoization-concentration process in the following distinct phases:

- Jews in the rural communities and the smaller towns were to be rounded up and temporarily transferred to synagogues and community buildings.
- Following the first round of investigation in pursuit of valuables, the Jews rounded up in the rural communities and smaller towns were to be transferred to the ghettos of the larger cities in their vicinity, usually the county seat.
- In the larger towns and cities Jews were to be rounded up and transferred to a specially designated area that would serve as a ghetto—totally isolated from the other parts of the city. In some cities, the ghetto was to be established in the Jewish quarter; in others in factories, warehouses, brickyards, or under the open sky.
- Jews were to be concentrated in centers with adequate rail facilities to make possible swift entrainment and deportation.

During each phase, the Jews were to be subjected to special investigations by teams composed of gendarmerie and police officials to compel them to surrender their valuables. The plans for the implementation of the ghettoization and deportation operations called for the launching of six territorially defined "mopping-up operations" *(tisztogatási akciók).* For this purpose, the country was divided into six operational zones, with each zone encompassing one or two gendarmerie districts.

The ghettoization-concentration-deportation program was carried out on a territorial basis determined by the location of the Jewish communities in the ten gendarmerie districts into which the country was divided (see map below). These districts, in turn, were divided into six operational zones determined by the priority attached to the deportation from particular areas. The bulk of the territory of Northern Transylvania belonged to Gendarmerie Districts IX and X, with headquarters in Kolozsvár and Marosvásárhely, respectively. Some of the northwestern parts of Northern Transylvania, including Máramaros County, were administratively considered to belong to Gendarmerie District VIII, covering Carpatho-Ruthenia and northeastern Hungary. The area of the two gendarmerie districts in the province was identified as operational Zone II (see figure 2).

The Ghettoization Conferences

Details of the procedures for the ghettoization of the Northern Transylvanian Jews were discussed at two top-secret conferences. The first was held in Szatmárnémeti on 26 April and was devoted to the dejewification operations in the counties of Gendarmerie District IX, namely, Bihar, Szatmár, Szilágy, Kolozs, Szolnok-Doboka, and Beszterce-Naszód. The second was held two days later in Marosvásárhely and was devoted to the concentration of the Jews in the so-called Székely Land, the counties of Gendarmerie District X: Maros-Torda, Csík, Udvarhely, and Háromszék.

Both conferences were chaired by Endre. They were attended by the heads and representatives of the civil service, gendarmerie, and police of the concerned counties. Among these were the deputy prefects (in some cases the prefects themselves), the mayors of the cities and their top assistants, and the chief officers of the gendarmerie and police units.

Endre's personal entourage included Albert Takács, his secretary; Géza Szanik, the chief of police of Aszód, who was later appointed prefect of Bereg County; Dr. Béla Rozsnyai, the supervisor of public welfare in Székesfehérvár; Dr. Ákos Simon, a military physician; and Dr. Sándor Tardi, the representative of the Ministry of Supply.[30] Among those present ex officio were the leading figures of the dejewification squad, including Lieutenant Colonel László Ferenczy and Dr. Lajos Meggyesi.

The size of the delegations from the various Northern Transylvanian counties and cities varied. Nagybánya, for example, was represented by the mayor of that city; Police Counselor Dr. Jenő Nagy, the head of the city's police department; and Gendarmerie Captain Tibor Várhelyi.[31]

Endre reviewed the procedures to be followed in the concentration of the Jews as detailed in Decree No. 6163/1944, dated 7 April. He informed the participants that the local Jewish Council was responsible for setting up the ghetto, but that drinking water, sanitary facilities, and hospital care had to be considered, and that the money and valuables of the Jews, "constituting the property of the state," should be taken from them. He expressed the hope that

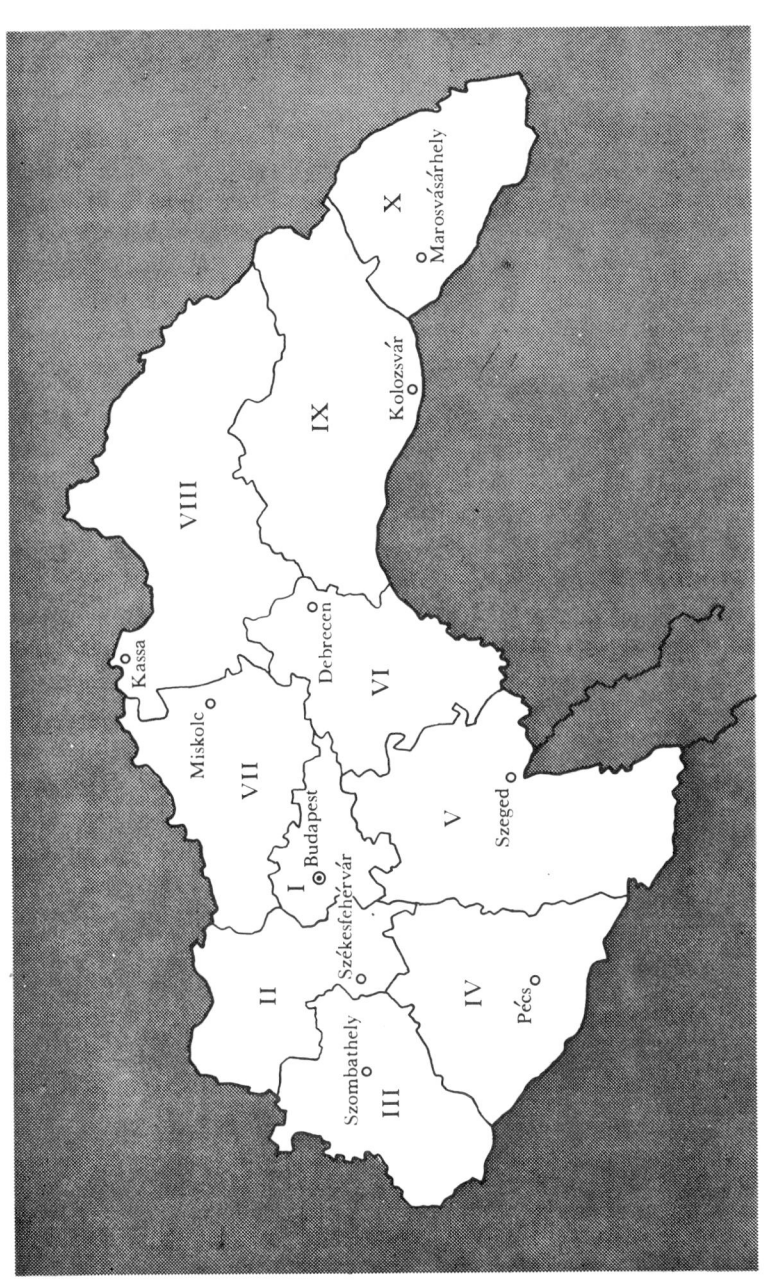

Figure 2. Gendarmerie districts and their headquarters, 1944.

the civil servants would cooperate in the implementation of "this work, which will perhaps only be appreciated by the succeeding generation."

Dr. Lajos Meggyesi emphasized that money, gold, silver, jewelry, typewriters, cameras, watches, rugs, furs, and valuable paintings taken from the Jews were to be listed in a form to be filled out in quadruplicate. One copy would remain with the city, the second would be given to the police, the third would be left in the apartment, and the fourth would be given to the Jews concerned. Since he was sure that many of the Jews had placed their valuables for safekeeping with Christians, he urged that Christians be warned by town criers, in newspaper announcements, and through posters to hand in those valuables under threat of internment. The mayors were made responsible for inventorying, storing, and safekeeping the valuables until the job could be assumed by representatives of the postal savings bank system. Ecclesiastical objects could be confiscated from both homes and synagogues. Cash and valuables were to be placed in separate sealed envelopes. Meggyesi also suggested that women should be hired to help in the search for hidden valuables.

Livestock belonging to Jews was to be given into the care of neighboring Christian farmers, and the food supplies left by the Jews were to be removed from their apartments and—in theory—used to feed them in the ghettos at a later time. (For the first two weeks the Jews were to eat the supplies they brought into the ghettos themselves.)

Lieutenant Colonel Ferenczy informed the participants of the beginning of the operation and announced the major concentration points in Gendarmerie District IX of Northern Transylvania: Nagyvárad, Szilágysomlyó, Szatmárnémeti, Kolozsvár, Szamosujvár, Dés, and Nagybánya. He advised them that in case of any difficulty they could telephone police headquarters in Kolozsvár between 10:00 and 11:00 A.M., where they could get instructions from himself, Dr. Meggyesi, or the German member of the committee.

The conferees then learned about the composition of the ghettoization commissions and the areas from which the Jews would be transferred to the various ghettos. In Nagybánya, the conferees were told, the concentration would be carried out under the command of Jenő Nagy with the assistance of Captain Tibor Várhelyi and SS-*Haupsturmführer* Franz Abromeit. The ghetto in Nagybánya would hold not only the Jews of that city, but also those of Felsőbánya and of the districts of Nagybánya, Nagysomkut, and Kápolnokmonostor in Szatmár County.[32]

The final plans worked out under the guidance of Endre called for the concentration of the Jews of Northern Transylvania (Gendarmerie Districts IX and X) into 11 cities, of which only one, Nagyvárad, was to have a ghetto within the city proper. The ten other cities with "suitable concentration camp areas" were identified as follows: Kolozsvár, Szamosujvár, Dés, Szilágysomlyó, Szatmárnémeti, Nagybánya, Beszterce, Szászrégen, Marosvásárhely, and Sepsiszentgyörgy.[33]

The Ghettoization Operation

In accordance with the decree and the oral instructions communicated at the two conferences, the chief executive for all the measures relating to the ghettoization of the Jews was the principal administrator of the locality or area. Under Hungarian law then in effect, this meant the mayor for cities, towns, and municipalities, and the deputy prefect of the county for rural areas. The organs of the police and gendarmerie as well as the auxiliary civil service organs of the cities, including the public notary and health units, were to be directly involved in the roundup and transfer of the Jews into ghettos.

The mayors, acting in cooperation with their subordinated agency heads, were empowered not only to direct and supervise the ghettoization operations but also to determine the location of the ghettos and to screen the Jews qualified for exemption. They were also responsible for seeing to the maintenance of essential services in the ghettos.

A few days before the scheduled 3 May start of the ghettoization drive in Northern Transylvania, the special commissions for the various cities and towns held meetings to determine the location of the ghettos and to settle the logistics relating to the roundup of the Jews. The commissions were normally composed of the mayors, deputy prefects, and heads of the local gendarmerie and police units. While nearly the same procedure was followed almost everywhere, the severity with which the ghettoization was carried out and the location of and the conditions within the ghetto depended upon the attitude of the particular mayors and their subordinates. Thus in cities such as Nagyvárad, Máramarossziget, and Szatmárnémeti, the ghettos were established in the poorer, mostly Jewish-inhabited sections; in others, such as Kolozsvár, Marosvásárhely, Szászrégen, Beszterce, and Szilágysomlyó, the ghettos were set up in brickyards. The ghetto of Dés was situated in the Bungur, a forest, where some of the Jews were put up in makeshift barracks and the others—the majority—under the open sky.

Late on 2 May, on the eve of the ghettoization, the mayors issued special instructions to the Jews and had them posted in all areas under their jurisdiction. The text followed the directives of the decree, though it varied in nuances from city to city. Typical of such announcements was the one issued by László Gyapai in Nagyvárad:

Jews who are obliged to wear the Yellow Star are forbidden to leave their homes after the publication of this announcement. For the time being and until the issuance of other instructions, Jews will be permitted to leave their homes only between 9:00 and 10:00 A.M. With the exception of this period, all of them must stay at home. At the order of the Royal Hungarian Government, I am placing into a ghetto all the Jews compelled to wear the Yellow Star in Nagyvárad. I call upon all non-Jews holding Jewish valuables to report them to the mayor's office within three days from the publication of this announcement. I shall be in charge of the receipt of such reported valuables. I warn the non-Jewish inhabitants of the municipality that all persons holding Jewish property who fail to declare it within the period cited above will be prosecuted with the greatest severity and immediate measures will be taken for their internment in camps.[34]

The roundup of the Jews was carried out by special units composed of civil servants, usually including local primary and high school teachers, gendarmes, and policemen, which were organized by the mayoral commissions and operated under their jurisdiction.

Immediate and overall command over the ghettoization process in Northern Transylvania was exercised by Gendarmerie Colonel Tibor Paksi-Kiss, who delegated special powers in Nagyvárad to Lieutenant Colonel Jenő Péterffy, his friend and colleague.

In some places the Jews were collected at smaller centers before their transfer to the ghetto. At each stage they were subjected to an expropriation process that assumed an increasingly barbaric character. It became particularly vicious during the few weeks prior to the beginning of the deportations. The search for valuables was the task of special investigative units, which normally consisted of local detectives who knew the economic status of their victims and of a few gendarmes and civil servants. These investigative units were legally under the immediate jurisdiction of the mayoral commissions.

May 3 was the first day of the ghettoization process in Northern Transylvania, and close to 8,000 Jews were rounded up in the territories of Gendarmerie District IX. During that day Paksi-Kiss visited the designated ghetto areas in Marosvásárhely, Szászrégen, Beszterce, Dés, and Szamosujvár. On 5 and 6 May he continued his tour by visiting the sites at Szatmárnémeti and Nagyvárad and spent some time observing the rounding up of the Jews in Nagykároly.

Around the same time, the major ghettos—the concentration centers—were also visited by László Endre. It was his second such tour; shortly after the end of the ghettoization conferences, he first visited Mátészalka. From there he went to Marosvásárhely, where he reviewed the local ghettoization details with the perfect, the deputy prefect, and the mayor. In Sepsiszentgyörgy he inspected the unfinished structure holding the Jews, in the company of the prefect of Háromszék, Dr. Gábor Szentiványi. Next he went to Kolozsvár, where he reviewed the ghettoization plans with Lieutenant General Lajos Veres, Mayor László Vásárhelyi, and deputy police chief Hollóssy. The next stop was Nagyvárad, where he dealt with László Gyapai and Deputy Prefect János Nadányi.[35]

Upon his return to Budapest, Endre gave an interview to a staff reporter of the Nazi-oriented *Uj Magyarság* (New Magyardom) in which he declared that the conclusion of the dejewification campaign represented a gigantic step calculated to defend the life of the Hungarian nation "by ridding it of the Jewish poison, a self-defense which will end Jewish predominance." He further asserted that in his view "the population in all cities and communities hailed the government measures with genuine delight." This was especially true, he claimed, in the cities of Munkács, Ungvár, Beregszász, and Máramarossziget, "which had borne the brunt of the flood of eastern Jews [and where] the population rejoiced and frequently supplied means of transportation to speed resettlement and get rid of the Jews."

Endre then proceeded to assuage the concern of the Hungarians by declaring:

> We adopted measures that were always carried out humanely and with consideration for moral factors. Really, no harm is befalling them. They can live among themselves in one group within the borders of the ghetto in accordance with their own folk and racial laws. We made it possible for them to cook with sesame oil, which enables them not to violate one of their important religious tenets. The ghettoization was carried out humanely with the avoidance of all rough conduct. I issued instructions that good care be taken for their safety.[36]

The ghettoization of the Jews was carried out smoothly, without major incidents of resistance on the part of either Jews or Christians. The Jewish masses, unaware of the realities of the Final Solution program, went to the ghettos resigned to their fate. Some of them rationalized their "isolation" as a logical step before the transformation of their territory into a battle zone. Others believed that they were being resettled at Kenyérmező in Transdanubia, where they would be employed on agricultural projects until the end of the war. Still others sustained the hope that the Red Army was not very far and that their concentration would be relatively short-lived. With the exception of some of the national leaders, none suspected that their ultimate destination would be Auschwitz.[37]

The Christians, even those friendly to the Jews, were mostly passive. Many cooperated with the authorities on ideological grounds or in the expectation of quick material rewards in the form of properties confiscated from the Jews. In practically every major community there were some Christians who denounced Jews in hiding.[38] On the other hand, there were also some Christians who helped either to hide Jews or to keep their valuables, although these cases were rare because of the fear instilled in the general population about helping Jews. Ferenczy was naturally impressed with the attitude of the Christian population. He noted in his report on the first day of the operations that the Christians were calm and in most places welcomed the campaign against the Jews. He also observed that the occasional expressions of sympathy came mostly from Romanians, who also suffered under the Horthy regime.[39] The smoothness with which the ghettoization and deportation program was effectuated in Northern Transylvania, as elsewhere, can be attributed in part to the absence of any meaningful resistance movement, let alone general opposition to the persecution of the Jews.

Neutrality and passivity were also the characteristic attitudes of the heads of the Christian churches in Transylvania, as reflected in the behavior of János Vásárhelyi, the Calvinist bishop, and Miklós Józan, the Unitarian bishop. The exemplary exception was Áron Marton, the Catholic bishop of Transylvania whose official residence was in Gyulafehérvár, in the Romanian part of Transylvania. In his sermon of 18 May in the St. Michael Church of Kolozsvár, Marton courageously condemned the ghettoization of the Jews and warned the Hungarians not to abandon the Jews to annihilation. He openly called on the Hungarian government to frustrate the intended deportation of the Jews. Unfortunately, his voice was echoed by only a few in the Catholic Church.[40]

The procedures for rounding up, interrogating, and expropriating property of the Jews, as well as the organization and administration of the ghetto, were basically the same in every county of Northern Transylvania. Everywhere they were in accord with the instructions and the spirit of the central and local dejewification authorities.

Here are some of the details pertaining to the individual ghettos and concentration centers:

Kolozsvár. In Kolozsvár as elsewhere the Jewish community was intimidated not only by the many discriminatory measures but also by the arrest and detention of many of its most distinguished members.[41] The Jews first learned about the ghettoization of Carpatho-Ruthenia on 28 April, when the local papers reported the transfer of the Jews of Kassa and the other communities in that region to certain specific areas allegedly threatened by air raids. The illusion that these measures affected only those areas with a large number of unassimilated Jews was short-lived, for a few days later they learned about the ghettoization decree affecting the country as a whole. The announcement pertaining to their own ghettoization, signed by Lajos Hollóssy-Kuthy, the deputy police chief, was posted throughout the city during the night of 2 May and published in the local press the following day.[42]

The Jews of Kolozsvár and of the communities in Kolozs County were concentrated in a ghetto established at the Iris Brickyard on Kajántói Road, in the northern part of the city. The specifics of the concentration operation were worked out at a meeting held on 2 May under the leadership of László Vásárhelyi, the mayor;[43] László Urbán, the police chief; and Paksi-Kiss. The meeting, attended by approximately 150 officials of the municipality who were assigned to the roundup operations, was devoted to the details of the ghettoization process as outlined in the decree and during the conference with Endre held at Szatmárnémeti on 26 April.

The Hungarian officials received expert guidance in the anti-Jewish drive from SS-*Hauptsturmführer* Stroschneider, the local commander of the German security services.[44]

The ghettoization was carried out at a rapid pace. By 10 May the number of those concentrated in the brickyard reached 12,000.[45] At its peak just before the deportations, the ghetto population, including the Jews transferred from the ghetto of Szamosujvár, reached close to 18,000.[46]

In addition to the officers cited above, József Forgács, the secretary general of Kolozs County representing the deputy prefect; Lajos Hollóssy-Kuthy, deputy police chief; Géza Papp, a high-ranking police official; and Kázmér Taar, a top official in the mayor's office, were also heavily involved in the ghettoization of the Jews. Overall command of the ghettoization process in Kolozs County, except Kolozsvár, was exercised by Ferenc Szász, the deputy prefect of Kolozs County, and by József Székely, the mayor of Bánffyhunyad. The Jews of the various towns and villages in the county were first concentrated in their localities, usually in the synagogue or a related Jewish institution. After a short while and a first round of expropriations, they were transferred to the ghetto in Kolozsvár.

In Bánffyhunyad, which had a Jewish community of considerable size, the ghettoization was carried out under the command and supervision of Székely, Pál Boldizsár, the city's supply official, József Orosz, the police chief, and police officers and detectives Ferenc Menyhért, András Szentkúti, András Lakatos, and Sándor Ojtózi.

The ghetto of Kolozsvár was under the direct command of Urbán. The overcrowding, shortage of washing and sanitary facilities, absence of hospitals, and tremendously inadequate food supply were typical of ghettos in Hungary.

The water supply for the ghetto's 18,000 inhabitants was provided by 15 faucets, many of which were often out of order for days on end. There was hardly enough water for drinking and cooking, let alone for washing. The brickyard consisted primarily of barns without walls, normally used as drying sheds for bricks and tiles. Four ditches were dug to serve as latrines for the entire ghetto—two for males and two for females. Each latrine was closed off on one side by a long board fastened to pillars.

A special building in the ghetto served as the "mint"—the place where Jews were tortured into confessing where they allegedly had hidden their valuables. Husbands were often tortured in full view of their wives and children; often wives were beaten in front of their husbands. The devices used were cruel and unusually barbaric. The victims were beaten on the soles of their feet with canes or rubber truncheons; they were slapped in the face and kicked until they lost consciousness. Males were often beaten on the testicles; females, sometimes even young girls, were searched vaginally by collaborating female volunteers and midwives who cared little about cleanliness, often in full view of the male interrogators. Some particularly sadistic investigators used electrical devices to compel the victims into confession. They would put one end of such a device in the mouth and the other in the vagina or attached to the testicles of the victims. These inhuman tortures drove many of the well-to-do Jews to insanity or suicide.[47]

The internal administration of the ghetto was entrusted to a Jewish Council consisting of the traditional leaders of the local Jewish community. In Kolozsvár the Council was headed by Dr. József Fischer,[48] the head of the Neolog community and Rezső Kasztner's father-in-law, and included Rabbi Akiba Glasner, Dr. József Fenichel, Gyula Klein, Dr. Ernő Marton, editor-in-chief of the *Uj Kelet* (New East), Zsigmond Léb, and Rabbi Mózes Weinberger.[49] Its secretary general was József Moskovits, while Dezső Hermann served as secretary.[50]

Dr. Kasztner visited Kolozsvár on 4–5 May in the company of Dr. Rudolf Sedlacek, an SS officer, allegedly to meet Dieter Wisliceny, who directed the ghettoization in Northern Transylvania as adviser at the Kolozsvár headquarters of the Dejewification Committee. He also met the leaders of the Jewish community. (What he did or did not tell them then about the reality of the Jewish situation became the subject of a heated controversy after the war.) As a result of Kasztner's dealings with the SS, permission was given to select 388 Jews from the ghetto and take them on 10 June by special train to Budapest. There they were placed in a special camp at the Wechselmann Institute for the Deaf-Mute on Columbus Street. The Columbus Street camp was a privileged camp: Its inmates were treated humanely, and it was protected by five SS guards under orders to prevent abuses. It is from here that the Kasztner group, including 1,684 Jews, left Budapest on 30 June 1944 and eventually reached Switzerland via Bergen-Belsen.[51]

According to one source, the group of 388 Kolozsvár Jews were put together on the basis of a recommendation by Zsigmond Léb, the leader of the city's Orthodox community, who happened to be in Budapest at the time, and of selections made in the ghetto by a group of local leaders and Zionists, including József Fischer, Hillel Dánzig, Dr. Lajos Marton, Dr. Jenő Kertész, and Dr. Sándor Weisz.[52]

No sooner was the ghettoization completed than the homes of these Jews, like practically everywhere else, became the target of looters. Unscrupulous Christians were eager to take over the businesses and shops of the Jews even before the deportations started. On 15 May the local press reported that no fewer than 1,500 Christians applied for 400 expropriated Jewish businesses.[53]

The deportations from the city began on 25 May and were completed on 9 June with the removal of 16,148 Jews in six transports (see Appendix 2). As if to celebrate this achievement, the city organized an "Anti-Bolshevik Exhibit," which was opened on 16 July by Baky. The occasion was not missed to identify the Jews with the menace of Bolshevism, providing the more sensitive stratum of the population with a rationale for the solution of the Jewish question.[54]

Szamosujvár. A small locality about 30 miles north of Kolozsvár, Szamosujvár had close to 1,600 Jews in its ghetto, which was located in the local brickyard. Nearly 400 of the ghetto inmates were from neighboring villages in Szamosujvár district, including Aranyszentmiklós, Böd, Buza, Coptelke, Dengeleg, Derzse, Devecser, Feketelak, Iklód, Kecsed, Kékes, Kérő, Lozsárd, Mányik, Mátéfalva, Naszoly, Ördöngösfüzes, Pujon, Szamoskend, Szentmárton, Szék, Szentgothárd, and Veresegyháza. The Jewish Council consisted of Dr. Sándor Köves and Dr. Edmund (Ödön) Abel. The ghetto population was transferred on 18 May to the brickyard at Kolozsvár and shortly thereafter deported from there.[55]

The ghettoization and subsequent transfer of the Jews of Szamosujvár and its environs were carried out under the immediate command of Lajos Tamási, the mayor; and Ernő Berecki and András Iványi, the chief police officers of the city.[56]

Dés. The county of Szolnok-Doboka, which was under the administrative leadership of Count Béla Bethlen,[57] was represented at the 26 April conference with Endre in Szatmárnémeti by János Schilling, the deputy prefect; Jenő Veress, the mayor of Dés,[58] Lajos Tamási, the mayor of Szamosujvár; Gyula Sárosi, the police chief of Dés; Ernő Berecki, the police chief of Szamosujvár; and Pál Antalffy, the commander of the gendarmerie in Szolnok-Doboka. The objectives and decisions of this conference were communicated to the chief civil service, gendarmerie, and police officers of the county at a special meeting convened and chaired by Schilling on 30 April. At this meeting Dés and Szamosujvár were selected as the two major ghetto sites of the county.

Among the civilian officials at the meeting were Lajos Krämer, a pharmacist; Dr. Jenő Vékás, a physician; and Dr. Zsigmond Léhnár (Lénárd), the health officer of Dés. Krämer's suggestion that the ghetto of Dés be set up in and around Kodor Street, the area of the city which was overwhelmingly Jewish, was vetoed on the insistence of Dr. Vékás and, above all, of Dr. Léhnár.[59] In accordance with the decision reached at this meeting, the ghetto was set up in Bungur forest, about two miles from the city, which was very close to a secondary railroad line that could be used for the later entrainment of the Jews. The local anti-Semitic organ, *Szamosvölgye* (Szamos Valley), edited by László Sztojka, had found even the forest too good for the Jews and would have preferred to see them placed "in a less beautiful area, in the open fields."[60]

Within a few days of the ghettoization drive, which was carried out under the overall command of Pál Antalffy, 7,800 Jews were brought into the Bungur.[61] Of these approximately half were from Dés.[62] Before their transfer to the Bungur, the Jews of Dés were concentrated at three centers within the city, where they were subjected to body searches for valuables. One of these centers was the large house of Miklós Bakay. The remainder of the ghetto population was brought in from the other communities in the county, many of whom were first concentrated in the district seats, including Bethlen, Magyarlápos, Nagyilonda, and Retteg.[63] The Jews in the county's rural communities were rounded up during 3–5 May. At first the authorities toyed with the idea of transferring them to the much larger ghetto of Szamosujvár.[64] However, by 6 May enough materials, including planks from Jewish-owned lumber yards, were found to keep the Jews in Bungur.[65] The ghetto, surrounded by barbed wire, was guarded by the local police who were supplemented by a special unit of 40 gendarmes assigned from Zilah.[66] Supreme command over the ghetto was exercised by Takács, a "government commissioner."

Sanitary conditions within the ghetto were miserable, as were the essential services and supplies. This was largely due to the malevolence of Veress and Léhnár, the mayor and the chief health officer of Dés. The investigative teams formed for the search of valuables were as cruel in Dés as they were everywhere else. Among those involved in the search who "distinguished" themselves by their cruelty were József Fekete, József Gecse, Mária Fekete, Jenő Takács, József Lakadár, and police officers Albert (Béla) Garamvölgyi, János Somorlyai, János Kassay, and Miklós Désaknai.[67] Abuses in the search for valuables also took place in the smaller towns of the county just before the transfer of the Jews to the Bungur. In Retteg, for example, Sándor Oláh and Rozália Jancsó were particularly zealous in their search, committing many brutal crimes. In Csicsó-Györgyfalra Ferenc Lakatos acted viciously not only against the Jews, but also against the Romanians.[68]

Although he attended the Szatmárnémeti conference and convened the meeting of 30 April in Dés, Deputy Prefect János Schilling backed out just before the beginning of the ghettoization. Feigning illness, he resigned his position on 2 May.[69] Needless to say, he failed to tip off the local Jewish leaders about the impending disaster. When he saw the columns of ragged Jews being driven into the ghetto, Schilling allegedly remarked to his subordinates: "Look, gentlemen, this is how thousand-year-old Hungary digs its grave."[70]

The internal administration of the ghetto was entrusted to a Jewish Council composed of the traditional leaders of the local community. The council included Ferenc Ordentlich (chairman), Lázár Albert, Samu Weinberger, Manó Weinberger, and Andor Ágai. Dr. Oszkár Engelberg served as the ghetto's chief physician and Zoltán Singer as its economic representative in charge of supplies.[71]

The Jews were kept in the ghetto for about four weeks under the most miserable conditions. The wealthier ones were subjected to especially cruel treatment at the hands of police and gendarme investigators. During the short lifespan of the ghetto, 25 Jews died of natural and other causes. Among these were a number of newborn babies and Dr. Samu Biró of Magyarlápos, who was beaten to death. (Their bodies were transferred from the Bungur to the Jewish cemetery after the war.) A small number of able-bodied Jews were taken to the city daily under special escort to work on various projects; some of them were put to work in the city's main synagogue, which had been transformed into a warehouse. The ghetto was liquidated between May 28 and June 8 with the removal of 7,674 Jews in three transports.[72] A few Jews managed to escape from the ghetto. Among these was Rabbi József Paneth of Nagyilonda, who eventually managed together with nine members of his family to get to safety in Romania. Other less successful Jews were caught and punished together with their Christian helpers.[73]

Szilágysomlyó. The ghettoization of the Jews of Szilágy County was carried out under the command and supervision of the officials who participated at the Szatmárnémeti Conference of 26 April: András Gazda, deputy county prefect; János Sréter, mayor of Zilah; József Udvari, mayor of Szilágysomlyó; Lieutenant Colonel György Mariska, commander of the gendarmerie unit of the county; Ferenc Elekes, police chief of Zilah; and István Pethes, police chief of Szilágysomlyó. Baron János Jósika, the prefect of Szilágy County, resigned immediately when he was informed by Gazda about the decisions taken at the conference.[74] He was one of the few Hungarian officials who dared to take a public stand against the anti-Jewish actions, deeming them both immoral and illegal. His successor, László Szlávi, an appointee of the Sztójay government, had no such scruples and cooperated fully in the implementation of the anti-Jewish measures.

Soon after their return from Szatmárnémeti, the conferees met at the prefect's office with Béla Sámi, the chief county clerk; Drs. Suchi and Ferenc Molnár, the chief health officials of Szilágy County and of Szilagysomlyó, respectively; László Krasznai, the head of Somlyó District; and István Kemecsey, the head of the technical services department of Szilágysomlyó, to select a site for the ghetto. They first thought of establishing it around Báthory Street and the synagogue in Szilágysomlyó, but eventually settled on the Klein Brickworks at Somlyócsehi, about three miles from the city.

The roundup of the Jews in Szilágysomlyó was carried out under the immediate command of István Pethes, in Zilah under the leadership of Ferenc Elekes, and in the other parts of the county under the direction of Gazda and the immediate command of Lieutenant Colonel György Mariska. Among the sizable Jewish communities affected were those of Tasnád[75] and Kraszna. By 6 May there were 7,200 Jews in the ghetto, including 313 from Zilah.[76] At its peak the ghetto had 8,500 inhabitants.

Despite the zeal of the commissions involved in the collection of the Jews, Ferenczy complained of some difficulties due to "the involvement of incompetent elements in the campaign." These were apparently ironed out soon after the assignment of a gendarmerie officer from Zilah. One of the difficulties Ferenczy mentioned was the discovery of a grenade in the luggage of one of the Jews.[77]

The brickyard was located in a marshy and muddy area. The brickdrying sheds in which the Jews were quartered had no walls and covered an area only 700 by 200 meters. As a consequence almost half of the ghetto population had to live outside. The ghetto was guarded by a special unit of gendarmes from Budapest and operated under the command of Krasznai, one of the most cruel ghetto commanders in Hungary. Under the guise of a search for valuables, he gave free rein to his sadistic instincts. In this and many other crimes, he had the full cooperation of many officials and *Nyilas* sympathizers: József Lázár, Miklós Sárközi, the gendarme commander of Zsibó, Ioan Anghea, László Petővári Petrik, Captain Sándor Horváth, János Vida, Ádám Kerekes, Sándor Nagy, Mihály Kovács, Sándor Farmati, Albert Szabó, Irén Duha, and Dezső Dénes. As a result of the tortures, poor feeding, and totally inadequate water supply in the ghetto of Somlyócsehi, the Jews of Szilágy County arrived at Auschwitz in very poor condition, so that an unusually large percentage was selected for gassing immediately upon arrival. The three transports that left Somlyócsehi between May 31 and June 6 included 7,851 Jews.[78]

Szatmárnémeti. The Hungarian authorities decided to establish two ghettos in Szatmár County: one in Szatmárnémeti and the other in Nagybánya. Nagykároly was at first also used as a concentration center for its local Jews and for those in the neighboring communities. The approximately 1,200 Jews gathered in Nagykároly were first housed in Hétsastoll, Debreceni István, Kazinczy, and Honvéd streets. The Jewish Council was composed of Dr. István Antal, Jenő Pfeffermann, Ernő Deutsch, and Lajos Jakobovics.[79] After a short while, the Jews concentrated in Nagykároly were transferred to the ghetto of Szatmárnémeti.

The county representatives at the Szatmárnémeti Conference of 26 April included László Csóka, the mayor of Szatmárnémeti; Endre Boér, the deputy county prefect; Zoltán Rogozi Papp, the deputy mayor of Szatmárnémeti; Ernő Pirkler, the city's secretary general, and representatives of the local police and gendarmerie.

The commissions for the apprehension of the Jews of Szatmárnémeti and its environs were established at a meeting held shortly after the conference. The meeting was chaired by Csóka and attended by representatives of the police and gendarmerie—among them Károly Csegezi, Béla Sárközi, and Jenő Nagy of the police and N. Deményi of the gendarmerie—and of the financial and educational boards of the city. The ghettoization in Szatmárnémeti was carried out under the direction of Csóka; in the rest of the county it was implemented under Boér.

The original plan called for the Jews to be concentrated at a special camp site. The final decision, however, was to establish the ghetto in and near Zrinyi, Petőfi, Báthory, and Tompa streets.[80] At its peak the ghetto of Szatmárnémeti held approximately 18,000 Jews, including those of Erdőd, Nagykároly, and Szatmárnémeti districts. The larger Jewish communities involved were those of Apa, Aranyosmeggyes, Avasfelsőfalu, Avaslekence, Avasujváros, Batiz, Beltek, Bikszád, Erdőd, Huta, Kacs, Nagykároly, Sarkod, Szamoskrassó, Szatmárhegy, Szinerváralja, Terep, and Vámfalu.[81] Health care in the ghetto was organized and provided by a group of Jewish physicians, including Drs. Tibor Kőváry, László Sárkány, and Ármin Fenyves.[82]

The commander of the ghetto was Béla Sárközi, the police officer in charge of the local KEOKH office.[83] The Jewish Council[84] was headed by Zoltán Schwartz and included Sámuel Rosenberg, the head of the Jewish community, Singer, Lajos Vinkler, and József Borgida, all highly respected leaders of the Jewish community of Szatmárnémeti.[85]

The searches for valuables were carried out with the customary cruelty by a team headed by Sárközi, Csegezi, and Deményi. In the wake of the ghettoization and of the tortures within the ghetto, several Jews committed suicide.[86] As was the case everywhere else, the ghettoization took place without any noteworthy incidents. The smoothness of the operation was due, according to Ferenczy, to the participation of a special unit of 50 gendarmes stationed at Merk.[87] Ferenczy was also comforted by the fact that he had managed to bring about the internment of three families who had received special exemption from Csóka[88] and to capture some Jews who had gone into hiding.[89] Many of those in hiding were denounced by Christian neighbors.[90] The six transports that left Szatmárnémeti between 19 May and 1 June included 18,863 Jews. (See Appendix 2)

Nagybánya. The ghettoization of the Jews of Nagybánya and of the various communities in the southeastern districts of Szatmár County (Nagybánya, Nagysomkut, and Kápolnokmonostor) was based on guidelines adopted a few days after the Szatmárnémeti Conference. The meeting of the local leaders was held at the headquarters of the Arrow Cross Party in Nagybánya and was also attended by László Endre. The city was first represented by Károly Tamás, the deputy mayor, but he was soon replaced by István Rosner, an assistant mayor, who was more pliable. Among the others present were Jenő Nagy, the police chief; Sándor Vajai, the former secretary general of the mayor's office; Tibor Várhelyi, the commander of the gendarmerie unit; Gyula Gergely, the head of the Arrow Cross Party in Northern Transylvania; and József Haracsek, the president of the Baross Association, the highly anti-Semitic association of Christian businessmen.

The ghetto for the Jews of the city of Nagybánya was established in the vacant lots of the König Glass Factory; those from the various communities in Nagybánya, Nagysomkut, and Kápolnokmonostor districts were quartered in a stable and barn in Borpatak (Valea Burcutului), about two miles from the city.[91] The apprehension of the Jews and the searches for valuables were carried out under the command of Jenő Nagy and Gyula Gergely under the guidance of SS-*Hauptsturmführer* Franz Abromeit.[92] The ghettoization took place at high speed: The Jews were given no more than 10 minutes to get ready.

The ghetto of Nagybánya held approximately 3,500 Jews and that of Borpatak over 2,000.[93] Of the latter only 200 found room in the stable and the barn; the others had to be quartered outdoors. The commander in chief of the ghetto was Tibor Várhelyi. The Jews in the ghetto of Nagybánya were subjected to the tortures and investigative methods customary in all ghettos. Among those responsible, under the leadership of Nagy and Várhelyi, were Károly Balogh and László Berentes, associates of the Phönix Factory of Nagybánya, as well as Haracsek, Péter Czeisberger, Zoltán Osváth, and detectives József Orgoványi, Imre Vajai, and István Bertalan. Overall responsibility for the administration of the county at the time rested with Barnabás Endrődi, who was appointed prefect of Szatmár County by the Sztójay government on 25 April

1944.⁹⁴ The 5,917 Jews in these two ghettos were deported in two transports (31 May and 5 June. See Appendix 2).

Beszterce. The approximately 6,000 Jews of Beszterce and of the other communities in Beszterce-Naszód County were concentrated at the Stamboli Farm, located about two to three miles from the city.⁹⁵ Close to 2,500 of the ghetto inhabitants were from Beszterce itself.⁹⁶

The ghettoization of the city's Jews was carried out under the command of Mayor Norbert Kuales and police chief Miklós Debreczeni. In the other communities of the county, the roundup was guided by László Smolenszki, the deputy prefect, and Lieutenant Colonel Ernő Pásztai of the gendarmerie. All four had attended the Marosvásárhely Conference with Endre on 28 April.

The ghetto, consisting of a number of barracks and pigsties, was ill-equipped from every point of view. The inadequate water and food supply was due primarily to the vicious behavior of Heinrich Smolka, who was in charge. Among those who cooperated with Smolka in the persecution of the Jews was Gusztáv Órendi, a Gestapo agent in Beszterce. In addition to the local police authorities, the ghetto was also guarded by 25 gendarmes from Nagydemeter ordered to Beszterce by Paksi-Kiss.⁹⁷ After 10 May 1944 the prefect of the county was Kálmán Borbély.⁹⁸ The deportation of the 5,981 Jews in Beszterce took place on 2 and 6 June. (See Appendix 2)

Nagyvárad. The largest ghetto of Hungary—except for the Budapest Ghetto, which was established only toward the end of November 1944—was that of Nagyvárad. Actually, Nagyvárad had two ghettos: one for the city's Jews, holding approximately 27,000 people and located in the neighborhood of the large Orthodox synagogue and the Great Market *(Nagypiac),* in the area surrounded by Mezei Mihály Street to the west, Kapucinus Street and Mussolini Square to the north, Frangepan K. Street to the east, and Szeptember 6 and Tompa Mihály Streets to the south. The other, for the approximately 8,000 Jews from the other communities in Bihar County, was at the city grange and in and around the Mezey Lumber Yards.⁹⁹

Overall command over the ghettoization and spoliation process in Bihar County was exercised by Lieutenant Colonel Jenő Péterffy of the gendarmerie, a close associate of Paksi-Kiss. Immediate command over the ghettoization in Nagyvárad was exercised by László Gyapai, the deputy mayor, who had just taken over for the mayor of the city, who had resigned.¹⁰⁰ One of his closest assistants in this drive was Lajos Cser. In the other parts of the county, the ghettoization was carried out under the supervision of János Nadányi, the county's deputy prefect.

The ghettoization was carried out at great speed, and completed within five days. The Jews were first gathered in the courtyard of the synagogue, where they were subjected to the customary searches, and then directed into the ghetto through a narrow entrance. Among the Jews in the ghetto of Nagyvárad were a considerable number of labor servicemen, who, though exempted and under the jurisdiction of the Ministry of Defense, were illegally picked up on orders of Péterffy.

Among the Jewish communities concentrated at the Mezey Lumber Yard area were those of Élesd, Érmihályfalva, Margitta, and Székelyhid. As in the other smaller localities, the Jews of these communities were first concentrated in their local synagogues or other "suitable" locations, where they were subjected to a thorough body search for valuables,[101] and then transferred to Nagyvárad.

The ghetto of Nagyvárad was extremely overcrowded. The Jews of the city, who constituted about 30 percent of its population,[102] were crammed into an area sufficient for only one-fifteenth of the city's inhabitants. The density was such that 14 to 15 Jews had to share a room.[103] The ghetto inhabitants also suffered from a shortage of food and essential services. The anti-Semitic city administration often cut off electric service and the flow of water to the ghetto.

The so-called commissions for the unearthing of Jewish wealth were established on 3 May at a meeting in the mayor's office chaired by Gyapai and attended by the heads of the city agencies and the top officials of the city government, the police, and the gendarmerie. Ultimate power over the two ghettos was assigned to a ghetto commission consisting of Péterffy, Gyapai, and Nadányi, which also had jurisdiction over the exemption provisions of the anti-Jewish laws.

Internally, the ghettos were administered by a Jewish Council consisting of Sándor Leitner (president); Chief Rabbi István Vajda; Dr. Sándor Lörincz, a lawyer; Dr. René Osváth, a physician; and Sámuel Metzen, a manufacturer.[104]

Both ghettos were tightly guarded by special units of the police and gendarmerie. During the first week (until 10 May), the Jews of Nagyvárad were under the immediate command of Imre Németh, a police captain. He acted under the guidance of Wennholz, the local Gestapo chief, and of Károly Rajnay (Reiner), the newly appointed pro-Endre prefect of Bihar.[105] Németh was assisted by István Kovács-Nagy, a fellow police officer. While the Jews were subjected to the customary searches and cruel treatment even during Németh's tenure, the real terror began after 10 May, when Péterffy[106] and his gendarmes took control. Péterffy began his reign of horrors by issuing an announcement titled *Discipline in the Ghetto,* which included no less than 80 punitive and discriminatory provisions. They provided, inter alia, for the execution of Jews leaving the territory of the ghetto, for Jews to stand at attention and bareheaded in front of any Hungarian or German officers; and for the ghetto to be "enveloped in the silence of the grave" from early evening to early morning ("from taps to reveille").[107] One of Péterffy's immediate subordinates in the ghetto was Captain István Garai.

The search for Jewish wealth was entrusted to a special unit of 40 gendarmes, assisted by the local police and detectives. Acting under the immediate command of Péterffy, the gendarmes conducted their searches in the "mint" at the Dréher Breweries immediately adjacent to the ghetto. The "mint" of Nagyvárad achieved notoriety not only because of the large number of Jews abused there, but also because of the especially sadistic behavior of the gendarmes. The victims were usually stripped naked and whipped mercilessly by their tormentors. Many of them were subjected to electric-shock torture in full view of their families, an act that drove some to suicide.[108]

Among Péterffy's assistants who distinguished themselves by their cruelty were gendarmerie officers Lieutenant Gyula Petri, who also served as a liaison with Theodor Dannecker, the local Gestapo chief; Lieutenant Ágoston Félegyházi Medgyesi, one of the top leaders of the investigative teams; Lieutenant Béla Rektor; Captain István Garai; and Lieutenant Endre Bodolai. Among those active at the Dréher Breweries were Ferenc Sziklai, András Medgyesi, Dezső Büss, Gyula Őri, György Fekete, Sándor Ilonka, János Teveli, István Szőllősi, Géza Szabados, József Tóth, Mihály Juhász, Sándor Posgai, Gábor Keresztesi, István Felföldi, Imre Garai, Sándor Fehér, Megyeri, Budai, Mihály Szabó, and József Horváth.[109] The investigative team in the mayor's office consisted of police officers Dr. Toperczel, Tapasztó, and Váradi.[110]

According to Péter Hain, the chief of the Hungarian Gestapo, Jewish wealth worth 41 million gold *Pengős* was "recovered" as a result of the "investigations," and suits were instituted against 2,004 Christians "for having concealed Jewish property."[111] As was the case in most ghettos, many of the policemen and gendarmes participating in the investigations succumbed to the temptation of easy loot and pocketed some of the confiscated valuables. So extensive was the practice in Nagyvárad that a special prosecutor of the Center for State Defense, Dr. Dénes Kovács, was called in to investigate.[112]

On 17 May Minister of the Interior Andor Jaross came to Nagyvárad to officiate at the inauguration of Dr. Károly Rajnay (Reiner) as the new prefect of Bihar County.[113] Speaking two days after the beginning of the deportations in Carpatho-Ruthenia, Jaross declared:

> Today I saw a new Nagyvárad emerge in the sunshine of May. I saw that here was the new nationalist Nagyvárad, where there are no Jews in the streets. I am convinced that there has been an appropriate segregation of the Jews in this city. Nagyvárad solved this problem and I notice with satisfaction that this solution is in accord with the requirements of the age. The Jewish problem, however, is not

ended with this. One must remove from the nation's bloodstream every infecting material and the possibility of any infection. In this regard the Hungarian government marches on step by step. I don't want to make any declaration on this; please follow events carefully.[114]

Endre also expressed great satisfaction over the achievements in the ghetto when he returned to the city on 18 May.[115] These "achievements" can be attributed largely to the advice the authorities received from Theodor Dannecker, the Eichmann-*Sonderkommando*'s representative in the city, who had already established his reputation in France and elsewhere in Nazi-occupied Europe.

The calvary of the Jews of Nagyvárad, which began on 31 March,[116] came to a climax on 23 May, when the first deportation train left the city.[117] The deportation of 23 May involved the rural Jews in the Mezey Lumber Yard. The first train from the ghetto proper left on 28 May and the last one on 3 June. Two additional transports left Nagyvárad on 5 June and 27 June with 2,527 and 2,819 Jews, respectively. The total number of Jews deported from Nagyvárad was 27,212.[118]

A small number of Jews managed to escape deportation by hiding in well camouflaged places within the ghetto.[119] Some, however, were discovered and deported with the transports from the gendarmerie districts cleared after Northern Transylvania.

The Székely Land

In Gendarmerie District X, the so-called Székely Land *(Székelyföld),* which covered Maros-Torda, Csík, Udvarhely, and Háromszék counties, the Jews were placed in three major ghettos: Marosvásárhely, Szászrégen, and Sepsiszentgyörgy.

The concentration of the Jews of the Székely Land counties was carried out in accordance with the decisions of a conference held in Marosvásárhely on 28 April 1944. The conference was chaired by Endre and attended by all prefects, deputy prefects, mayors of cities, heads of districts, and top police and gendarmerie officers of the area. As decided at this conference, the ghetto of Marosvásárhely held not only the local Jews but also those from the communities in Udvarhely County and the western part of Maros-Torda County. The ghetto of Szászrégen held the Jews of the communities in the eastern part of Maros-Torda County and in the northern part of Csík County. The ghetto of Sepsiszentgyörgy was established for the Jews of Háromszék County and the southern part of Csík County. As was the case everywhere else, the Jews of the various communities were first concentrated in the local synagogues, schools, or police headquarters, and then transferred to the assigned ghettos.[120]

Marosvásárhely. The ghetto of Marosvásárhely was located in a dilapidated brickyard at Koronkai Road. Encompassing an area of approximately 20,000 square meters, it had one large building with a broken roof and cement floors; since it had not been in use for several years, it was also extremely dirty. The ghetto had a population of 7,380 Jews,[121] of which around 5,500 were from the city itself[122] and the remainder from the communities in the western part of Maros-Torda County and from Udvarhely County. Among these were the 276 Jews of Székelyudvarhely[123] and the Jews of Bözödújfalu, descendants of the Székely who had converted to Judaism in the early days of the Transylvania Principality. Allegedly these Jews were given an opportunity to escape the ghettoization if they would declare that they were in fact Christian Magyars, but, according to one source, they refused to do so.[124]

In the brickyard, the largest ghetto in the area, approximately 2,400 of the 7,380 Jews found accommodation in the brickdrying barns.[125] The others had to make do in the open. The commander of the ghetto was police chief Géza Bedő; his deputy was Dezső Liptai. The Jewish Council, which did its best to alleviate the plight of the Jews, included Samu Ábrahám,[126] Mayer Csengeri, Mór Darvas, Ernő Goldstein, József Helmer, Dezső Léderer, Jenő Schwimmer, Ernő Singer, and Manón Szofer.[127]

Conditions in the ghetto were as miserable as everywhere else, the water supply being particularly bad. Responsibility for the failure of health and sanitary services in the ghetto must be borne by Dr. Ádám Horváth, the city health officer, and his deputy, Dr. Mátyás Talos.

The Marosvásárhely Jews were concentrated under the overall guidance of Mayor Ferenc Májay, who had attended the conference with Endre. In fact, Májay proceeded with the implementation of Endre's directives the day after the conference, when he ordered that the main synagogue be converted into a makeshift hospital. The police and gendarmerie units directly involved in the ghettoization process were under the direct command of Colonel János Papp, the head of the Gendarmerie Inspectorate in the four counties of the Székely Land; Colonel János Zalantai, the commander of the Legion of Gendarmes of Maros-Torda County; and Géza Bedő. Leadership roles were also played by Colonel Géza Körmendi, the head of the *Honvéd* units in the city and the county, and General István Kozma, the head of the so-called Székely Border Guard *(Székely Határőr)* paramilitary organization. The involvement of these *Honvéd* officials was exceptional, inasmuch as regular military units were not normally involved in the ghettoization process. Kozma claimed that he had gotten involved at the personal request of Endre. Technical advice in the course of the anti-Jewish operations was provided by the local representative of the Gestapo, Major Schröder.[128]

The harshness and effectiveness of the local military-administrative authorities notwithstanding, Paksi-Kiss found much wanting in their operations and provided a special unit of gendarmes for their assistance.[129] The concentration of the Jews was carried out with the help of the local chapter of the Levente paramilitary youth organization. Several of its members were caught taking money from the Jews for forwarding letters and messages.[130]

Májay's immediate collaborators in the initiation and administration of the anti-Jewish measures in Marosvásárhely were Ferenc Henner, the head notary in the mayor's office, and Ernő Javor, the head notary of the prefecture. Within the county of Maros-Torda, the concentration was carried out under the direction of Andor Joós and Zsigmond Marton, prefect and deputy prefect, respectively.

In Udvarhely County and the city of Székelyudvarhely, the county seat, the ghettoization was carried out under the general guidance of Dezső Gálfy, the prefect. Immediate command in the county was exercised by Deputy Prefect István Bonda and Lieutenant Colonel László Kiss, the commander of the gendarmerie in the county. In Székelyudvarhely, the roundup was directed by Mayor Ferenc Filó, and police chief János Zsigmond.

As in all other major ghettos, the Marosvásárhely ghetto had a "screening commission" whose function was to evaluate petitions from Jews, including those claiming exemption status. The commission, whose position toward the Jews was absolutely negative, consisted of Májay, Bedő, and Colonel Loránt Bocskor of the gendarmerie. In Marosvásárhely there was also a "mint," located in a small building within the ghetto. Among the torturers active in the drive for Jewish valuables were Ferenc Sallós and Captains Konya and Pintér of the gendarmerie. In one respect the "mint" of Marosvásárhely was unique: It had a Jewish informer working with the officials. He was József Lax, a jeweler with close ties to the local police and the counterintelligence service, who reportedly had personal knowledge of the jewelry owned by the wealthier Jews. Occasionally he "intervened" with the authorities on behalf of Jews in return for large sums of money, which were then shared with the officials.[131] The first transport was entrained for Auschwitz on 27 May. By 8 June, when the third and last transport departed, 7,549 Jews were removed from these local ghettos.[132]

Szászrégen. The ghetto of Szászrégen was established in a totally inadequate brickyard selected by Mayor Imre Schmidt and police chief János Dudás. Both of them had attended the Marosvásárhely Conference with Endre on 28 April. They were assisted in this decision, as in the roundup of the Jews, by Major

László Komáromi, the head of the *Honvéd* forces in Szászrégen; Lieutenant G. Szentpáli Kálmán, the commander of the local gendarmerie unit; and Jenő Csordácsics, a counselor in the mayor's office and the local "expert" on the Jewish question.

Most of the Jews were housed in brick-drying sheds without walls. A number had to live in the open, and a few were allowed to stay in houses at the edge of the city right next to the brickyard. At its peak, the ghetto population was 4,000,[133] with approximately 1,400 from the city itself.[134] The remainder were brought in from the eastern part of Maros-Torda County and from the northern part of Csík County.

The Jews of Gyergyószentmiklós in Csík County were rounded up under the direction of Mayor Mátyás Tóth and police chief Géza Polánkai. (Polánkai's predecessor, police chief Örményi, had resigned rather than become involved in such immoral activities.) Here even exempted Jews were picked up and held together with the others in a local primary school, where searches for valuables were conducted by Béla Ferenczi, a member of the local police department. After three days in the school, where they were given practically no food, the Jews were transferred to the Szászrégen ghetto.

The ghetto was guarded by a special unit of 40 gendarmes sent in from Szeged[135] in addition to the local police. The conditions in the ghetto were similar to those elsewhere. The searches for valuables were conducted by the police and gendarmerie officers mentioned above, assisted by Pál Bányai, Balázs Biró, András Fehér, and István Gősi, members of a special gendarme investigative unit. To help with the "interrogation" of the Jews from Gyergyószentmiklós, Béla Ferenczi was summoned from that city. Vaginal searches were performed primarily by Irma Lovas. Immediate command in the ghetto was exercised by János Dudás, though two others vied for a while for this infamous position—Komáromi and György Füleki Kugler, a leader of the local Arrow Cross party. As a consolation for their defeat by Dudás, they were allowed to participate in the "search parties," during which they gave vent to their sadistic instincts.[136]

During the short lifetime of the ghetto, a number of the men were put to work in the construction of a nearby airport. About 20 Jewish women were assigned every day to the Germans for kitchen and household work.[137] The ghetto was liquidated with the deportation of the Jews on June 4. (See Appendix 2)

Sepsiszentgyörgy. The ghetto of Sepsiszentgyörgy held the local Jews as well as those from the small communities in Háromszék County and the southern part of Csík County. The total ghetto population numbered only 850.[138]

The commission for the selection of the ghetto site consisted of Dr. Gábor

Szentiványi, the prefect of Háromszék County, who behaved quite decently toward the rural population; Dr. Andor Barabás, the deputy prefect; Dr. András Virányi, the mayor; Dr. István Vincze, the chief of the Sepsiszentgyörgy police; and Lieutenant Colonel Balla, the commander of the gendarmes in Háromszék County. All of them had attended the Marosvásárhely Conference with Endre. The ghettoization of the few hundred Jews of Sepsiszentgyörgy differed from the procedure followed elsewhere. On 2 May the Jews were informed by the police to appear the following morning at 6:00 at police headquarters with all members of their families. One member of each family was then allowed to return home in the company of a policeman to pick up the essential goods permitted by the authorities. After this operation the Jews were transferred to an unfinished building that had neither doors nor windows.

The Jews of Csík County, including those of Csíkszereda, were rounded up under the general command of Ernő Gaáli, the prefect of Csík County; Dr. József Ábrahám, the deputy prefect; Gerő Szász, the mayor of Csíkszereda; Pál Farkas, the city's chief of police; and Lieutenant Colonel Tivadar Lohr, the commander of the gendarmes at Csíkszereda. Like the city and county leaders of Háromszék County, these leaders also attended the Marosvásárhely Conference.

The conditions in the Sepsiszentgyörgy ghetto, which was under the immediate command of an unidentified SS officer, were harsh. The Jews from this ghetto were transferred to the ghetto of Szászrégen a week later. On this occasion they had a foretaste of the kind of transportation they would be subjected to later in the month during their deportation to Auschwitz, for they were packed 70 to a freight wagon without regard to sex, age, or state of health.[139]

Máramarossziget Although Máramaros County belonged geographically to Northern Transylvania, it was considered part of Carpatho-Ruthenia and northeastern Hungary for purposes of dejewification.[140] As it contained one of the largest concentrations of Orthodox and Hasidic Jews in Hungary, the German and Hungarian officials were particularly anxious to clear the area of Jews.

The details of the anti-Jewish measures enacted in Máramaros County, as in Carpatho-Ruthenia as a whole, were adopted at the conference held at Munkács on April 12. Máramaros County and the municipality of Máramarossziget were represented in Munkács by the following officials: Dr. László Illinyi, the deputy prefect, Dr. Sándor Gyulafalvi Rednik, the Mayor of Máramarossziget, Dr. Lajos Tóth, the chief of police, Colonel Zoltán Agy, the commander of the local legion of gendarmes, and Colonel Sárvári, the commander of District IV of the gendarmerie. On the morning of April 15, Illinyi held a meeting in Máramarossziget with all the top officials of the county to discuss the details of the ghettoization process, including the selection of ghetto sites. That same afternoon, Tóth chaired a meeting of the civilian, police, and gendarmerie officials of Máramarossziget, in which the details of the operations were reviewed. This meeting also established the 20 commissions entrusted with the roundup of the Jews. Each commission was composed of a police officer, two policemen, two gendarmes, and one civil servant.

The ghetto of Máramarossziget was established in two peripheral sections of the city, inhabited primarily by the poorer strata of Jewry. They were located in and around Timár, Kigyó, and Ipar Streets up to Hajnal Street and included Kamarai Road between Timár and Ipar Streets. The ghetto included over 12,000 Jews, of whom a little more than 10,000 came from the city itself. The remainder were brought in from the mostly Romanian-inhabited villages in the neighboring Drágomérfalva, Aknasugatag, and Felsővisó districts, including those of Barcánfalva, Bárdfalva,[141] Budfalva, Desenfalva, Farkasrev, Gyulafalva, Kracsfalva, Nánfalva, Szerbfalva, Szurdok, and Váncsfalva.

The ghetto was extremely crowded, with practically every room in every building, including the cellars and attics, occupied by 15 to 24 persons. The windows of the buildings bordering the ghetto had to be whitewashed, reportedly to prevent the ghetto inhabitants from communicating with non-Jews. To further assure the isolation of the Jews, the ghetto was surrounded by barbed wire and guarded not only by the local police but also by a special unit of 50 gendarmes assigned from Miskolc under the command of Colonel Sárvári. The commander of the ghetto was Tóth; József Konyuk, the head of the local firefighters, acted as his deputy. The ghetto was administered under the general authority of Sándor Gyulafalvi Rednik, whose expert advisor on Jewish affairs was Ferenc Hullmann. It was Hullmann who rejected practically all requests forwarded by the Jewish Council asking for an improvement in the lot of the ghetto inhabitants.

The Jewish Council was composed of Rabbi Dr. Samu Dánzig (the father of Hillel Dánzig, the noted Transylvanian journalist and Zionist leader), Lipót Joszovits, Jenő Keszner, Dr. Ferenc Krausz, Mór Jakobovits, and Ignátz Vogel.[142]

Like every other ghetto, Máramarossziget also had a "mint" (the place where Jews were tortured into confessing where they had hidden their valuables). It was directed by Tóth and Sárvári, who were assisted by János Fejér, a police commissioner, and by József Konyuk. The head of Máramaros County at the time of the anti-Jewish drive was László Szaplonczai, a leading member of Imrédy's *Magyar Megújulás Pártja* (Party of Hungarian Renewal).

The ghetto of Máramarossziget was among the first to be liquidated after the beginning of the mass deportations in Hungary on May 15. The ghetto was liquidated through the removal of 12,849 Jews in four transports that left the city between 16 and 22 May.[143] The local Jewish physicians and the few Jews who were caught after the departure of the transports were deported from the ghetto of Szlatina (also known as Aknaszlatina), near Máramarossziget. The Szlatina ghetto, which also held the Jews from the neighboring villages of Alsóróna, Felsőróna, Hosszumező, Karácsonyfalva, Nagybocskó, Remetefalva, Rónaszék, and Szaplonca, was liquidated on 25 May with the deportation of 3,317 Jews.[144]

There were two other ghettos in Máramaros County. The one in Ökörmező, which included 3,052 Jews, was liquidated on May 17. A much larger ghetto was in operation for a short while in Felsővisó, which also included the Jewish communities of Borsa, Havasmező, Leordina, Majszin, Petrova, and Ruszkova. Their entrainment took place at Alsóvisó from where they were deported together with the Jews from the villages of Alsóvisó, Botiza, Glod, Izakonyha, Izaszacsal, Jod, Rozália, Sajófalva, and Szelistye. The number of Jews deported from Alsóvisó and Felsővisó was 12,079. These were removed in four transports between 19 and 25 May.[145]

The Ghettoization in Northern Transylvania: An Overview

The campaign for the concentration of the Jews in Gendarmerie Districts IX and X of Northern Transylvania, which began on 3 May 1944, was generally completed within one week. By noon of 5 May 16,144 Jews had been concentrated; their number increased to 72,382 by 6 May, and to 98,000 by 10 May.[146]

The effectiveness of the anti-Jewish drive, which in Máramaros County began even earlier, was assured not only by the cooperation of the local administration and police authorities and by the direct involvement of the gendarmerie, but also by the guidance provided by the SS-*Sonderkommando* and the central Hungarian authorities, especially those under the direct command of Baky and Endre. Contact between the dejewification field offices in Northern Transylvania and the central organs in Budapest was provided by two special gendarmerie courier cars that traveled daily in opposite directions, meeting in Nagyvárad—the midpoint between the capital and Kolozsvár, the headquarters for the ghettoization and deportation program in Northern Transylvania.[147]

A few days after the completion of the ghettoization and the transfer of the Jews from the smaller communities into the larger ghetto centers, the dejewification authorities turned their attention to the finalization of deportation plans.

The top administrative, police, and gendarmerie officers of the various counties and county seats in Northern Transylvania were informed about the details of the planned deportations at a conference chaired by László Endre, held in Munkács on 8 May. The participants were told the procedures to be used in the entrainment of the Jews and the schedule of the transports from the various ghettos. More detailed instructions were also given "in the field," normally by Lieutenant Colonel László Ferenczy, the gendarmerie officer in charge of the ghettoization operations throughout Hungary. During 18-20 May, for example, he held a conference with the civilian, police, and gendarmerie leaders of the counties around Kolozsvár, giving them final instructions relating to the deportations from Gendarmerie Districts IX and X.[148] A few days later the liquidation of the Jewish communities of Northern Transylvania began.[149]

Because of the priority attached to the liquidation of the basically unassimilated Jewish communities in the northeastern parts of the country—areas that were also closest to the fast approaching Soviet front—the dejewification authorities decided to deport the Jews in Zones I and II first. The deportations began on 15 May, and by 9 June these areas were, with the exception of the few exempted Jews and the labor servicemen in companies stationed there, *Judenrein.*[150]

Notes

1. The province is identified as Transilvania or Ardeal by the Romanians, as Erdély by the Hungarians, and as Siebenbürgen by the German-speaking people.

2. For details on the Charter of Rights of 18 July 1623, see Mózes Carmilly-Weinberger, ed., *A kolozsvári zsidóság emlékkönyve* [The memorial volume of the Jews of Kolozsvár] (New York: The Editor, 1970), pp. 7-28, 263-68.

3. *Encyclopaedia Judaica,* Jerusalem, 1971, vol. 15, columns 1341-1342.

4. For details on this era, see Randolph L. Braham, *The Politics of Genocide. The Holocaust in Hungary* (New York: Columbia University Press, 1981), pp. 1-12. (Cited hereafter as *The Politics of Genocide.*)

5. For details on the Congress, see Nathaniel Katzburg, "The Jewish Congress of Hungary, 1868-1869," in *Hungarian-Jewish Studies,* vol. II, ed. Randolph L. Braham (New York: World Federation of Hungarian Jews, 1969), pp. 1-33.

6. For further details on the Zionist movement in Transylvania, see Livia Bitton, "The Zionist Movement in Transylvania," in *A kolozsvári zsidóság emlékkönyve,* ed. Carmilly-Weinberger, pp. 277-85.

7. General Werth outlined his ideas in a memorandum dated 12 December 1939. Reportedly, he also instructed General Gábor Faraghó, the Hungarian military attaché in Moscow, to discuss with his Soviet counterpart the possibility of a coordinated attack against Romania. C. A. Macartney, *October Fifteenth. A History of Modern Hungary, 1929-1945.* (Edinburgh: Edinburgh University Press, 1957, vol. I), pp. 386-87, 389.

8. According to some reports, Molotov assured József Kristóffy, the Hungarian minister in Moscow, that the USSR supported Hungary in its demands against Romania. These assurances were reportedly repeated during the Romanian-Hungarian negotiations at Turnu Severin on 16-26 August 1940. Stephen D. Kertesz, *Diplomacy in a Whirlpool. Hungary Between Nazi Germany and Soviet Russia* (Notre Dame, Ind.: University of Notre Dame Press, 1953), p. 50.

9. *Horthy Miklós titkos iratai,* [The confidential papers of Miklós Horthy], ed. Miklós Szinai and László Szücs (Budapest: Kossuth, 1963), pp. 221-25.

10. For further details see Braham, *The Politics of Genocide,* pp. 165-91. See also Daniel Csatári, *Dans la tourmente; Les relations hungaro-roumaines de 1940 á 1945* (Budapest: Akadémiai Kiadó, 1974), 418 p.

11. See, for example, Ernő Ligeti, "Erdély zsidósága" [Transylvania's Jewry), in *Ararát. Magyar zsidó évkönyv az 1941. évre* [Ararát. Hungarian-Jewish Yearbook for 1941], ed. Aladár Komlós (Budapest: Országos Izr. Leányárvaház, 1941), pp. 81-88.

12. C. A. Macartney, *October Fifteenth,* p. 423.

13. Ernő László, "Hungarian Jewry: A Demographic Overview, 1918-1945," in *Hungarian-Jewish Studies,* vol. II, ed. Randolph L. Braham (New York: World Federation of Hungarian Jews, 1969), pp. 165-67.

14. Ernő László, "Hungarian Jewry: A Demographic Overview, 1918-1945," p. 171.

15. Ibid., p. 173.

16. Ibid.

17. See Decree No. 2.220/1941.M.E. of the Council of Ministers dated 21 March 1941, *Budapesti Közlöny* [Gazette of Budapest] 70 (27 March 1941): 1-3.

18. The *Uj Kelet* was launched in 1918 (first as a weekly and later as a daily) under the editorship of Ernő Marton, a leading Transylvanian Zionist figure. The paper resumed publication in Tel Aviv in 1948. For further details see Béla Vágó, "The Destruction of the Jews of Transylvania," in vol. I, *Hungarian-Jewish Studies,* ed. Randolph L. Braham (New York: World Federation of Hungarian Jews, 1966), pp. 171-221.

19. For further details see M. Carmilly-Weinberger, "Jewish Education in Transylvania in the Days of the Holocaust," *A kolozsvári zsidóság emlékkönyve,* pp. 269-76.

20. Arthúr Geyer, "Az első magyarországi deportálás" [The first deportation in Hungary], *Uj Élet Naptár, 1960–1961* [New Life Calendar, 1960-1961] (Budapest: Magyar Izraeliták Országos Képviselete, 1960), pp. 75-76.

21. For details see Braham, *The Politics of Genocide,* pp. 199-207.

22. All Jewish males born between 1 January 1894 and 31 December 1924 were required to register with the military authorities during December 1942 and supplied with a photo identification. For further details see *Székely Nép* [Székely people], Sepsiszentgyörgy (29 November 1942): 2.

23. For details see Randolph L. Braham, *The Hungarian Labor Service System, 1939–1945* (Boulder, Col.: East European Quarterly, 1977), 159 p. (distributed by Columbia University Press). See also Braham, *The Politics of Genocide,* pp. 285-361.

24. For details on the Wannsee Conference, see Raul Hilberg, *The Destruction of the European Jews* (Chicago: Quadrangle Books, 1961), pp. 263-66.

25. For details on the Kállay era, see Braham, *The Politics of Genocide,* pp. 222-54.

26. For details on the background and composition of the Sztójay government, see ibid, pp. 400-17.

27. For details on the council's activities see ibid., pp. 418-79.

28. Early in September 1944, when the combined Soviet-Romanian forces were already fighting in Transylvania, Ricsóy-Uhlarik was replaced as government commissioner by Count Béla Bethlen, the prefect of Szolnok-Doboka County. For further details on this and the other measures

relating to the ghettoization and concentration of the Jews, see ibid., pp. 528–38. On Count Bethlen's appointment see *Ellenzék* [Opposition], Kolozsvár (5 September 1944), p. 3.

29. For further details see Braham, *The Politics of Genocide,* pp. 534–37.

30. Statement by László Endre given on 17 December 1945 in connection with the preparation of the prosecution by Dr. Endre Pollák of the cases against László Gyapai, László Csóka, and László Vásárhelyi, the mayors of Nagyvárad, Szatmárnémeti, and Kolozsvár, respectively. The original Endre statement is in the possession of this author. See Appendix 4.

31. Endre statement cited above.

32. Ferenczy Report F. I. Israel Police, Bureau 06, Eichmann Trial Doc. no. 1314.

33. Ferenczy Report dated 3 May 1944. Israel Police Bureau 06, Eichmann Trial Doc. no. 1315. Ferenczy sent his reports on the operations in Northern Transylvania to Department XX of the Ministry of the Interior with copies to Secretaries of State Baky and Endre, the head of Department VII of the Ministry of the Interior, the commander of the investigative unit of the gendarmerie, and Béla Ricsóy-Uhlarik, the government commissioner for Northern Transylvania.

34. Tribunalul Poporului, Cluj. *Hotă rârea Nr. 8. Şedinţa Publică din 31 Mai 1946* [Judgment No. 8. Public Session of 31 May 1946], p. 21. (Cited hereafter as *Judgment.* All references are to the official Romanian version of the document.)

35. Endre's statement of 17 December 1945.

36. *Uj Magyarság,* 15 May 1944. The interview was reproduced in the *Völkischer Beobachter* of 17 May 1944.

37. For details on what the Jewish and the non-Jewish leaders did or did not know about the realities of the Nazis' Final Solution program, see Braham, *The Politics of Genocide,* pp. 691–731.

38. For incidents of denunciations, see *Judgment,* pp. 58–65, 81–88.

39. Ferenczy Report of 3 May. Israel Police Bureau 06, Eichmann Trial Doc. No. 1315. For details on the treatment of the Romanians during the Hungarian era, consult *Tribunalul Poporului, Cluj. Completul de judecată. Hotărírea No. 1. Şedinţa Publică din 13 Martie 1946* [Judgment. Decision No. 1. Public Session of March 1, 1946], 59 p. Judgment rendered against 63 individuals accused of war crimes. See also Ion Spălăţelu; "The Horthyist Occupation of Northern Transylvania (1940–1944)," in *Romanian News,* Bucharest, 4, no. 8 (9 May 1978): 8–9.

40. Marton's stand in behalf of the Jews was rebuked by the government. He returned to Alba Iulia at the end of May and was not allowed back to Kolozsvár until after the war. Béla Vágó, "The Destruction of the Jews of Transylvania," pp. 192–93. For details on the attitudes and reactions of the Christian churches, see Braham, *The Politics of Genocide,* pp. 1027–56.

41. For a partial identification of those arrested, see *Ellenzék,* 21 April 1944, p. 4.

42. For text of the announcement, see *Ellenzék,* 3 May 1944, p. 3.

43. Vásárhelyi, a city councillor, was appointed mayor early in April after Tibor Keledy was assigned to serve as mayor of Budapest. Lajos Marton, *A Svájcba 1944 augusztusban és decemberben érkezett bergen-belseni csoport eseményeinek rövid kronográfiája* [A Short Chronology of the Bergen-Belsen Group that Arrived in Switzerland in August and December 1944] (Geneva, 1945), p. 6 (manuscript).

44. The German security police unit arrived in Kolozsvár on 30 March 1944 and established its headquarters in the Péter-Pál villa at 24 Apácai Csere János Street. Ibid.

45. Ferenczy Report of 10 May. Israel Police. Bureau 06, Eichmann Trial Doc. no. 1317.

46. Kasztner claims that 18,000 Jews were in the ghetto of Kolozsvár. *Der Kastner-Bericht über Eichmanns Menschenhandel in Ungarn* [The Kasztner Report on Eichmann's Trade in Men in Hungary], ed. Ernest Landau (Munich: Kindler, 1961), p. 107. (Cited hereafter as *Der Kastner-Bericht*). According to the census of 1941, the city had a total population of 110,956, of which 16,763 were Jews. In 1947 the city had a Jewish population of about 6,500, consisting not only of the local survivors of the Holocaust, but also of persons who moved in from neighboring rural

communities and from such Southern Transylvanian towns as Turda and Uioara. *Aşezările evreilor din România. Memento statistic* [The Settlements of the Jews in Romania. Statistical Synopsis] (Bucharest: Congresul Mondial Evreesc. Secţiunea din România, 1947). (Cited hereafter as *Aşezările evreilor.*)

47. *Judgment,* pp. 74–92.

48. Fischer was born in 1887 in Tiszaujhely. He came to Kolozsvár in 1913. In 1920 he was elected head of the Zionist Association of Transylvania and the Banat *(Erdély-Bánáti Cionista Szövetség).* Shortly thereafter he was also elected president of the Neolog community and as a Jewish party representative in the Romanian Parliament. He headed the so-called Kasztner group both in Bergen-Belsen and in Switzerland. He died in Israel in 1952. Carmilly-Weinberger, *A kolozsvári zsidóság emlékkönyve,* pp. 86–88.

49. Carmilly-Weinberger, *A kolozsvári zsidóság emlékkönyve,* p. 223. Following the council's reorganization late in April, the membership included Fischer, Marton, Léb, and the following new members; Ernő Kasztner (Rudolph Kasztner's brother), Pál Klein (Joel Brand's brother-in-law), and Dr. Jenő Weisz (Fischer's brother-in-law). Ibid., p. 225. Zoltán Glatz claims that the council was composed of Fischer, Endre Balázs, and Sándor Weisz. See his statement in Yad Vashem, Archives M-20/95.

50. Marton, *A Svájcba 1944 augusztusban.*

51. For details on the so-called Kasztner transports and the controversy they evoked after the war in Israel, see Braham, *The Politics of Genocide,* pp. 951–76.

52. Report of Zoltán Glatz. Yad Vashem, Archives M-20/95. For further details on the fate of the Jewish community of Kolozsvár and its environs, see Carmilly-Weinberger, *A kolozsvári zsidóság emlékkönyve.* See also *Zikkaron netsah le'kehila ha'kedosha Kolozhvar-Klauzenburg asher nehreva ba'shoa* [Everlasting Memorial to the Martyred Community of Kolozsvár Which Perished in the Holocaust], ed. Sh. Zimroni and Y. Schwartz (Tel Aviv: Former Residents of Kolozsvár in Israel, 1968), 118 p. Mimeographed in Hebrew and Hungarian. See also the personal accounts of Ester Pollák (YIVO, 770/184), Ferdinand Salamon (774/2872), and S. Weisz (775/3115).

53. *Ellenzék,* 15 May 1944, p. 5.

54. Ibid., 17 July 1944, p. 3.

55. Personal communication by Michael Bar-On. For further details see *Szamosujvár, Iklód és környéke* [Szamosujvár, Iklód, and Environs], ed. Michael Bar-On (Deutsch) (Tel Aviv: Izsák Efrájim és Fia, 1971), 90–190 pp. Pages 157–82 contains the lists of the martyred Jews of the various communities in Szamosujvár District.

56. *Judgment,* p. 142.

57. Until the German occupation, Count Bethlen also served as the prefect of Beszterce-Naszód County. Late in April 1944, when the new pro-Sztójay prefects were appointed in Northern Transylvania, Bethlen's role in Beszterce-Naszód County was taken over by Kálmán Borbély. *Ellenzék,* 27 April 1944, p. 2.

58. Mayor Veress' virulent anti-Semitism was revealed even before the German occupation. As early as the summer of 1942 he applied to the government in Budapest for authorization to requisition Jewish business establishments in the city. Ibid., 1 September 1942, p. 2.

59. *"Volt egyszer egy Dés..."* [There Was Once Upon a Time a Dés...], ed. Zoltán Singer (Tel Aviv: A Dés és Vidékéről Elszármazottak Landsmannschaftja, n.d.), pp. 426–27, 432. Vékás committed suicide after the war.

60. Ibid.

61. Ferenczy Report of 10 May. Israel Police, Bureau 06, Eichmann Trial Doc. no. 1317.

62. In 1941 Dés had a total population of 16,353, of which 3,719 were Jews. In 1947 there were 1,020 Jews in the city, including those who moved in from the neighboring villages and from

elsewhere in Romania. *Aşezările evreilor,* pp. 201–7. At the time of the ghettoization, the community consisted of 3,266 people. (Several hundred additional males were serving in labor service companies.) A list of the 3,266 Jews (a copy is in possession of this author) was prepared by order of the authorities shortly before the beginning of the anti-Jewish operations. Only 239 of them returned after the war. Singer, *"Volt egyszer egy Dés...,"* p. 459. For a partial list of the martyred Jews of Dés, see Ibid., pp. 465–542.

63. For details on the Jewish communities of these district seats and of the neighboring villages, including Alőr, Alsó-Ilosva, Apanagyfalu, Domokos, Felőr, Galgó, Ispánmező, Kaczkó, Kosály, Mikeháza, Somkerék, and Szöcs, see Ibid., pp. 291–459, 616–25. The same source lists all the Jewish settlements of Szolnok-Doboka (Szamos) County with some statistical data for 1857, 1886, 1891, 1930, 1944, and 1946 (pp. 178–86), and gives the names of the martyred Jews of Bethlen, Magyarlápos, Nagyilonda, Retteg, and some neighboring smaller communities (pp. 543–90).

64. Ferenczy Report of 5 May 1944.
65. Ibid., 6 May 1944.
66. Ibid., 7 May 1944.
67. For details on the activities of these individuals, see *Judgment,* pp. 135–40.
68. Ibid., pp. 140–42.
69. Ferenczy Report of 6 May 1944. Schilling's successor as deputy prefect of Szolnok-Doboka County was Géza Czanik, who was officially appointed early in July 1944. *Ellenzék,* 5 July 1944, p. 3. In his telegram dated 8 May 1944, Veesenmayer claimed that Count Béla Bethlen, the prefect of Szolnok-Doboka County, had also resigned. *The Destruction of Hungarian Jewry. A Documentary Account,* comp. and ed. Randolph L. Braham (New York: World Federation of Hungarian Jews, 1963), 2 vols., Doc. No. 264. (Cited hereafter as *RLB.*) Ferenczy, however, does not mention Count Bethlen at all. Singer, in turn, mistakenly asserts that Bethlen had cooperated with the authorities and been condemned by a postwar People's Tribunal to ten years of forced labor. (*"Volt egyszer egy Dés...,"* p. 422). In fact it was Schilling rather than Bethlen who was condemned to 10 years' imprisonment.*Judgment,* p. 173.
70. Singer, *"Volt egyszer egy Dés...,"* p. 422.
71. Ibid., p. 432, and personal communication to this author by Singer dated 11 January 1973.
72. Ibid., pp. 446 and 450. See also Appendix 2. For further details on the fate of the Jews of Szolnok-Doboka County, see Singer's account cited above and the statements of Andreas Havas (Yad Vashem, Jerusalem, 015/17-3, 1016/55) and Ephraim (Ferenc) Singer (Yad Vashem, 0-3/1756).
73. Among these was Mrs. Izsák Klermann, who was hidden by Romanians, and Mrs. Regina Fuchs, who tried to escape with the aid of István Molnár, a Hungarian policeman. See *Ellenzék,* 21 July 1944, p. 5, and 27 July 1944, p. 4.
74. Andrei Paul [Endre Pollák], *Az északerdélyi zsidó lakosság deportálása 1944-ben* [The Deportation of the Jewish Population of Northern Transylvania in 1944]. Manuscript, pp. 9 and 48. Andrei Paul was one of the chief prosecutors in the war crimes trials held in Kolozsvár in 1945–46.
75. For an account of the Jewish community of Tasnád, which numbered about 800 in 1944, see Abraham Fuchs, *Tasnád* [Jerusalem: The Author, 1973], 276 pp. (Hebrew).
76. Ferenczy Report of 6 May 1944.
77. Ibid., 5 May 1944.
78. See Appendix 2. For further details on the ghetto and the activities of the Hungarian officials active in the drive against the Jews of Szilágy County, see *Judgment,* pp. 115–33. See also statement by Dr. Joseph Szerényi, YIVO Institute for Jewish Research, New York, Archives 772/2593.

79. Jenő Lévai, *Zsidósors Magyarországon* [Jewish Fate in Hungary] (Budapest: Magyar Téka, 1948), p. 410.

80. Ferenczy Report of 3 May 1944. Israel Police, Bureau 06, Eichmann Trial Doc. 1315. See also Lévai, *Zsidósors Magyarországon,* p. 410.

81. Ibid. Also personal communication by Lea Merksamer (neé Lili Markovits), a former clerk of the Jewish Council in Szatmárnémeti, who settled in Israel after the war.

82. Communication by Lea Merksamer cited above.

83. Sárközi surfaced during the Hungarian Uprising of October–November 1956. Recognized by survivors of the Holocaust, he was arrested, brought to trial, and hanged in Budapest in 1960. Communication by Lea Merksamer, who served as one of the witnesses in the trial.

84. The composition of the council is based on a personal communication from József Borgida, who served as deputy head of the council.

85. Szatmárnémeti had a large Jewish community before the war. According to the census of 1941, the city had a population of 52,011, of which 12,960 were Jews. In 1947 the city had 7,500 Jews, including those who moved there from other parts of Romania after World War II. *Aşezările evreilor,* p. 194. See also Lévai, *Zsidósors Magyarországon,* p. 410.

86. Ferenczy reported the suicides of Dr. Oszkár György and his mother, and of Mr. and Mrs. Albert Weisz. Ferenczy Report of 6 May 1944.

87. Ibid, 7 May 1944.

88. The mayor of Szatmárnemeti had exempted Sámuel Engel and nine members of his family because they were raising 250 pigs, which were deemed economically essential for the country. Ferenczy, however, saw to it that the task was entrusted to a Christian by the name of Géza Papler, and Engel and his family were interned. Ferenczy Report of 9 May, Israel Police, Bureau 06, Eichmann Trial Doc. 1316.

89. Among these was András Wohl, a converted university student, who had sought refuge in the local Roman Catholic Seminary. Ferenczy Report of 10 May, Israel Police, Bureau 06, Eichmann Trial Doc. 1317.

90. For further details on the Szatmárnémeti ghetto and the officials associated with its establishment and operation, see *Judgment,* pp. 51–65. On the denunciation of Jews, see pp. 58–65. See also the following personal narratives available at the YIVO Institute for Jewish Research in New York: Eugene Sernthal (Archives. 768/3637), Mirjam Perl (770/133), Béla Rosenberg (774/2716), and H. Moskovits (776/40).

91. *Judgment,* p. 63.

92. Israel Police, Bureau 06, Eichmann Trial Doc. 1314.

93. *Judgment,* p. 64; Ferenczy Report of 10 May 1944. Among the Jews at Borpatak were the 246 Jews of Felsőbánya. Ferenczy Report of 6 May 1944.

94. *Judgment,* pp. 51, 63–74. See also the personal narrative of Herman Jeger at the YIVO Institute for Jewish Research, New York, Archives 775/3172. For further details, see *Baia-Mare, Nagybánya mártirjainak emlékkönyve* [Memorial Book of the Martyrs of Nagybánya], ed. Naftali Stern (B'nei B'rak, Israel: The Editor, 1979), 245 p. (mimeographed).

95. *Judgment,* pp. 142–43. In his report of 10 May 1944, Ferenczy claims that the number of Jews in the ghetto was approximately 6,000 and that the ghetto was established in a brickyard located at Borgó Prund, about 4 miles from the city.

96. In 1941 Beszterce had a population of 16,282, of which 2,358 were Jews. The city's Jewish population in 1947 was 1,300, including those relocated there from the neighboring communities and from elsewhere after the war. *Aşezările evreilor,* p. 178.

97. Ferenczy Reports of 5 and 7 May 1944.

98. *Judgment,* pp. 142–45.

99. Ferenczy Reports of 7 and 10 May 1944. For a detailed historical overview of the Jewish

community, including the Holocaust period, see Dezső Schön et al., *A tegnap városa. A nagyváradi zsidóság emlékkönyve* [The City of Yesterday. The Memorial Book of the Jews of Nagyvárad] (Tel Aviv: Lahav Printers for the A Nagyváradról Elszármazottak Egyesülete Izráelben, 1981, 446 p). Includes, inter alia, a thorough historical overview by Dezső Schön (pp. 18–147) and the Hungarian version of the diary of Sándor Leitner, the former head of the Orthodox community, covering the 19 March through 6 June 1944 period (pp. 261–319). It also contains shorter accounts on the Jewish communities of Székelyhid, Nagyszalonta, Nagybárod, Élesd, Fugyivásárhely, Diószeg, Szalárd, Mezőtelegd, and Biharpüspöki (pp. 323–25) as well as the lists of martyrs of Nagyvárad (pp. 388–429), Szalonta (pp. 430–32), and Nagybárod (pp. 433–34). The map of the ghetto of Nagyvárad may be found at the University of Haifa, Center of Historical Studies, File H3h28-A.M.E.1/25.

100. Gyapai was formally appointed mayor of Nagyvárad early in July 1944, about three months after his predecessor, István Soós, had retired. At the same time, Dezső Borbély, the town-clerk, was appointed as Gyapai's deputy. *Ellenzék,* 7 July 1944, p. 3.

101. One of the women involved in the search for valuables at the Érmihályfalva ghetto was Rozália Zeffer Kiss. *Judgment,* pp. 50–51. The Jewish women of Margitta were searched vaginally by Erzsébet Valkó and Erzsébet Mutza Medgyesi. The latter was especially cruel, violating virgin girls. Ibid., pp 49–50.

102. In 1941, 21,337 of the city's population of 92,942 identified themselves as Jewish. (If one includes converts, the number of Jews was much larger.) In 1947 the city had a Jewish population of 8,000, including those who moved in from other parts of Romania *Aşezările evreilor,* pp. 159–64.

103. *Judgment,* p. 27.

104. For details on the Jewish Council and the ghetto of Nagyvárad, see Alexander Leitner (Sándor), *Die Tragödie der Juden in Nagyvárad* [The Tragedy of the Jews of Nagyvárad], manuscript, Yad Vashem, Jerusalem, Archives JM/2686. The English version is available at the Central Zionist Archives, Jerusalem, File No. S26/1469.

105. Rajnay was relieved of his position by the Lakatos government on 5 September 1944 and replaced by Dr. Károly Barcsay, the county's chief prosecutor. *Budapesti Közlöny,* no. 204, 7 September 1944, p. 1.

106. Péterffy was associated with the Royal Hungarian Gendarmerie Cadet School of Nagyvárad [*Magyar Királyi nagyváradi csendőriskola*], which was headed by Paksi-Kiss. He was arrested soon after the war and held for trial at the Márkó Street prison of Budapest. He hanged himself shortly before his scheduled extradition to Romania to stand trial for his crimes in Northern Transylvania. Paul, *Az északerdélyi zsidó lakosság deportálása 1944-ben,* p. 47.

107. For the text see Dezső Schön et al., *A tegnap városa,* pp. 258–61.

108. One of those who committed suicide in the wake of the tortures was Dr. Osváth of the Jewish Council.

109. For details on their background and activities in the ghetto, see *Judgment,* pp. 26–51.

110. Ibid.

111. Lévai, *Zsidósors Magyarországon,* pp. 108, 409.

112. Ferenczy Report of 6 May 1944. Among those suspected was Pál Krasznay, the police chief counselor of Nagyvárad. Ferenczy Report of 7 May 1944.

113. For details on Rajnay's culpability in the destruction of the Jews of Nagyvárad and Bihar County, see *Judgment,* pp. 41–47.

114. Lévai, *Zsidósors Magyarországon,* pp. 137–38.

115. *Egyedül Vagyunk* [We Are Alone], an anti-Semitic organ, satirically observed that although Endre walked in the ghetto in the company of only one gendarme, none of the ghetto's 30,000 Jews dared touch him. Jenő Lévai, *Fekete könyv a magyar zsidóság szenvedéseiről* [Black book on the suffering of Hungarian Jewry] (Budapest: Officina, 1946), pp. 134–35.

116. On this date the SS entered the city and immediately confiscated the Jewish Hospital. The Jewish leaders were asked to have it refurbished within two days for transformation into a German military hospital. Alexander Leitner, *Die Tragödie der Juden in Nagyvárad,* pp. 14–16.

117. For details on the Nagyvárad ghetto, see Alexander Leitner's *Die Tragödie der Juden in Nagyvárad.* Leitner and his family were taken to Budapest early in June and included in the Kasztner group that left the country on 30 June 1944. For further details, consult the personal narratives of Frida and Ella Leser (YIVO, 772/2487), Thomas Bárdi (775/311), and B. Eisenberg (776/5), as well as Béla Katona, *Várad a viharban* [Várad in the Storm] (Nagyvárad: Tealah Korháztámogató Egyesület, 1946), 363 p.

118. See Appendix 2. For the schedule of the deportations, including details about the sequence of the parts of the ghetto involved, see also Dezső Schön et al., *A tegnap városa, op. cit.,* p. 322.

119. *Ellenzék,* 15 June 1944, p. 5, and 17 July 1944, p. 3.

120. *Judgment,* pp. 93–94.

121. Ibid., p. 94. In his report of 10 May 1944, Ferenczy claims that 6,050 Jews were interned by that day.

122. In 1941 the city had a population of 44,933, of which 5,693 were Jews. In 1947 Marosvásárhely had 2,420 Jewish inhabitants. *Aşezările evreilor,* p. 173.

123. Ferenczy Report of 6 May 1944.

124. Jicchak Perri (Friedmann), *Prakim be'toldot ha'yehudim be Transylvania b'et hehadasha. Korot yehudei Marosvásárhely ve'hasviva* [Chapters From the History of the Jews of Transylvania in Modern Times. History of the Jews of Marosvásárhely and Environs] (Tel Aviv: Bet Lohamei Hagetaot, 1977), 2:207. For further details see Róbert Dan, "Az erdélyi szombatosság vége" (The End of Sabbatarianism in Transylvania), in *Évkönyv 1973–1974* (Yearbook, 1973–1974), ed. Sándor Scheiber (Budapest: Magyar Izraeliták Országos Képviselete, 1974), pp. 217–29.

125. Perri claims that in addition to the brickyard at Koronkai Road, the synagogues of the Orthodox and Status Quo communities also served as ghettos Ibid., p. 204.

126. Samu Ábrahám, a wholesale grocer, was the head of the Orthodox Jewish community. He was subjected to much harassment by the local anti-Semitic elements even before the German occupation. See, for example, *Székely Nép* [Szekely People], Sepsiszentgyörgy, 29 November 1941, p. 7, and 4 December 1941, p. 9.

127. Perri, *Prakim be'toldot,* p. 203. This source—with one volume in Hungarian and one in Hebrew—contains a detailed, though not fully documented, history of the Jewish communities of Marosvásárhely and its environs. The Hungarian volume includes a partial list of the martyrs of Marosvásárhely (pp. 213–55) and 34 neighboring communities, including Bergenye, Mezőbánd, Erdőszentgyörgy, Nyárádszereda, Parajd, Székelyudvarhely, Szováta, and Székelykeresztur (pp. 256–64). According to Dr. Adalbert (Béla) Charap, the council was composed of Ábrahám, Szofer, and Krausz, representing the Orthodox, and of Darvas, Léderer, and Rabbi Ferenc Loewy, representing the Status Quo. See his statement signed in Bucharest on 9 February 1945 at the University of Haifa, Center of Historical Studies, File H3h17-A.M.E.1/5.

128. *Judgment,* p. 97. According to Dr. Charap, the commander of the SS units in Marosvásárhely was Captain Sotzki.

129. Ferenczy Report of 7 May 1944.

130. Ibid., 5 May 1944. See also *RLB,* Doc. 263.

131. *Judgment,* pp. 94–102. See also the personal narrative of M. Grün at the YIVO-Institute for Jewish Research, New York, Archives 776/10.

132. See Appendix 2. See also Perri, *Prakim be'toldot,* p. 209. According to Dr. Charap, whose statement was cited above, the deportations took place between 25 and 27 May.

133. Ferenczy Report of 10 May 1944. Israel Police, Bureau 06, Eichmann Trial Doc. no. 1317.

134. In 1941, 1,635 of the city's 10,165 inhabitants were Jewish. In 1947 there were 820 Jews in Szászrégen. *Aşezările evreilor,* p. 173.

135. Lévai, *Zsidósors Magyarországon,* p. 410.
136. *Judgment,* pp. 103–8.
137. Lévai, *Zsidósors Magyarországon,* p. 410.
138. Ferenczy Report of 9 May 1944. In the same report Ferenczy noted that the one Jewish family authorized to remain in Sepsiszentgyörgy—that of Izsó Silberstein—was also placed in the ghetto at his insistence.
139. *Judgment,* pp. 108–9.
140. For details on the anti-Jewish drive in Carpatho-Ruthenia and northeastern Hungary, see Braham, *The Politics of Genocide,* pp. 538–549.
141. According to one account, the ghetto of Bárdfalva included approximately 3,000 Jews before the transfer to Máramarossziget. Among those first taken to Bárdfalva were the Jews of Aknasugatag and 18 other smaller villages in Máramaros County. Lévai, *Zsidósors Magyarországon,* pp. 175 and 408. See also the following personal narratives at the YIVO: I. Berkovits (770/182) and Rose Szabó (770/307).
142. Personal communication, March 1, 1976, from Kálmán C. Kahán, the New York representative of the *Uj Kelet* (New East), the Hungarian-language daily of Tel Aviv.
143. See Appendix 2. See also *Judgment,* pp. 109–15, and Lévai, *Zsidósors Magyarországon,* p. 408.
144. See Appendix 2.
145. Ibid. For further details concerning the deportations from Máramarossziget and the neighboring communities were supplied by Kálmán Kahán, cited above. See also Rosman, *Sefer Zikhron Kedoshim le'Yehudei Karpatorus-Marmarosh.* For personal accounts by survivors, see the following narratives at the YIVO in New York: M. Moskovits (770/168), M. Drummer (770/384), Helene Beck, et al. (774/2813), and A. Káhán (776/91). For a moving though somewhat fictionalized account of the community's destruction, see Elie Wiesel's *Night* (New York: Avon Books, 1969), 127 p. The Jewish community of Máramarossziget was reestablished after the war. In 1947, it consisted of 2,308 members, many of whom had settled in the city after their return from the camps. *Aşezările evreilor,* p. 171.
146. Ferenczy Reports of 6, 7, and 10 May. The figures for Northern Transylvania do not include the Jews of Máramaros and the neighboring counties of the northeast, which were administratively considered to belong to Gendarmerie District VIII, i.e., to Carpatho-Ruthenia and northeastern Hungary.
147. Ferenczy Report of 3 May 1944. Israel Police, Bureau 06, Eichmann Trial Doc. 1315.
148. *Judgment,* pp. 146–47.
149. In addition to the references cited for the various communities discussed in this chapter, see *Toldot ha'kehilot b'Transylvania* [History of the Communities of Transylvania], ed. Yehuda Schwarz (Tel Aviv: Ha'aguda yad Le'Kehilot Transylvania, 1976), 294 p. The book contains brief historical review notes on a large number of communities, including Alőr, Bánffyhunyad, Bárdfalva, Beszterce, Betlen, Biharnagybajom, Borsa, Csárda, Derecske, Dés, Érmihályfalva, Felső visó, Halmi, Havasmező, Hidalmás, Iklód, Ilonda, Kiskalota, Kissármás, Kolozsvár, Kraszna, Magyarlápos, Máramarossziget, Margitta, Marosvásárhely, Mezőtelegd, Mócs, Nagybánya, Nagykároly, Nagysomkut, Nagyszalonta, Nagysármás, Nagyvárad, Naszód, Náznánfalva, Retteg, Sepsiszentgyörgy, Szamosujvár, Szaplonca, Szászrégen, Szatmárnémeti, Szilágycseh, and Szilágysomlyó. Of these communities, Kissármás and Nagysármás—both in Southern Transylvania—were affected in the wake of the Hungarian invasion of the Romanian-held territories in September 1944. See also Hans Holzträger, "Ghettoisierung und Deportation der jüdischen Bevölkerung Nordsiebenbürgens April bis Juni 1944" [The Ghettoization and Deportation of the Jewish Population of Northern Transylvania from April to June 1944], in *Siebenbürgisches Jahrbuch, 1979* [Transylvanian Yearbook, 1979], Munich 1979, pp. 57–68.
150. For a statistical overview of the deportations from Northern Transylvania, see Appendix 2.

II THE JUDGMENT OF THE PEOPLE'S TRIBUNAL OF KOLOZSVÁR (CLUJ): 31 MAY 1946, JUDGMENT NUMBER 8

Ministerul Afacerilor Interne. *Dos. Mr. 40029. Ancheta Abraham Josif și alții* [Dossier No. 40029. The Inquest of József Abraham et al.]. Vol. 1, Part II, pp. 891–1068.

România
TRIBUNALUL POPORULUI
Completul de judecata Cluj

Dos.Lot Nr.8/1946.

Proces verbal
Sedinta publica dela 22 Mai 1946.

Tribunalul Poporului Cluj,completul de judecata compus din:

Presedinte Dl.Dr.Nicolae Matei,Presedintele Tribunalului Cluj,delegat la Tribunalul Poporului Cluj,prin delegatia No.21788/1946 a Ministerului Justitiei.

Asesor dl. Dr.Nerva Hărăguș,judecator la Judecatoria de Munca Cluj,delegat la Tribunalul Poporului Cluj prin delegatia No. 21788/1946 a Ministerului Justitiei.

Judecatori ai poporului Dnii:
Pavel Bojan,dela partidul Frontul Plugarilor.
Belovai Stefan,dela partidul Comunist Roman.
Dan Gheorghe,dela Confederatia Generala a Muncii.
Meseșan Augustin,dela partidul Frontul Plugarilor
Covaciu Mihaiu,dela partidul Frontul Plugarilor.
Gligorin Alexandru,dela partidul Social Democrat.
Taflan Victor dela partidul National Liberal Tatarascian

Acuzatori publici Dnii:
Dr.Andrei Paul,
Grigore Rapeanu,
Dr.Simion Pop și
Ghiran Moraru.

Grefier fiind dl.Gavril Stanca
§§§§§§§§§§§§§§§

In sedinta publica de azi,data de mai sus, s-a luat in cercetare actiunea publica pusa in curgere prin actul de acuzare al acuzatorilor publici de pe langa Tribunalul Poporului Cluj din 14 Mai 1946 aprobat de Consiliul de Ministri prin procesul verbal No.12 dresat in sedinta plenara a Consiliului de Ministri din 17 Mai 1946,in contra acuzatilor :Dr.Gyapay Ladislau și complicii,trimisi in judecata pentru dezastrul tarii si crime de razboiu prevazute de dispozitiunile art.2 din legea No.312/1945,pentru urmarirea si sanctionarea celor vinovati de dezastrul tarii sau de crime de razboiu.

La apelul nominal facut au raspuns acuzatii arestati si anume: Dr.Schilling Ioan,Dr.Pirkler Ernest,Szmolka Henrich,Szabó Coloman,Cziefzperger Petru,Bathori Elena,Janoso Rozalia,Szilagy Stefan si Olah Alexandru,personal, asistati de dl.avocat Richard Filipescu numit aparator din oficiu pentru acuzatii:Olah Alexandru,Szilagy Stefan si Dr.Schilling Ioan,si ales pentru ceilalti acuzati.

Acuzatii: Schmiedt Americ,Fekete Elisabeta,Georg Iosif și Petővari Petrik Vasile și Osvath Zoltan,personal asistati de dl.avocat Dr.Nagy Grigore,aparator ales pentru acuzatul Osvath Zoltan si numit din oficiu pentru ceilalti acuzati.

Acuzatii:Dr.Inczádi Lokszman Edmund,Dr.Szentiványi Gavril personal asistati de dl.avocat Dr.Szatmari Ioan, numit aparator din oficiu.

Acuzatii: general Rajnay /Reiner/ Carol,Parmati Alexandru, Anghea Ioan, si Vancea Ioan,personal asistati de dl.avocat Dr.Amiras Aladar,numit aparator din oficiu pentru acuzatii Vancea Ioan și general Rajnay Reiner Carol si aparator ales pentru ceilalti acuzati.

Acuzatii: Dr.Mayai Francisc și Dr.Csoka Vasile /Ladislau/ personal, asistati de dl.avocat Dr.Sari Stefan,numit aparator din oficiu pentru acuzatul Dr.Csoka Ladislau și ales pentru celalalt acuzat.

Acuzatul Botos Ioan, personal, asistat de dl.avocat Dr. Botos Stefan, aparator ales.

Acuzatii : Vadas Iosif,Orgoványi Iosif și Lazar Iosif,personal, asistati de dl.avocat Dr.Blazsek Alfred,aparator ales pentru acuzatii Vadas Iosif si Orgovanyi Iosif si din oficiu pentru celalalt acuzat.

The Panel of Judges of the Kolozsvár People's Tribunal, which was organized by Law No. 526 of 10 July 1945, is composed of:

President: Dr. Nicolae Matei, tribunal head, assigned to the People's Tribunal by virtue of Decision No. 21788/1946 of the Ministry of Justice.

Assessor: Dr. Nerva Hăgăduş, judge at the Kolozsvár Labor Court, assigned to the People's Tribunal by virtue of Decision No. 21788/1946 of the Ministry of Justice.

People's judges:
Pavel Bojan of the Ploughmen's Front *(Frontul Plugarilor);*
Ştefan Belovai of the Romanian Communist Party *(Partidul Comunist Român);*
Gheorghe Dan of the General Confederation of Labor *(Confederaţia Generală a Muncii);*
Augustin Meseşan of the Ploughmen's Front;
Alexandru Gligorin of the Social Democratic Party *(Partidul Social Democrat);*

Victor Taflan of the National Liberal Party of Tătărescu *(Partidul Național Liberal Tătărăscian);*
Mihai Covaci of the Ploughmen's Front.

Drawn by lot in accordance with Decision No. 21789/1946 and Decision No. 45958 of the Ministry of Justice:

Public Prosecutors:
Dr. Andrei Paul,
Grigore Răpeanu,
Dr. Simion Pop, and
Ghiran Morariu.

Recorder: Gavril Stanca.

The order of the day being the passing of judgment on the accused in the penal cases listed in the 14 May 1946 indictment submitted by the public prosecutors associated with the Kolozsvár People's Tribunal as approved in Minutes No. 12 of 17 May 1946 of the Romanian Council of Ministers against the accused: Dr. László Gyapai, Dr. János Nadányi, Dr. Imre Németh, Lajos Cser, Ágoston Félegyházi Medgyesi, Dr. Gyula Petri, János Frater, Dr. Béla Rektor, István Garai, Dr. Endre Bodolai, Ferenc Sziklai, András Medgyesi, Dezső Büss, Gyula Őri, György Fekete, Sándor Ilonka, János Teveli, István Szőllősi, Géza Szabados, János Tóth, Mihály Juhász, Sándor Posgai, Gábor Keresztesi, István Felföldi, Imre Garai, Sándor Fehér, József Horváth, Mihály Szabó, the gendarme Megyeri, the gendarme Budai, Dr. Miklós Toperczel, Mrs. József Medgyesi née Erzsébet Mutza, the widow of János Kiss née Rozália Zeffer, József Vadász, Melánia Szilárszki née Kosári, Irén Kosári, Dr. László Csóka, Dr. Ernő Pirkler Dr. Zoltán Rogozi Papp, Dr. Béla Sárközi, Károly Csegezi, N. Demény, Barnabás Endrődi, Endre Boér, Erzsébet Fekete, Ioan Vancea, István Kerényi, Dr. László Vásárhelyi, Dr. László (Ferenc) Urbán, Tibor Paksi-Kiss, Dr. József Forgács, Dr. Géza Papp, Kázmér Taar, Dr. Lajos Varga, Sámuel Császár, Zoltán Horkai, Dr. József Székely, Ferenc Menyhárt, Dr. József Orosz, András Szentkuti, Dr. Pál Boldizsár, András Lakatos, Sándor Ojtózi, Dr. Ferenc Szász, Ödön Inczedi-Joksmann, Victor Capesius, János Botos, Irén Ujvári, Irma Enyedi, Vilmos Horák, Ilona Báthori, Andor Joós, Dr. Zsigmond Marton, Dr. Ferenc Májay, Dr. Ferenc Henner, Dr. Ernő Jávor, Colonel Dr. János Papp, Colonel János Zalantai, Dr. Géza Bedő, Colonel Géza Körmendi, Army Corps General István Kozma, Major Schröder, Gendarmerie Captain Konya, Gendarmerie Captain Pintér, Quartermaster Ferenc Sallós, József Lax, Dezső Gálfy, Dr. István Bonda, Dr.

JUDGMENT OF THE PEOPLE'S TRIBUNAL

Ferenc Filó, Dr. János Zsigmond, Lieutenant Colonel László Kiss, Dr. Imre Schmidt, Major László Komáromi, János Dudás, Gendarmerie Lieutenant Kálmán Szentpáli G., Jenő Csordácsics, György Kugler (Füleki), Quartermaster Pál Bányai, Quartermaster Balázs Biró, First Sergeant András Fehér, First Sergeant István Gősi, Irma Lovas, Dr. Mátyás Tóth, Dr. Géza Polánkai, Béla Ferenczi, Kálmán Szabó, Ernő Gaáli, Dr. József Ábrahám, Gerő Szász, Pál Farkas, Dr. Gábor Szentiványi, Dr. Andor Barabás, András Virányi, Dr. István Vincze, Lieutenant Colonel Balla, Tivadar Lohr, Dr. János Schilling, Dr. Jenő Veress, Dr. Zsigmond Léhnár, Dr. Gyula Sárosi, István Takács, János Somorlyai, János Kassay, Albert Garamvölgyi, Miklós Désaknai, József Gecse, Mária Fekete, József Lakadár, Sándor Oláh, Rozália Jancsó, Pál Antalffy, Ernő Berecki, András Iványi, Lajos Tamási, Ferenc Lakatos, István Szilágyi, Dr. István Rosner, Sándor Vajai, Dr. Jenő Nagy, Károly Balogh, József Haracsek, Captain László Berentes, József Orgoványi, Imre Vajai, István Bertalan, Péter Czeisberger, Zoltán Osváth, Lajos Ormos, Dr. László Szlávi, Dr. András Gazda, Dr. János Sréter, Dr. József Udvari, Ferenc Elekes, Lieutenant Colonel György Mariska, István Pethes, Gendarmerie Captain Dr. Sándor Horváth, Dr. László Krasznai, József Lázár, Quartermaster Miklós Sárközi, Quartermaster János Horváth, János Vida, Ádám Kerekes, Mihály Kovács, Sándor Farmati, Ioan Anghea, László Petővári Petrik, Albert Szabó, Irén Duha, István Nagy, Dr. Ferenc Molnár, Dr. Béla Sámi, Dr. Dezső Dénes, Dr. László Illinyi, Dr. Sándor Gyulafalvi Rednik, Ferenc Hullmann, Dr. Lajos Tóth, János Fehér, Colonel Miklós Sárváry, Florea Tascan, János Biró, György Varga, Gusztáv Sarkadi, István Bede, Dr. László Szaplonczai, István Komán, Kálmán Borbély, László Smolenszki, Dr. Norbert Kuales, Dr. Miklós Debreczeni, Heinrich Smolka, Gusztáv Orendi, Lieutenant Colonel Ernő Pásztai, Lieutenant Colonel Miklós Jakab, and against the accused Károly Rajnay (Reiner), Retired Brigadier General, sent to trial by virtue of indictment 2 of 26 February 1946 as approved by the Council of Ministers, Minutes No. 4 of 1 March 1946; all of the above were indicted for their role in the disaster of the country caused by the war crimes stipulated in paragraphs *e, f, g, h, l, m, n,* and *o* of Article 2 of Law No. 312/1945[1] as specified in the indictment for each accused separately. These crimes were committed inasmuch as some of them carried out the illegal establishment of Jewish ghettos; others subjected the Jewish population to tortures and other illegal means of coercion and to forcible searches to compel them to confess where they had hidden their movable goods, especially their valuables; others carried out the regulations resulting from the state of war, and the political and racial measures, in an intentionally excessive manner, while others engaged in reprisals for the same reasons; others were engaged in the displacement and removal of people for purposes of extermination, while others, acting as ghetto commanders, subjected the unfortunate people to inhumane treatment; others illegally acquired fortunes by profiting from the racial laws and measures; and, finally, others placed themselves in the service of fascism and Hitlerism, contributing by their own deeds to the realization of their political goals.

Some of the accused carried out these crimes as direct perpetrators, other as instigators, and still others as accomplices. Which of the accused committed which of the crimes and the role played by each of the accused in the perpetration of these crimes are shown in the indictment that brought the accused before this People's Tribunal.

The following of the accused responded to the call for appeal at the time of the judgment: Lajos Cser, Mrs. József Medgyesi née Erzsébet Mutza, the widow of János Kiss née Rozália Zeffer, József Vadász, Melánia Szilárszki née Kosári, Irén Kosári, Dr. László Csóka, Dr. Ernő Pirkler, Erzsébet Fekete, Ioan Vancea, Kázmér Taar, Ödön Inczedi-Joksmann, János Botos, Irma Enyedi, Vilmos Horák, Ilona Báthori, Dr. Ferenc Májay, József Lax, Dr. Imre Schmidt, György Kugler (Füleki), Kálmán Szabó, Dr. Gábor Szentiványi, Dr. János Schilling, Dr. Zsigmond Léhnár, József Gecse, Mária Fekete, Sándor Oláh, Rozália Jancsó, Ferenc Lakatos, István Szilágyi, József Orgoványi, Péter Czeisberger, Zoltán Osváth, József Lázár, János Vida, Mihály Kovács, Sándor Farmati, Ioan Anghea, László Petővári Petrik, Albert Szabó, Irén Duha, István Nagy, Dr. Ferenc Molnár, Dr. Béla Sámi, Dr. Dezső Dénes, Ferenc Hullmann, Gusztáv Sarkadi, Kálmán Borbély, Heinrich Smolka, and Károly Rajnay (Reiner), all under arrest, as well as the following defense lawyers: Dr. György Nagy for the accused Erzsébet Fekete, József Gecse, László Petővári Petrik, and Imre Schmidt as court-appointed defense lawyer, and for the accused Zoltán Osváth as personal lawyer; Dr. Felician Vaida for the accused János Vida, Mihály Kovács, Dr. Béla Sámi (court-appointed) and for the accused Irén Duha and István Nagy (personal); Dr. Alfred Blazsek for the accused József Vadász and József Orgoványi (personal) and for József Lázár (court-appointed); Dr. István Sary for Dr. László Csóka and Dr. Ferenc Májay (court-appointed); Dr. Richard Filipescu for Dr. Ernő Pirkler, Ilona Báthori, Kálmán Szabó, Péter Czeisberger, Rozália Jancsó, and Heinrich Smolka (personal) and for Sándor Oláh, István Szilágyi, and Dr. János Schilling (court-appointed); Dr. Aladár Amiras for Ioan Vancea and General Károly Rajnay (court-appointed) and for Sándor Farmati and Ioan Anghea (personal); Dr. László Gyenge for György Kugler, Lajos Cser, Ferenc Lakatos, Albert Szabó, Gusztáv Sarkadi, and Irma Enyedi (court-appointed) and for Kázmér Taar, Irma Kosári and Melánia Szilárszki (personal); Dr. János Szatmári for Ödön Inczedi-Joksmann, Dr. Gábor Szentiványi and the wife of János Kiss (court-appointed); Dr. István Botos and

Dr. E. Dunca for János Botos (court-appointed); Dr. Ernő Pásztai, represented by Dr. Zoltán Német, for Zsigmond Léhnár and Ferenc Hullmann (court-appointed) and for the wife of József Medgyesi née Erzsébet Mutza (personal); Dr. Alois Nemecz for Dr. Ferenc Molnár and Dr. Dezső Dénes (personal); Dr. Teodor Criveanu for Vilmos Horák (personal) and for Mária Fekete (court-appointed); Dr. Constantin Xantorpol for Kálmán Borbély and József Lax (personal); Dr. Aurel Socol for István Komán (personal). The other accused were absent.

The People's Tribunal

In regard to the penal action before it:
Whereas the accused listed above were brought to trial before this People's Tribunal on the basis of the indictment mentioned above and Council of Ministers Minutes No. 12 of 17 May 1946 and No. 4 of 1 March 1946 for war crimes stipulated in Article 2 of Law No. 312/1945, as detailed in the indictment for each of the accused.

Whereas the defenders of all of the present accused raised the issue of the constitutionality of Law No. 312/1945.

Whereas the People's Tribunal, finding that the constitutionality of a law can be determined only by the Highest Court of Appeal sitting in Plenary Session *(Înalta Curte de Casaţie în Secţiuni Unite),* has restricted itself to taking note of this action and is leaving it for the Highest Court of Appeal to review this issue.

Whereas the defense lawyer Dr. Sándor Begosi, appearing for Margit Rosner, the widow of the accused Dr. István Rosner, requested the separation of the case of this accused, arguing that since he is dead the accusation directed against him is moot and any judgment affecting the property of the accused cannot be pursued against the heirs unless legal proceedings are instituted against these heirs, and that this procedure was not invoked in the case of the heirs of the accused Dr. István Rosner, the separation of the case of this accused is well taken.

Whereas the public prosecutors did not object to this request and the prosecution itself requested the separation of the case of the accused Dr. Ferenc Szász, the former deputy prefect of Kolozs County, on the same grounds.

Whereas the prosecution also requested the separation of the case of the accused Ödön Inczedi-Joksmann on the ground that new facts were discovered against this accused—facts that will place the guilt of this accused in greater light—and the prosecution needs more time to prove these facts.

Whereas the defender of this accused did not oppose the separation of this case.

Whereas the People's Tribunal, appreciating the validity of these requests, decided on the separation of the cases of the deceased accused Dr. István Rosner and Dr. Ferenc Szász as well as of the accused Ödön Inczedi-Joksmann.

Whereas the defender of the accused István Komán also requested the separation of the case of this accused on the ground that his presence in this group of accused is not justified at all since the deeds imputed to him have nothing to do with the deeds of the other accused, and that exactly for this reason, given the charged atmosphere, the trial of this accused may be influenced in the general ghetto trials.

Whereas the prosecution requested the rejection of this request for separation on the ground that the acts perpetrated by this accused were part of the anti-Jewish measures.

Whereas the People's Tribunal also considered the acts imputed to this defendant as connected with and similar to the acts of the other accused, inasmuch as all of these acts constituted the implementation of the anti-Jewish racial measures ordered by the Hungarian government and authorities, and thus rejected the petition submitted by the defender of the accused István Komán.

Whereas at the interrogation of the accused these responded as follows:

The accused Lajos Cser denied the facts imputed to him, maintaining that his task as an agent of the mayor's office of Nagyvárad was to take over the homes vacated as a result of the roundup of the Jews, to seal the apartments, and to take over money and valuables for safekeeping, and that the removal of the Jews was the function of the policeman whom he merely accompanied as a delegate. Thus, it was the policeman rather than he who had arrested the wife of János Puțovan.

The accused Erzsébet Medgyesi née Mutza admitted that she carried out vaginal searches of some Jewish women on the occasion of their internment in the ghetto, but denied that she carried out these searches brutally and especially denied that she deflowered young Ica Glück.

The accused Rozália Zeffer similarly denied that she caried out vaginal searches in a brutal manner, and specifically that she deflowered Olga Danzinger.

The accused József Vadász, Erzsébet Fekete, Vilmos Horák, Kálmán Szabó, József Gecse, Mária Fekete, Sándor Oláh, Rozália Jancsó, Ferenc Lakatos, István Szilágyi, József Orgoványi, Péter Czeisberger, Zoltán Osváth, József Lázár, János Vida, Mihály Kovács, Sándor Farmati, Ioan Anghea, László Petővari Petrik, Albert Szabó, Irén Duha, István Nagy, György Kugler

(Füleki), Gusztáv Sarkadi, and Heinrich Smolka denied the deeds imputed to them.

Whereas the accused Melánia Szilárszki née Kosári and Irén Kosári also denied that they took the two little girls of pharmacist Roth to Nagyvárad with the intention of turning them over to the Gestapo and maintained that having had to go to Nagyvárad they only served as guides for them so that the little girls would not stay apart from their parents.

Whereas the accused Dr. László Csóka declared that he confirms what he said to the public prosecutor with certain modifications, namely, that he had no knowledge that the orders of László Endre concerning the establishment of the ghettos had no legal basis. Had he received an order from László Endre, the Under-Secretary of State of the Hungarian Ministry of the Interior, to also intern citizens of Hungarian ethnic origin, he would have carried out this order, since he was firmly convinced that whatever emanated from Under-Secretary of State László Endre was based on law. This accused also declared that when Decree No. 1610/1944 M.E.[2] concerning the regulation of certain questions relating to the designation of areas in which Jews could live and Jewish homes was issued, he believed that the order signed and issued by Under-Secretary of State Baky on 7 April 1944[3] was merely the instruction for carrying out Decree No. 1610/1944 M.E. published in the *Budapesti Közlöny* (Gazette of Budapest) of 28 April 1944. Finally, this accused admitted that when the Jews were interned in the ghetto in the city of Szatmárnémeti he was in possession of the *Gazette of Budapest* that carried Decree No. 1610/1944 M.E.

The accused Dr. Ernő Pirkler declared that he had not been involved at all and took no position with regard to the ghetto, admitting nevertheless and in contradiction to this that he participated at the conference held by Under-Secretary of State László Endre at Szatmárnémeti and that around the middle of April he was involved on behalf of the accused Dr. László Csóka in the exploration of the city's terrain, to find a suitable place for the establishment of the ghetto. This accused also admitted that it was his task to supply the ghetto population with food, and, finally, he declared that he feels guilty for having signed the decision rejecting the request of the Jewish Council of the ghetto to enlarge the area of the ghetto—a signature which he provided in his position of expert adviser *(referent)*.

The accused Ioan Vancea denied that he beat the Jews during their concentration in the ghetto, but admitted that he picked up the two-year-old girl of Jewish origin who had been adopted by Adela Lidenthal, declaring he did so on orders.

The accused Kázmér Taar declared during the examination that he had no assignment other than to receive money and valuables in the ghetto, for which he gave receipts, and denied that he beat the Jews to obtain these objects from them, as he also denied that he appropriated any Jewish goods.

The accused János Botos declared that his function as administrative secretary of the *Erdélyi Párt* (Transylvanian Party) was not a political but simply an administrative function, that he was not involved in journalism, and that the article that appeared in *Ellenzék* (Opposition) of Kolozsvár under his by-line and that contained a report on the life of the Jews in the ghetto was not wholly written by him and that he only submitted a report on the life of the Jews in the ghetto, a report that was amplified and altered by the editors of the publication in such a way that this report did not represent his own views.

The accused Irma Enyedi denied that she denounced the Salamon family who lived at the Aszupatak farm near Kolozsvár and maintained that it was only after the family was discovered by the authorities early in June 1944 that she reported to the police, where she had an acquaintance, in order to prevent any harm to her cousin Bonyhay, who had hidden these Jews, and she succeeded in registering them prior to their arrest to create a misleading impression.

The accused Ilona Bárthori admitted that when she was asked by a Hungarian police officer where Olga Tanner lived she gave him the address even though she did not suspect the reasons for his question.

The accused Dr. Ferenc Májay tried to maintain during the interrogation that Decree No. 1610/1944 M.E. did not pertain to ghettos, and that the only ordinance on the basis of which the administrative organs proceeded with the establishment of ghettos was the one issued by Under-Secretary of State Baky on 7 April 1944. The accused also declared that the roundup of the Jews into the ghettos was carried out by the police organs and that he, as mayor of the city of Marosvásárhely, was only entrusted with designating the location of the ghetto.

That after the internment of the Jews in the ghettos, he reported orally to the deputy prefect that the situation there was untenable. The accused admitted that he was also a member of the screening commission, which handled approximately 1,500 petitions, of which almost 100 were approved. The accused explained the fact that in the ghetto of Marosvásárhely, as in the rest of Hungary, even persons not required to wear the Yellow Star were interned, by saying that this internment was carried out pursuant to an oral order of László Endre, and that he considered this order to apply to ghettos while Article 14 of Decree No. 1610/1944 M.E., which exempted persons not obliged to wear the Yellow Star, regulated matters other than ghettos. The accused admitted that as early as 28 April 1944, on the occasion of the conference held with László Endre at Marosvásárhely, he was told that the

Jews would have to take with them into the ghetto enough food for 14 days, after which time the obligation to maintain them would fall on the respective mayoral office until such time as they would be deported; the accused admitted specifically that from this date forward he was aware that the Jews were being rounded up for eventual deportation. The accused Ferenc Májay denied that he was a government commissioner after his escape into Trianon Hungary, and maintained that he was only an expert adviser to this commissioner on questions of food supply, and that he resigned even from this position after the Szálasi government assumed power, not being active any longer after this date and returning to Northern Transylvania, reaching the region ahead of the advancing Soviet-Romanian troops.

The accused József Lax denied that he was an informer for the investigators on Jews who owned jewelry, maintaining on the contrary that since he was acquainted with one of them, namely Saros, he was able to intervene in behalf of many Jews, whom he saved from beatings and tortures. He stated that he did only good for the Jews in the ghetto, bringing them food that he bought with his own money whenever he was able to leave the ghetto.

The accused Dr. Imre Schmidt, the former mayor of the city of Szászrégen, admitted that together with Komáromi he selected the location of the ghetto and that he carried out the establishment of the ghetto on the basis of a written order received from Gendarmerie Lieutenant Colonel Ferenczy.

The accused Dr. Gábor Szentiványi declared during the interrogation that he did not know of the illegality of the order regarding the ghettos and that had he known of it he would have intervened.

The accused Dr. János Schilling admitted that he participated in László Endre's conference to discuss instructions for the establishment of ghettos and that upon his return from the conference he convened the county chiefs to transmit to them what he had heard at the conference. He denied, however, that he gave any orders to the county chiefs, maintaining that the civil administration had nothing to do with the question of ghettos and that the roundup of the Jews was the exclusive function of the police and gendarmerie. With regard to the sending of Romanians to Germany in 1943, he maintained that no such conscription was handled by the administrative authorities; in the summer of 1944, when such a conscription did indeed take place, he stated that he was no longer deputy prefect, not having returned to his office after 2 May 1944 when he entered the hospital, and subsequently retiring.

The accused Dr. Zsigmond Léhnár denied that he was a coworker in the selection of the location for the ghetto, and maintained that as the physician entrusted with supervision of the ghetto, he took all the hygienic measures that it was possible to take.

The accused Dr. Ferenc Molnár denied the acts imputed to him, maintaining that he did his duty as physician of the ghetto of Szilágysomlyó, doing whatever was possible under the circumstances to assure a satisfactory sanitary condition. Furthermore, he stated that he brought about the vaccination of everyone in the ghetto, something that did not occur in any other ghetto in Transylvania.

The accused Dr. Béla Sámi denied that he had been the expert on Jewish affairs or that he had had any involvement with ghetto matters, but admitted nevertheless that he had prepared the circular for the deputy prefect of the county that prohibited the acceptance of requests from Jews to convert to the Christian religion.

The accused Dr. Dezső Dénes admitted that after the end of the military administration in Kraszna, Szilágy County, he carried out some of the expulsion measures initiated by the military command. He also admitted that in his capacity as secretary general of the Zilah mayor's office, he issued an ordinance prohibiting Jews from shopping in the market and that he also signed several ordinances and acts of an anti-Jewish nature in the name and in the absence of the mayor. He insisted, however, that these measures had been decided on in advance by the mayor.

The accused Ferenc Hullmann denied that he had been the expert on Jewish affairs, without, however, being able to justify why he resolved various questions relating to this topic. For example, on the petition by the Jewish Council to approve the release of three cows from among the cattle owned by the Jews to provide milk for the children in the ghetto, the accused made the notation: "Without merit."

The accused István Komán denied that he was involved in any way in the expulsion of 34 Jews from Borsa in the spring of 1942, maintaining that these expulsions were ordered by the county authorities and by chief district administrator Kadicsfalvi of Felső Visó. He stated that the lists of persons to be expelled were prepared by notary József Farkas, who had been entrusted with this task directly by chief district administrator Kadicsfalvi, because this notary, being of Hungarian origin, had the confidence of his superiors. This accused denied that he requested or received money from Jews to keep them off the list of those to be expelled.

The accused Kálmán Borbély demonstrated that he took over the county office only on 10 May 1944, by which time the ghetto had already been established. The accused could not explain why he did not intervene to put an end to the deplorable condition of those interned in the ghetto, although he admitted that he was personally aware of the miserable state in which the ghetto internees found themselves.

The accused Károly Rajnay (Reiner) declared during the interrogation that he had carried out the expulsion of Romanians in 1940 on higher orders and that as a military man he could not disregard orders. He maintained that he did not exceed his orders, and to his best recollection he expelled not 100 families but 100 persons as he had been ordered . . . the persons who were to benefit from these measures having been designated by Budapest, and that he himself had not been involved in the selection or initiation of these activities.

The accused maintained that with regard to the ghetto he had not had any functions in his position as prefect, since this problem was handled by Under-Secretary of State László Endre with the aid of Lieutenant Colonel Jenő Péterffy, the Gendarmerie Commander of Nagyvárad.

The People's Tribunal

Considering the documents and the materials on file;
Considering the administrative investigations before this court as well as the oral and written summaries of the parties, the following was in fact concluded:

The Jewish people, who were forced through the centuries to live dispersed over the entire globe without having a country of their own, have suffered innumerable persecutions throughout these centuries.

The social sciences have established that anti-Semitism is not just a political diversion; that is, instead of a real solution of social problems being pursued, the solution was pursued by following the line of least resistance.

Anti-Semitism in the Middle Ages at the time of the Inquisition was based on the religious segregation of the Jews.

The new anti-Semitism, which erupted at the beginning of the century, was based on the racial theory that distinguishes between superior and inferior races, with the aim that the people considered superior be in a position to subjugate, humiliate, and despoil the races deemed inferior.

This form of oppression of peoples had become part of German imperialism, the mortal enemy of progress and democracy, which destroyed not only millions of Jews but also tens of millions of people, the best sons of liberty-loving nations.

The oldest form of fascism in Europe was in Horthyite Hungary, which, as early as 1920, was the first to introduce anti-Jewish laws by adopting the *Numerus Clausus* system in the universities of Hungary. The same regime was engaged in the oppression of workers and progressive elements and in political assassinations, having relations with the Hitlerite regime in Germany from the moment it came to power. As a consequence of this Fascist regime, a series of anti-Jewish measures were adopted in Horthyite Hungary; among the inhumane measures that were carried out were the deportation of a number of Jews to Kamenets-Podolsk in the summer of 1941,[4] the expulsions ordered by the military commands in Transylvania in 1940, the Ujvidék pogrom,[5] and other similar deeds.

Nevertheless, these measures could be considered local and sporadic until

May 1944, when the government of Berlin's lackeys brought about the total persecution of the Jews in Hungary by plundering, removing, and deporting them for extermination.

As the documents of this trial will show, the chauvinism of the hooligans of the Sztójay government surpassed even the expectations of the German Hitlerites.

Since the German armies, in the course of their advance in the territories of the Soviet Union, committed cruelties forbidden by the laws of warfare, the Soviet Union established as early as in 1941 an extraordinary state commission to systematize the information received from various parts of the areas conquered by the Hitlerites.

Here is how the pamphlet entitled *The Atrocities of the Fascist German Invaders* (published in the USSR by the G.P. Military Publishing House in 1942, serial 4, p. 14) describes these atrocities committed by the Germans:

> A reprisal detachment of SS troops arrived in the village of Checarevo on 21 October 1941. All of the inhabitants were forced out into the street and arranged in rows and by groups; the men and boys were separated from the women, with the use of fists and rifle butts. The officer declared: "We will not kill your men and sons; take out your things from your homes because we will set them afire." All of us then saw that the village had already begun to burn. The women started to run screaming toward their homes and the children, clinging to their mother's skirts, ran after them crying. Some of them remained frozen in fear and horror and no longer had the strength to move. At this time the shooting of the men and boys began. They were lined up against the walls of a burning building and shot on the spot from a short distance.
>
> In the village of Protasovo, Dubnensk District, Tula region, the Hitlerites undressed farmer Norozou, the president of the local kolchoz, and kept him on his knees for 24 hours in the cold, then carried him through the village, and half-buried him in the ground, and forbade the burying of the corpse for over a week.
>
> In the village of Procovski, Cheremishinov District, Kursk region, the Fascists undressed the farmer Alehin and ordered him to dig his own grave, forcing him to lie in the grave a number of times for measurement. After the grave was completed, they tore off both of his arms, cut off his ears, took out his eyes, and then shot him.

Aside from these cruelties, the Hitlerite armies carried out several others; thus in the Stalino region, no less than 25,000 peaceful Soviet citizens killed by the Hitlerite armies were buried, and in the Kiev region the same army tortured, shot, and poisoned in murder wagons over 195,000 Soviet citizens. Through these tortures and exterminations, the Hitlerites aimed at decreasing the Russian, Ukrainian, Byelorussian, and other populations of the Soviet Union in order to depopulate these areas so they could colonize them later with Germans.

In the occupied territories, the Hitlerite armies behaved even more bloodily toward the Jewish population. Here is what the communique of the Information Bureau of the People's Commissariat for Foreign Affairs of the Soviet Union writes in this respect:

> With respect to the atrocities committed against the Jewish population in the territories occupied by the Hitlerites, the system of destruction to the last man, which is practiced by them, has acquired proportions that the human mind cannot conceive.
> In two days, on 26 and 27 August, alone, the German Fascist bandits organized a bloody massacre in several Ukrainian cities.
> In the city of Lutzk they shot 20,000 Jews who had been concentrated on the pretext of being registered, while in the city of Sarnii, where only last spring they executed 18,000 Jews in addition to the thousands of Ukrainians and Russians, they again concentrated 14,000 Jews from the surrounding areas and executed them on 26 August. At Kiev and Dnyepropetrovsk they exterminated over 60,000 people during the German occupation.

This entire range of cruelties and illegal acts committed in flagrant contradiction of the International Conventions of the Hague came to the attention of the United Nations, which dealt with them in several conferences beginning in 1942. Thus the 19 December 1942 communique of the Information Bureau of the People's Commissariat for Foreign Affairs of the Soviet Union, taking note of the fulfillment by the Hitlerite authorities of their plan to destroy the Jewish population of Europe, includes a warning to these torturers stating that "heavy will be the hand of the peoples that will punish the German Fascist occupants after they throw off their yoke. Neither the leading Hitlerite clique nor the vile executants of their bloody and criminal orders will escape the vengeance of the liberated peoples." (See pp. 9 and 10 of Professor A. Trainin's *The Penal Responsibility of the Hitlerites.*)

Along the same lines, the House of Representatives of the United States of America adopted the following resolution on 19 March 1942:

> Whereas the American people view with indignation the atrocities committed against the civilian population of the countries occupied by the Nazis and especially the mass murder of Jewish men, women, and children, and keeping in mind that this Nazi policy lies in cruelties and in terror and resulted in the destruction of the people of Poland and of other countries in East Central Europe, the House determines that these bestial crimes committed against defenseless men, women, and children cannot be justified, must be condemned and are condemned as activities unworthy of any country or government striving for a place among the civilized nations. . . .
> The House resolves that the persons found directly or indirectly responsible for these criminal acts must be held accountable and punished in terms of the crimes of which they are found guilty.[6]

The American Senate also adopted a resolution, even before the House of Representatives, a resolution that ends with the following statement:

> When the hour of retribution comes—and it is fast approaching—the Hitlerites will bear the entire responsibility for this murderous policy relating to the extermination of the Jewish people as well.[7]

All of these warnings were broadcast by the United Nations and appeared even in the papers of nations with which the United Nations were not in a state of war, so that not only the leaders but any other persons who read a newspaper were aware of them.

One must also note that on 2 November 1943 the United Nations issued through the joint voice of the Big Three an important warning to the Hitlerites and their satellites, a warning issued in the name of 32 United Nations. Here is what this warning states:

> The Germans who took part in the mass shooting of Italian officers or in the execution of Dutch, Belgian, and Norwegian hostages or of peasants on Crete as well as those who took part in the extermination of the Polish people or in the destruction of the population in the territories of the USSR, which are currently being cleared of the enemy, must know that they will be judged on the spot by the people they have brutalized.

The proclamation particularly emphasized the following:

> Those who did not soil their hands with innocent blood should beware that they do not somehow find themselves among the guilty ones, because the three allied powers will certainly find the real criminals even at the end of the world and will give the accusers a free hand to provide justice.[8]

It was proven that this joint declaration of the Big Three was reproduced in its entirety in the *Pesti Hirlap* (News Journal of Pest) and the *Magyar Nemzet* (Hungarian Nation) of Budapest so that not only the Horthyite leaders but all other citizens could have taken note of it.

In spite of this, horrible crimes were committed by all who had any power, however little, and even by some who had no official function but were simple citizens who did not have to engage in such acts, yet volunteered to commit them.

The acts in themselves, as they were committed, may be classified under the penal provisions of common law. Even at the time of their commission they were clearly illegal and offenses; thus, those who committed them cannot exculpate themselves with the excuse that they were not aware of the nature of their acts and that, should they be condemned, they would suffer penalties for deeds that at the time of their commission were not incriminatory.

With respect to the characterization of these acts under Law No. 312/1945, the offenders again cannot complain that this constitutes something that was unforeseen by them because, as was shown above, all of them could have been aware of the repeated warnings issued at the time by the United Nations in this respect.

Shortly after the Döme Sztójay government came to power in Hungary, the sporadic anti-Jewish measures were transformed into total measures, and the Hungarian government began to issue ministerial decrees aimed at the regulation of these anti-Jewish measures.

One of the first measures taken by the Sztójay government was that authorized by Decree No. 1240/1944[9] under which all Jews above the age of six were compelled to wear a distinguishing sign, namely a yellow-colored Star of David sewn visibly on their clothing.

Simultaneously with this discriminatory measure, which was taken with a well-determined objective, Minister of the Interior Andor Jaross empowered László Endre, who at the beginning of April was serving as deputy prefect of Pest-Pilis-Solt-Kiskun County, to organize, as a delegate of the Ministry of the Interior, the concentration of the Jews from the entire territory of the country into ghettos and to prepare the instructions required for this operation.

Judgment No. B.X. 4419/1945, rendered by the People's Tribunal of Budapest on 7 January 1946 in the case of the three war criminals Andor Jaross, László Endre, and László Baky, reveals that these instructions, which were issued by the Hungarian Ministry of the Interior under No. 6163/1943 Kes. on 7 April 1944 and which aimed at designating the areas to be inhabited by Jews, were prepared by the two under-secretaries of state in the Ministry of the Interior, namely László Endre and László Baky, but that the spiritual parent of these instructions was László Endre; since he did not have the title of under-secretary of state in the ministry on 7 April 1944, the instructions were signed by László Baky, who was at the time the only under-secretary of state in the Ministry of the Interior.

These observations of the Budapest People's Tribunal are also supported by the fact that at the successive conferences held at Szatmárnémeti, Marosvásárhely, and Munkács to provide oral instructions and to explain the content of the written instructions to the heads of all the administrative and police authorities, it was László Endre who appeared and not László Baky, the signer of the instructions.

The preamble of the instructions states: "The Royal Hungarian Government will shortly clear the country of Jews. I order the clearing to be carried out by regions; for the attainment of the objective, Jewry will be taken into specially designated concentration camps without regard to age or sex. In cities and larger towns, a part of Jewry will later be located in Jewish buildings or in a ghetto so designated by the authorities of public order."

Further on, after paragraph II of the instructions which deals with the exemption from these measures of Jews considered necessary for the war economy, paragraph III stipulates that the people described in Decree No. 1240/1944 M.E. are to be considered as Jewish.

The roundup of the Jews was to be effectuated by the police and gendarmerie having jurisdiction over the particular territory, and, when necessary, the armed forces could also be called upon; also recommended was harmonious cooperation with the German security service that was to be assigned, as the situation required, to work in the field as an advisory body.

The instructions also direct the county administrative authorities to establish concentration camps in proportion with the number of Jews to be assembled in those camps, and to identify the selected places for the under-secretary of state of Public Security.

According to the written conception of these instructions, the first measure to be taken was the rounding up of the Jews without regard to age or sex into common camps; the second measure was the screening of the Jews with the aim of retaining in the camp only the Jews deemed dangerous to public safety, with the others to be placed within 30 days in a specially designated section of the city, i.e., into a ghetto. Since the Jews were dispersed in various communities in the country and the concentration camps designed for screening were to be set up only in certain centers, the transportation from the various localities to the centers was to be effectuated by trains along the manner used for POWs or, in the absence of rail facilities, by other means of transportation made available by the local administrative authorities.

The Jews that were to be concentrated in this manner were not permitted to take along anything except the clothing they were wearing, a single change of underwear, food for each person for at least 14 days, and luggage, including bedding, weighing a maximum of 50 kilograms; under no circumstances were they allowed to take along money, jewelry, or other valuables.

Simultaneously with the campaign for the roundup of the Jews, the local administrative authorities were instructed to assign commissions to accompany the police and gendarmerie organs to Jewish homes and shops in order to close and seal them. They had to present the keys, marked with the exact name and address of the Jew, to the ghetto commander in a sealed envelope. Items subject to spoilage and animals other than those used for reproduction purposes were to be taken over by the administrative authorities and to be used primarily by the army and the security organs and finally for local supply.

These instructions were communicated to all the deputy prefects, mayors, commanders of gendarmerie legions, prefects, and police chiefs, with the stipulation that these instructions were absolutely confidential and that the authorities and commands were responsible for keeping the secret until the beginning of the roundup.

The documents on file, the depositions of the witnesses, and even the admission of the witnesses reveal that not even these strictly confidential instructions were observed by the authorities entrusted with their implementation; this is surely because at the conferences held at Szatmárnémeti, Marosvásárhely, and Munkács, László Endre issued them other oral orders that changed these instructions in many respects, and the heads of the administrative authorities were told that the goal in the concentration of the Jews was, in the last analysis, their deportation to Germany.

That this was the case was also admitted by the accused Dr. Ferenc Májay, who confessed during the interrogation before the court panel that at the conference held in Marosvásárhely on 28 April 1944, they were informed by Under-Secretary of State László Endre that after the expiration of the 14 days the Jews would be maintained in the ghetto by the mayor's office until the time of their deportation. Thus as early as 28 April 1944, at the conference in which the under-secretary of state explained the procedural details to be followed in the roundup of the Jews, this under-secretary of state communicated orally instructions that surpassed even those included in Order No. 6163 of 7 April 1944, which appeared under the signature of László Baky.

But since these instructions, whose contents were analyzed above, were nevertheless strictly confidential instructions that contained provisions that were not to be publicized, the Hungarian government felt obliged even before the beginning of the ghettoization to concretize the anti-Jewish measures in a decree by the presidency of the Council of Ministers, in order to make it appear that these measures were adopted within the legal framework of a decree of the government issued by virtue of the provisional power granted to it by the Hungarian Parliament in matters of legislation in time of war. Reference is made to Decree No. 1610/1944, which was published in the *Hungarian Official Gazette* of 28 April 1944 under the title "Concerning the Regulation of Certain Questions Relating to the Determination of the Jews' Apartments and Living Quarter."

In accordance with Article 8 of this decree, the principal administrative official of a locality with a population of under 10,000 had the power to order the removal of the Jews to another locality determined by this official, and in accordance with Article 9 of this decree, the principal administrative official of a community with a population of over 10,000 or of a city had the power to determine that the Jews live only in certain sections or certain streets or even in certain buildings. Both in the first case and in the second, the principal official of the municipality had the duty to see to it that the necessary apartments were placed at the disposal of the relocated Jews.

Article 14 of the same decree stipulates that its provisions are not applicable to the Jews who by virtue of Decree No. 1240/1944 M.E. are not obliged to wear the distinctive badge, that is, the Yellow Star.

In the course of the court proceedings it was in fact established that László Endre, the inspirer of Order No. 6163/1944, convened two preparatory conferences for Northern Transylvania, the first on 26 April 1944, in Szatmárnémeti, and the second in Marosvásárhely on 28 April of the same year. Both conferences were attended by all the deputy prefects, all city, county seat, and municipality mayors, the chief district administrators, the commanders of gendarmerie legions, and the highest police officers. On this occasion they received oral instructions, which in large measure went beyond even the provisions of the confidential instructions referred to above; that this was the case is proved by the manner in which the Jews were rounded up.

Moreover, it was stated at the end of the instructions mentioned above that they were being handed to all deputy prefects, mayors, and police and gendarmerie units, so that there is no doubt that these were the organs that were entrusted with the implementation of all the measures relating to the so-called "clearing of the country of its Jews."

And these organs carried out their mission to the hilt. Here is how the judgment of the People's Tribunal of Budapest, handed down in the Endre, Baky, Jaross trial on 7 January 1946 under No. B.X. 4419, characterizes the role of the Hungarian administration in the roundup of the Jews into ghettos:

> There can be no doubt that the concentration and deportation across the border of 434,351 Jews from homes throughout the country within a bare two months were only possible because of the active collaboration of Hungarian authorities acquainted with the local situation. This is noted in the testimony of Dr. Márton Mandel Bolyai and Miksa Domonkos, former leading officials of the Budapest Jewish Council; according to them several leading German officials (Eichmann, Wisliceny) told them at the time that the situation in Hungary was special because Endre and Baky insisted on a quicker tempo in Jewish affairs than the Germans themselves. And according to the deposition of Veesenmayer, Adolf Eichmann, the German official in charge of Jewish affairs in Hungary, told him at the time that the essence of the deportation procedure rested on the gendarmerie and the Hungarian administration because he only had a small detachment. In his subsequent deposition, Veesenmayer declared that without the Hungarian contribution the liquidation could not have been either quick or obstacle-free, and he noted, moreover, that when Horthy declared that there would be no more deportations, nothing was done afterward in this matter.

The court proceedings reflected in the documents on file, the interrogations of the accused, and the depositions of witnesses clearly reveal that this administration's roles were well distributed among its members, with well-determined functions for each member of the state administration.

Thus, according to the instructions included in Order No. 6163/1944 issued by László Baky, Decree No. 1610/1944 M.E., and finally even the oral instructions given at the conferences held for this purpose, the person directly entrusted with the execution of the measures relating to the roundup of the Jews into the ghettos was the principal official of the municipality, which according to the Hungarian administrative laws was the mayor for cities, county seats, and municipalities, and the deputy prefect for the territory of the county.

All the other organs of the police and gendarmerie, which are together identified in Hungarian legislation as law enforcement organs *(Rendészeti hatóságok),* as well as the organs subordinated to the principal officials of the municipality—for example the district administrators, notaries, and the city and health district physicians—served only as auxiliary organs for the officials directly entrusted with the roundup of the Jews, that is, in the case before us, for the principal officials of the municipalities.

This truth is revealed in Articles 8 and 9 of Decree No. 1610/1944 M.E., articles which leave to the free will of the *principal official of the municipality* the moving of the Jews from localities with populations under 10,000 and the establishment of ghettos in cities with populations exceeding this number.

The instructions included in Order No. 6163/1944 also reveal that only the operations involving the use of armed force in the roundup of the Jews were entrusted to the law enforcement organs—i.e., the police and gendarmerie—but that the guidance of these operations, and the designation of the ghetto areas—a designation that had to take into account the number of those to be rounded up—and the ultimate decision in determining exemptions were the prerogatives of the principal officials of the municipalities, who were also the presidents of the ghetto commissions whose functions will be described below.

This is also revealed by the fact that these instructions were given in the first place to the deputy prefects and mayors, i.e., the heads of the respective administrations.

Finally, the principal officials of the municipalities were the ones who, on the eve of the roundup of the Jews into the ghettos, issued announcements over their signature ordering the roundup of Jews into the ghettos and forbidding them freedom of movement until the beginning of the roundup operations. Here is a part of the announcement issued by the accused László Gyapai, the principal official of the municipality of Nagyvárad in his capacity as deputy mayor, acting for the mayor who had resigned at the time:

> I forbid the Jews obliged to wear the Yellow Star from leaving their homes beginning with the publication of this announcement. For the time being, until the issuance of other provisions, the Jews will be allowed to leave their homes between 9:00 and

10:00 A.M. With the exception of this period, all must remain at home. On order of the Royal Hungarian Government, I place all the Jews in Nagyvárad compelled to wear the Yellow Star into a ghetto. I call upon all the non-Jewish citizens who are safekeeping Jewish valuables to report this to the mayor's office within three days from the publication of this announcement. I shall take care of these notifications. I draw the attention of all non-Jewish inhabitants of the municipality that I shall proceed with the greatest severity against those who possess Jewish property and do not report it within the deadline cited above, and shall take immediate measures to intern them in camps.

This being the case, there is no doubt that the assertion of the accused deputy prefects and mayors that their task was restricted to supplying food and construction materials to the ghettos and that they were involved neither in the establishment of the ghettos nor in the roundup of the Jews is without foundation and cannot be taken into account.

If this is the case, then even if one accepts the assertion of the accused identified above that the roundup of the exempted persons was carried out by the law enforcement organs without their knowledge and involved an abuse of power, this circumstance does not relieve them of responsibility, because as the heads of their particular administrations they had to know that not a single old man, nor a sick person, and especially not a single Jewish child remained in their cities or counties even though Decree No. 1610/1944 exempted children under six years of age from wearing the distinguishing Yellow Star, and, according to Article 14 of the same decree, they were exempted from internment into the ghetto.

But in addition it was also proved, and even the accused stated this during their interrogation (see the interrogation of the accused Dr. Ferenc Májay), that special screening commissions were established in every city that had a ghetto, consisting of the deputy prefects, mayors, commanders of the gendarmerie legions, and police chiefs; these commissions received innumerable petitions and complaints concerning the abuses perpetrated against exempted persons, petitions and complaints which, however, found the doors of reason and the hearts of these commission members closed.

Thus in addition to the fact—as will be shown for each ghetto separately—that the principal officials of the municipalities are responsible for the establishment of the ghettos, for the inhumane manner in which the specific ghettos were established, and the failure to supply them with necessities, they are also responsible for the culpable omission of not having seen to it that the subordinated organs and especially those of public force did not commit abuses during the removal of the Jews from their homes.

With respect to the law enforcement organs, a term which includes the police and gendarmerie organs, it is indisputable that these organs are responsible for all the maltreatments, all the tortures, and all the beatings they used in the course of these operations.

With respect to the role played by the prefects in these operations, there is no doubt, and it is impossible to believe, that even though they did not participate in the admininstrative conferences convened by László Endre, that they were not informed by the deputy prefects after their return about what was discussed there; and it is inconceivable that they themselves did not ask the deputy prefects about the aim for convening these conferences. Moreover it was proven—and even the accused admitted it (see the interrogation of the accused Dr. Gábor Szentiványi and Ödön Inczedi-Joksmann) —that in the course of his travels through the various cities to advise on the establishment of ghettos, László Endre always established contact with the prefects as well. It is obvious that these contacts did not aim to tackle cultural or some other problems, but were connected with László Endre's special mission.

The county prefects, knowing in advance what was about to be implemented and, especially after the beginning of the concentration of the Jews in ghettos, seeing the way in which this concentration was carried out and cognizant of the legal provisions in effect, should have taken measures to redress the abuses and, if they wanted to abide by the legal framework, should have suspended these operations or at least the abuses and reported the situation to the Ministry of the Interior.

Again, the prefect had to be the person who was informed about the tortures and horrors that were inflicted upon the Jews to compel them to declare where they had hidden their money and valuables. This is all the more clear since each prefect admitted during the interrogation that he had visited the ghetto. On the occasion of these visits, the prefect had to see the miserable state in which the Jews lived in the ghetto, in terms of housing as well as feeding and sanitation. These prefects failed to take notice, even when they saw with their own eyes how births occurred on the wet ground under the open sky or when they saw that nursing children were dying of starvation, as they could no longer suck anything from mothers whose breasts were desiccated by the lack of nourishment.

With respect to the satraps of the other accused, among them mayoral officials entrusted with the inventorying of Jewish goods—simple citizens of the city who were trained and assigned to the police organs to close and seal the homes of the Jews immediately after their removal—it was proved that these accused did not restrict themselves to the fulfillment of the functions assigned to them, but exceeded them and turned into organs for the forced removal of the Jews, often abusing and exceeding the instructions received from the law enforcement organs, and at other times turned into investigators, torturing and maltreating the Jews to compel them to confess where they had hidden their money and valuables.

As was shown above, the initiative for the establishment of the ghetto came from above, and those who had to carry it out concretely were suddenly confronted with the anti-Jewish decrees and the written and oral instructions described above.

It remains for us to examine how the organs of public administration and order, including the control and supervisory personnel such as the prefects, were required to act toward this entire complex of provisions.

As a matter of principle, it must be pointed out from the beginning that all the prefects, deputy prefects, and mayors accused in this trial hold diplomas from law schools and that as lawyers they cannot invoke the excuse that they were unable to evaluate the legality of the orders and instructions they had received or of the decrees that were published.

This being the case, they were in a position to know, and they certainly also realized, that Decree No. 1610/1944 M.E., which regulated the question of the establishment of ghettos, was itself an *unconstitutional decree*.

It is known and incontestable that the Hungarian government received full power from the Parliament to regulate current questions by means of decrees of the Council of Ministers, decrees that had the power of law. It is no less true, however, that these decrees could not be issued in violation of the Hungarian constitution, any more than the laws voted by the Parliament could be in contradiction of the fundamental law of the state.

The deprivation of rights regulated by the decrees in question pertains to the equality of rights of all citizens, which is an essential constitutional question, rights that may not be violated by a presidential decree. There did not even exist a legislative authorization for limiting by means of a decree the equality of rights of a group of citizens defined as a race, and separated as such. Thus these decrees must be considered unconstitutional in terms of constitutional law. (Observations by the People's Tribunal of Budapest in the trial of the initiators of these racial measures.)

But even admitting that one could not expect these administrative organs to verify the constitutionality of a law or a decree with the power of law, had these administrative organs remained strictly within the legal framework of Decree No. 1610/1944 M.E., they would have seen that the establishment of the ghettos was stipulated for them as an *optional provision;* this being the case, they should have noted that, this question having been left to their discretion, there was no call for them to take such a serious measure, which plucked an entire category of people, or better stated an entire nation, from their homes and accustomed environment in such a record quick time period and without the slightest human consideration for the old, the ill, and the children. Since, within the framework of Decree No. 1610/1944—if we admit that they had to abide by this measure—those to whose discretion the evaluation of the applicability of the ordinance was left are guilty of excessive implementation of certain laws and measures resulting from the state of war . . . leading to their taking some serious measures that can be construed as an actual initiative on their part.

But these administrative organs even exceeded the framework of Decree 1610/1944, which itself was clearly unconstitutional as well as immoral, and lent themselves to the execution of instructions written and issued by the Ministry of the Interior as No. 6163/1944 over the signature of László Baky —instructions that were not even formally mandatory, since a person holding a juridic title and having legal experience could determine at first sight that such instructions could not be executed.

The Hungarian administrative organs, however, transcending this consideration, also went beyond even these instructions and carried out the orders and oral suggestions of the under-secretary of state in the Ministry of the Interior, László Endre.

It was shown above that, according to Article 14 of the Decree 1610/1944 M.E., those who were exempted from wearing the Yellow Star were not to be interned in the ghetto. The article also provided that if the Jews were to be separated from the rest of the population, they were to be housed only in dwellings fit to be inhabited, with no more than three persons per room. Nevertheless, in most cases the quarters used were brickyards, amid indescribable crowding and promiscuity; where the ghetto was established in a section of the city, i.e., in homes, 14 to 15 people were crowded into a room, as for example in the ghettos of Nagyvárad, Szatmárnémeti, and Máramarossziget. At the administrative conferences, it was first stated that those exempted from wearing the Yellow Star would not be interned in the ghettos, but later, toward the end of the conference, László Endre nevertheless ordered that all Jews without distinction be interned in the ghetto, and the participants at the meeting did not protest and acquiesced to this order as well. (See the interrogation taken during the preliminary investigation of the accused Dr. Ferenc Májay.) The interrogation of this accused also reveals that some of the oral instructions were in flagrant contradiction with even the written instructions issued on the spot by László Endre and his staff, and that these contradictions were noted by the accused on the written instructions that were in a more legalistic spirit.

The interrogation of the accused Dr. László Csóka reveals that on 8 May 1944 a new conference was convened at Munkács, which was attended by the same persons as at Szatmárnémeti and Marosvásárhely, when the participants were informed about the conditions under which the Jews were to be deported to Auschwitz. Furthermore, it appears that the participants were already informed during the first administrative conference at Szatmárnémeti and Marosvásárhely that the Jews were being rounded up for deportation. Only thus can one explain that these administrative organs were of the opinion that it was unnecessary to provide better housing for the Jews and were not disposed during the subsequent days to take measures to improve conditions in the ghetto, since, knowing that the Jews would be deported anyhow, they felt it superfluous to take measures on behalf of persons already destined for deportation. Here is how the accused Dr. László Csóka revealed this mentality at his interrogation during the preliminary investigation:

> I know that the leaders of the Jewish population in the ghetto submitted a petition to me in which they asked for an expansion of the ghetto, on the grounds that space was insufficient and that sanitation was very poor. However, I did not act on this request because I already knew that transportation would follow.

Further on, the same accused admits:

> I also know, and this corresponds to the truth, that I decided that all milch cows which the Jews brought into the ghetto and which were needed to supply the children and the sick should be taken.

He surely took them because it was superfluous to give milk to those destined for deportation, even if it was from their own cattle.

After all the above, the natural question arises: Did these representatives of the Hungarian administration have to perform the roles that were assigned to them, and to carry out the orders they were given and those contained in the published decrees, or did they not? The answer to this question is clear and unequivocal: Had the prefects had the slightest humane sentiments, they would have had to refuse to support these horrible acts, and the deputy prefects and mayors, although career officials, would nevertheless have been able to resist, substantiating their resistance by the circumstance that these orders and decrees were not legal. And if we admit their moral compulsion as due to the threat that they would be fired from their jobs, one could still not justify the excesses when the questions were left to their own discretion, as in the cases provided for in Articles 8 and 9 of Decree No. 1610/1944, nor the manner in which they carried out the operations, especially their responses to the various requests for ameliorating the life of the oppressed, a humane response about which the higher organs of the type of László Endre or László Baky would certainly not have known.

After the above exposition, it will be shown how the various ghettos were established in Northern Transylvania, the treatment of the Jews in these ghettos, as well as the guilty persons, demonstrating each person's personal contribution to the violations. Thus:

The Nagyvárad Ghetto

In the ghetto of Nagyvárad were concentrated all the Jews from this city as well as those living in Bihar County. The first act by which the establishment of the ghetto was brought to the knowledge of the Jewish population was the publication issued by the accused Deputy Mayor Dr. László Gyapai, who replaced the resigned mayor—an announcement that was issued and posted on the night of 2–3 May 1944. Parts of this announcement have already been quoted above; this time, let us note that by this announcement the accused Dr. László Gyapai himself ordered the moving of all Jewish inhabitants of Nagyvárad into a special section of the city called "the ghetto," and this order—says the accused in his announcement—is issued pursuant to certain oral instructions he received on the matter.

In Nagyvárad, as in Máramarossziget and Szatmárnémeti and in contradistinction to the other Transylvanian cities, the ghetto was established in a poorer section of the city, so that in this respect one could say that those who set up the ghetto were somehow led by more civilized feelings, since here the Jews were accommodated in homes and not in brickyards or cleared forests or gardens under the open sky.

However, this argument in support of more humane sentiments is refuted by the manner in which the borders of the ghetto were established. It is enough to note that a population representing over 30 per cent of the city's total was placed in an area sufficient for at most 1/15th of the city's population, so that the Jews were compelled to live 14 and 15 people per room. (Deposition of the witnesses Dr. Lajos Jakab and Béla Nussbaum) In consequence of this overcrowding, no one could rest and the sanitary situation became disastrous, since neither the water supply nor the toilet facilities were sufficient for the needs of those in the ghetto. As the witness Dr. Lajos Jakab stated, if one adds that the city authorities intentionally shut off the electricity in the ghetto and reduced the water supply, shutting it off entirely in the early hours, one can imagine how deplorable the situation of this large population crowded into such a restricted area was.

On 3 May 1944 the accused László Gyapai convened a meeting at city hall attended by the chiefs of the various services, officials of the mayor's office, and the police chief of Nagyvárad, at which the accused Dr. László Gyapai handed the participants written instructions dated 3 May 1944 and entitled "Instructions for the Commissions." In accordance with these instructions, this accused set up special commissions entrusted with the roundup of the Jews from their homes. These commissions consisted of police representation and one or two delegates from the mayor's office. The police had the function of removing the Jewish families, and the delegates from the mayor's office were to take over the money and valuables found in the apartments, lock up the apartments, seal them off, and take the keys.

Even the manner in which the accused Dr. László Gyapai conceived the roundup of the Jews by these commissions reveals that it was his intention that this roundup be carried out in the greatest haste, without allowing the Jewish population to take along the most necessary items or to take the most urgent measures in connection with things to be taken along or in connection with the administration or preservation of the goods being left behind. And this is how matters proceeded, since these commissions did not disappoint those who established them—in this case the mayor of the city of Nagyvárad, the accused Dr. László Gyapai—and what is more in their excess of zeal they even exceeded the instructions given to them. For example, not only were these commissions very strict about the time granted for preparations, but they surpassed one's imagination even with respect to the transportation of the small amount of baggage the Jews were allowed to take along, forbidding them to hire means of transportation or porters and making them drag their belongings along the streets from their homes to the ghetto. In some cases the members of this commission even forbade a merciful neighbor who wanted to help a Jewish family with the transportation of the baggage, threatening the Christians with the statement that "it is not permitted for a Hungarian to carry the baggage of a Jew." (This was the case of the accused Lajos Cser of Nagyvárad, according to the deposition of the witness Rozália Nagy.)

Led by the same intentions, these commissions engaged in even more serious excesses. Many a time they did not allow the Jewish families to take along even a small spoon or fork or knife or any type of underwear. Other families were forbidden to take along even the 50 kilograms of baggage that were authorized by the orders and were taken from their home without any baggage and with only the underwear and clothes they had on. The transportation from the home to the ghetto took place in the most demeaning manner, and while it was going on there was no lack of shouting, cursing, shoving, and even beatings by the policemen and gendarmes. The internment of the Jews of Nagyvárad into the ghetto was carried out in record time, concentrating approximately 30,000 people during a mere five days. They were concentrated in the courtyard of the synagogue and from there they were pushed into the interior of the ghetto through a narrow door. On this occasion even children under six years of age, the aged, and sick people from homes and hospitals were rounded up and taken into the ghetto.

This was the case of a patient who had been operated on only two days earlier for appendicitis at St. Joseph's Hospital, who was removed and made to walk to the ghetto and was allowed to be taken in a vehicle only after the intervention of some nursing nuns.

The culmination of the horrors committed against the Jewish population of Nagyvárad, like those committed against the Jewish population in all parts of Hungary, came in the searching of this population for hidden valuables. The maltreatment and tortures committed in the ghetto for this purpose surpassed the most bestial tortures of the Middle Ages and of the Inquisition, and the perpetrators of these cruelties and tortures surpassed in ferocity even Torquemada in the Middle Ages. A particular specialty of the Nagyvárad ghetto, which distinguishes it from all other ghettos in Transylvania, was started by the accused Jenő Péterffy: Although, according to the general regulations, the Jews in the labor service companies did not have to be interned in the ghetto, the accused Péterffy through his agents brought about the concentration of the Jews in the labor service companies stationed in some communities in Bihar County and the city of Nagyvárad, and often participated personally.

This being, in general outline, what happened to the Jewish population of Nagyvárad between 3 May and 3 June 1944, it remains for us to examine below the contribution of each of the accused to these horrors.

Thus the accused Dr. László Gyapai is guilty because, although as a lawyer he was aware of the decrees in effect and should have known that the only decree that was legal was Decree No. 1610/1944 M.E. according to which the establishment of a ghetto was a purely optional matter for him, he intentionally accepted the oral instructions and suggestions of László Endre and decided on the establishment of a ghetto, issuing an announcement that shows that he ordered the measures personally and merely on the basis of oral orders received in the matter.

Although the accused knew that there were persons exempted from having to go into the ghetto, he nevertheless instructed his special commissions entrusted with the roundup of the Jews to remove all Jews without distinction, even children, women, the sick, and the aged; and in his capacity of supreme commander of these operations within the city, he did not supervise the activities of the commissions entrusted with the removal of the Jews, abstaining from this supervision intentionally and with the aim of permitting these commissions to engage in all kinds of abuses. This accused also did not see to it that the size of the ghetto be appropriate to the number of people to be interned there, which caused suffering, privation, and even the death of numerous people. The borders of this ghetto were designated by this accused, as was shown in the preceding section, in such a way that a population representing 30 per cent of the city's total population was assigned an area no larger than 3 per cent of the urban territory of the city of Nagyvárad.

Further, the accused Dr. László Gyapai did not see to it that this population interned in the ghetto would have at least the minimum food required for existence, but on the contrary provided for the cutoff of electricity in the ghetto and the considerable reduction in the volume of water and in the hours of operation of the water supply system.

All of these measures were taken by the accused Dr. László Gyapai in the knowledge of what was to happen to the Jewish population, a knowledge he had acquired at the conference called by László Endre, which he attended. The soul of the accused was such that instead of shuddering at the fate of those interned in the ghetto, he preferred to display his racial hatred whenever the occasion arose.

Thus, when a delegation of Jews from the ghetto appeared on behalf of better hygiene in the ghetto, the accused rejected this appeal indignantly; and when another delegation of the leading Christian public figures of Nagyvárad, who were horrified by what was going on in the ghetto, appeared before the accused Dr. László Gyapai and requested an improvement of ghetto conditions, pointing out the deplorable sanitary situation there, the accused Gyapai responded: "Gentlemen, all of these are bluffs. Take note that the ghetto is not a resort." (Deposition of the witness Béla Katona)

Animated by these sentiments and knowing that the Jews were condemned not to return to their homes again, the accused Dr. Gyapai in his capacity as mayor allowed the emptying of the Jewish homes and the removal of furniture from these homes, on which occasion he made it easy for the regime's people, in the absence of serious supervision, to acquire all the valuables from the closets and chests.

But listing only the deeds ordered by this accused and his culpable supervisory omissions would create the appearance that this accused, being mayor and thus an administrative career official, did nothing else in this capacity than carry out the orders of his superiors, which, even if these orders were illegal, cannot make him responsible of an intentional crime but at most only of negligence. However, the accused László Gyapai unveiled his soul and his outbursts of race hatred whenever he had an occasion. Thus on the very day when the ghetto was established, he issued the following statement to the local press:

> We had to solve this problem for the existence of the nation and for the victory we must win together with our German comrades. The primary condition for this is the need to clear Christian society of Jews. I saw to it that the Jews will be able to

live a normal life within the ghetto. Even if they have to sacrifice some of their current comfort, they won't lack the necessities.

Also, the 4 May 1944 issue of *Magyar Lapok* (Hungarian Papers) published the following declaration of this accused under the title: "The Deputy Mayor Took Severe Action Against Christians Who Circumvent the Jewish Law." Here is part of this article:

> Dr. László Gyapai, the deputy mayor, gave statements to the press on the Jewish questions. The placement of the Jews in the ghetto is taking place as fast as possible. We have learned that Christian elements are trying to thwart this process in behalf of the Jews, i.e., to make it difficult. They enter clandestinely into agreement with the Jews, they move into their apartments, without the approval of the authorities, and hide their valuables. I call upon the Christian population to abstain from these deeds, as I shall take severe measures against those who disobey. I evacuated the apartments occupied without the approval of the authorities, and those who moved into them, i.e., those who are guilty of hiding Jewish wealth, will be interned.

That the accused László Gyapai was aware that the Jews would not return to their homes is proven by the article in *Magyar Lapok* of 5 May 1944, which contains his declarations—declarations by which this accused aimed to earn the popularity of the poorer strata and especially of the Aryan population of the city of Nagyvárad. Here is the content of this article:

> The linen confiscated from the Jewish homes will be distributed to the population at a reduced price. The tasks associated with the transportation of the Jews into the ghetto were completed today. In regard to the expulsion of the Jews, Deputy Mayor László Gyapai declared: "I instructed the appropriate authorities that the firewood confiscated from the Jews be taken to a wood warehouse. In a short while I shall determine the firewood needs of the Christian workers and will issue instructions for the delivery of wood in accordance with their needs. I placed the animals taken from the Jews—cows and poultry, of which there are a considerable number—into the city farm. I shall assign the cows to the agricultural workers of Nagyvárad on the condition that they deliver the milk to the OMTK branch, and by this measure, I believe that the milk supply of the city will be improved. I ordered that the horned cattle be taken to the market, and they will be placed at the disposal of the Christian population."

The accused László Gyapai also bares his soul through his speech at the meeting of the KABSz (*Keleti Arcvonal Bajtársi Szövetség;* Alliance of the Veterans of the Eastern Front) organization, an association that in reality was composed of Imrédy's partisans. Here is how the *Magyar Lapok* of Nagyvárad renders this speech in its issue of 23 June 1944:

> "We will no longer tolerate the humiliation of our heroic ideal. You who have seen what Stalin did in his own country, how he has killed 30 million Russians, you know

what we Hungarians can expect from him. The answer is not a secret. It was given clearly by the Jewish people's commissar for foreign affairs in Moscow. The Hungarians will have to be exiled to Turkestan. Let no one believe that we could obtain even cattle cars for this exile. Blood and tears, the old and children, men and women, with their corpses will mark the trek of these new exiles toward Asia. And who would it be, with whip in hand, that would beat those staggering on bloody feet? The Jews, and in the first place our Hungarian Jews. Bolshevism and Jewry are the same thing. A society that wants to fight against them must extirpate this species because the Jew does not want to, and cannot, assimilate." Here, Mayor Gyapay justified the damaging character of Jewry with irrefutable data.

On the basis of the items analyzed above, it is abundantly clear that the accused László Gyapai has intentionally, and motivated by race hatred, placed himself completely in the service of Hitlerism and fascism and intentionally brought about the establishment of the ghetto of Nagyvárad on 3 May 1944 and patronized the entire gamut of tortures and cruelties committed in this ghetto, even failing to exempt from this suffering the persons who, according to the orders and instructions received, should not have been taken to the ghetto.

Concomitantly with the roundup of the Jews in the city of Nagyvárad, Dr. János Nadányi, the deputy prefect of Bihar County, carried out this evil work in Bihar County; on 3 May 1944, without having received any legal order and only on the basis of the oral orders and suggestions received from László Endre, he ordered the roundup of the Jews from all of Bihar County.

As a result of this order, the Jews of the city of Szalonta and of the communities of Élesd, Margitta, Érmihályfalva, and Székelyhid were rounded up; they were taken from their homes by the same process that was used in Nagyvárad: first concentrated in local camps, then taken in a completely inhumane manner into a ghetto separately established in Nagyvárad; the guarding of this camp and the maintenance of public order within it were provided by the accused, Gendarmerie Lieutenant Colonel Jenő Péterffy.

With respect to the treatment within the two ghettos of Nagyvárad and especially with regard to the tortures used to compel the Jews to confess where they had hidden their valuables, no distinction can be made between the two ghettos since their guarding as well as the operations of coercion aimed at the disclosure of valuables were carried out in both ghettos by the subordinates of the same accused, that is, Lieutenant Colonel Jenő Péterffy.

In the ghetto of Nagyvárad proper, it is true that until 10 May 1944 public order was maintained by the state police organs of Nagyvárad under the command of the accused police officer, Dr. Imre Németh (police captain) who lived in Budapest, 12 Nádor St.; starting on 10 May 1944, however, command over the law enforcement forces entrusted with guarding both ghettos was transferred to the gendarmes, whose highest commander was Gendarmerie Lieutenant Colonel Jenő Péterffy.

Concurrently with the assumption of command by this latter accused, the so-called "ghetto commission" was also established; it consisted of the accused Péterffy, Deputy Prefect János Nadányi, and the mayor, László Gyapai. This commission had to supervise all the measures taken against the Jews and to give its approval to all of these measures, and had special competence in determining dispensations for Jews exempted from internment into the ghetto. By the manner in which it evaluated the exemptions, this criminal trio supported the internment of children under six years of age, of women in the last stages of pregnancy, of the elderly, of freshly operated and thus immobile hospital patients, as well as of tens of people who had the right to be exempted from these measures even under the Hungarian racial ordinances.

At the People's Tribunal of Budapest, Under-Secretary of State László Endre was interrogated before he was condemned to death and asked to reveal details about the meetings he had had with the various executive organs of Transylvania. In this declaration László Endre confessed that he had held meetings with the accused Gyapai and Nadányi with respect to the ghetto of Nagyvárad and that he gave them instructions to treat those interned in the ghetto humanely.[10]

It was in the same vein that Under-Secretary of State László Baky, who was the supreme chief of the organs of internal order, also testified; on this occasion he also declared that no higher order had been issued to the effect that the Jews within the ghetto be beaten or tortured, and that if such cases took place the various commanders and supervisors of the ghettos must be personally responsible.[11]

In contrast even with these instructions of Endre and Baky, who cannot be praised for their humanitarianism, the supervising commanders of the ghettos invented the most extraordinary persecution and torture measures. The avowed purpose of these tortures and cruelties was to compel the Jews to declare where they had hidden their money and jewelry; however, in the course of the preliminary investigation and the trial of this case it was often proved that this aim was but a pretext, for the real aim was to torture the Jewish population in order to hasten the extermination of the Jews, something that all of these commanders and supervisors realized was a well-determined plan.

Thus even before 10 May 1944, a series of inhumane acts were committed under the command of the accused police officer Imre Németh. Women were subjected to vaginal searches. The people taken into the ghetto were deprived of everything they had without receiving receipts for the items that were confiscated. In this manner their watches, penknives, fountain pens, utensils, and the more valuable clothing were taken away from them. However, the real terror in the ghetto of Nagyvárad began after 10 May 1944, when command was assumed by the accused Jenő Péterffy. During his first few days, he issued an ordinance entitled "Discipline in the Ghetto," listing about 80 prohibitions of various kinds and decreeing that death by shooting would be the penalty for violating almost all of these prohibitions.

In the preamble to this ordinance, the accused Péterffy states:

> The ghetto is guarded by gendarmes. Anyone attempting to leave the ghetto illegally and without the escort of gendarmes will be shot by the gendarmes.

With regard to the proper attitude for those in the ghetto and the respect they, even women, must show to members of the Hungarian and German armed forces, here is what the ordinance provides:

> Whenever a Hungarian or German officer appears in the ghetto, the men will salute by removing their hats in a polite gesture. They may stand in front of officers only with their hats removed, and at attention. If an officer enters a room, whoever sees him first must shout: "Attention!" Standing at attention is required for everybody, including women.

The end of the ordinance reads as follows:

> In the ghetto quiet must be maintained even during daytime. Noise, singing, shouting, quarrels, are forbidden. Between lights-out and reveille, the silence of the grave must prevail in the ghetto.

During the approximately 30 days of the ghetto's existence in Nagyvárad, all of the unfortunate inhabitants of the ghetto could experience on their own skin the discipline imposed by the gendarmerie of the accused Jenő Péterffy. Thousands of persons were tortured, beaten, and maltreated by a savage group of torturers consisting of gendarme officers and noncommissioned officers who were specially trained for this purpose. In the course of these tortures and as their direct result, 17 people were killed outright and many more persons died later as a result of this treatment.

One of the adjutants of the accused Péterffy was the accused Dr. Gyula Petri, a former lawyer and public notary in Nagyvárad, who as reserve gendarmerie lieutenant was entrusted by the accused Péterffy with all Jewish affairs. Here is what his former supervisor, the accused Péterffy, testified about the accused Dr. Gyula Petri in his 20 December 1945 testimony before the People's Tribunal of Budapest: "When I was entrusted with the handling of Jewish questions, this part of my functions was performed by him as my adjutant. The above-named was aware of everything, took part in all the discussions, and knew all of my orders. I do not recall that Dr. Gyula Petri intervened with me at any time in behalf of any Jew or to request a concession or moderation of the measures taken by me."

In the same statement, the accused Péterffy also admitted that he personally established the special team entrusted with the search for hidden valuables and that he entrusted Gendarmerie Lieutenant Ágoston Félegyházi Medgyesi, also an accused in this trial, with the command of these operations.

János Frater, a former gendarmerie lieutenant, was entrusted with supervising the investigations and in this capacity, as revealed in the deposition of witnesses, he not only did attend the torture sessions but occasionally applied these measures himself.

A similar role was also played by Dr. Béla Rektor, one of Péterffy's gendarmerie lieutenants.

Here are a few proofs concerning the activity of these criminals:

The deposition of the witness Ernő Schwartz, Minutes of 8 August 1945:

> The special investigation section was comprised of about 40 people in civilian clothes, all of them noncommissioned gendarmerie officers. Their procedure was as follows: They summoned from among the Jews several who were better off, as well as some poorer people, for interrogation. When the summoned person entered, he was harshly beaten with rubber truncheons and fists. Then the victim was compelled to undress completely by the command: "Undress, Jew." He was again beaten, especially on the soles of the feet and again with the rubber truncheons. If the prisoners were male, electrical current was applied to the testicles, along with the beating. In the case of women, a usual means of investigation was to place one terminal of the electric current generator in the vagina, and the other in the mouth of the victim. Another preferred procedure was to have the prisoner stand in a basin of water, and to pump the water into the mouth of the victim through a hose until the victim fainted. Another usual means of inquisition was to stuff the mouth of the victim with a blackboard eraser. I know a number of victims who committed suicide with poison because of the horror of the tortures, among them the physician Dr. Osváth, the physician Dr. Stolz, and many others whose names I cannot recall. It was customary when their interrogation did not bring results by torture of the husband, to bring in the wife and the children who were tortured before the husband or father to elicit a declaration of the hidden valuables. I know of a case when an inmate, in order to escape the beatings and tortures, declared in advance what valuables and money he had burned. Nevertheless, he was beaten bloody. I know that there were many who died in the wake of this treatment, among them one by the name of Leopold Weisz. The number of victims that were beaten, tortured, and abused in this institution of inquisition approached several thousand. On occasion when there was no longer any information to be gained by the interrogators, they stood by the window, and picked out a few of the women who came to pick up their bread rations, brought them there, undressed them, and beat them. The terror was so strong that the people renounced their only food, that is, bread, rather than to be exposed to these tortures.

The witness Béla Nussbaum said the following concerning the procedure used by the special team:

Immediately after I entered I was taken into the cellar and with the question, "You, soldier of Stalin, where did you hide your valuables?" they began to beat me with unheard-of ferocity; after that they placed my feet on a wet rag; they stuffed my mouth with my socks; brought in an electrification machine, attached one terminal to my penis and the other to the little finger of my left hand and then started the machine, interrupting the current to make it more painful. The pain drove me to jump a meter toward the ceiling. After this procedure they took a red pencil out of my pocket and said: "We caught you as the person who drew red stars and engaged in propaganda in the city" and then proceeded to beat me again. The second day a gendarmerie lieutenant arrived. It seems to me that his name was Rektor, originally from Nyíregyháza; he addressed me with the following words: "Do you admit finally, you Jew, that you were engaged in propaganda with Soviet stars?" and without waiting for any answer he gave me around 16 to 18 slaps in the face that were so powerful that I could not eat for a few days because of a nervous tick in the cheek. Throughout the beatings and the tortures, the loudspeakers were set at an unusually high level so as to drown out the groans of the victims. I know that the electric machine was applied to women so that one pole of the current was attached to the breast and the other to the little finger of the left hand, thus torturing them with interrupted current. I heard this from the wife of László Bárdos, who was investigated at that time. I also know from this woman that she was forced to undress and to dance undressed before the investigating gendarmes, who whipped her during the dance. I was tortured in this manner for five days, after which I was put to work preparing an inventory of the goods plundered from the lawyer Imre Balázs, who died in deportation; he was beaten here so severely that he could not stand on his feet, which were treated with cold water compresses. This was also the case with Lajos Káhán, Ferdinand Káhán, Dr. Elek Elovics, and many others.

I was taken away on 27 May 1944 in a freight car in which 75 people were crowded with one bucket of water and one bucket for our needs. It was very hot, and the situation was unbearable. We were unloaded in Auschwitz, where we were separated from our families and taken to various camps and liberated by the American forces on 5 May 1945. Of the approximately 7,000 men from Nagyvárad in the work camps, as far as I know only four remained alive; the others were killed by beatings, famine, or disease, or were destroyed in the gas chamber.

The witness Dr. Endre Fehér declared the following among other things:

At this special police I was tortured in the crudest manner. The first day I was tortured continuously for two and a half hours. At first the order was issued by a young lieutenant, who, reading my exemption document, declared that it had no value and instructed the inspector [the beater] who investigated me not to return it to me. This Group VIII inspector to which I was assigned was called József Horváth, and, having been instigated by his superior, without letting me say a word he began to turn the handle of the electrification machine; I was compelled to pick up the positive electrode with one hand and the negative one with the other, and thus the shocks were administered to my body. His aide played the radio even louder so that my shouts could not be heard. I received about 40 blows on my soles, 50 slaps in the face, and electric shocks in various forms. At the beginning I only had to hold the electrodes in my two hands; then I had to put one of the electrodes that was built as a bridle bit in my mouth. It was horrible when all my teeth felt the oscillation of the electric current. When I was unable to hold the electrode tight enough or when I dropped it because of the excruciating pain, I was beaten with extraordinary cruelty by fists and sticks. They also used other means of electrification, of which I remember that in the last half hour, when eight hangmen took part in my torture, they tied me to a pole with strings. They introduced one electrode in my anus and with the other they touched my organ. During this torture two young gendarmerie lieutenants, whose names I don't recall, also took part as spectators. Not only during this phase when I was constantly beaten and one danced on my body, but even earlier, a gendarmerie lieutenant was almost always present.

I heard the women were also cruelly tortured, especially with electrification. I do not know it personally, but while I was in the ghetto and even in Auschwitz where we were deported I heard from those from Nagyvárad that police commissioner Németh, who supervised the ghetto, behaved brutally not only to the interned Jews but also to the members of the so-called Jewish Council.

Here is the deposition of a female victim of the investigations, the wife of Manó Guttmann, who declared the following:

I was investigated in the torture chambers of the Dréher factory for six days after the establishment of the ghetto. When they took me there, I found many people, even acquaintances of mine, lying on the ground in horrible excruciating pain, following the beatings and tortures to which they had been subjected. The first day I entered the torture chamber, the three men who were there asked me what my name was and where my jewelry was and then they ordered me to undress. As I was hesitating they tore off my clothes and began to hit me with their rubber truncheons. When I turned to one side, they hit me on the other side. They ordered me to take my shoes off, which I did, but then I fell down because of the beatings. They began to hit my soles with their rubber truncheons until I lost consciousness; when I came to they threw my clothes at me, and I had to run into the courtyard. The second day began the same way as the first day; then they squeezed my nails with the door and began the electrification torture.

They handed me a handle connected to a small electric generator, which I had to hold close to my heart; they attached the other to my tongue. They also tried to introduce the electric cable into my vagina, but changed their minds because I was bleeding as a result of the beatings. They did the same things in the days that followed until I revealed where the jewelry was, and they took me to the city by car to fetch them. During the inventory of the jewelry, Péterffy was also present.

During my torture a gendarmerie officer with the rank of captain was present.

I know that among the torturers there was one called Szabó with the rank of standard-bearer and one called Teveli who gave the orders.

After they finished torturing me because I revealed where the jewelry was hidden, I had to go to the factory to prepare food for the torturers who ate and worked there, even nights. I also had to clean up the room after each torture. As I was there I saw hundreds of torture cases; that is, I saw through the open doors, I heard the screaming, and I saw the wounds caused. At the beginning they tortured only the rich, but later they turned to everyone in the order of their homes, and the tortures were even more horrible. I also saw people in a state of unconsciousness in the torture chambers, because I had to clean up the blood, vomit, and feces of the victims who could not control themselves in the wake of the tortures.

The files of this case contain a series of similar depositions. The deposition of the witness Dr. Lajos Jakab is conclusive with respect to the intention of the torturers to hasten the end of these people destined for death; it reveals that the investigators addressed the victims several times more or less as follows: "Why do you cling to these little things and why don't you reveal where you have hidden them? Within a few days you will be buried in the lime ditch anyway."

The depositions of the witnesses Péter Csurka, a former gendarmerie officer, Miklós Heller, Zoltán Rothbart, Ignác Deutsch, Hermann Grünfeld, Dr. Miksa Kupfer, Manó Weisz, Arthúr Spitzer, and József Áron reveal that:

All of the police and gendarmerie officers were aware of the bestialities committed in the torture chambers of the Dréher factory.

These inhumane acts were so scandalous that at the time, to investigate the case, the Ministry of the Interior sent a prosecutor who submitted a report urging the punishment of Lieutenant Colonel Péterffy and Lieutenant Ágoston Medgyesi.

Lieutenant Dr. Gyula Petri played the most important role by maintaining contact, as Péterffy's adjutant, with Demeter, the Gestapo officer in Nagyvárad.

At the officers' meetings, the accused Ágoston Félegyházi Medgyesi spoke openly and in detail about the tortures, the use of electrification and other inhumane methods, and Péterffy's concern only that care be taken to prevent anyone from the outside from somehow learning what was going on at Dréher.

The accused Gendarmerie Lieutenant János Frater (originally from Berettyóujfalu), Gendarmerie Lieutenant Dr. Béla Rektor (originally for Nyíregyháza), Gendarmerie Captain István Garai, and former Gendarmerie Lieutenant Dr. Endre Bodolai took part in the beatings and tortures at Dréher.

The following were identified as part of the torturers at the Dréher factory: Quartermasters Ferenc Sziklai and András Medgyesi, both gendarmerie agents from Budapest; first sergeants Dezső Büss and Gyula Ori, M.Á.V.

(*Magyar Államvasutak;* Hungarian Railroads) agents; Quartermasters György Fekete and Sándor Ilonka from the special agents section of Debrecen; Quartermasters János Teveli, István Szőllősi, Géza Szabados, and József Tóth, from the special agents section of Transdanubia (Dunántul); and First Sergeants Mihály Juhász, Sándor Posgai, Gábor Keresztesi, István Felföldi, Imre Garai, and Sándor Fehér from the Battalion of the Gendarmerie School of Nagyvárad. Also identified were noncommissioned gendarmerie officers named Megyeri, Budai, and Mihály Szabó originally from Szentes, as well as József Horváth, a gendarmerie noncommissioned officer from the punitive Section VIII.

Similar tortures were perpetrated in room 28, on the second floor of City Hall, by Police Commissioner Dr. Toperczel, detective Tapasztó, and detective Váradi.

One of the executive organs of the mayor of Nagyvárad was the accused Lajos Cser, a former official of the mayor's office in Nagyvárad. In this capacity he attended the conferences for the instruction of the commissions entrusted with the roundup of the Jews and was assigned to the police organs that rounded up the Jews from the section of Nagyvárad called the Józsa Colony. In the execution of this mission, he went to the home of shoemaker János Puțovan, whose wife was of Jewish ethnic background but had converted to Christianity during that summer and who had a seven-year-old girl who was born Christian. Because of this situation, the policeman whom the accused accompanied was opposed to the removal of the woman, but the accused Lajos Cser, showing an extraordinary excess of zeal, vehemently insisted that she be removed, and not only she but also her daughter who was Christian. When the neighbors began to cry at the sight of this tragic scene, the accused told them: "It doesn't pay for you to cry for a stinking Jew." When the wife of János Puțovan, weakened by emotion and horror, could not carry her baggage and little girl, the neighbors wanted to help her but they were prevented by the accused, who said: "It is forbidden for a Hungarian to carry the baggage of a Jew." One must mention that all of this took place while the husband of the unfortunate woman was not at home, so that she found herself in an extremely unfortunate situation; the accused did not even have the compassion to postpone the operation until after the return of the woman's husband in the evening.

Although he was only a delegate of the mayor's office with well-determined functions relating to the acceptance of valuables and the sealing of apartments, the accused Lajos Cser, motivated by race hatred, exceeded his functions and assumed the role of the policeman, contributing in this manner to the misfortune of the Jews.

It was proved that the little girl of the shoemaker János Puțovan was removed from the ghetto after two weeks, but his wife was deported to Auschwitz with the Jews and didn't return from there until the summer of 1945.

All of these facts are proved abundantly in the depositions of the witnesses Rozália Nagy, Ilona Buia, and János Puțovan.

The person who bears responsibility for the above deeds, in conformity with the usual motives, is the prefect of the city of Nagyvárad and of Bihar County, i.e., the accused Károly Rajnay.

The accused Károly Rajnay (Reiner), reserve brigade general, was brought to trial before this People's Tribunal on 26 February 1946 under the indictment of Trial Group 2 by the public prosecutors associated with this People's Tribunal.

At the time of the trial of Group 2, the accused claimed that he was to be exempted in the matter being judged, maintaining he had already been tried by the People's Tribunal of Budapest for the deeds being tried by this People's Tribunal and had been condemned to six years' confinement. The People's Tribunal at the time accepted this exemption on principle, subject to proof of the affirmation by the accused.

But since the accused is also charged, among other things, with complicity in war crimes perpetrated during the establishment of the ghetto of Nagyvárad, the People's Tribunal—considering the connection between these serious deeds with which the accused is charged and the acts through which the ghettos of Northern Transylvania, and especially that of Nagyvárad, were established, and considering also Article 89, Paragraph 4 of the Penal Code —decided to include the file of the accused Károly Rajnay (Reiner) and to try him within the framework of Group VIII (ghettos) brought before this Tribunal.

Whereas since the separation of the accused's case from Trial Group 2, Dossier No. IX. 502/1945 of the People's Tribunal of Budapest, has been received, and it in fact reveals that the accused Károly Rajnay was condemned on 19 February 1946 to six years' confinement for the same deeds for which he is also being brought to trial before this People's Tribunal.

Whereas this decision is not final and is being appealed both by the accused and the Hungarian public prosecutors, with these appeals to be judged by the Hungarian National Council of People's Tribunals of Budapest.

Whereas, moreover, by a note of 21 December 1945, relating to the accused Károly Rajnay, the Hungarian Ministry of Justice informed the People's Tribunal of Kolozsvár that on the basis of the evidence placed at the disposal of the Hungarian Ministry of Justice, this ministry agreed in principle to the extradition of the accused Károly Rajnay to Romania as a war criminal.

Whereas through telegraphic communication No. 908/1946 of the same

Ministry of Justice, the accused Károly Rajnay (Reiner) was definitively extradited to Romania to be tried as a war criminal.

Considering that in accordance with Article 2 of Decree No. 81/1945 M.E. of the Hungarian National Provisional Government, which aims at people's justice:

> For offenses caused outside the territory of the Hungarian state, as well as with regard to any perpetrator who is to be extradited, the jurisdiction of the People's Tribunal is exercised until the extradition of the perpetrator is ordered. (*Magyar Közlöny. Hivatalos Lap,* Debrecen, No. 3, 5 February 1945)

Thus, once the extradition of the accused Károly Rajnay was ordered as shown above, the jurisdiction of the People's Tribunal of Budapest ceased; from the point of view of the trial of this accused before this Tribunal, it makes no difference whether this accused was or was not condemned by the People's Tribunal of Budapest, especially since Judgment No. Nb IX. 5070/1945/6 of 19 February 1946 of the People's Tribunal of Budapest is not final, but it is being appealed to the Hungarian National Council of People's Tribunals. This being the case, it is evident that even if the accused was indeed condemned in the first instance to six years' confinement for acts that took place in Northern Transylvania and for which he was brought to trial before this People's Tribunal as well, the Hungarian National Council of People's Tribunals cannot fail to take into account, when judging the appeal of the accused, the fact of the accused's extradition and thus the termination of the Hungarian People's Tribunals' jurisdiction over the accused as per Article 2 of Decree No. 81/1945 M.E. cited above, which regulates people's justice in the Hungarian Republic.

Whereas in the first place and especially in connection with this group, the accused Károly Rajnay is charged, while prefect of the municipality of Nagyvárad and of Bihar County, of having cooperated since the beginning of May 1944 in the establishment and organization of the ghetto of Nagyvárad, with the entire procession of horrors that took place there as described earlier in the present judgment.

That by this act, as the indictment maintains, the accused is guilty of having committed war crimes stipulated in Article 3, Paragraph *n* of Law No. 312/1945.

Taking into consideration that:

The proceedings and the file in this case reveal that the accused Károly Rajnay assumed the position of prefect only on 9 May 1944, i.e., after the ghetto had been established.

Even after the establishment of the ghetto, persons who were exempted from internment, and even from wearing the distinctive Yellow Star, continued to remain interned in this ghetto.

In his capacity as prefect of the municipality of Nagyvárad and Bihar County and on the basis of the power conferred upon him by the administrative laws then in effect to supervise and oversee any and all measures taken in the city and county, the accused Károly Rajnay should have intervened to free from internment in the ghetto those who were exempted from this measure, especially children under six years of age. But the accused was content to leave things as they were, since as will be shown below he shared that inclination.

The accused Károly Rajnay was also engaged in a culpable omission through which he aided and abetted the torturers and the investigators involved in the search for hidden valuables.

Indeed, while he knew that there were beatings and maltreatments in the ghetto, even sometimes causing death, in the search for hidden valuables, he nevertheless took no measure to halt these atrocities—atrocities of which even the Hungarian Council of Ministers took notice.

The accused Károly Rajnay saw everything that went on in the ghetto and did not inform the Ministry of the Interior in time to take corrective measures. His failure to report is revealed by the deposition of former Minister of the Interior Andor Jaross, who, in his deposition as a witness before the People's Tribunal of Budapest, declared:

> On the basis of my knowledge of public law, I maintain that Rajnay's supervisory powers as prefect were also in effect with respect to Gendarmerie Colonel Péterffy, the commander of the ghetto, especially since Péterffy was carrying out an administrative police mission in the ghetto, and the ghetto did not constitute an autonomous unit, but was part of his administrative assignment; had he believed that Péterffy was inept he certainly would have had to report this.

But the accused Károly Rajnay neither supervised nor controlled life in the ghetto, i.e., the activity of the Mayor Dr. László Gyapai. Along these lines, the accused failed to control or check that electricity was cut off in the ghetto, that the volume of water was severely restricted, that the food was insufficient, and that the size of the ghetto was disproportionately small in comparison with the number of those interned in the ghetto—omissions through which he aided and abetted the accused Dr. László Gyapai and the persons entrusted with sanitation measures in the ghetto to perpetrate these war crimes.

The accused was aware of all of these facts, for here is what the *Erdélyi Néplap* (The People's Journal of Transylvania) of Nagyvárad wrote under the title "The Municipal Administrative Committee Held a Meeting with the Presidency of the Prefect Károly Rajnay" (No. 111 of 19 May 1944):

> In the course of the reports of the sections many problems arose in connection with the provisions relating to the Jews and especially to the internment of the Jews in the ghetto . . .

Prefect Károly Rajnay emphasized that the hygienic and sanitary conditions in the ghetto were totally satisfactory.

This is how the accused Károly Rajnay saw the situation in the ghetto of Nagyvárad. And this point of view proved to be the direct consequence of his political conceptions, which were expressed publicly in various communications while he functioned as prefect. And indeed during his inauguration, the accused Rajnay stated as follows:

> But I do not ask for the usual support, but for a collaboration with a totally different nuance—on the idea *that this may be the last hour when it is possible for us to embrace the ideology of the Right and to transplant it not only to our little circle in Bihar County and the city of Nagyvárad but to the entire country as well.*

On the same day, in his speech at Nagyvárad City Hall, he stated: "We have aligned ourselves with the Right, and we must put a definitive end to the ideology and activity of the Left."

At a press reception on 11 May 1944, the accused Károly Rajnay declared among other things: "I noted the tone of the pre-19 March 1944 Hungarian press with stupefaction. This press had forgotten its mission; it failed to come out openly in support of our ally's cause. My appointment gave new impetus to the fighting units. My presence here denotes changed conceptions and circumstances. I am not inclined to tolerate drives that weaken the powers of the nation in its battle against the horror from the East."

On 1 June 1944, at the meeting of the county assembly, the accused Károly Rajnay responded as follows to the interpellation by the deputy János Szabó on whether the prefect was aware that several members of the county council had hidden Jewish goods:

> Yes, I am aware. In each uncovered case the investigation is proceeding and the guilty parties will be punished.... Here in Nagyvárad, the procedure has been and will continue to be more severe.

This reveals the mental state of the accused Károly Rajnay with which he started out when he was named prefect of Nagyvárad, and explains why he did not take any measures to right matters in the ghetto.

The accused Károly Rajnay was also engaged in another activity in 1940, when in his capacity as brigadier general he was the military commander of the municipality of Nagyvárad.

In this capacity he engaged from the very first in the dispossession of and the withdrawal of licenses and authorizations from various Jewish and Romanian citizens. Thus, for example, by Decree No. 3946/1940 he withdrew the license of the Palace firm, and by Decree No. 3298/1940 he withdrew the authorization from the Astoria firm.

Here is how the accused justified the withdrawal of the authorization from the Palace firm: "Because serious misgivings arose against the activities of Palace."

The accused was involved in all aspects of Nagyvárad's professional and economic life. Thus he was involved in the dismissal of Jewish and Romanian employees from private enterprises and public offices and establishments, and prohibited the practice of law and medicine for the majority of Romanian and Jewish lawyers and physicians.

But the culminant aspect of his activity as military commander of the city of Nagyvárad was his expulsion of 100 familes from Nagyvárad.

Although he had received an order for the expulsion of 100 persons, the accused called for the expulsion of 100 families, raising the number of those expelled to approximately 400 people in Nagyvárad alone.

Although the order dealt with the expulsion only in principle, leaving unspecified the manner in which this expulsion was to be carried out, the accused Károly Rajnay intentionally carried this order out in an excessively inhumane manner, giving free vent to the race hatred of his agents.

Here, in brief, is how these events took place:

All those affected were arrested by gendarmes and escorted to the penitentiary of Nagyvárad. Here they were first questioned and then crowded into cells; toward the end of the first day, the agents carried out a mock mass execution of the inmates to torture them mentally. After this simulated execution, all of those arrested, including Dr. Nicolae Popovici, the bishop of Nagyvárad, were taken to the station under strong escort and in the midst of maltreatment. At the station they were entrained into cattle cars full with dung and without seats or light or water; during the entrainment the railroad officials and the people at the station booed them, making fun of this situation; then the cars were sealed off and sent to Romania via the Békéscsaba-Lökösháza-Curtici route.

The wealth of the expelled people was taken over by Hungarian curators especially selected by the accused.

Had he had the slightest humane feelings and not been dominated by race hatred, the accused Károly Rajnay, even if he had received an expulsion order, could have carried out this expulsion in a humane manner. Thus in the first place he did not have to expel 100 families instead of 100 persons; in the second place he could have allowed the expellees to take along the most necessary things and could have taken measures for the administration and preservation of the goods they left behind; and finally, he should have effectuated the expulsion in suitable vehicles and not by a long route that caused unmeasurable hardship and suffering but through the Băile Felix-Mirau border point, which was only two kilometers from the city of Nagyvárad.

That he did not carry out this expulsion under humane conditions shows that the accused intentionally performed these political and racial measures in an excessive manner.

The accused Károly Rajnay (Reiner) gave free hand for, and even ordered, the torture, maltreatment, and internment of several Romanians in the Püspökladány camp. This was the case of the victim Vasile Oraş, who was taken from his home on 20 September 1940 to the military command, where his hands were tied with a wire that was then electrified; he was then beaten so severely with a rubber truncheon that he lost seven teeth, the eardrums in both ears were punctured, and the ribcage was broken.

The same kind of maltreatment was used on Coriolan Bucico, the former mayor of Nagyvárad, who was afterward interned at Püspökladány camp.

Here is how Dr. Kálmán Turi, the former administrative adviser of the accused at the time of the military administration of Nagyvárad, described the attitude and activities of the accused Károly Rajnay during this administration:

> He did not hide his chauvinist nationalist and anti-Semitic attitude. These sentiments were behind his arbitrary acts. When on 26 November 1940 he said good-bye I told him to his face that his activities were unfortunate; to this the accused replied that he would always take responsibility for his acts.

Whereas with respect to the acts shown above committed by the accused, the People's Tribunal had to change the particulars given in the indictment and to determine that the acts of the accused Károly Rajnay (Reiner) constitute complicity in crimes stipulated by Article 2, Paragraphs *h* and *m,* and commission of war crimes stipulated by Article 2, Paragraph *o* of Law No. 312/1945.

As shown above, in addition to the administrative and police authorities who carried out the internment of the Jews into the ghetto, a part of the Hungarian population, animated by the same race hatred as the state administration, helped this administration whenever it had the chance, denouncing those who were able to hide from the fury of the executors of these racial measures.

One of these auxiliary informers for the state administration was the accused József Vadász of Nagyvárad, formerly living at 41 Tompa Mihály Street. The accused, an electrician by profession, was sent to work at Episcopiei Street.

In this street two Jews, Oszkár Dávid and Imre Balázs, were hiding in the home of Imre Bene. They had gone into hiding in April 1944 because they were being sought for Communist activities, and starting at the beginning of May 1944 they no longer left this hiding place, knowing that if they were seen in public they would be interned in the ghetto. It happened that on 6 September

1944, Imre Bene's house was damaged by an Allied bombing, on which occasion Oszkár Dávid was wounded by debris from a wall and was only saved from death with great difficulty.

The Electric Works of Nagyvárad decided to send electricians to the bombed homes to retrieve the meters so they would not be lost. In the performance of this task, the electricians Schmack and Szentmiklósy arrived along their route to the house of Imre Bene, where they recognized the two Jews who were hiding there. Leaving this house, the electrician Szentmiklósy brought their discovery to the attention of the accused József Vadász, and about an hour later two policemen accompanied by the accused József Vadász appeared at the home of Imre Bene; following identification of the Jews, Ozskár Dávid and Imre Balázs, by the accused József Vadász, the policemen arrested the two Jews as well as Imre Bene and his wife. All of them were condemned to two months in prison, with the stipulation that following the completion of their imprisonment the two Jews were to be interned; because of the intervening war events and the imminent liberation of Nagyvárad by Soviet-Romanian troops, the two Jews were handed over to the military command to be executed, but through the intervention of some comrades of theirs they managed to escape from the military prison.

It is true that during the preliminary investigation the workmate of the accused Vadász, Ferenc Schmack, maintained that following the discovery of the two Jews his colleague Szentmiklósy revealed this discovery to a policeman on the street.

This testimony by F. Schmack is also to some extent supported by the witness Gusztáv Kala, who stated that while working with this witness the accused József Vadász was called from the workplace by a boy from the civil defense, and that only after this call did the accused József Vadász go to the home of Imre Bene.

But these depositions are not worthy of belief since they were made in a spirit of solidarity with the accused, inasmuch as if one accepts what the witness F. Schmack stated, namely that it was László Szentmiklósy who first informed the police, then how can one explain that the policemen did not immediately enter the home of Imre Bene but called for László Szentmiklósy to serve as a guide?

Moreover, the deposition of the witness Gusztáv Kala also reveals that Schmack and Szentmiklósy came to the house where the accused József Vadász worked and spoke with the accused, telling him that they had discovered two Jews in Imre Bene's home. At the same time, the witness F. Schmack maintained in his deposition that he did not meet the accused József Vadász that day, but only the following day. From this contradiction one can conclude that both witnesses, F. Schmack and Gusztáv Kala, intentionally tried to save their colleague, i.e., the accused, and their deposition cannot be worthy of belief.

In contrast to their testimony, there is the fact admitted by the accused and proved by the witnesses Imre Bene, Oszkár Dávid, and Imre Balázs, that the accused József Vadász was the one who accompanied the two policemen to the home of Imre Bene and insisted on identifying them, and that this took place approximately one hour after the departure of the electricians F. Schmack and László Szentmiklósy; now, if Szentmiklósy had been the direct informer to the policemen immediately after leaving Imre Bene's home, then an hour would not have been needed between the discovery and the arrival of the policemen, and there would have been no need to call on the accused József Vadász for identification when Szentmiklósy was there and could have offered information to identify the two Jews.

What happened is quite different; namely, when Szentmiklósy and Schmack discovered the two Jews, they left Imre Bene's home after finishing their work there, then stopped where the accused József Vádasz worked as an electrician in another house in the neighborhood, informed him about their discovery, and left, while the accused József Vádász, remaining in the same street and motivated by race hatred, intentionally went to look for the police and did not give up until he had led two policemen to arrest the people in hiding.

Another category of accused in this trial are the public midwives or other women not licensed as midwives who helped the investigators in the search for hidden valuables in the most intimate parts of the investigated persons' bodies. Obviously if these midwives had performed their professional tasks conscientiously this would not be classified as a war crime, since being in public service they could not have refused to perform body searches within their specialty. But being poisoned by the Fascist poison of race hatred and animated by an appetite for enrichment, they intentionally engaged in a series of tortures during the body searches, and not infrequently in the course of these searches they dishonored virgin girls, performing acts that were both morally and legally forbidden.

Such a public midwife in Margitta, Bihar County, was Erzsébet Medgyesi, who together with another public midwife of the same town called Erzsébet Valkó, was appointed to search the women interned in the ghetto for money and jewelry. The accused, as was proved, only had the task of searching through certain items, namely shoes and clothing, and the other midwife was to search the vaginal organs. However, while midwife Erzsébet Valkó did not exceed the humane bounds of searching, the accused Erzsébet Medgyesi at all times behaved extremely brutally with those whom she searched.

While the vaginal examinations were being performed, midwife Erzsébet Valkó was called to a patient in the town, and the accused replaced her for the vaginal searches. On this occasion she examined the young Icu Glück, 16 years old, and although she was a virgin the accused examined her by tearing her hymen with her hands and causing a hemorrhage, so that when midwife Erzsébet Valkó returned the accused was found by her with her hands full of blood. The witness in this case revealed how the accused Erzsébet Medgyesi, when she examined the young Icu Glück and felt that she had something hidden in her intimate parts, furiously exhorted her to push out the hidden object, and then in the same furious tone asked for a knife. It was not proved, however, that she actually used a knife in cutting the hymen, and it seems she tore it with her bare hands. In fact it was proved that Icu Glück had a roll of banknotes in the value of 1900 *Pengős* hidden in her anus, and thus the accused, not being sure whether the object was in the vagina or the rectum and driven by anger, made this unplanned move of tearing the hymen of the young girl and causing a hemorrhage but without finding the banknotes. It can be seen that the other midwife had greater expertise, for upon her return it was she who removed the roll of banknotes from the rectum of the victim Icu Glück.

It is probable that under normal conditions Icu Glück, had she received the necessary care, would have escaped with her life, but since the day after her search she was taken to Nagyvárad with the other Jews of Margitta, where they were entrained and taken to Auschwitz three days later, she no longer had the possibility to take care of herself and consequently suffered a general infection and died in the freight car on the way to Auschwitz. The witnesses reveal their conviction that this death was due to general septicemia, and that it was precipitated by the miseries endured in the ghetto and especially in the freight car on the way to Auschwitz, which was very overcrowded and unbearably hot.

The accused Erzsébet Medgyesi also had desires for enrichment. Thus she requested jewelry and shoes from the Jewish women who were to be interned in the ghetto, promising that she would not harm them during the investigation.

All of these deeds attributed to the accused were proved by the declarations of the witnesses Erzsébet Valkó, Berta Berkovits, Lujza Pollák, Sarolta Herskovits, Ilona Grünfeld, Aranka Grünfeld, and Mrs. Ábrahám Preisler.

A colleague of the accused Erzsébet Medgyesi—of the same profession as well as lawlessness—in Érmihályfalva was the accused widow of János Kiss née Rozália Zeffer, the local midwife entrusted with the internal investigation of the women that were to be interned in the ghetto of Érmihályfalva. This accused too exceeded her mission by checking the vaginas of the women with unheard-of brutality and extending these searches even to young girls 13 to 14 years of age. The above facts have been proved by the depositions of the witnesses Mária Patos, Ágnes Bauer, and Margit Weinberger.

The Ghetto of Szatmárnémeti

In Szatmár County two ghettos were established: one in the county seat, Szatmárnémeti, and the other in the city of Nagybánya. In addition to these two ghettos, there was also a concentration camp in Nagykároly, from which the concentrated Jews were taken to the ghetto of Szatmárnémeti.

On 27 April 1944 Szatmárnémeti was the seat of László Endre's conference, which was attended by Dr. Endre Boér, the county deputy prefect; Dr. László Csóka, the mayor; Dr. Zoltán Rogozi Papp, the deputy mayor of Szatmárnémeti; Dr. Ernő Pirkler, the secretary general of the mayor's office of Szatmárnémeti; and the heads of the police and gendarmerie authorities. The tone of these discussions and the information acquired by the participants were shown above, and there is no need to mention them again.

It is, however, sufficient to show that the mayor of Szatmárnémeti also issued an announcement—No. 12150 of 3 May 1944—whose content is summarized as follows:

> I inform the Jews living in the territory of the municipality who, in accord with my Decree No. 12080 Eln., are obliged to wear the distinctive badge, that beginning at 5:00 A.M. on 3 May they cannot leave their homes. Those Jews who do not live in the designated quarter—the Jewish camps—may not leave their homes from 4 May until the issuance of new directives, except daily between 9:00 and 11:00 A.M. exclusively to acquire drinking water, strictly necessary food, and the essentials for their existence. Those who violate this provision will be interned.

In Szatmárnémeti as in Nagyvárad, the mayor, together with the secretary general and the deputy mayor, called a conference at city hall to be attended by the entire administration of police, gendarmerie, state revenue, financial administration and city hall personnel as well as the primary and secondary teachers. The conference was presided over by the accused Dr. László Csóka, who issued instructions in connection with the roundup and internment of Jews in the ghetto. As assistants to the mayor, the following attended this conference: Dr. Béla Sárközi, police officer; Károly Csegezi, the commander of the police guard personnel; Dr. Ernő Pirkler, the secretary general of the mayor's office; Dr. Jenő Nagy, the police chief; and N. Deményi, the commander of the gendarmerie legion. It was on this occasion that the commissions for the roundup of the Jews were formed.

The decrees and instructions relating to exempted persons were not respected in Szatmárnémeti either, and thus here also all the Jews without exception—i.e., including children under six years of age, the aged, the ill, and those exempted from wearing the Yellow Star generally—were interned.

It was pointed out in the general part of this discussion that all those entrusted with the concentration of the Jews were aware of what would happen to the Jews, as well as of the illegality of the internment orders, so there is no reason to repeat this point. It is nevertheless edifying and conclusive to point out that the accused Dr. László Csóka, the mayor of Szatmárnémeti, had the frankness to admit during the preliminary investigation that he realized he was carrying out an illegal operation. Here is verbatim what he declared during the preliminary investigation:

> As a lawyer with long administrative experience, I realized that the decision taken and transmitted by Secretary of State László Endre had no legal basis because it regulated an unconstitutional matter which cannot be regulated by such orders. . . .

To the question of the public prosecutor, he also declared that had he received similar orders relating to people of Hungarian nationality, he would not have executed them.

As in Nagyvárad, the ghetto of Szatmárnémeti was established in a section of the city, i.e., in apartments, but here too the area of the ghetto was in flagrant disproportion to the 19,000 Jews that were interned there.

The food supply of the ghetto population was intentionally designed to underfeed the internees, whereby those entrusted with this operation contributed to causing an unbearable life for the ghetto inhabitants. Here is how the witness Dr. József Borgida describes this state of affairs:

> Before the transfer of the Jews from the province, the Jews were quartered so that about 10 to 15 were assigned to an average room. Afterward, 3,000 other Jews and several thousand Jews from the county's villages were brought in, so that the situation became unbearable; many of the people were placed in cellars and attics under miserable conditions. I personally intervened with the leaders mentioned above, but they refused to honor my requests for expanding the ghetto territory. Upon entering the ghetto, all the people were subjected to searches, and the women were also vaginally searched under shameful conditions. We were compelled to surrender all our valuables to a police or gendarmerie officer.
>
> As far as feeding was concerned, we received so little food from the mayor's office that one could not live on it. Therefore, from funds collected for communal purposes, we once paid Counselor Pirkler 200,000 *Pengős* to get us supplies from outside. I must note that he accepted this sum the day before the beginning of the deportation.

JUDGMENT OF THE PEOPLE'S TRIBUNAL

Here, too, tortures and torments were aimed to compel the Jews to confess where they had hidden their money and jewelry. The authors of these torments and tortures were the police officer and commander of the ghetto Dr. Béla Sárközi, police inspector Károly Csegezi, and Gendarmerie Lieutenant Colonel N. Deményi, but the chiefs of administration were not strangers to what was going on in the ghetto in the pursuit of goods and valuables. Here is what the witness Dr. József Borgida declared with respect to the maltreatment, intimidations, and chicaneries perpetrated by the Hungarian authorities:

> The guarding of the ghetto was particularly strict. To intimidate us at night they drove trucks with their beams on and with mounted machine guns. I know of a number of simulated escape cases, which aimed to grab the last items of value that had been hidden at such great risk. This is the case of Mrs. Markovics, who surrendered many hidden valuables to a policeman who pretended to have caught her while trying to escape. The victims were brought to the police, where they were harshly beaten and then brought back to the ghetto. The valuables, on the other hand, were retained. On orders from ghetto commander Béla Sárközi, the police commissioner, extraordinary pressure was exerted upon the people to intimidate them into surrendering all their valuables. Following an intensive propaganda campaign of intimidation launched by Sárközi and Csegezi, they placed a basket in front of the People's Council building, claiming that up to a specified deadline all the people had the right to throw their valuables into this basket without being watched or punished. As a result of this magnanimity of the policemen, large values in watches, jewelry, bracelets, etc., were collected from the intimidated internees. The ghetto was visited several times, especially by police inspector Csegezi and Gendarmerie Lieutenant Colonel Deményi, who came to visit us in the ghetto and were delighted with our miserable situation.

The cruelties perpetrated by the special group involved in the torture and searches for hidden wealth in the ghetto of Szatmárnémeti were so great that the ghetto internees jostled toward the deportation trains to escape the maltreatment in the ghetto. In this respect the deposition of Mrs. Endre Delmann is edifying:

> Here we were handed over to some special investigators, young men in civilian clothes, who were part of the special frontline gendarmerie. At first everybody was told that it made no sense for us not to admit everything because they had sufficient means to compel us to state the truth. We waited in the courtyard where we heard the shouts and moans of the victims. After a short while there came my turn. I was led before a commission of three which tried to induce me to declare where my persian fur coat was, something which I never had, as well as some valuables, stating that they well knew that I had many things hidden. In the meantime their chief entered, a small blond man also in civilian clothes, who said that there was no sense in talking with me, but that they should proceed to action. Then I was caught and

forced to remove my shoes, they laid me down on a bench, one of them held me by my knees and the other began to beat me on my soles with a long stick until he got tired, and then they raised my dress and hit me where they could. I shouted and moaned in pain. I was beaten horribly, and then I was obliged to run around the room and to put on my shoes, which was painful. I was investigated once again for me to reveal where I had hidden my valuables and when I did not they repeated the same procedure. Again barefooted I was again beaten and tortured. During the beating, their leader entered saying that they should beat me even harder. Then I was sent out and waited in another courtyard until I was recalled and sent back to the ghetto. I was so crushed that my entire body was full of bruises and I could not walk, having been carried by two people. After a week I was again called for investigation and then, from fear of the beating, I voluntarily joined a transport to be transported as urgently as possible and it is in this manner that I escaped further tortures.

These investigators and torturers had their own inquisitional methods to squeeze out the confessions they needed. These methods consisted in beating the soles and hands with rubber truncheons and in squeezing the testicles in the case of men. As the investigations on file show, many of the Jews were maltreated in this manner. The witnesses who were heard in this case recall the cases of the jeweler Samu Grosz, Leopold Lebovits, Béla Spitz, Heinrich Salamon, József Princz, Imre Reiter, and Sándor Gerő, a grain merchant who was terribly tortured one day and, when he was again called the following day, committed suicide for fear of the tortures.

Following the evaluation of the acts that were perpetrated in the ghetto of Szatmárnémeti, it is necessary to analyze the personality of those who contributed to the establishment of this ghetto as well as the role played by each and every one of them.

The head of the city of Szatmárnémeti was the accused mayor Dr. László Csóka. This accused is originally from Debrecen and became mayor of the municipality of Szatmárnémeti following the Diktat of Vienna, as a result of his personal merits acknowledged by the Horthyite-Fascist regime of Hungary. It was mentioned above that the guilt of the accused career mayors could not be established so easily if one did not know the mentality of these accused, which is revealed by their demonstrations. Thus one could easily come to the view that being career officials, they had to carry out certain orders even if they were immoral, under the moral compulsion that otherwise they would have been threatened with the loss of jobs, i.e., of their and their families' existence.

However, this is not the case with mayor Dr. László Csóka, who demonstrated his race hatred and typically Fascist feelings even before the establishment of the ghetto by a series of acts taken on his own initiative, which were not based on any order or law.

Along these lines, the accused Dr. László Csóka issued Announcement No. 3038 of 14 November 1942, which appeared in the newspaper *Szamos,* in which he forbade the Jews from buying more than 100 kilograms of firewood weekly.

As a result of the persecution launched by this alien mayor, the *Szamos* of 30 October 1942, praising the activities of the accused, was in a position to provide a balance sheet in the sense that 74 Jewish business establishments were transferred into Christian hands in a single year. The article is titled "A New Settling Down in Szatmárnémeti."

The same paper, dealing with the same problem, wrote the following in an article entitled "Changing of the Guard":

> It is natural that it was not possible to temporize much during the introduction of the civilian administration. The change had to be effectuated in fire and iron. The problem was that many had in their possession a contract valid for one year. We had to wait longer, until the expiration of the contract. Work began on 1 January of this year. That Mayor Dr. László Csóka, together with the entire communal council, performed a job, not a small one at that, is proven by the list which shows that the changing of the guard was effectuated without any reservations. On Horthy Square 23 Jewish establishments went into Christian hands . . .

But the accused, consistent with himself, not only was concerned with business establishments, but pursued with tenacity the dispossession of the Jews of any means of existence. Here is how the *Szamos* described the activity of the accused with respect to carriage and taxi drivers:

> Two years ago when the traveler arrived in the station, it was the bearded Jewish drivers who took him into the city. In this area too the leader of the city cleaned up the situation. At that time, 42 of the 68 carriage drivers were Jewish and 20 of the 25 taxi owners were Jewish. Today there is not a single Jewish taxi owner left in Szatmárnémeti. On the carriage seat and behind the wheel there are now Christians.

The accused Dr. László Csóka is also the person who on 6 March 1943 issued an ordinance regulating the operation of the communal swimming beach of Szatmárnémeti whose Section 3 classified the Jewish population of the city along with persons of loose morals—persons suffering from visible venereal diseases and persons suffering from infectious skin diseases—forbidding their access to the communal swimming area. This ordinance can be found on page 63 in the file relating to the ghetto of Szatmárnémeti.

On 29 April 1944 this same accused, without receiving any instructions from his superiors, forwarded his note 11870/1944 to the local post office to prohibit telephone conversations by Jews and to forbid the issuance of money orders to them. He based this order on the contention that the Jews would probably try to hide their valuables through money orders or by using telephone calls or telegrams. The head of the post office responded to this note in the negative, arguing that he could not take such measures in the absence of direct orders from his superiors. These documents may be found on pages 90–91 of the appendix file.

Fearing that they would not be able to gather into the ghetto all the Jews of Szatmárnémeti as quickly as possible, the accused and Deputy Mayor Dr. Zoltán Rogozi Papp sent a note (No. 12456 of 7 May 1944) to the director of the Reformed High School of Szatmárnémeti, inviting him to place at their disposal all the instructors of the high school for the operation relating to the roundup of the Jews, substantiating their request with the following sentence, which reveals their true feelings:

> We are convinced that you recognize, Mr. Director, the total importance of this patriotic obligation.

This document is in the same file under page 96.

This is the soul, and these are the feelings that animated the former mayor of Szatmárnémeti at the time he received the instructions and orders for the concentration of the Jews in the ghetto. The excessive zeal he showed during these operations is therefore not surprising.

But the accused Dr. László Csóka was also concerned with molding public opinion against the Soviet Union, for here is the content of his 30 June 1944 speech as published in the *Szamos:*

> The soldiers who are beating the red hordes that are prepared to overpower us, to destroy us, still have a blow ahead of them. Another attack, which must be a powerful last one, after which there is no more recuperation. We trust in the steeled arms of our soldiers. We trust in the unflinching power of Hungarian ancestral bravery and we trust that just as we once escaped from the epidemic of the infamous red domination and nihilism, we shall once again be able to save all of Europe in collaboration with our allies.

One of the most intimate collaborators of the accused Dr. László Csóka was the accused Dr. Ernő Pirkler, the general secretary of the Szatmárnémeti city hall. The latter, together with Deputy Mayor Zoltán Rogozi Papp, was entrusted with designating the location and size of the ghetto. At the interrogation the accused Dr. László Csóka affirmed that the accused Pirkler attended, together with him, the conferences at Szatmárnémeti and Munkács; the accused László Csóka emphasized at his interrogation during the preliminary investigation that the actual executor of the decisions relating to the ghetto was Ernő Pirkler, and that at the Szatmárnémeti conference László Endre's written instructions had been received by both the accused Ernő Pirkler and Deputy Mayor Dr. Zoltán Rogozi Papp.

The accused Dr. Ernő Pirkler was entrusted concretely with the supply of food for the Jewish population of the ghetto. If this supply was provided as described above, then it is evident that the accused also bears direct responsibility in the matter. Moreover, it was also proved that the accused Dr. Ernő Pirkler received 200,000 *Pengős* collected from the Jews on the day that the deportations started. The accused was unable to explain what he did with these funds.

Witness József Borgida declared that he personally had complained in the name of the Jewish Council to the accused Pirkler about the beatings and tortures taking place in the ghetto, but that the accused did not take any measures to end these beatings and tortures, just as he did not take any steps to inform those in the ghetto about the fate that awaited them; had the Jews of the ghetto known for sure that they would be deported, they would have tried as hard as possible to escape. The accused Dr. Ernő Pirkler was aware of the fate envisioned for the Jews; and despite the fact that he earlier had had good relations with the Jews, he failed to warn them and, on the contrary, continuously assured them that they would not be deported, which caused them harm. (Deposition of witness Dr. József Borgida)

This accused is also revealed as the signer of several notes and decisions rejecting requests by the Jews in the ghetto for enlarging the size of the ghetto and for permission to receive underwear, firewood, etc., of their own from the outside. This request was settled by a decision of Mayor László Csóka on 16 May 1944 by stating that "the expansion of the camp for the Jews is not within my power because, according to the opinion of the experts, the current territory is perfectly sufficient for the existing number of Jews."

It is true that the mayor allowed the issuance of food from the stocks of the Jews, but he only did so because he was informed by Army Corps IX of Kolozsvár that in some places the Jews had poisoned their food; in the belief that these stocks were also poisoned, the mayor ordered that they be given to the Jews for their own consumption. This decision by Mayor Dr. László Csóka, bearing No. 13123 of 15 May 1944, was also communicated to the accused Dr. Ernő Pirkler, as revealed by Documents 19–20 in the file. Thus the accused Pirkler was also pacified with the idea that the poisoned food was good enough for the Jews. Here is the declaration of the witness József Borgida:

> We did not even know what our fate would be and the representatives of the authorities did everything possible to mislead us. We were encouraged to continue our construction work to bring in electric current, water, sewers, etc., to mislead us that we would be living here and would not be transported. Nevertheless, just a few days before the deportation the rumor spread among the internees that we would be taken across the frontier. The masses showed an inclination to revolt, resolving that they would rather die there than allow themselves to be deported. In

this situation, conscious of the responsibility of a leader, I asked for an audience with Prefect Barnabás Endrődi through the intermediation of policeman Csegezi, to obtain an authentic statement about our fate. I was not received by the prefect, but rather by Lieutenant Colonel Deményi whom I asked, after telling him about the rumors and our concern, precisely what he knew about our fate. He declared, on his word of honor as an officer, that we would not be transported across the frontiers of the country.

With respect to the attitude of the accused Pirkler in this connection, this witness stated the following:

Pirkler played the role of an actual executor. In connection with my personal situation, he promised my brother-in-law Frigyes Princz, who was exempted according to the provisions then in effect, that he would arrange for my and my family's exemption as well. Toward this end he accepted from my brother-in-law a very valuable gold cigarette case but did not do anything, even though I held five decorations and could have been granted exemption. This Pirkler always told us to rest assured that we would not be transported; when the transportation of the Jews from the provinces began he deluded us by saying that only the Jews from the provinces, and not those from Szatmárnémeti, would be deported. This accused in general acted with us as a protector of the Jewish population, but always only in appearance. To throw dust into our eyes, he once brought a number of cigars.

The accused Dr. Ernő Pirkler, moreover, also played an evil role in the military administration of the municipality of Szatmárnémeti in the fall of 1940, under the command of General Bajor, when as administrative councillor he ordered the withdrawal of the licenses of several Romanian and Jewish inhabitants, as for example wood merchants and coach drivers.

With respect to the accused Dr. Zoltán Rogozi Papp, the deputy mayor of the city of Szatmárnémeti, it is noted from the file that includes the documents from the archives of Szatmárnémeti's municipal office that this accused was the expert adviser on forbidding Jews from going to the city beach. It was also shown that this accused, together with Ernő Pirkler, designated the locality of the ghetto and generally supported the accused Dr. László Csóka in everything.

The files of this case reveal that the supreme commander in the ghetto of Szatmárnémeti was Lieutenant Colonel Deményi, who knew of all the tortures and cruelties taking place in the ghetto and thus is responsible for them.

The accused Károly Csegezi was police inspector of Szatmárnémeti, and the accused Dr. Béla Sárközi was a police officer and the head of the Alien Control Office. Both ordered and supervised the brutalities committed in the ghetto for the purpose of finding hidden valuables, an act for which the People's Tribunal established their responsibility.

The Schwartz family of Szatmárnémeti, having previously met with two Polish Jews who had experience with Jewish deportations, decided not to allow themselves to be interned in the ghetto and for this purpose built an underground hiding place in a cellar. After bringing in enough food for about one year they closed the entrance to the cellar, camouflaging it in a very ingenious manner; at the same time they dug a tunnel from the cellar to the woodshed on the opposite side of the candle factory, hiding the exit of this tunnel with a block of earth and connecting the hideout to the factory chimney as a means of letting in air. However, because the hideout was poorly ventilated through the factory chimney, the 14 hideaways in this shelter had to take turns during the night at the end of the tunnel in the woodshed to get air. At night they also removed the block of earth in order to produce a draft to air the hideout. It was the misfortune of these Jews that next to the woodshed was the apartment of the accused Erzsébet Fekete, who had a pantry with a small window overlooking this woodshed. This accused heard the noise being made at night by these Jews when they left for air and denounced the matter to the police, which under the leadership of the accused Ioan Vancea removed the 14 Jews from the hiding place and had them deported to Auschwitz. In the course of the transportation by train, this group of 14 Jews jumped from the cars in Czechoslovak territory (Russian Sub-Carpathia), but ten of them were caught and executed, so that only four returned.

The accused Erzsébet Fekete tried to defend herself before the People's Tribunal by claiming that it was not she who denounced the group of Jews hidden in the shelter, but that this group had used electricity in the hideout and the personnel of the electric power plant discovered the consumption of electricity from the meter, a fact that made them suspect that there were people hidden in the cellar. However, this defense is not justified, since it was proved through the witnesses Hermann Schwartz and Jenő Schwartz that when the 14 Jews were taken from the hideout the accused Erzsébet Fekete was on the spot and even boasted by declaring that she was proud to have been the one who denounced the case to the police. This is also admitted in part by the accused Ioan Vancea, the detective at the time, who stated that he went to the house at 37 Kölcsey Street following a denunciation by a private person.

Against the accused Erzsébet Fekete, it was also proved that when the Jews were taken from the hideout and a Jewish woman seemed to be adjusting her underwear, the accused denounced her on the spot to the accused Ioan Vancea, pointing out that she might have hidden some objects in her underwear; this led to an order for the searching of this Jewish woman, and it was the accused herself who carried out this search.

Moreover, aside from the testimony of the witnesses Jenő Schwartz and Mr.

and Mrs. Hermann Schwartz, there are two circumstances that totally contradict the defense of the accused; thus when the Jews in this hideout were being looked for, the accused Ioan Vancea stood with loaded pistol at the opening of the shelter into the woodshed, close to the home of the accused, while others began to dismantle the floor that had been built at the entrance to the cellar in the warehouse of the cement factory. This proves that the police had been informed about the opening from the hideout into the woodshed, and that this information could not have come from the personnel of the electrical power plant who had checked the meters, but rather by the neighbor to the woodshed, namely the accused.

A second circumstance that overturns the accused's defense is an article published in the newspaper *Szamos* of 18 June 1944 in connection with the discovery of this group of Jews. This article states that the trail from which the police started was the suspicious noise that some neighbors of the house at 37 Kölcsey Street heard every night. But the only close neighbor to this house was the accused. In the course of the preliminary investigation, moreover, it was proved that the accused had shown her race hatred before this affair. The witness Mrs. Hermann Schwartz states that three days before the Jews entered the cellar this accused, seeing a Hungarian beating a Jew, came out and also hit this Jew, constantly calling him "stinking Jew." This having been the spiritual makeup of this accused Erzsébet Fekete at the time, it can be explained that when she heard suspicious noises from the courtyard of the candle factory she did not hesitate for a moment to denounce them, and when her informing led to positive results she could not control the manifestation of her joy and pride at beting the author of this discovery.

The accused Ioan Vancea was the head of the Corps of Detectives of the Szatmárnémeti police, and in this capacity had a particularly rich activity, especially in Jewish questions. Thus, as he himself admits, he took part in the roundup of the Jews to be interned in the ghetto, distinguishing himself as a specialist in the search for Jews hiding in underground hideouts. This is the case of the hideout at 37 Kölcsey (today Decebal) Street where he picked up the 14 Jews that were hidden there, cheating them out of a large sum of money when he promised the family of Jenő Schwartz that he would rescue them in exchange for 100,000 *Pengős;* when Jenő Schwartz's brother heard this promise he went with the accused into the hideout and showed him where their money was hidden, but after the accused took their money he did not keep his promise to save them, showing that this promise was only a ruse to get the Jews to reveal where they had hidden their money and jewelry. (Deposition of witnesses Jenő Schwartz and Hermann Schwartz)

The accused Ioan Vancea, moreover, methodically pursued the uncovering of valuables hidden by Jews. This is the case of the objects left by Miksa Edelmann with Mrs. Kálmán Jakner née Jolán Nagy, which the accused took after discovering them. This is also the case with Sándor Izráel, whom the accused Vancea visited in search of money and jewelry even after the wife of Sándor Izráel had been deported. (Witness Mrs. Antal Lakli née Borbála Berkovics) This is also the case of Márton Simermann, where the accused discovered jewelry buried in the ground and carpets hidden in a double-bottomed barrel.

The same accused also discovered in Szatmárnémeti the hideout in which Edmond Lefkovits, Wilhelm Freud, and I. Weisz were hiding with their families at 6 Vajay Street, a hideout built by them with the aid of bricklayer János Krammer of Szatmárnémeti. After about four weeks in the shelter these Jews, having been informed that the accused Ioan Vancea suspected the bricklayer Krammer whom the Jews had induced to live on the ground floor of their building, moved their families elsewhere, and only Edmond Lefkovits and his brother-in-law Wilhelm Freud remained in the hideout. On 24 June 1944 the accused Ioan Vancea arrested Krammer as a suspect and in the course of his searches discovered the hideout, where he found the two Jews. On the basis of their past friendly relations they asked the accused not to denounce them and to help them leave for Turkey, promising their jewelry and diamonds in exchange. The accused took this jewelry but was not disposed to yield on the question of denunciation.

The accused Ioan Vancea also carried out brutalities during the roundup of the Jews into the ghetto. This is the case of the family of Miklós Weisz, when he forced the mother to carry a 50-kilogram bundle on her back even though she was a woman of 59 and in poor health.

In accordance with these sentiments animating this accused, when he was informed by the accused István Kerényi that the woman Adela Lidenthal had the two-year-old little girl of the Jewish Mrs. Goldfinger, the accused Vancea went to Adela Lidenthal, who had adopted the little girl, took both to the police station, and after some maltreatment took the little girl and had her interned in the ghetto. Being of German ethnic origin, Adela Lidenthal had agreed with Mrs. Tibor Goldfinger to adopt the two-year-old little girl, which in fact took place in March 1944. Toward the end of May 1944, the adoptive mother of the little girl went to the market to shop and during this time left the adopted daughter with István Kerényi and his wife. When Adela Lidenthal returned from the market, she found police agents in Kerényi's courtyard, namely the accused Vancea and agent Vida. The little girl was separated from her adopted mother and deported to Auschwitz, from where she did not return. The extermination of this young child is attributed to the accused István Kerényi, who denounced this case to the accused Ioan

Vancea when the little girl was left with him, and is also attributed to Ioan Vancea, who did not take into account that this little girl had already been adopted by a Christian in March 1944. The same accused also knew that children under six years of age were not obliged to wear the Yellow Star or to be interned in the ghetto, and in this particular case he also knew that the little girl had already been adopted and baptized in the Roman Catholic religion in March 1944.

But the accused Ioan Vancea had the same chauvinistic and Fascist behavior even before the internment of the Jews into the ghetto; this is the case, for example, with Sándor Friedmann, who was harshly beaten by Ioan Vancea on 17 April 1944 because he had not sewn the Yellow Star on his chest in the required manner. On this occasion he behaved in an extremely brutal manner with Sándor Friedmann, pursuing him perseveringly for a long time.

The same vengeful and perseverant behavior of the accused was also shown toward the minor children of a Jakab Zelmin who had been repatriated to Romania, whom he pursued on suspicion that they were engaged in espionage; he did everything possible to have them deported to Kamenets-Podolsk in Galicia, from where they did not return. The witness David Lustig stated during the preliminary investigation that Zelmin's mother-in-law intervened in Budapest to save the children and that the police commissioner had agreed to postpone their deportation until the arrival of a decision from Budapest, but that the accused Ioan Vancea insisted so much against awaiting this decision that the commissioner changed his mind and ordered the children sent across the border on the morning of the same day. Shortly after the expulsion, a telegram arrived from Budapest authorizing a six-month extension of the children's permission to remain in Hungary, but it was already too late as the children had been expelled. No one knows the fate of these three children, even today. It is highly probable that they were exterminated together with the 30,000 Jews at Kamenets-Podolsk.

This, in broad outline, is the evil activity of the accused Ioan Vancea. As shown by the depositions of the witnesses, the accused Ioan Vancea was a man who did not miss a single occasion to cause harm to his fellow man while he held power, and not because he feared for his job—since it was proved that in fact he was more zealous than his superiors and did not overlook anything even when he could have done so because nothing would have happened to him, as no one would have known of the particular instance.

What the Mayor Dr. László Csóka did in the city of Szatmárnémeti, the accused Dr. Endre Boér, the deputy prefect of Szatmárnémeti, did in the territory of Szatmár County, by establishing the concentration camp of Nagykároly and the ghetto of Nagybánya.

However, in Nagykároly there was only a camp for the concentration of the Jews, who were subsequently transferred to the ghetto of Szatmárnémeti, while in Nagybánya, an independent ghetto was established.

Here, in chronological order, are the facts underlying the establishment of this ghetto.

Approximately two to three days after the Szatmárnémeti conference, i.e., toward the end of April 1944, László Endre went to Nagybánya to issue directives in the field about the internment of the Jews in the ghetto. The meeting, which was held at the headquarters of the Arrow Cross Party, was attended by the deputy of Mayor Dr. Károly Tamás, who, not having received orders to participate in the establishment of the ghetto, had left the city and was thus replaced by Dr. István Rosner, who served as assistant to the mayor of Nagybánya. The meeting was also attended by Dr. Jenő Nagy, the police chief; Sándor Vajai, the former secretary general of the mayor's office; Gyula Gergely, the commander of the gendarmerie legion; Captain Dr. Tibor Várhelyi, the President of the Arrow Cross Party in Transylvania; and József Haracsek, the President of the Baross Association.

The participants at this conference then went to the spot and selected the area of the ghetto: for the Jews of Nagybánya in a vacant lot consisting of three or four sheds of the König Glass Factory, and for the Jews from the districts of Nagybánya, Nagysomkut, and Kápolnokmonostor, a farm consisting of a stable and barn in Borpatak, a village located about two to three kilometers from Nagybánya.

As in the other ghettos mentioned so far, here too squads were established for the roundup of the Jews and the acquisition of money and valuables, etc., under the leadership of police chief Dr. Jenő Nagy and Gyula Gergely, the president of the *Nyilas* party. The Jews were rounded up at an extremely fast rate and among unheard-of brutalities, the people being allowed only ten minutes to leave their homes and prevented from taking along food and baggage.

The ghetto was established so that approximately 3,500 Jewish inhabitants were crowded into an area that could hardly hold 250 people. The search squads began their body searches the moment the people entered the ghetto; here too the vaginal searches and the brutalities associated with these searches were not missing.

No measure was taken to house these unfortunate people so as to prevent their suffering from wind and rain; they were left to sleep on the wet ground under the open skies, so that after a few days the young children and the women became ill and had to be placed in the hospital, which was established in the synagogue with the permission of the authorities.

Here is how the witness Dr. Ákos Gazda described this state of affairs:

The mayor's office took no measures to safeguard the communal living of the Jews in the ghetto; it merely had a few holes dug, which, provided by some primitive fences, served as outhouses, and surrounded the ghetto with a ditch.

For three weeks, the drinking water was also not made safe; the 3,500 Jews were compelled to drink dirty water from a dirty well. Because of the dirty water there were several infectious cases.

The investigations and the searches for hidden valuables were carried out in the ghettos of Nagybánya by a special squad led by the accused police chief Jenő Nagy. The methods of torture were among the most ingenious. Thus after the investigated person was undressed to the skin, he was placed on his stomach on the floor. Some of the investigators would then tie his legs, placing wooden logs behind his knees, hang him upside down, and beat his soles and face with a rubber truncheon or horse whip. They did not omit the squeezing of testicles, or the placement of needles under the nails. Because of these tortures, several families committed suicide, among them the families of László Benedek and László Gottlieb.

Here is how the witness Béla Gellért described the method of torture used by one of the investigators, namely the accused detective József Orgoványi:

> My mother-in-law and my sister-in-law, who have not yet returned from deportation, were taken into these torture chambers one by one. My mother-in-law, who was then 70 years of age, was beaten by the accused with a horsewhip because she refused to reveal the whereabouts of the jewelry of her son with whom she lived. The manner in which they applied these beatings was horrible; each of those called in was fully undressed and beaten until they lost consciousness. I and my sister-in-law, whose turn it was to go in, waited in horror for the passage of the moments of horror, hearing the shouts coming from the torture chamber where my mother-in-law was. While she was inside, the accused came out and went to the back of the courtyard. We all breathed a sigh of relief that my mother-in-law's maltreatment had come to an end, but our hope was not realized; the suspect returned after a few minutes with a new horsewhip in his hand. My mother-in-law was kept inside for about an hour but to us it seemed like an eternity, especially since we heard her screams of pain and pleas for help, but there was nothing we could do. After my mother was pushed out, it was the turn of my sister-in-law, Berta Gellért, but when mother, hearing the name of her daughter called and knowing what was to follow, began to shout as loudly as she could not to let her enter. My mother was horribly beaten and was left with bruises all over her body and unable to talk. To ease her pain she was kept all the time in wet shawls, inasmuch from the day of her beating she was unable to walk and we had to drag her along on the day we were entrained. They acted the same way with my sister-in-law, subjecting her to the same tortures and beatings and cursing her all the time using obscene language, because of her refusal to declare where she had hidden valuables.

JUDGMENT OF THE PEOPLE'S TRIBUNAL

The fate of the Jews concentrated in the Nagybánya, Nagysomkut, and Kápolnokmonostor districts and interned in a barn at Borpatak was no less sad. Here too about 200 people were crowded into a barn and stable, and those who could not be placed were left outdoors. These internees too were tortured by József Orgoványi and his comrades. Tens of people died because of the inhumane conditions in which they were held, as did all the newborn babies.

The commander of the ghetto was Captain Dr. Tibor Várhelyi.

This state of affairs is reflected in the depositions of the witnesses Dr. Ákos Gazda, Sarolta Friedmann, Margit Lázárovics, Julia Berger, Izidor Palkovics, and Margit Goldberger.

In addition to Deputy Prefect Dr. Endre Boér, who ordered the establishment of the Nagybánya ghetto, the following participated in these operations: the accused Dr. István Rosner, who has since died and whose case was separated at the request of his heirs' lawyer, with the material consequences relating to his goods to be investigated and decided later.

The accused Sándor Vajai, the former first notary of the mayor's office in Nagybánya, was entrusted by the mayor with the handling of Jewish questions, and in this capacity he behaved extremely inhumanely in every respect; he handled each and every just request of those interned in the ghetto in an unfavorable manner, leaving the Jews to suffer from hunger for weeks on end, and he showed particular zeal during the roundup of Jews in the ghetto and in the establishment of the commissions entrusted with their roundup as well as in the training of the search commissions.

The accused Dr. Jenő Nagy, the chief of the Nagybánya police, subjected the Jews to particularly cruel treatment in his capacity as commander of the ghetto. He led the search and investigative teams, approving all the beatings. Here is how the witness Velemin Wilhelm described the role of the accused Jenő Nagy:

> Since my wife and other members of my family were interned, I and some friends went to take them some food. After we entered, the former police chief Jenő Nagy did not allow us to leave; on the contrary, to punish us he had us—all six—undress and ordered a strong Jew to give us 25 strokes on our rears. He was dissatisfied because the beatings were not hard enough and called upon a *Nyilas,* who gave us 25 blows in a manner that left us numb.

The accused Jenő Nagy was also the person who pursued Jews in the labor service companies who came with permission to visit their relatives; the accused apprehended and interned them in the ghetto and then had them deported together with the other Jews, even though the Jews in the labor service companies were exempted from internment and deportation (as was the case of the Jew Móric Rosenfeld). The accused also ordered the roundup and internment in the ghetto even of immobilized hospital patients.

The accused Károly Balogh, a former official of the Phönix factory, volunteered to participate in the searching of Jews for hidden valuables, even though he had no official position. For this purpose he went to the ghetto daily, either alone or in the company of armed German soldiers, and maltreated the Jews by slapping them in the face if they did not stand at attention when he passed by. He also had a mania for ordering stronger Jews to beat up the weaker ones. From the fact that he used to go into the ghetto in the company of armed German soldiers, one can assume that he also had contacts with the German Gestapo, which he kept informed about what was going on in the ghetto.

A similar activity with respect to the concentration of the Jews in the ghetto and the search for their hidden valuables was also engaged in by the accused József Haracsek, the then president of the Baross Association (the association of Christian merchants), who, as a member of the Arrow Cross Party without a public position, volunteered for this sinister operation. The manner in which this accused acted can be presupposed, given the fact that he volunteered for this service.

As president of the Baross Association, he began as early as 1942 to prepare lists of the Jews of Nagybánya, which he forwarded to the recruiting centers for the concentration of these Jews into labor service units, which were designed to exterminate the Jews; he distributed the shops and professional offices of the Jews thus removed from economic life among various Hungarian Fascists.

One of the most sinister figures of Nagybánya during the Horthyite occupation was the accused József Orgoványi, a detective in the political investigations section of the Nagybánya police between October 1941 and October 1944. It was mentioned tangentially above that this accused formed part of the special commission that investigated the Jews interned in the ghetto.

This accused was indeed the terror of the ghetto of Nagybánya in his capacity as specialist in tortures. Incited by the gendarmes and civilians, he subjected the Jews suspected of having hidden their goods to horrible tortures. He especially maltreated the wives of rich Jews; thus, for example, he cruelly beat the wives of the lawyers Toploncs and Bernárd. He beat the members of the Izsák family so horribly that they died within a few days while being deported, as revealed by the witnesses Dr. Ákos Gazda and Margit Lázárovics. As mentioned above, because of these unheard-of tortures, the families of Dr. László Benedek and László Gold committed suicide.

On the occasion of his frequent raids into the ghetto, this accused was in the habit of taking food and clothing from the Jews. (Depositions of the witnesses Velemin Wilhelm and Béla Gellért) He would also tip over the cauldrons containing cooked food, in order to starve the Jews. On one occasion he requested the Jews in the ghetto to deposit five million *Pengős* if they did not want him to institute his method of tithing, i.e., to shoot every tenth Jew.

The Jews Avram Szinetár, Béla Gellért, and Berta Gellért were beaten with a horsewhip on the soles of their feet and over their entire bodies, which had previously been covered with wet sheets, to compel them to confess where they had hidden their goods.

But the activities of the accused József Orgoványi did not begin with the internment of the Jews in the ghetto. He had already begun in 1941, in close collaboration with the Hungarian counterespionage service, to pursue and arrest Communist fighters; after their arrest, he subjected them in the course of the investigations to the most horrible cruelties, horsewhipping them, squeezing their testicles, pushing needles under their nails, setting fire between their toes, binding them by the hands and feet, and hanging them with their heads down; after that he would draw up documents and send them to the Szamostalva and Garany camps or put them on trial before a traveling court.

The accused Orgoványi also had close relations with the accused Captain László Berentes, the military commander of the Phönix factory of Nagybánya, who supplied him with torture objects in the form of workers suspected of Communist activity.

Thus in August 1941, Lajos Filipás, who was associated with the Petroşani company of Nagybánya, was handed by the accused László Berentes to the accused József Orgoványi to be maltreated because he was suspected of communism and had refused the proposal of the accused László Berentes to enter his service as a spy denouncing Communists in the Petroşani factory. The accused József Orgoványi kept him locked up at the police station for 11 days, during which time he cruelly tortured him, causing this Lajos Filipás several wounds that were later treated by the physician Dr. Liviu Pop of Nagybánya. After these maltreatments, the accused József Orgoványi compelled him to appear before the Nagybánya police for three years to be kept under police surveillance; he was also forbidden from occupying any position because he was considered a danger to national security. Here is how this Lajos Filipás described the cruelties he endured from the accused József Orgoványi during the investigations:

> When I was locked up in August 1941 following the denunciation by László Berentes, the former manager of the Petroşani and Phönix works who escaped with the Hungarian army and who tried to induce me to change my political views and enter into his service to denounce my Communist comrades, he arrested me personally because I refused and took me in his automobile to the police and handed me over to Orgoványi, who kept me under arrest for 11 days. During this time I was maltreated by the suspect almost daily; at the beginning he beat both of my hands

with a horsewhip and when he could no longer hit me on the hands I had to remove my shoes and they beat both of my feet so much that they both became very swollen. In this state of great pain they ordered me to dance around the room in which they tortured me, and when I could not they beat me with the rubber truncheon. When they beat my soles, they tied my feet with strings, then they tied my hands to my feet and placed a thick stick under my knees which was balanced on the backs of two chairs or placed on the floor and in this manner they beat me all over the body. When these beatings led to no result, I was undressed and the accused in his sadism squeezed my testicles until I lost consciousness.

After 11 days of such tortures, the accused set me free, but in the wake of the tortures I had suffered I fell ill and had to be under medical care for several months, during which time I was treated by Dr. Liviu Pop, a physician from Nagybánya.

Also, because of the tortures inflicted upon my testicles I remained impotent for eight months. My hands were tied with wire so that when my body was hanged over the backs of the two chairs my flesh was cut from the weight of my body.

In February 1944 the accused József Orgoványi handed the witness Lajos Filipás over to the political camp at Szamosfalva where he was held for four weeks and subjected to various types of maltreatment, sometimes even in the presence of the accused József Orgoványi, who, showing up at this camp, also participated in beating the victim.

It was in the same manner that in June 1941 he treated Zoltán Lévi, whom he had sent to the internment and labor camp at Garany only to be brought back to Nagybánya to be again subjected to tortures by the accused József Orgoványi; in the presence of László Berentes of the Phönix factory, this accused placed papers between his toes and then set them afire. The accused again sent Zoltán Lévi to the camp at Garany, where he remained until May 1943, when he was placed on trial before the "council of five" (*Kolozsvári ötös tanács;* the Council of Five of Kolozsvár), which condemned him to five years' imprisonment.

He proceeded in the same manner toward other people suspected of communism; thus he arrested Piroska Roth and five of her comrades as well as Rudolf Lázárovics and others.

Here is how a victim of Orgoványi described the suffering endured at the hands of this accused. This is the declaration of the witness, the victim Iuliu Cetățeanu of Nagybánya:

> Having a sister in Dorohoi, Romania, I crossed the border to visit her; when I returned to Nagybánya, the accused Orgoványi, having found out about it, began to suspect me. He offered me a chance to become his agent and secret informer, but I refused. For this reason, he arrested me on 11 November 1942 on the ground that I was a spy and took me to the Nagybánya police where I was tortured horribly. They placed handcuffs on my hands, placed a stick under my knees and tied my

hands to the stick, and after my body was so hanged, they beat me on my soles and tortured me so that I fainted twice; after I fainted they would pour water over me for me to come to. They tortured me this way all day long and at night they put me in a cell, threatening me with the arrest of my father and mother. Horrified, I cut the artery of my left hand; then I was taken to the hospital where I was treated. From Nagybánya I was returned to Ungvár and from there, after three and a half months of suffering and beatings, I was taken to Budapest where I was imprisoned for about two years. I was returned to Nagybánya around March 1944. Here I was tried before a commission sent from Budapest, which included as I recall a judge named Tarda, and on the ground that I was allegedly a spy and a Communist, I was condemned to 15 years' imprisonment. When the accused József Orgoványi beat me he also hit me on my genital organs.

This is the activity of the accused Orgoványi. He was brought to Nagybánya by the Hungarian authorities from Budatetény to provide proof on how these authorities were treating the coinhabiting nationalities.

The supplier of the accused József Orgoványi, as was already shown above, was the accused Captain László Berentes, the military commander of the Phönix and Petroşani factories of Nagybánya, who, as a member of the Arrow Cross Party and a collaborator of the Hungarian counterespionage service, occupied himself with the discovery of Communist workers in the two factories and with their transfer to the political investigation section of the accused József Orgoványi. Thus, in 1941 he submitted to this section a list with the names of 80 Communist workers, and in 1942 he forwarded to the recruitment center at Nagybánya a list with the names of suspected Jewish workers in the factories whom he proposed to be placed in special labor service companies for purposes of extermination.

The same accused organized a workers' school at the Phönix factory, where he gave anti-democratic and chauvinistic lectures and distributed among the workers a number of newspapers containing Hitlerite propaganda.

The collaborators of the accused József Orgoványi in beatings and tortures in the ghetto were the accused Imre Vajai and István Bertalan, both detectives associated with the Nagybánya police. In addition to the searches for hidden valuables, these detectives also occupied themselves with the capture of Jews in the forests where they had hidden at the beginning of May to escape internment in the ghetto. Those so caught were interned in the ghetto, where they were subjected to cruel tortures to compel them to denounce those still hidden in the forests. Here is how the witness Jenő Bak described the maltreatment to which he was subjected by the accused Imre Vajai and József Orgoványi on that occasion:

> When one of us wandered away he was seen by someone and when the Hungarian gendarmes pursued our traces we were discovered and interned in the ghetto in

Nagybánya on 20 May 1944. One day after our internment we began to be interrogated to reveal who among us was still hiding in the forest. The interrogations were conducted in a room near the ghetto and each detective investigated one of us in turn. I was interrogated by the detective Vajai of the Nagybánya police, who asked me why I had hidden, but I could not even answer his questions because he ordered me to take my shoes off and beat me on the soles with a rubber truncheon. The above named also implanted needles under my fingernails to torture me even more. I had to put my fingers on the desk and after he tied my hands to the table with an especially prepared device, he began to insert needles under ny fingernails. Because of these tortures I lost consciousness so that I could no longer be interrogated, and I was thrown out into a woodshed where they left me for almost half a day until I regained consciousness, after which I was taken back to the ghetto. I was held in the torture chamber for two hours.

A short while after me, Miklós Fischer, the lumber dealer from Nagybánya who died at Auschwitz, was taken in. The moment Fischer entered the torture chamber, the detective Vajai left the place and I heard him address Orgoványi, who had just arrived from the city, with the following words: "Come because a rich noon hour is awaiting you too." Vajai then left the room where I was beaten and Orgoványi entered. I heard shouts for help and of pain, but what he did with the man inside I do not know because I did not see. In the evening when I was in the ghetto I saw Fischer on the ground with a swollen head and three bruises on the top of his head, in a state of complete loss of consciousness. When he came to a little I asked him who beat him and he said Orgoványi, but because he was constantly feverish I could not discuss details. It was in this state that we were entrained for Auschwitz, where we arrived on 2 June 1944. When we were detrained, the healthy ones were assigned to the right and the ill and the old were sent to the left and subsequently taken to the crematorium. Among these was the businessman Fischer, who still had fever during the selection and was taken with the infirm.

Another tool of the organizers of the ghetto of Nagybánya was the accused Péter Czeisberger, who was a member of the Arrow Cross Party. In this capacity, without being a public official, he, like all the *Nyilas,* participated in the roundup of Jews in the ghetto and in the search for hidden goods, on which occasion he put into practice his education as a *Nyilas.* Here is how the witness Adolf Klein described the behavior of this accused:

At the end of April 1944, when the Jews were being interned in the ghetto, I was concentrated in Kolozsvár. I succeeded in obtaining a permit to visit my family. When I approached the ghetto, which was within a former iron factory, I was observed by the accused Péter Czeisberger, who picked up a stick and came to me asking what I was doing there, since he knew me from before. He then began to beat me with the stick, hitting me all over the body indiscriminately. After he got bored with the beating, he locked me up with 18 other Jews in a room without windows, and kept us for two days under police guard without food or water. Meanwhile Czeisberger took everything I had from me—my fountain pen, a wallet with 50

Pengős, my handkerchief, a pencil, and a briefcase with food. From the other comrades he also took everything they had. Finally I was sent to the commander's office and from there back to the unit I had come from.

A fate similar to that described above by Adolf Klein, was also suffered by the witness Lajos Lembel.

The accused Péter Czeisberger also belonged to Division 9 in charge of trains in Nagyvárad, a division that consisted of *Nyilas* people and was entrusted with supervising the transportation of Jews from Szőnyű, near Győr, to Germany.

In this capacity they . . . took Jewish women from the ghetto and raped and robbed them of their clothes, as revealed by the deposition of the witnesses Tivadar Magyar, József Kretz, and Endre Kocsibár. The commander of the Jewish camp in Szőnyű, near Győr, was the accused Lajos Ormos, a Hungarian originally from Nagyvárad, who, during the transports organized by Division 9 of Nagyvárad, was entrusted—as were Czeisberger and Osváth—with supervising the deportation of Jews to Germany.

While he was the commander of the Szőnyű camp, he treated the Jews in the camp in an inhumane manner, robbing them and participating with the accused Czeisberger and Osváth in the raping of women.

He intentionally neglected the feeding and housing of the camp internees. Once he housed Jews in the attic of a building that collapsed because the beams were rotten, and several Jews died. In his investigation it was also proved that several Jews died in the wake of beatings administered by him.

His deed were proved by the deposition of the witnesses Kocsibár, Tivadar Magyar, Kálmán Sáska, Szilveszter Decsey, and others.

The role played by Dr. Endre Boér, the then deputy prefect of the county —an executive role pertaining to measures for the establishment of the ghetto in Szatmár County—was shown above. His responsibility is similar to that of other deputy prefects. It is not necessary to repeat the considerations for which he is responsible; it is sufficient to point out the horrors perpetrated in the ghetto of Nagybánya, horrors that denote that the then deputy prefect did not acquaint himself with these shortcomings and that thus denote that he must be responsible for these culpable omissions.

Another person who had to be aware of the insufficient feeding and defective housing and especially of the tortures and illegalities committed in the ghettos of Szatmárnémeti and Nagybánya was the accused Barnabás Endrődi, a retired lieutenant colonel, who was appointed on 25 April 1944 by the Sztójay government as prefect of the city of Szatmárnémeti and of Szatmár County.

But how could this prefect be aware of what was happening in the city and in Szatmár County when he was overwhelmed with Imrédyist and *Nyilas* feelings, for here is how the *Szamos* (issue 102 of 6 May 1944) published the appeal launched by this accused for the solidarity of the Hungarian nation:

> I beg all the sons and daughters of my city not to permit the disunity of our front, not to allow themselves to be cheated by the cunning maneuvers of the external enemy and especially of the internal one, who tries to provoke compassion for himself by engaging in slanders, and finally to assure our solidarity for there are so few of us. Between Hungarians and Hungarians there is and should be no difference, even when one is in the National Socialist party and the other in the *Nyilas* party or in the Imrédyist party, for all of them fight for the happiness of the nation and for liberty.

Again, how could this prefect be aware and consider that there was no decree based upon law with reference to the roundup of the Jews when these are the words he used on 6 May 1944 during his solemn inauguration as prefect of Szatmárnémeti:

> The enemy aims at our destruction not only with his arms but also, through his allies that coinhabit here, with demeaning forms of destruction, sabotage, and alarmism; they want to destroy our internal front, which would bring in its wake a defeat of our external front. According to the service regulations, the soldier who uses words of despair or throws away his rifle in battle must be executed, and whoever here in the interior tries to disturb the unity of the second front—whether with alarmism, or destruction, or failure to perform his work with the greatest devotion at the post to which he was assigned—is engaged in sabotage and deserves no other procedure then the one stipulated in the service regulations.

As far as his political attitude is concerned, he declared the following:

> I shall strive with all my strength to see to it that no one shall hinder us in our work to build the new state, the National Socialist work for the final victory in the struggle against the Judeo-Bolshevik-Capitalist enemy . . .
>
> Our responsibilities along this road are specified by the government and we shall execute them without any reservations and in the spirit of the new times . . .

The depositions of the witnesses reveal that the accused Barnabás Endrődi went to the ghettos of Szatmárnémeti and Nagybánya almost daily, on which occasions he declared that he would not tolerate the presence of a single Jew in the county's territory.

Furthermore, he launched a veritable persecution of the Jews who were exempted from internment in the ghetto, as was the case with the family of Weisz who, although a 75 percent war invalid, was picked up in the village of Secas and locked in the ghetto. This was also the case with the children of József Fekete and many other persons.

In the fall of 1944, the accused Barnabás Endrődi launched a hunt against Jews who had returned to the county from their labor service companies, ordering that any Jew found in the territory of the county be executed without pity. Thus it was on the basis of this order that the labor serviceman Márton Fekete was executed on 22 October 1944, as is revealed by the death certificate on file.

This is the pretext, the foundation of the Fascist administration of the Hungarian state.

The Ghetto of Kolozsvár

The first one to carry out the instructions of László Endre in the municipality of Kolozsvár was Dr. László Vásárhelyi, the mayor. He called a meeting for 2 May 1944, which was attended by 150 officials of the municipality of Kolozsvár; Dr. László Urbán, the chief of police; and Tibor Paksi-Kiss, the commander of the gendarmerie district. On this occasion the accused László Vásárhelyi read the instructions of László Endre and issued oral instructions to the officials on how to proceed with the roundup of the Jews into the ghetto beginning on 3 May 1944.

In contrast to Nagyvárad and Szatmárnémeti, the ghetto in Kolozsvár was set up in a brickyard. As will be shown below, this also determined the location of the ghetto for other cities that were in the neighborhood of Kolozsvár, since the authorities of these cities, imitating the accused Vásárhelyi, also designated brickyards or other unsuitable places. This was the case in Marosvásárhely, Szászrégen, Beszterce, and Szilágysomlyó. The designated ghetto area was unsuitable from the sanitary point of view as well as in terms of size—the area was so small that it could not possibly hold the 18,000 people concentrated in Kolozsvár.

In this respect the deposition of the witness István Kovács, given during the preliminary investigation, is enlightening:

> The space for sleeping was so small that the people were bunched together and it was impossible to have any rest. In an area of six square meters, nine people were crowded together with their baggage and everything else they had. For a population of about 17,000 Jews, the mayor's office installed a water pipe with approximately 15 faucets to be used for washing, cooking, and cleaning. These faucets operated only from time to time. Often they were, in fact, closed for a whole day.
>
> For this reason most of us suffered from thirst, and we could not wash or clean ourselves. The people were compelled to steal water, and it frequently happened that while someone left his barrack to find firewood his cooking water was stolen. We received food only once a day, so that we had to supplement what we were given

with whatever we could cook ourself. Milk was not distributed to children or adults, and the small quantity of milk the Jewish hospital succeeded in bringing into the ghetto was nowheres nearly sufficient for the at least 1,000 small children and ill people.

For physiological needs, they dug four ditches which served as latrines, two for men and two for women. These latrines were constructed by placing a board on top of supports at the edge of the ditch, so that the people took care of their necessities one next to the other; about 20 could find room on the boards. The ditches were open and surrounded by boards. During rainy and hot weather the atmosphere was saturated with the stench that emanated from these ditches. Many were ill. . . . There was an infirmary in which the ill were treated, and pregnant women were taken to give birth.

It is in the same vein that Miklós Hevesi testified:

We were gathered in the IRIS brickyard where there was not a single house or other covered place except for the barns used for drying bricks. These barns, however, had no walls. This is where about 18,000 people—children, men, and women—stayed in dust, rain, and wind. The hygienic conditions were below any criticism. Latrines were dug only after the first week had passed, so that taking care of one's needs was a pain and a misfortune.

The primary official of the municipality, Mayor Dr. László Vásárhelyi, had discretionary power to select a suitable place for the ghetto, but he did not have the decency to search for such a place. Since he knew the ultimate fate of the Jews and was complacent about it, he did not take the trouble to find something appropriate, selecting instead the place described in the above depositions.

The commissions for rounding up the Jews in the city were also set up by the accused Dr. László Vásárhelyi. The depositions of the witnesses reveal that the mayor instructed the 150 members of the commissions charged with the roundup of the Jews to behave as sternly as possible with them, to search them for valuables, and even to carry out vaginal searches.

Here is what the witness István Kovács declared in this respect:

On the basis of the Hungarian racial laws, I was exempted from the regulation affecting nonbaptized Jews, and on the basis of the nine decorations I earned during the previous world war, I was exempted from the anti-Jewish racial measures. . . . In spite of all this, in the evening of 25 May 1944, I was picked up by three individuals, namely, Brasan, Bodi—a young man from the industrial establishment —and a detective, whose name I do not recall, and I was taken to the ghetto with my entire family. On this occasion they took away from me two high-precision cameras, a magnifying apparatus, photoelectric cells and instruments, a compass, other professional instruments, and a bicycle, without giving me a receipt. Upon entering the ghetto we were searched. They took from us the few valuable objects we had left, and let us settle where we wanted. The ghetto was under the open sky and we settled in some barns in which the burnt bricks and tiles were kept. The ground was covered with five centimeters of dust and it was exposed to the wind and rain, against which we tried to protect ourselves by hanging shawls and blankets on piles.

The witness Mihály Geller testified in the same vein.

With respect to the vaginal searches and especially the personal participation of the accused László Vásárhelyi as a guide to them, it is interesting to reveal the testimony of Julianna Nagy, who declared:

> The second day at six o'clock in the morning, I and my group went to city hall, where a taxi was placed at our disposal. We went with Vásárhelyi to the city's brickyard. Upon arrival at the brickyard, two of us were assigned to each of three rooms—two for women and one for men. The mayor, Vásárhelyi, together with his secretary, Szacsvay, personally assigned us to the rooms, telling us that three of us would have to carry out body searches to find the jewelry or other valuable objects the deportees were hiding.
>
> In the afternoon, Ilus Vigh, whom I know personally, arrived and brought us some rubber gloves and told us that there was an order for us to perform vaginal searches. I accepted the gloves, but did not use them. However, from Camila Krenner's room which was near ours, I had in the meantime heard Camila Krenner shouting at the deportees and I also heard the cries of the Jewish women.

Aside from his involvement in the establishment of the ghetto in Kolozsvár, the accused Dr. László Vásárhelyi was also involved in personal persecutions motivated by personal hatred and especially by the drive for personal enrichment. Thus he persecuted Dr. Endre Schreiber, the owner of the New York Hotel in Kolozsvár, because the latter did not want to give up his coffee shop for the establishment of a pub in which Vásárhelyi was also interested. As a consequence of this persecution, Endre Schreiber, although exempted from the racial measures, had to hide in Budapest, where, however, he was shot by a group of *Nyilas* and thrown into the Danube. To establish the responsibility of the accused László Vásárhelyi for the acts revealed above, it is sufficient to note here his quality as mayor of the municipality of Kolozsvár at the time the ghetto was established.

Nevertheless, to illustrate the gravity of his participation, one must mention that approximately 5,000 children under the age of six were interned in the Kolozsvár ghetto—children who were not obliged to wear the Yellow Star and thus in accordance with Article 14 of Decree No. 1610/1944 M.E. did not have to go into the ghetto.

This accused, together with Dr. József Forgács, the general secretary of Kolozsvár County representing the County's deputy prefect; Tibor Paksi-Kiss, the gendarmerie colonel representing the Legion of Gendarmes; and Dr. Géza Papp, the police commander representing the police, constituted the commission that handled all requests from exempted Jews demanding their rights. It acted in an inhumane and arbitrary manner, even bypassing the racial laws in effect.

The law enforcement organs in Kolozsvár included Tibor Paksi-Kiss, the gendarmerie colonel and former commander of the Kolozsvár District No. IX; Dr. László (Ferenc) Urbán, former officer of the Hungarian state police in Kolozsvár; and Dr. Géza Papp, the police commissioner of Kolozsvár.

They are responsible for all the tortures and all the maltreatments committed by them personally as well as by their agents. The accused Tibor Paksi-Kiss, as the commander of Gendarmerie District IX with headquarters in Kolozsvár, was the superior of all the law enforcement organs of Northern Transylvania that operated in the ghettos of this area. In this capacity he even issued orders and instructions to the infamous Gendarmerie Lieutenant Colonel Jenő Péterffy of Nagyvárad, as revealed in the report of Gendarmerie Lieutenant Colonel László Ferenczy, the liaison officer sent to Kolozsvár by Section XX of the Ministry of the Interior of Budapest. The report contains the following passage:

> Kolozsvár, 9 May 1944.
> I report on the events relating to the roundup of the Jews in the area of District 19 as follows:
> 1. In Nagyvárad, because of the very large number of Jews, the roundup was carried out with some difficulty. The number of policemen proved insufficient and the home and body searches were not performed by specialists, so that many opportunities were afforded for hiding valuables. Because of these circumstances, by order of Colonel Paksi-Kiss the leadership of the entire operation in Nagyvárad was taken over by Lieutenant Colonel Jenő Péterffy, the commander of the gendarmerie school.

We are also reproducing an order issued by the accused on 13 May 1944 with respect to the sequestration of food from the Jews:

> According to our information, the Jews distributed poisoned sample razor blades in the country. Thus one may assume that the food sequestered from the Jews during the roundup operation, especially the fat and flour, was also poisoned. To avoid any misfortunes that might arise from the poisoning, it might be desirable to have the food sequestered from the Jews used exclusively for feeding Jews and not to have any of it distributed to Christians, with the exception of the fat, which would have to be tested.

That the accused Tibor Paksi-Kiss held supreme command over the gendarmerie forces in all of Transylvania also results from his order issued on 13 May 1944 with respect to the foods sequestered from the Jews.

There can be no doubt that in his capacity as supreme commander of the gendarmerie forces in Northern Transylvania, this accused was the inspirer of all the inhumanities committed in the ghetto.

Another tool of the accused Mayor Dr. László Vásárhelyi was the two-star police officer Dr. László (Ferenc) Urbán, a man about 30 years old, originally from Miskolc or Komárom and a polytechnical school graduate. As Vásárhelyi's tool, he performed the duties of commander of the Kolozsvár ghetto. Here is how the witness Miklós Hevesi described the behavior of this ghetto commander:

> He called the roll every morning. Those who claimed that they were infirm or ill were gathered separately and one of them was slapped in the face by Urbán and obliged to pass on the slap to the other unfortunates. If the slapping by the first person was not sufficiently strong, Urbán would slap him even harder, demonstrating how a person had to be slapped in the face. This is how he amused himself, watching the unfortunates hitting and mocking each other.

The accused Dr. László Urbán personally beat the witness Katalin Markovics as well as other Jews in the ghetto. The executive organs of this ghetto commander were gendarmes dressed in civilian clothes. These torturers were so harsh that the screams of the victims could be heard far from the torture place; those investigated there left the place so broken that they had to be carried by two persons, and, in several cases, those beaten in the torture chamber had to be taken out on stretchers.

A strange and moving sight was the mass of baby carriages and wheelchairs of the infirm that were left in the brickyard at the time of the entrainment of the Jews for Auschwitz, baby carriages that were left behind because the then authorities of Kolozsvár were aware that the little children would no longer need the carriages.

To describe the state of affairs in the ghetto, especially with respect to the tortures and maltreatments perpetrated, a few of the edifying testimonies by witnesses will be reproduced below.

Here is what the witness Margit Deutsch declared:

> I also was led before the special investigating group. Here the gendarmes worked in civilian clothes. Even though I told them that my husband had been in the Ukraine for two years, I was nevertheless harshly beaten with a rubber truncheon. My father-in-law, Gy. Deutsch, 70 years of age, was beaten and tortured so gravely that he could no longer stand on his feet.

Here is what the witness Samu Felszner declared:

> In the ghetto I was investigated by a gendarme investigator dressed in civilian clothes and I was asked where I had hidden my valuables. During the investigation I was hit with the fist a number of times and then I was threatened that I would

be beaten on my soles if I did not confess. The investigators were acquainted with this technique, and there were cases when people were beaten harshly and after the beating had to be taken away on stretchers. I am aware of the case of Lidenthal. I know that some committed suicide because of the beatings.

Declaration of the witness Sándor Frankovics:

When I returned home I found the house bombed and very little furniture in some places. My wife, child, and mother had been killed. While still in the ghetto about 20 to 30 people were called into the separate room daily, where they were asked to declare where they had hidden their properties, especially their valuables. I personally was also called in, but did not report because I joined the fourth deportation group even though I had been assigned to the fifth; I was afraid to show up because those who came out of the investigation room had been beaten and tortured. My uncle, Dr. Aladár Simon, and his wife poisoned themselves in the ghetto and died because of the miseries and fear.

Deposition of the witness Mihály Geller:

I was left in peace for three days and then was called through a service courier, a young Jew, to the camp commander, where I was taken over by three gendarmes from Kassa and was subjected to inhuman tortures aimed at making me confess where I had hidden valuables. I was totally undressed, tied hand and foot, beaten with a rubber truncheon by one of the gendarmes while the other kicked me and the third got on top of my chest and beat me with his fists. I lost consciousness as a result of these tortures, so they poured buckets of water over me to revive me. This happened three times, without their getting a confession. Then I was taken through the courtyard of the ghetto and shown to the people with these words: "Look, this was Mihály Geller. He was, because now he is only a rag. Learn from him, because all of you who hide the truth and don't confess where your things are hidden will end up like him."

Not only Jews were beaten to make them confess where they had hidden things, but also Christians, especially when the concealer was Romanian. Thus, Iosif Câmpean was beaten because he kept a Persian rug and 5,000 *Pengős* from his brother-in-law.

After these brutalities and excesses, there came the deportation of the Jews, a deportation that was carried out under the most brutal possible conditions. There were cases when as many as 92 people were crowded into a freight car. The cars were locked, and they had to stand throughout the trip in the June heat without food and without water; they even had to take care of their basic needs in the car. To all of these brutalities the accused Dr. László Urbán and the accused Dr. Géza Papp, the police commissioner, made their own contribution.

One of the commissioners entrusted with accompanying the police for the roundup of the Jews into the ghetto of Kolozsvár included the accused Kázmér Taar, an official of the mayor's office of Kolozsvár. If on that occasion this low-ranking official had performed his function without excessive zeal and without manifesting race hatred, he would not be called to account today. But the accused Kázmér Taar was merciless, excessive and cruel, and at the same time had an ambitious appetite to enrich himself. He had no consideration for anyone; for example, he picked up the physician Dr. Jenő Király, who was his family doctor and in this capacity had saved the brother of the accused, from his home in such a hurry that he did not even allow him to change his rain-soaked clothes. He took from this physician and his wife everything they had, including their wedding bands.

The witness Izidor Molnár declared about this witness that in order to induce the Jews to hand over their valuables, he staged a mass execution with a machine gun in the ghetto.

Here is how the witness Aliz Gurkovschi described the procedure of the accused Kázmér Taar:

> I, my mother, and my grandparents appeared before Taar, who asked us to hand over to him all of our valuables and jewelry. When my turn came I declared that I had no jewelry and then he jumped at me shouting "but what about that watch?" Then I recalled that I had a watch on my left hand, which I removed and handed over, and he put it in his pocket. Neither my mother, nor I, nor my grandparents received any receipt for the valuables we handed over to Taar.

The witness Julia Kos declared about the same accused:

> Being a friend of the wife of the pharmacist Bezdan, I passed by to chat with her; I found her very agitated and depressed, telling me that some agents of the mayor's office had been there and asked her for her identity papers and told her to get ready, as they would come to take all of her family into the ghetto. Shortly afterward, three civilian officials indeed came, and among these was Kázmér Taar. Two of these officials began to question the Bezdan family after Mrs. Bezdan submitted the identification documents. At this time, Kázmér Taar asked me what I was doing there. I told him that I was there as a friend of the Bezdan family. Kázmér Taar then told me to leave immediately, for otherwise he would take me to the ghetto as well. Because of Taar's severe attitude I became so emotionally upset that I did not even say good-bye to the Bezdan family.

The same facts are also revealed by the witness Margit Krausz, who described in her deposition how the accused Kázmér Taar stood with other officials at the gate of the ghetto and searched those taken into the ghetto, taking their money, jewelry, watches, and other objects without giving them receipts. This witness also stated that, being acquainted with the accused Taar, she begged him to let her go to the ghetto of Szászrégen where her parents were interned, a request that the accused Kázmér Taar answered with the sarcastic statement that it would not be necessary because all the Jews would be together.

The accused Kázmér Taar acquired many things on the occasion of the searches; only thus can one explain that when he was arrested, three hunting rifles and much elegant clothing were found, as revealed by the witness Ioan Chifor. The accused Kázmér Taar, executing his functions in the roundup of the Jews into the ghetto with excessive zeal, also mixed himself into questions relating to the apprehension and internment into the ghetto of Jews that were exempted. Here is what the witness Sándor Müller said in this connection:

> In Kolozsvár, while in front of my house in which my mother-in-law was also staying, I saw all my relatives being loaded into a truck, and on the spur of the moment I jumped into the truck myself as well, reaching the ghetto with them. As I entered I came across Kázmér Taar, a ghetto official; hearing from me that I was assigned to community public work, which I proved with documents, he nevertheless refused to take this into consideration, declaring: "You don't have to return there and must remain here in the ghetto." Thanks to some friends I was able to escape from the ghetto the next day. However, I was caught at the station by the security organs and returned to the ghetto. Before reaching the ghetto, I was taken to the police station, where I met Taar, who told me: "The Jews will see that it is no longer possible to escape from the ghetto . . ."
>
> Showing that I had only 500 *Pengős,* I was led into the ghetto where I was brought before Kázmér Taar, who took all my valuables and the 500 *Pengős,* and ordered the quartermaster to have me taken to the "massage" section. Reaching this special room, they descended upon me without saying a word and hit me cruelly with their rubber truncheons all over the body and even on the head, so that I fell several times; then I was lifted up and maltreated again, only to fall down for good when I fainted. This vile affair lasted almost an hour. Leaving, or more exactly after being taken out of the "massage room," I was met by Kázmér Taar, who addressed me as follows, looking very satisfied: "At least now you will learn that it's not so easy to escape from the ghetto." Thanks to Taar I too got into the camps at Auschwitz and Buchenwald, where only my wife and I survived.

Kolozsvár also was not without a horde of informers on the persons who tried to escape from internment in the ghetto and from deportation to a sure death.

One of these informers was the accused Irén Ujvári née Varga of Kolozsvár. Her activities can be summarized as follows: In May 1944, when the Jews of Kolozsvár were being interned into the ghetto, the husbands Zoltán Kőrösi and Ernő Stössel, coming home on furlough from a labor service company at Borgoprund, found out that their wives were already interned in the Kolozsvár ghetto; with the aid of a German officer in the ghetto whom they bribed with a sizable amount of money, they were able to remove their wives along with another woman, Roza Herskovits, and took them to work near the Neolog

Jewish church on Horea Street; from the Neolog Jewish church, the three women went to the Herskovits home at 34 Horea Street with the intention of not returning to the ghetto but instead of escaping to Romania, as they had decided the day before.

However, their plan was frustrated by the accused Irén Ujvári, who, as they were entering the Herskovits home, saw them through the door of her shop, which was across Horea Street from the home where the three women who had left the ghetto went. As the People's witness Gheorghe Albon shows, as soon as the accused saw the women entering the Herskovits home she went to the back of the store where there was a telephone and informed the police about what she had seen. The same witness talked to the policeman, who said that he had been sent on the basis of a telephone denunciation. The result was that a very short time later a police agent arrived in the Herskovits house and, with the assurance of the well-informed and even knowing the names of the women, picked up all three and took them to the police station together with Kőrösi and Stössel, where Stössel's wife was beaten. At the police station Stössel and Kőrösi were freed since they were serving in a labor service company, but the women were sent back to the ghetto from which they were not able to escape again, so that they were deported to Germany from where they did not return.

The above facts are revealed in an undoubted manner in the depositions of the witnesses Gheorghe Albon, Zoltán Kőrösi, Ernő Stössel, József Pakai, Márton Binder, the wife of Gáspár Lázár née Erzsébet Pakai, and Zseni Berkovits. In other words, from the above one can conclude with certitude that the accused's role was that of an informer, without whose activities the three Jewish women could have saved their lives.

Another informer whose activities resulted in the extermination of 11 people was the accused Irma Enyedi of Kolozsvár. The facts are as follows:

At the Aszupatak estate near the city of Kolozsvár, which had been held on leasehold by the resident István Bonyhai and the Jewish brothers Ernő Salamon and Árpád Salamon since long before the internment of the Jews into the ghetto, the families of the two Jewish brothers settled in the estate residence during May 1944; in addition to the families of the Salamon brothers, a few of their relatives also came to live at this estate, so that a total of 11 people lived there.

As is revealed by the deposition of the witness József Millich, with the goodwill of certain Kolozsvár police officials, these 11 people had succeeded in escaping internment into the ghetto, an internment process that began on 3 May 1944, and they would have succeeded in saving themselves had not the criminal activity of the accused Irma Enyedi intervened.

István Bonyhai, the associate of the Salamon brothers, did not live at the

Aszupatak estate and went there only very rarely; because of the bombing of the city of Kolozsvár, however, on 2 June 1944, István Bonyhai decided to move to the estate with his mother.

As a result of this decision, the Bonyhai family, joined by the accused Irma Enyedi, a relative of theirs, went to the estate on the same day, 2 June 1944. At that time István Bonyhai was assigned as a lieutenant in the quartermaster section of the Hungarian Army in Kolozsvár, and the brothers Árpád and Ernő Salamon were in a labor service company that at that time was working at the Nagyvárad station.

Arriving at the estate, the members of the Bonyhai family notified the Salamon brothers through István Bonyhai that all the Jews who were there should leave immediately to wherever they thought they could, threatening the wives of the Salamon brothers that if they didn't leave they would arrange worse things for them.

Indeed, István Bonyhai and Sándor Bonyhai together with the accused Irma Enyedi decided on the denunciation of the 11 Jews on the estate to the Kolozsvár police. Following this decision, on 3 June 1944 at 2 P.M. the accused Irma Enyedi went to Kolozsvár and on that same day, following the denunciation, a truck with three policemen arrived at the estate; these first looked for István Bonyhai and after a short talk with him and on his invitation, went to the areas inhabited by the 11 Jews, whom they picked up, put into the truck, and took to the police station. The next day at the police station these Jews were maltreated; the wife of Árpád Salamon was beaten especially harshly by police agents Szatmári and Gömbös to make her reveal where the family jewelry was hidden; at the time of these investigations, the accused Irma Enyedi was seen by the wife of Árpád Salamon looking for Szatmári at the police station.

On 6 or 7 June the 11 Jews who had been picked up at the Aszupatak estate were entrained and deported with other Jews to the camps at Auschwitz, from where none of them returned.

The above is revealed unquestionably from the acknowledgment of the accused, corroborated by the depositions of the witnesses Ella Bonyhai, Ernő Salamon, Manó Neulender, József Millich, Árpád Salamon, Eszter Tessler, and others.

The accused Irma Enyedi attempted to show that she made the denunciation to the police only after the members of the Salamon family had been discovered, and only did so to protect her cousin Bonyhai from the consequences he might have suffered if he had been accused of sheltering a Jewish family. The accused also maintained that as a result of her connections at the Kolozsvár police station, she succeeded in registering this denounciation under a date earlier than the date when the Jews were found at the estate.

In opposition to this position of the accused is the deposition of the witness Ernő Salamon, who declared that being in a labor service company assigned to the Nagyvárad station and curious to see which Jews were being deported from Kolozsvár on a train that had stopped at the Nagyvárad station, he saw his wife and the rest of his family although he had thought that he had left them safe and hidden at the Aszupatak farm. The wife of this witness told him that it had been the accused who denounced them to the police and that even the police detective had told her so.

Moreover, even the logic of the matter leads to this conclusion. In truth, until 2 June the Salamon family was able to stay peacefully at Aszupatak, a farm that was under lease to the Salamon family who used the camouflage name of Bonyhai, and which had living quarters consisting of three rooms and a kitchen. But after the bombing of Kolozsvár on 2 June, the Bonyhai family, fearing a repetition of the bombing, decided to move to the Aszupatak farm. At that point it became the story of the mole and the hedgehog. The Salamon family of 11 people, and in the absence of its head Ernő Salamon who was in a labor service company, was purely and simply kicked out of the home by the Bonyhai family and obliged to move to a barn on the farm; apparently, not even this satisfied the Bonyhai family, who did not wish to be inconvenienced by the presence of these Jews even in the barn. The accused was Bonyhai's cousin and had connections with the police commissioner of Kolozsvár, and herself offered to do this task for her cousin and denounced the 11 Jews. The accused carried this out especially eagerly since, not having any property, she lived with her cousin Bonyhai and was convinced that only if they got rid of the family of Ernő Salamon could they be comfortable in the three rooms of the Aszupatak farm.

Another denouncer of the Jews of Kolozsvár was the accused Vilmos Horák. The antecedents of the denunciation by this accused can be summarized as follows:

When the internment of the Kolozsvár Jews into the ghetto began, many of them—aware of the calvary awaiting them because of this measure—tried to escape by any means at their disposal. Some of those who succeeded in escaping took advantage of the humanity of some acquaintances, who sheltered, hid, fed, and protected them as much as they could. If at the end they nevertheless failed to escape, their misfortune was due to some heartless persons who had been poisoned by doctrines of hatred that beclouded their minds and perverted their souls.

Among the Jews who were interned in the ghetto from the beginning were those belonging to the Schwartz and Schönhaus families, which included the husbands Sándor Schwartz and Miksa Schönhaus, the wife (Hermina) and daughter (Marian) of the former, and the wife of the latter. When the internment took place, Hermina Schwartz was in the hospital, having been ill, and all the others were left in their homes on 27 Iașilor Street because of the goodwill of police physician Dr. Tibor Konczwald and the head of the alien control office in the municipal police, Dr. Ernő Borkay, who protected them and kept them up to date on everything that was of interest to them.

However, it happened that the street warden was the accused Vilmos Horák. It must be mentioned that this organization of street wardens was a typical Fascist creation of the Horthyite regime and had been established specifically so that these street wardens would serve as the eyes and ears of the regime so that nothing could escape unobserved by this regime. The depositions of the witnesses with respect to the activities of the accused Vilmos Horák are contradictory. On the one hand there are the depositions of the witnesses Zsuzsa Deutsch and Miksa Schönhaus, according to which near the end of May a police car went to the Jewish hospital at Iașilor Street, i.e., the street in which the accused and the Schönhaus and Schwartz families lived. While the car was parked in front of the hospital, according to the depositions of the witnesses Zsuzsa Deutsch and Miksa Schönhaus, the accused Vilmos Horák came out and informed the Gestapo agents that the two families of Schönhaus and Schwartz were still there, not yet picked up, because these families had connections with the police. Also, according to this version, the driver of the car told Miksa Schönhaus that the street warden must have hated him, to denounce him to the Gestapo agents in front of the Jewish hospital.

A second version of depositions is represented by that of the driver Tibor Șuteu, who denied that he had told Miksa Schönhaus that the street warden had denounced him. This deposition is somewhat supported by the deposition of the witness Julia Fábián, who maintained that on the day the police and the Gestapo picked up the Schönhaus and Schwartz families, Vilmos Horák was at home and that later some woman came and she heard her ask Borkay to go with her to the Schönhaus house to help her get her personal belongings so that these would not be locked and sealed in Schönhaus's house.

From these depositions it might appear that the accused Vilmos Horák had nothing to do with the roundup of the two Jewish families and that thus the depositions of Miksa Schönhaus and Zsuzsa Deutsch would have to be set aside.

The People's Tribunal, however, set aside the depositions of the two witnesses Tibor Șuteu and Julia Fábián as not being worthy of belief, since the former contradicted himself in his confrontation with the witness Miksa Schönhaus as well as in connection with the deposition made during the investigation, and Julia Fábián lives with the sister of the accused Vilmos

Horák and it is presumed that she wanted to perform an act of kindness with her deposition.

The reasons for which the People's Tribunal established the guilt of the accused Vilmos Horák are as follows:

The files in this case contain a declaration by Mrs. István Horváth née Ana Serföző of Debrecen, which was made before a notary public in Debrecen; it reveals that this woman brought food to the Schönhaus and Schwartz families, who were not interned in the ghetto during the first half of May 1944, having been left home on the excuse that they were needed for clearing rubble in the wake of the bombings.

This assistance of Mrs. István Horváth by providing food was observed by the accused, who threatened her that if she continued with the delivery of food for these Jewish families she too would be interned as punishment.

It was in the same vein that the witnesses Endre Sebestyén and Rozália Sebestyén testified in the investigation office of the public prosecutor; although they were not directly threatened by the accused, they were nevertheless alerted at the time by the Schwartz and Schönhaus families to be careful when bringing food so that they would not be seen by the street warden, i.e., by the accused, because he was following them.

The fact that the accused pursued these two Jewish families was known to these families through police commissioner István Borkay, their protector, who also told them that the police were continuously receiving denunciations from the accused against these two families, but at the same time assured them not to be afraid because he, commissioner Borkay, would suppress them.

That these depositions of the victims Miksa Schönhaus and Sándor Schwartz include much truth results also from the fact that the accused himself admitted in the course of the investigations that Mrs. Borkay, the police commissioner's wife, asked him why he denounced the Schönhaus and Schwartz families in writing and even denounced her on suspicion that she was harboring hidden Jews in her home.

All of these depositions, taken together, make it abundantly clear that the accused Vilmos Horák was no stranger to the roundup and internment into the ghetto of the Schwartz and Schönhaus families, all the more so since this accused in his capacity as street warden in the wardens' organization had exactly the mission not to leave anything awaiting further execution with respect to the anti-Jewish laws relating to the internment of the Jews in the ghetto.

Another person involved in the operation relating to the internment in the ghetto was the accused Ilona Báthori. It happened that in her immediate neighborhood there lived Olga Tanner, of Jewish ethnic origin, who was engaged to Dezső Istvánovits. To avoid internment in the ghetto—in order not to be recognized and denounced by neighbors from 30 János Zsigmond Street, the neighborhood of the accused—she moved to an apartment at 30 Gh. Barițiu Street, where she registered under the name of Olga Istvánovits so as to erase her traces.

The measure taken by this woman was indeed effective, for nothing happened to her until 27 June 1944. And it is possible that nothing would have happened to her thereafter had she not had the misfortune of meeting her former neighbor of János Zsigmond Street, i.e., the accused Ilona Báthori, who after recognizing her denounced her to the first policeman she met. The policeman, looking for Olga Tanner, contacted the doorwoman of the house at 30 Gh. Barițiu Street, but the doorwoman said that there was no such person in the building, although there was a person by the name of Olga Istvánovits. The policeman was satisfied with this answer and was ready to leave, but in the street the accused Ilona Báthori convinced him that Olga Istvánovits was the same person as Olga Tanner; thus he returned to the building and arrested Olga Tanner, who, after her arrest, was interned in various camps and prisons in Budapest and then deported to Germany to Dachau and Belsen from where, after endless adventures, she returned to the country in January 1946.

The role of the accused Ilona Báthori in this denunciation was proved by the deposition of the witness Ana Farkas née Maczalek, who was a woman in the street talking with the policeman and overheard Olga Tanner, while being taken to the police, tell this woman in the street: "Are you satisfied now that they picked me up?"

It is true that the witness Ana Farkas did not at the time know who this woman in the street was who talked to the policeman and identified the victim, but her deposition is substantiated by the admission of the accused Ilona Báthori during the investigation that she had denounced the victim to a policeman, having been urged by her husband and having been frightened by a stranger who told her that if she did not denounce her she would suffer the consequences of the laws. It is true that in the course of the oral arguments before this People's Tribunal she reconsidered this admission, declaring nevertheless that she admitted that she was the one who revealed the address of the victim at 30 Gh. Barițiu Street, but denying that she had accompanied the policeman to that house. This denial, however, is weakened by the deposition of the absolutely disinterested witness Ana Farkas, who declared that she had seen a woman in the street talking to a policeman and had heard and even seen the victim addressing that woman with the words cited above.

This being the case, there can be no doubt that the person who caused the misfortune of the victim Olga Tanner was the accused, by acts through which she intentionally contributed as an accomplice to the internment of this victim in a camp and consequently to her deportation to Germany.

The executors of the measures relating to the internment of the Jews of Kolozs County into the Kolozsvár ghetto were Dr. Ferenc Szász, the deputy prefect of Kolozs County, and Dr. József Székely, the mayor of Bánffyhunyad.

Both took part in the preparatory conferences that were held by László Endre at Szatmárnémeti and Marosvásárhely, carrying out faithfully all of the instructions received.

Deputy Prefect Dr. Ferenc Szász died on 2 June 1944 and since his heirs were not involved in the case, the People's Tribunal had to order the separation of the case involving this accused, with the stipulation that the case against the heirs of this accused for the consequences provided in Paragraph 2, Article 9 of Law No. 312/1945 be subsequently adjudicated.

With respect to the roundup of the Jews in Bánffyhunyad, this operation was carried out in an inhumane manner by the police authorities with the participation of subordinates of the mayor, including first of all Dr. Pál Boldizsár, the former supply counselor of Bánffyhunyad.

This latter accused, who did not have any official connection with the roundup and internment of the Jews, nevertheless participated in this evil campaign with excessive zeal and committed many brutalities. He walked around all the time with a whip in his hand hitting innocent people, ordering the searching of everyone, including infants and suckling babies.

On the part of the police, these measures where carried out above all by chief of police Dr. József Orosz, police officer Ferenc Menyhért, detective András Szentkuti, police officer András Lakatos, and police commissioner Sándor Ojtózi.

The depositions of the witnesses Sándor Pocsai, Irén Noti, János Ambrus, István Hunyadi, and Sámuel Knok—all residents of Bánffyhunyad—reveal that the police officers carried out searches among the Jewish population as well as among the Christian population who wanted to save some objects from the organized theft of the Hitlerites. Thus police officer Orosz used a stick to beat Sándor Pocsai until it broke in the course of the beatings. Police officer Ferenc Menyhért hit the testicles of the same witness with his sword until he lost consciousness. The accused Pál Boldizsár was excessively brutal. He referred to Jewish women as "stinking whores"; when the witness Irma Knok wanted to get on the truck that carried her mother, the accused pushed her away with the following words: "Get lost, you stinking whore, before I kick you in the ass until you turn into a flower." The same witness tells how little children cried during the internal examinations ordered by this hangman.

The wife of János Ambrus was investigated by detective András Szentkuti by order of the police chief in the search for objects that had been given to her for safekeeping by the deportee Klára Nussbecher. This woman was so cruelly tortured that she lost her mind in the wake of the tortures she suffered. He behaved similarly toward István Hunyadi, the former rail stationmaster of Bánffyhunyad, who after being beaten and tortured at the police station was interned in a concentration camp.

The deposition of the witness Ferenc László, who was an official of the Royal Hungarian Police, reveals that all the valuables robbed from the Jews were divided among the accused József Orosz, Ferenc Menyhért, and András Lakatos, the police cashier, and were shipped to Budapest for their own purposes.

After the Jews were taken to the ghetto of Kolozsvár, the accused Pál Boldizsár, Ferenc Menyhért, József Orosz, and András Szentkuti appeared each morning at the ghetto command station and began the investigation of the Jews from Bánffyhunyad at the special torture unit in the Kolozsvár ghetto. After each investigation, the Jews were taken out of the torture chamber unconscious, in a wheelbarrow. One of the torture victims, named Margit Fischer, described the torture process as follows:

> When my sister entered the office, Pál Boldizsár confronted her with a question: "Do you know me?" My sister naturally answered, "yes." To this Boldizsár responded laughingly, "But of course you know me, you Jewish whore, and you will get to know me even better from now on," and asked her where she hid her valuables, to which my sister answered that she did not hide them anywhere. In response to this, Boldizsár slapped her twice in the face, as a result of which two of her teeth were knocked out. After that, he took a list from which he began to read the inventory of the items given to Károly Ilosvai, an inhabitant of Bánffyhunyad. After this, without waiting for any answers he grabbed her by the hair, threw her to the ground and kicked her with his feet. My sister, driven by pain, began to wail, but Boldizsár ordered her to remove her stockings with which he stuffed her mouth, and then he beat her bare feet with a rubber truncheon. Then my sister lost consciousness; after she came to, at the order of Boldizsár, they placed pencils between her fingers and then squeezed her hands so that she fainted. When she regained consciousness she was already in the barracks.
>
> Boldizsár threatened my sister that he would continue the investigation in a few days, but this did not come to pass because in the meantime she was deported.

Dr. József Székely, the mayor of Bánffyhunyad—an expert on matters relating to public administration—was aware of the illegality of the orders but nevertheless issued them and insisted on their implementation. This accused must have known that the execution of orders contradicting moral precepts had to be stopped.

JUDGMENT OF THE PEOPLE'S TRIBUNAL

This was the deplorable state of the Jews in the city of Kolozsvár and Kolozs County in May 1944. The state of housing and feeding of the Jews in the Kolozsvár ghetto was shown above, but in contrast to this state of affairs, the accused János Botos, the secretary of the Kolozsvár section of the *Erdélyi Párt* (Transylvanian Party), in order to mislead Hungarian public opinion so that no one should take pity on the Jews and eventually come to their aid, went to the ghetto located in the Kolozsvár brickyard and, although he could observe things that were more than tragic, wrote an article in the 17 May 1944 issue of *Ellenzék* (Opposition) titled "I Was at the Ghetto." He also wrote articles titled "How Do the Jews Live in Their Compulsory Homes in Kolozsvár?" and "A Short Visit to the Brickyard Where People Play Football and Rummy and Nobody Wants to Work."

Here are extracts from some parts of this report:

> I am like the overwhelming majority of the Kolozsvár Hungarians. I never had any closer relationship with them. They caused this themselves when around 1925 they voluntarily cut themselves off from the tortured body of Magyardom. For two decades the Hungarians of Kolozsvár behaved toward them the way one normally behaves toward strangers. . . .
>
> Nevertheless, I went into the ghetto, because I felt that there has been enough of the exaggeration that twirls around us; clearly it's enough of this real and masked sentimentalism, enough of this irresponsible and harmful slander. . . .
>
> I can immediately reassure all those who are upset. In the Jewish camp nobody froze, nobody committed suicide, and nobody lifted as much as a finger against the iron authority of the Hungarian policemen. In the Jewish camp there is not a single person suffering from an infectious disease, and 26 physicians guard the health of the camp's inhabitants. . . .
>
> The sanitary situation in the camp is adequate, and opportunities for cleaning were placed at their disposal. A visible sign is the immense amount of washed laundry that flutters in the spring air. . . .
>
> Among those from Kolozsvár are some Jews wearing kaftans and traditional fur hats. On the other hand, among them may also be many hundreds who for several generations have severed themselves from Tarnopol and Warsaw, although their ancestral instincts still come gushing out when rough times visit them. There already is no difference whatsoever between the behavior of the Jews from Galicia and those of Kolozsvár. . . .
>
> Leaning against the barbed-wire fence, smaller and larger groups were talking and putting their heads together. This is typical of Galicia. This is how the men who were at the front in the cities of the Eastern country know them.
>
> Since their housing was arranged so that the families and relatives would be together, one person from these groups normally brings food in a bucket, which is then divided among them in the barracks. Each of them receives a complete portion; thus no one suffers from hunger; no one is in want of anything. They are also

supplied plentifully with canned food, since each person could bring into the camp 50 kilograms of luggage plus food for several days. The camp commander inspected the baggage leniently, so that several brought in 100 and even 150 kilograms.

In good times too they played cards; now they can play cards until they are surfeited.

They have lined the brick-drying barns with kerchiefs and bed covers. From a distance the camp looks like a piece of clothing with a thousand patches. Around the tent, however, life continues calmly. Everyone continues calmly with his distractions or his work, if he wants to work. The council also established a technical bureau which includes well-known engineers, but I have heard that they work in vain to prepare the most beautiful plans, as these are only sparingly put into practice or not at all. Somehow this is the spirit of the ghetto. But it is theirs, and the Hungarian authorities have no inclination or plan to interfere. The mayor of the municipality has indeed satisfied all rational requirements; this would have to be their business.

Although in his capacity as secretary of the Transylvanian Party he was conscious of the fate ordained for the Jews, he concluded his article with the following paragraph:

I arrived exactly to the point from which I left the ghetto, set up by them according to their nature, in which life is not comfortable but neither is it bad. At any rate, it is much better than the life of the bombed-out Hungarian and of the Hungarian soldier who fights at the front and who, aside from the lack of comfort, also risks his life in this battle which is being fought not only for us but because of them.

As this paragraph shows, the accused made the Jews guilty even for the launching of the war. This shows clearly that the accused János Botos intentionally put himself at the service of Hitlerism and fascism, his article and his activity as secretary of the Transylvanian Party being so many acts by which he contributed to the realization of the political goals of Hitlerism and fascism.

A sinister figure who played a large role in the selection of the Jews at the Auschwitz camp was the accused Victor Capesius, a pharmacist from Sighişoara (Segesvár) and a salesman for Transylvania for the German I.G. Farbenindustrie.

This accused contributed to the misfortunes of all the Jews from all the ghettos of Transylvania; he was seen at Auschwitz by the witness Dr. Jenő Király of Kolozsvár when he was active in the selection of those who were sent to the crematorium near Auschwitz. This selection was performed in such a way that the young who were deemed able to work were sent to the right, and the children, the old, the sick, and generally those who appeared to be weak, as well as mothers who did not leave their little children, were sent to the left. Those sent to the right were undressed, passed through special sheds to be deloused, put into prison uniforms, and sent to various labor camps. Those sent to the left were crowded into chambers equipped for extermination by means of gas where they were gassed, and their bodies were incinerated in the crematoria of Auschwitz and Birkenau.

As the people used for labor became exhausted from the hard work, they were sent to various selection hospitals, and those considered no longer suitable for labor over a longer period, or those whose physical rehabilitation would cost too much, were also gassed and then burned in the crematoria. Although the accused Victor Capesius was supported by the Jewish physicians in the cities of Transylvania while he was the salesman of the I.G. Farbenindustrie company, when he arrived in Auschwitz as a captain pharmacist he reneged on all his acquaintances with Jewish physicians, and proceeded with the greatest cruelty to the selection of the unfortunate victims. This accused behaved with unbelievable cruelty in his capacity as captain of the SS Army, when on the occasion of the arrival of transports of tens of thousands of Jews from Northern Transylvania, he mercilessly ordered their evacuation from the freight cars and the taking from them of their last absolutely necessary goods which they held in their hands; then he ordered that they be grouped into two columns, one of men and the other of women and children; finally he always took part in the selection operations described above.[12]

The Ghettos in the Székely Land

Three ghettos were established in the Székely Land:

1. The ghetto of Marosvásárhely for the city of Marosvásárhely, the western part of Maros County, and Udvarhely County;
2. The Szászrégen ghetto for the eastern part of Maros County and the northern part of Csík County; and finally
3. The ghetto of Sepsiszentgyörgy for Háromszék County and the southern part of Csík County.

A conference was held on 28 April 1944 at Marosvásárhely concerning the establishment of the ghettos in the Székely Land: It was presided over by László Endre, the under-secretary of state of the Ministry of the Interior, and was attended by all the prefects, deputy prefects, mayors of urban communities, district chiefs, police chiefs, commanders of the gendarme legions, and higher officials of the civil administration, as well as the commanders of the more important military units. Here in the Székely Land also, as in Szatmárnémeti, the participants received written instructions signed by Under-Secretary of State László Baky, the head of the organs of public order in Hungary, as well as oral instructions given by László Endre; not to repeat what was said above in connection with the examination of these instructions, they will not be analyzed again here.

One must mention, however, that a number of problems were raised here by the participants, as was admitted by Dr. Ferenc Májay, the former mayor of Marosvásárhely, himself. These objections were raised with regard to children and food.

With respect to the first question, a participant objected that he would not round up and intern children under six years of age in the ghetto, because this was against Decree No. 1610/1944 M. E., but László Endre interrupted the questioner with the words: "Certainly all the children will also be rounded up; not a single family member will remain." Another participant raised the objection that the Jews would not be able to acquire food for 14 days because food was distributed by ration card, so that no one could provide himself with food to last a longer period. This was an objection to which László Endre responded most sharply that he wasn't interested.

These objections reveal that those who so desired could have raised any question without danger of being called to account, and if these objections had been presented forcefully, it is more than certain that no excesses would have taken place.

The interrogation of the accused Ferenc Májay also reveals that it was already known on 28 April 1944 that the Jews would be deported, because László Endre informed them that the mayor's office would have to be concerned with feeding the Jews until they were transported away from the locality.

In the Székely Land the operations relating to the roundup of the Jews and their internment into the ghettos were carried out with the same harshness and brutalities as in the other ghettos. Here too one did not do without the convocation of the implementation organs by the mayor Dr. Ferenc Májay, nor the division of roles among squads, nor the cooperation in the operations by *Nyilas* elements without an official public role who volunteered for these operations. Neither was there an absence of the searches for hidden valuables, which were accompanied by the usual vaginal searches.

In the cities in which a ghetto was located, the Jews were rounded up and placed into the ghetto, but in the other Székely cities the Jews were assembled in schools or the police station and taken from there as prisoners by train, cars, or even horsecarts to the ghetto closest to their locality.

Following these general observations applying to all the ghettos in the Székely Land, we shall examine below each ghetto separately.

The Ghetto of Marosvásárhely

In the city of Marosvásárhely the ghetto was set up in a ruined brick factory. The factory building was in the middle of a field measuring approximately 200,000 square meters. The roof of the building was mostly broken, it was paved with cement, and as it had not been used for years the pavement was very dirty and wet. The interior of the building consisted of galleries and furnaces, which, being decayed, wet, and dirty, looked like pits and catacombs. Here there were crowded together about 7,380 persons, constituting the Jewish population of the western part of Maros County, Udvarhely County, and the city of Marosvásárhely.

The commander of the ghetto was the police questor, the accused Dr. Géza Bedő, who appointed Commissioner Dezső Niptai as his deputy. Since the factory building had room for only about 2,400 people, the rest had to stay under the open sky, in rainy and cold weather, forced to build a sort of tent out of the few belongings they brought with them.

The lack of food made itself felt in the ghetto even in the first days and later this lack became frightening. The food sent to the ghetto by the mayor's office was insufficient and of bad quality, being only the withered and rotten remnants taken off the market. The only food that improved the situation somewhat was bread, due to the fact that one of the co-owners of the bakery in Marosvásárhely was Jewish, so that the bread was delivered in more humane conditions.

In the first week after the internment, there were no cooking facilities and individual families prepared their meals as best they could, by their own means. After a week, at the intervention of the Jewish Council, the municipal authorities allowed the Jews to bring eight bathtubs into the ghetto in which they could heat their meals, but even then, because of the lack of firewood, the meals could hardly be prepared properly since the authorities did not allow the Jews to bring firewood from their homes.

The situation with regard to drinking water was no better. In the beginning, the ghetto had only a small spring that drained through a very thin pipe, which wasn't nearly enough for the entire ghetto population. After a few days the municipal authorities allowed the Jews to use the water pump in the factory courtyard, but even this pump could not satisfy the normal water needs; thus the Jews were also forced to consume the undrinkable water from a dirty reservoir and from a lake with stagnant water. Only very late and after many and persistent complaints was water brought to the ghetto in a firemen's water truck, but even then not regularly and not in sufficient quantities.

But the most shameful thing in the ghetto of Marosvásárhely was the lack of toilet facilities. Although the Jews were rounded up in the greatest haste, the municipal authorities did not concern themselves with arranging beforehand for setting up the necessary toilet facilities. Only after the assembly of the Jews was finished, did teams of Jews dig ditches in the back of the courtyard, which they fenced in with pieces of rotten planks and with pieces of tarred paper found in the factory yard. The witnesses testified that in the first three days, until these toilet ditches could be lengthened, terrible scenes took place. The people, men and women together, stood long hours in line, waiting to satisfy their most elementary needs.

In these conditions of existence, it is self-understood that very many people became sick. Although by 29 April the mayor, Dr. Ferenc Májay, had ordered that a small hospital be set up inside the Jewish synagogue, it turned out to be too small, so that many of the sick had to remain in the ghetto. Dr. Ádám Horváth, the physician who was in charge of the medical supervision of the ghetto, was completely uninterested and made no effort to improve the conditions in the ghetto. Most of the time he would not even set foot in the ghetto but would send physician Dr. Mátyás Talos in his place.

This is the main outline of the tragic situation of the housing and food supply of the almost 7,500 Jews in the ghetto of Marosvásárhely. The state of affairs in the ghetto was fully testified to by the witnesses heard at the office of the public prosecutor as well as by the witnesses József Vancea, Márton Haus, Gábor Kraus, Blanka Steier, Dr. László Kovács, and others heard before the court.

As shown above the man in charge of the housing and feeding of the Jews in the ghetto was the accused Dr. Ferenc Májay, the city's mayor.

This defendant had already arranged on the second day after László Endre's conference, i.e., on 29 April 1944, on instructions received from him, for setting up a small hospital at the Jewish synagogue. The defendant Ferenc Májay himself admitted at his questioning during the preliminary investigation that he took this measure to give the Jews something to worry about concerning the measures that were going to be taken against them. In fact, a delegation of the Jewish Council, consisting of Darvas, Léderer, and Schwartz, presented itself before the accused, asking him not to set up a camp in the city of Marosvásárhely, but, at most, a ghetto in a part of the city, in houses, and the accused promised them this but did not keep his word. When, after the ghetto was established at the brick factory, the same delegation tried to contact the accused Májay again, but was not allowed to enter his office, since the secretary general of the mayor's office, the accused Ferenc Henner, informed them that Jewish matters were not open to discussion.

The accused Májay himself admitted during his questioning that he gave orders to put up announcements that he would not receive anyone concerning Jewish matters, explaining that there appeared to be too great an accumulation of Jewish demands and that too many were seeking him out directly instead of addressing themselves to the secretary general of the mayor's office.

During the preliminary investigation it has already been proved that the ban on receiving anyone concerning Jewish matters was applied not only by the accused Májay but also by the Prefect Joós, by the Deputy Prefect Marton, and by the secretary general of the prefect's office, Jávor.

The accused Ferenc Májay's collaborators were the first notary of the mayor's office, Dr. Ferenc Henner, and the first notary of the prefect's office, Dr. Ernő Jávor, each of whom acted as the adviser on Jewish affairs in his area.

The law enforcement agencies responsible for the rounding up of the Jews were led by Colonel Dr. János Papp, the commander of the Inspectorate of Gendarmes of the four Székely counties; Colonel János Zalantai, the commander of the Legion of Gendarmes of Maros County; and Dr. Géza Bedő, the chief of police of Marosvásárhely.

Beside these, however, there also meddled in these operations Colonel Géza Körmendi, the commander of the operational troops in the city and the county, as well as general István Kozma, the commander of a paramilitary organization called *Székely Határőr* (Székely Border Guards), a formation later incorporated into the regular army with the coming into power of the Szálasi government. The accused Májay himself declared at his interrogation that he asked General Kozma why he involved himself in the concentration of the Jews in the ghetto since this was not a military problem and that General Kozma had answered that he had been especially asked to do so by László Endre on the occasion of his visit to Marosvásárhely.

The German Gestapo was also represented on this higher commission that directed the internment of the Jews in the ghetto, the German Gestapo's representative being Major Schröder.

At Marosvásárhely also, there was no lack of the usual announcement on the day before, informing the Jewish inhabitants that they were no longer allowed to leave their dwellings. And here also, squads for rounding up the Jews were organized. The squads, as elsewhere, consisted of soldiers, paramilitary police, and municipal officials.

Even though those rounded up were told that they were allowed, in theory, to take with them 50 kilograms of luggage per person and food for 14 days, in practice, the Jews could not take with them even these few things, since the time for preparation granted them was so limited that most of them had to leave empty handed, some even undressed, as they had been taken out of bed. (Deposition of the witness Aladár Gárdos)

It also appears from the interrogation of the accused Ferenc Májay that at first they were granted an eight-day period for rounding up the Jews, and on the morning of 3 May, an officer (probably the defendant Géza Körmendi) informed Májay that the roundup time was reduced to three[13] days and he also asked for 80 city officials so that the internment could take place at a faster rate. The accused Ferenc Májay did not object to this request, as he did not object when László Endre inquired on the telephone about the progress of the operation and he hastened, instead, to answer that everything was proceeding in an orderly manner and he was trying hard to please this chief. Neither did the accused Ferenc Májay object to the disregard of orders concerning those exempted from internment in the ghetto. He also disregarded these orders in regard to the provisions specifying that the internment in the ghetto take place in livable houses and with a certain number of tenants in each house. It was actually shown that members of the roundup squads themselves, often more kindhearted than their superiors, allowed for these exemptions that were stipulated in the decrees and even in the instructions that were issued to them. This is how such a case is narrated by the lawyer Dr. Lázár Schwartz, 75 percent invalid from the First World War, saved from internment in the ghetto only because of the humane interpretation that a member of the roundup squad gave to the instructions he carried in his pocket:

> The next morning at five o'clock a policeman accompanied by two paramilitary men appeared at my house, ordering me to get ready to leave with my family in ten minutes. I replied to the guard that I was among the Jews who had been exempted by government order, since I was not obliged to wear the Yellow Star as a 75 percent war invalid. The guard replied that he did not know of the dispositions regarding those exempted, but that he would make inquiries to clarify my case. . . .
>
> The guard returned after two hours and then I had a discussion with him asking him to show me the order to pick me up he had on him; the guard took out of his pocket a typewritten copy of the order which I read in its entirety. The order provided for the evacuation and internment into camps of all the Jews in the city . . . with the exception of those who, according to Decree No. 1240/1944 M.E., were exempted from wearing the Yellow Star and with the exception of those sick in bed and those . . . from family . . .
>
> I succeeded in persuading the guard . . .

The accused Ferenc Májay failed to carry out the letter and spirit of the decrees, for he was always ready to execute the written and oral orders of Under-Secretary László Endre even though they had no legal basis; and the accused proceeded in this manner because he himself proved to be a man devoid of the most elemental humanity. To illustrate the real nature of the accused Májay, it is necessary to cite the cases that follow as examples.

The inhabitant Miksa Elekes was exempted along with his entire family because he was a war invalid. Nevertheless, his daughter was taken into the ghetto. He appealed to the screening commission, explaining the situation.

This request, though just and legal, was rejected. (See the declaration of M. Elekes and the rejection document on file)

The physician Dr. László Kovács, born of a Christian father and a Jewish mother, wanted to save his mother from the ghetto. Since there was a decree that the immediate family members of those mobilized for public labor service were exempted from camp internment and since the physician Kovács had been mobilized for public labor service, he submitted to the mayor a petition that included a favorable report from Dr. Ádám Horváth, the county medical examiner. After two days he received the response, which is in the files, in which the accused Májay informed him that his mother could not be considered as a close relative and only his wife and children could be so considered. (See also the deposition of László Kovács on file)

The screening commissions consisted of County Deputy Prefect Zsigmond Marton, Mayor Ferenc Májay, Gendarmerie Colonel Loránt Bocskor, and Police Inspector Géza Bedő. The accused Májay himself admitted at the interrogation that this commission handled approximately 1,500 petitions for exempted people and that only about 47 of these were approved, as were about 20 submitted by Székely people who were of the Jewish faith but obviously of Hungarian ethnic origin.

This screening commission operated with the greatest severity, and not in accordance with the decrees issued by the presidency of the Council of Ministers, which were known to all, but in accordance with the written and oral instructions of László Endre.

The accused Dr. Ferenc Májay defended himself in the case by claiming that as a career mayor he could not have opposed the orders of László Endre. This defense of the accused could not be taken into account since the conduct of this accused had shown an excessive execution of the orders received. It is sufficient to mention anew the case of Dr. László Kovács who had only his mother—he was not married—but where the accused Májay interpreted the decree in effect, which stipulated that the immediate family members of a public labor service worker could be exempted from internment into the ghetto, by arguing that only the wife and children but not the mother could be considered as immediate members.

Even without the fact that the accused Ferenc Májay carried out the illegal orders of László Endre in flagrant contradiction of Decree No. 1610/1944 M.E., and even if there were not the absence of measures relating to housing, feeding, and hygiene in the ghetto of Marosvásárhely and the other abuses, but there were only this single case of Dr. László Kovács's mother, it would have been sufficient proof for the accused Dr. Ferenc Májay to be condemned as one who, having a perverted soul, carried out the laws and measures derived from the state of war in a totally excessive manner.

The well-known squads of gendarmes which had the mission to investigate and search for hidden valuables were not absent in the Marosvásárhely ghetto either. This squad had as its commanders the accused Captain Konya, Captain Pintér, and Quartermaster Ferenc Sallós. On their orders, the gendarmes beat the Jews in the course of the investigations for hidden valuables in a terrible fashion and applied these beatings to men, women, and children alike.

The torture took place in a house within the factory's courtyard, two of whose four to five rooms had been placed at the disposal of the gendarmes (gendarme investigators; *csendőrnyomozók*); the tortures were perpetrated here. Here is how the witness György Réti described one of these torture scenes:

> I too was among the Jews taken into the ghetto and was cruelly beaten seven times by the agents of the counterintelligence or of the investigative gendarmerie to reveal where I had hidden my wealth. I know only the name of Sallós, who was a man of brown complexion, medium in height, weak, about 45 years of age. This one beat me badly on my soles, hands, and body with a rubber truncheon. He beat me twice. Two of his comrades, whose names I do not recall, beat me until I fainted, having tied me hand and foot. All of these bullies also hit me on my testicles.

The manner in which these beatings were applied was corroborated in the depositions of the witnesses Aladár Gárdos, József Adler, Acațiu Kohn, Roza Rosenfeld, Ernő Rosmann, Dr. Béla Charap, Aranka Landau, and Márton Krausz.

Concomitantly with the searches for hidden valuables, they collected from the Jews all their watches, fountain pens, and furs and even their wedding bands, whose weight, according to the estimate of the witness Aladár Gárdos, came to five and a half kilograms of gold, and the Jews were compelled to sign statements declaring that they surrendered these valuables of their free will.

An instrument of the investigators in the Marosvásárhely ghetto was the accused József Lax, a Jewish jeweler. As a jeweler, this man knew all the Jews of Marosvásárhely who had valuables, especially jewelry, and provided these data for the investigators. This accused was so feared in the ghetto that the place where he lived in the ghetto was a veritable pilgrimage site for people soliciting his intervention to help them escape the claws of the investigators in return for certain sums of money in exchange. This accused was always seen in the two torture chambers mentioned above, and the witness Márton Krausz stated in his declaration made during the investigation that while he was being beaten by the investigating gendarmes, the accused József Lax was in the hall of the torture chamber and that when the investigators became bored with the beatings and realized that they could not wring any declaration out of the witness, the accused József Lax said loudly to the gendarmes: "Continue to beat the witness, for then he will surrender the jewelry."

The deposition of the witness Márton Krausz also reveals that the accused József Lax had been busy even earlier with the denunciation of various people and then intervening in their behalf to save them, an intervention he undertook in exchange for certain sums of money.

The accused Lax was also in the service of the counterintelligence bureau as a secret informer, as well as a secret informer for the treasury guard. In 1942 he denounced Márton Krausz for possession of jewelry, as a result of which a part of it was confiscated. The accused József Lax offered to save it, but the witness Márton Krausz had no confidence in him, for the public rumor in the city had it that József Lax occupied himself with denunciations and then with interventions to counterbalance the effects of the denunciations, in order to provide material profit to himself. These accounts by the witness Márton Krausz are also corroborated by the declaration of his brother, i.e., the witness Gábor Krausz, who also testified before this court panel.

The depositions of the witnesses István Gál and Mrs. Jakab Steier née Blanka Weintraub are in the same vein.

The accused József Lax tried to defend himself before this court panel by claiming that he did not denounce the rich Jews in order that they be searched for valuables and jewelry, but rather that since he had some contacts with the police of Marosvásárhely he had intervened without payment and in a disinterested manner to save them, and that if he occasionally took money for these interventions he used the funds to bribe the investigators to save those being tortured. Toward this end the accused presented a number of witnesses who were heard by the People's Tribunal.

The depositions of these witnesses only reveal, however, that the accused József Lax intervened to save some people from torture whenever he was asked and that he was paid specific amounts of money for these interventions.

The witnesses did not say and the accused himself did not affirm that he ever told these witnesses that these amounts of money were to be given to the investigators as bribes for stopping the tortures, and thus the whole world believed—and rightly so—that these sums were flowing into the pockets of the accused József Lax. Also, the accused József Lax could not explain to the court panel of the People's Tribunal the origin and reasons of his close relations with the Marosvásárhely police, both during the internment in the ghetto and before the establishment of the ghetto.

The depositions of the prosecution witnesses also reveal that József Lax was always in the halls of the torture chamber, even when the person being beaten and tortured had not solicited his intervention. (See the deposition of witness Blanka Steier)

This being the case, the People's Tribunal, evaluating the evidence, reached the conclusion that the accused József Lax maintained close relations with the Marosvásárhely police, the Hungarian counterintelligence service, the finance unit, and the investigating gendarmes in the Marosvásárhely ghetto, denouncing anybody about whom he knew something before the establishment of the ghetto, making these denunciations to draw material benefits, and during the time of the ghetto both to obtain these benefits and to ingratiate himself with the ghetto commander so that he and his family would attain a better fate.

The person responsible for supervising and checking the entire operation relating to the roundup of the Jews in Marosvásárhely and the western part of Maros County was the prefect of Maros County, the accused Andor Joós. To avoid repetition, we shall omit the reasons why this accused is penally responsible, inasmuch as these reasons were detailed above within the framework of the general considerations of this judgment. In this context it will be shown, however, that this accused Andor Joós was appointed prefect of Maros County by the Fascist government of Döme Sztójay, only after the previous prefect, Dr. Mikó, resigned, probably to disassociate himself from the regime that was about to be installed.

In the city and county of Udvarhely, activities relating to the ghetto similar to those carried out in Marosvásárhely by the accused Dr. Ferenc Májay and his collaborators were carried out by the accused Dr. István Bonda, deputy prefect of Udvarhely County; Dr. Ferenc Filó, mayor of Udvarhely; Dr. János Zsigmond, police chief; and Lieutenant Colonel László Kiss, commander of the legion of gendarmes at Udvarhely—all under the supervision, on the basis of the general control law, of the accused Dezső Gálfy, prefect of Udvarhely County.

All of these accused took part in the preparatory conference called by László Endre at Marosvásárhely on 28 April, received their instructions and carried them out without any reservation, surpassing and even violating the provisions of Decree No. 1610/1944 M.E. in that they even picked up and took into the ghetto persons who were exempted from wearing the Yellow Star.

The behavior of these accused from the beginning of the roundup of the Jews until their transfer to the Marosvásárhely ghetto does not differ in any way from the behavior of the authorities in Marosvásárhely with respect to their inhumanity. (Deposition of witness Jenő Schwechter)

The Ghetto of Szászrégen

The top officials of Szászrégen had been invited to the 26 April 1944 conference of László Endre at Nyíregyháza (sic), which they attended, but since László

Endre also came to Marosvásárhely in accordance with a subsequent decision, these Szászrégen functionaries also attended the Marosvásárhely conference. The other representatives of the authorities in the Székely Land, though called to Nyíregyháza (sic), had received the countermanding telegram in time and thus awaited László Endre's arrival in Marosvásárhely.

The mayor of the city of Szászrégen was the accused Dr. Imre Schmidt, the chief of the Szászrégen police was the accused János Dudás, and the commander of the troops in the area of Szászrégen was Major László Komáromi. Aside from these three, Gendarmerie Lieutenant Kálmán Szentpáli G., commander of the group of gendarmes, and Jenő Csordácsics, counselor in the mayor's office in Szászrégen, were also involved in the establishment of the Szászrégen ghetto.

They were the ones who decided on the location of the ghetto, as in Marosvásárhely, selecting for this purpose a dilapidated and too-small brick factory. In Szászrégen, as in Marosvásárhely, squads were formed in the usual way, which proceeded with the roundup of the approximately 1,400 Jews in the city. The squads proceeded with the same cruelty, preventing the Jews from taking into the ghetto even the quantities of food and baggages allowed under László Endre's instructions. These squads picked up even the exempted Jews.

Life in the ghetto was as miserable as in that of Marosvásárhely. The accused Dr. Imre Schmidt himself declared during his interrogation: "I know that the brick factory was in ruins.... I did not ever go there, because I could not bear to see the horrible scene I imagined."

Thus the Jews were housed in sheds that had no side walls in this factory in ruins. Only a small number of them were taken into a few buildings on the edge of Szászrégen.

In Szászrégen, as in Marosvásárhely, there were no toilets at the beginning; later a few ditches were dug for this purpose by the Jews. They also lacked water, and it was only after a few days that water was brought in in a firemen's tank car, but this was insufficient and the Jews were compelled to drink nonpotable water from a marsh.

Food supplies were provided by the mayor's office, also in a defective manner. The Jews often received only 100 grams of bread a day and some potato soup.

It is self-understood that under these conditions of housing and feeding, many among the people and especially the children, being in the rain in the cold weather of early May, became sick; the Jewish physicians could not help them because of the absence of drugs. Here is how the Christian physician, Dr. Sándor Belteki, described the sanitary conditions in the Szászrégen ghetto:

> After receiving the written order, I visited the ghetto and saw how the Jews lived under very bad conditions, some of them in buildings, some of them outdoors in the

cold and rain; they did not have sufficient and potable water, nor toilets, or kitchens, or milk for the children, nor soap for washing or any of the most necessary things.

And if one adds the circumstance that the Jews from the countryside, i.e., from the eastern part of Maros County and the northern part of Csík County, were also brought into the ghetto of Szászrégen—raising the total number of Jews in the ghetto of Szászrégen to about 4,000—one can easily understand the intolerable conditions under which the Jews found themselves. The person who brought about the establishment of the ghetto in accordance with the decrees of the Council of Ministers and the written and oral instructions of László Endre was the first official of the municipality, who in Szászrégen was none other than the mayor, Dr. Imre Schmidt; he was assisted on questions of housing and feeding by his city counselor, the accused Jenő Csordácsics, who had been appointed by the accused Dr. Schmidt as his expert adviser on Jewish matters. The accused Dr. Schmidt and his aide, aside from the fact that they were obliged to verify the legality of the orders relating to the establishment of the ghetto, are guilty especially of the fact that they brought about the establishment of the ghetto of Szászrégen in a totally inhumane manner, without seeing to it that those interned in camps were housed in a satisfactory manner and without seeing to it that they were assured the necessary food and potable water. The accused Dr. Imre Schmidt cannot exculpate himself by stating that he had no heart to see what was going on in the ghetto; on the contrary, he had a duty to go to the ghetto and see the state of affairs there and take humane measures to correct them, and even more it was his elementary duty to go to the ghetto before the roundup of the Jews to assure in advance humane living conditions for them.

But as the investigation shows, this did not concern the accused. Indeed, the accused Jenő Csordácsics, the city counselor of Szászrégen, having been asked by the accused Dr. Imre Schmidt to be his expert adviser on Jewish matters, worked directly in the field as one of the organizers of the ghetto, and after the deportation of the Jews he created a source of income for himself by having himself named curator of Jewish wealth. This accused Jenő Csordácsics mixed himself into matters that were of no direct concern to him. Thus he was the one who ordered the internment into the ghetto of the Jew Mózes Rosenberg, a 100-percent war invalid, who was freed by the camp commander himself after 24 hours of internment inasmuch as his status as an exempt person was evident. (Deposition of the witness Mózes Rosenberg)

By right the leadership of the ghetto was supposed to be entrusted to the local chief of police, János Dudás, but the accused Major László Komáromi, commander of the troops in the Szászrégen region, installed himself by force as camp commander and forbade the accused János Dudás from getting involved in this matter. It was only after Dudás complained at the Ministry of the Interior that he was installed as ghetto commander. It must be noted, moreover, that according to Imre Schmidt's declaration during the investigation, this Major László Komáromi was recommended to Mayor Schmidt by the prefect of Maros County himself, the accused Andor Joós, to assist the mayor on all questions of interest to him.

But aside from the two accused who argued over the command of the ghetto, there was a third pretender to this odious function. This was the accused György Kugler, known as Füleki, who had no public office whatsoever; he was a private white-collar worker, but a leading member of the Arrow Cross Party. This accused appointed himself as leader of the ghetto of Szászrégen, initiating searches and investigations for hidden valuables and issuing instructions for the maintenance of discipline. Numerous witnesses describe the odious deeds of this accused. Thus, for example, the witness János Fazakas showed how the accused Kugler beat and cursed the Jews, calling them "stinking Jews." Declarations of this kind were also made during the investigation by the witnesses Katalin Kőműves, Samu Kisselstein, Béla Herschkovits, József Heisler, Miksa Leopold, and others.

The responsibility of the accused György Kugler is even greater since he cannot invoke an order of the higher authorities, for as a private functionary he was not obliged to get involved in these operations, let alone become excessive and issue orders on his own initiative.

Aside from the maltreatment administered by the accused György Kugler, the ghetto of Szászrégen also did not lack the special squads searching for hidden valuables. Here too there were corporal searches and vaginal searches of the women, and all of them were subjected to beatings in a cellar that was especially equipped for this purpose. Here is what the witness Sándor Schmuck declared in this respect:

> The interrogation was conducted in the office and the cellar of a house. Those who did not want to admit or those who had nothing to admit were beaten in the following manner: All were ordered to take their shoes off their feet and then they stuffed the socks in their mouths to prevent them from shouting. They were laid on their stomachs, their hands and feet were tied so that their soles pointed upward, and then they were beaten on their soles with a rubber truncheon. Those beaten were then thrown out where they had to dance. The leader and principal beater of this team was Pál Bányai. The women and girls were beaten in the same manner. Two girls from Szászrégen went mad as a result of the beatings. They beat an old woman named Berkovits so hard that her entire body was full of bruises. Mendel Moskovits of Gyergyószentmiklós was beaten so badly that for three weeks he urinated only blood. He was beaten by Béla Ferenczi.

The witness Irma Schmuck declared in the same vein:

We were taken to Szászrégen and interned in the ghetto. They started the corporal and baggage searches at six o'clock in the evening, separating the men from the women and children so that no one knew of each other; since the searches lasted until after midnight, we spent the night under the open sky in the rain until four A.M., when the searches were finally ended. While we stayed in Szászrégen, a squad of detectives began the maltreatment of the Jews on the basis of information received from the authorities in Gyergyószentmiklós; they were taken one by one to a torture chamber to identify the persons and places where they had hidden their valuables. Thus they beat Mendel Moskovits so horribly that he began to spit and urinate blood. They beat the wife of Jakab Berkovits so harshly on three separate occasions that she died in the ghetto, where she was also buried; and they maltreated and tortured a girl from Szászrégen many times so seriously that she went mad and the torturers themselves who could no longer bear hearing her screams took her out of the ghetto.

On the basis of the above witnesses and the witnesses Zsiga Lupu, Miksa Diamantstein, Dr. Menyhért Weisz, Kálmán Márk, and Albert Grün, the following torturers could be identified: Quartermaster Pál Bányai, Quartermaster Balázs Biró, Major András Fehér, and István Gősi, as well as the detective from Gyergyószentmiklós police, Béla Ferenczi.

The vaginal searches were performed with great cruelty by the communal midwife, the accused Irma Lovas, who, because she worked with dirty hands, infected a large number of women. She did not even spare virgin girls from these searches. (Deposition of the witnesses Mrs. László Neumann, Helén Mendelovits, Magda Rosenbaum, Frida Richtenberg, and others)

In the Szászrégen ghetto there was a commission for the screening of exempted persons, which was composed of the accused Dr. Imre Schmidt, the chief of police János Dudás, and the commander of the gendarmerie Kálmán Szentpáli.

The accused Dr. Imre Schmidt declared during his interrogation that he could not carry out his mission in accordance with the decrees in effect because Major László Komáromi in effect terrorized this commission, urging the rejection of all exemption requests, even of well-founded ones.

This was the case of Sándor Schmuck who, although exempted as a 75-percent war invalid, had his exemption petition rejected and thus was transported together with the other Jews to the Hungarian-German border where the German commander, seeing his documents, removed him from the freight car and allowed him to go home.

Here is a case when the German commander in charge of transports of Jews to Germany himself proved more humane and legalistic than the Szászrégen accused.

The Jews from the northern part of Csík County were also brought into the ghetto of Szászrégen.

Also in this area was the city of Gyergyószentmiklós whose mayor, the accused Dr. Mátyás Tóth, attended László Endre's conference and accepted all the measures taken by him. He carried out the roundup of the Jews through the police chief, i.e., the accused Dr. Géza Polánkai, since police chief Örmény refused to take part in this monstrous crime. The Jews of this city were assembled in an elementary school, where they were held for eight days without almost any food and then taken to Szászrégen. All the exempted individuals, including children, were also picked up. Among the exempted persons was Sándor Schmuck, about whom we shall speak below. Also among them was Jenő Kondor, a 70-year old man who had converted to Christianity a long time ago; he was picked up in the hospital and taken away by stretcher, and then received the sacraments in accordance with the Christian rites from the priest Ignác László in the very place where the Jews were interned. (See deposition of witness Irma Schmuck)

The roundup, the baggage and body searches, and the vaginal searches of women were carried out under the directives of the accused Dr. Polánkai.

The accused prevented the Christian population from bringing food and milk for the children into the school where the Jews were assembled, shouting that "the Jews do not deserve any mercy and they ate enough." On the day the Jews were transported to Szászrégen, the accused, at the peak of his happiness, stated before everyone: "Now I have completed the greatest work of my life and now I can die." (See deposition of the witness Dr. László Hermann)

In the same police of Gyergyószentmiklós there was a detective who played an important part in torturing the Jews, namely the accused Béla Ferenczi. He was sent into the ghetto of Szászrégen to collaborate with the team of policemen there in the searches for hidden jewelry. On this occasion, the accused participated in the barbaric maltreatment of the Jews. He especially beat the Jews of Gyergyószentmiklós. (See depositions of the witnesses Irma Schmuck, Sándor Schmuck, Zsiga Lupu, and Ferenc Weinstein)

We may mention in passing that although a separate ghetto was established in the city of Sepsiszentgyörgy, it was later decided to transfer all of the Jews interned there to the ghetto of Szászrégen.

The Ghetto of Sepsiszentgyörgy

The roundup and internment of the Jews of Sepsiszentgyörgy were carried out somewhat differently from the other ghettos of Transylvania. Specifically, on the evening of 2 May 1944, the police forwarded summons to all the Jewish inhabitants of Sepsiszentgyörgy specifying that the following morning at 6:00 they should appear at the police station with all members of their families, taking along documents proving their Hungarian citizenship. In the morning of 3 May, all the Jews appeared at the police station; they were detained and only one member of each family was allowed to return to their homes together with the squads to pick up the permitted goods, and afterward all the Jews were taken into an uncompleted building at the edge of Sepsiszentgyörgy.

The Jews of Háromszék County, Csíkszereda, and the southern part of Csík County were also brought here, so that approximately 700 people were crowded into this building.

This building was far from being able to satisfy the needs of 700 people for housing. In the first place it was unfinished, and then the flooring on the first floor consisted merely of boards. The building had no doors and no windows and was exposed to wind currents, so that a considerable part of those housed here became sick. The people interned here lacked food, water, and the necessary clothing, and generally suffered from the same deprivations as the Jews in the other ghettos; from the sanitary point of view also, their situation was no better than in the other ghettos. At Sepsiszentgyörgy too there were body and vaginal searches for hidden valuables and jewelry. The commander of the ghetto was a German SS second lieutenant who remains unidentified. He was aided by other German and Hungarian officers.

The commission for the establishment of the Sepsiszentgyörgy ghetto was composed of the accused Dr. Gábor Szentiványi, county prefect; Dr. Andor Barabás, county deputy prefect; Dr. András Virányi, mayor of Sepsiszentgyörgy; Dr. István Vincze, police chief of Sepsiszentgyörgy; and Lieutenant Colonel Balla, commander of the legion of gendarmes in Háromszék County. All of these accused participated in László Endre's conference at Marosvásárhely and received and carried out his orders without any reservation.

The responsibility of the accused Dr. Gábor Szentiványi was the same as that of all prefects. Nevertheless, since it was shown through the witnesses Károly Gál and Antal Becze that he behaved well toward the rural population and toward the refugees from Bukovina who passed through the county, and since the ghetto of Sepsiszentgyörgy was in existence only one week after which all the Jews were taken to Szászrégen, the People's Tribunal took into account all of these circumstances in the determination of the penalty.

As shown above, it was in the ghetto of Sepsiszentgyörgy that the Jews from the southern part of Csík County and the city of Csíkszereda were concentrated. Those responsible for the roundup of the Jews in this region, and especially for the inhumane manner in which this roundup was effectuated, which does not differ in any particular from the other ghettos, were the accused Ernő Gaáli, prefect of Csík County; Dr. József Ábrahám, deputy prefect of the same county; Gerő Szász, mayor of Csíkszereda; Pál Farkas, police chief of

Csíkszereda, and Lieutenant Colonel Tivadar Lohr, commander of the legion of gendarmes at Csíkszereda.

All of these accused took part in László Endre's conference, accepting and carrying out all of László Endre's instructions without any reservations.

The transfer of the Jews from Sepsiszentgyörgy to Szászrégen was carried out in an excessive manner, crowding people 70 to a freight car and transporting all the Jews without regard to sex or age, even the sick that were unfit to travel.

The Ghetto of Máramarossziget

In the city of Máramarossziget, the ghetto was established in two peripheral quarters of the city, enabling the internees to live in the buildings of these quarters; since the number of the interned surpassed the housing capacity within the area of the ghetto, the people were compelled to live even in cellars, attics, and sheds.

The border of the ghetto was surrounded by barbed wire, and the windows were whitewashed to prevent the inhabitants from looking outside.

As was proved in the course of the preliminary investigations before this court panel, the ghetto of Máramarossziget was established somewhat earlier than the other ghettos in Northern Transylvania.

Indeed, inasmuch as Máramaros County was considered part of Sub-Carpathian Ruthenia, it shared the fate of this province with which László Endre was particularly concerned.

Thus László Endre called a meeting for 12 April 1944 at Munkács to discuss the establishment of ghettos and the organization of the deportation of Jews from this province.

The conference was attended on the part of Máramaros County by Deputy Prefect Dr. László Illinyi; the mayor of Máramarossziget, Dr. Sándor Gyulafalvi Rednik; the chief of the Máramarossziget police, Dr. Lajos Tóth; the commander of the legion of gendarmes, Zoltán Agy; and the commander of the Fourth Gendarmerie District, Colonel Sárváry.

Deputy Prefect Dr. László Illinyi called a meeting for 15 April 1944, at which he assigned the roles of the Máramarossziget authorities along the model of the other ghettos.

Already in the afternoon of the same day, the chief of the Máramarossziget police, Dr. Lajos Tóth, held a meeting with the officials of the mayor's office, the police officials, and the gendarmes, on which occasion he informed them about the establishment of the ghetto and at the same time put together 20 squads, each of which was composed of a police chief, two policemen, two gendarmes, and one administrative official, and issued them the necessary instructions on the manner in which they were to proceed toward the roundup of the Jews. The first operation undertaken by these squads was the confiscation of the valuables, jewelry, precious dishes, furs, and monies, following the issuance of an order that the Jews were not permitted to leave their homes after 6:00 P.M.

After the five to six days that the confiscation of goods lasted, they proceeded with the roundup and internment of the Jews into ghettos. Here too they proceeded in an inhumane manner, forbidding them to take along even absolutely necessary things except for 50 kilograms, which had to include both clothing and food. They picked up even the sick who were not fit for travel and those exempted from wearing the Yellow Star.

Police chief Dr. Lajos Tóth was appointed commander of the ghetto.

The mayor's office, represented by the accused Dr. Sándor Gyulafalvi Rednik and his deputy, the accused Ferenc Hullmann, who was chief notary of the mayor's office, failed to provide supplies for those interned in the ghetto, leaving them without food. These communal authorities refused to place cows that were owned by Jews at the disposal of the internees to provide milk for the infants.

Because of these actions relating to housing and feeding, there were many cases of typhus as revealed by Report No. 8982 of 8 May 1944, submitted by the mayor to the Ministry of the Interior.

Here as in the other ghettos an important activity involved the searches for hidden valuables undertaken by the squads of Colonel Zoltán Agy and the accused Lajos Tóth. Additionally, the gendarmes, policemen, and officials of the mayor's office engaged in body searches of men and women upon their entry into the ghetto, not overlooking vaginal searches even for eight-year-old girls, and on these occasions they confiscated things they deemed valuable.

In her deposition the witness Margit Rosenberg stated that the women were placed along the wall completely undressed and were threatened with shooting as their vaginas and rectums were searched.

Similar accounts were given by the witnesses Fáni Perl, László Werner, István Paláti, János Perl, Teréz Megsi, and Ferenc Dávidovits.

In addition to the accused Dr. Lajos Tóth and his policemen, 50 student gendarmes were brought from the Gendarmerie School of Miskolc under the command of Colonel Sárváry, commander of the Fourth Gendarmerie District of Máramarossziget, for guarding the ghetto. This squad also, with its commander in front, maltreated and tortured the Jews, robbing them of the things they still had, as evidenced during the interrogation by the accused Ferenc Hullmann himself.

As shown above, the main municipal officials who played an evil role in the establishment of the ghetto of Máramarossziget were the accused Mayor, Dr. Sándor Gyulafalvi Rednik, for the city of Máramarossziget and Dr. László Illinyi, the county deputy prefect, for Máramaros County.

The former accused excelled himself as mayor of the city even before the establishment of the ghetto through a series of racial measures against the Jews, specifically, taking over of shops, withdrawal of licenses, prohibition of shopping in the market, assignment of compulsory places of residence, and, finally, expulsions from the city.

With respect to the establishment of the ghetto, like the other mayors he must have known that the oral orders and written instructions received at Munkács from László Endre had no legal basis whatsoever and as such did not have to be executed. In spite of all this, they proceeded with the establishment of the ghetto and with the crowding in a totally inhumane manner in an extremely restricted area. This same accused supported the commission, which was headed by accounting chief Dr. István Nagy, and which was entrusted with inventorying the goods left behind after the internments in the ghetto.

As far as food supplies are concerned, he left this matter to the head of the economics section of the mayor's office, István Paláti, and entrusted the solution of all matters pertaining to the Jews to the first notary of the city, the accused Ferenc Hullmann, allowing him a free hand without supervising him or taking any measures to improve matters.

The accused Ferenc Hullmann was the mayor's right-hand man, having been entrusted with the solution of Jewish questions. Aside from the fact that he did not concern himself with the supply of food for those interned in the ghetto, failing to supervise the head of the economics division, his great guilt was that he solved all requests advanced by the Jewish community through its council in a Fascist manner and full of racial hatred.

Thus, the repeated requests of the Jewish Council for milk from the cows of the Jews for suckling children whose mothers could no longer give any milk because of the starvation and for the sick elderly people were of no interest to him and he rejected them; although he received the petition of the Jewish Council registered under No. 9030 on 4 May 1944, in which three cows were requested for the ghetto from among the cows confiscated from the Jews, in order to provide milk for the suckling children, he acted only on 11 May 1944, writing on his resolution on the petition: "To be disregarded" *(Tárgytalan)*. In a similar manner he rejected petition No. 9654 of 13 May 1944 of the Jewish Council requesting the freeing of furniture from the various Jewish children's homes in order to establish a children's home in the ghetto to avoid the danger of disease.

He rejected, by specifying "To be disregarded," petition No. 99.656 of 13

May 1944 of the Jewish Council, which requested disinfecting materials and drugs to combat the typhus epidemic that was raging in the ghetto.

He rejected petition No. 8872 of 1 May 1944 of the Jewish Council, which requested indemnity payments for the families of those mobilized in labor service companies, not by resolving it but simply transferring it on 26 May 1944, i.e., after 26 days, to the economics section of the mayor's office, where it was classified as "To be disregarded," the Jews being deported at the time.

Having received petition No. 8873 of 1 May 1944 of the Jewish Council, requesting 20 sewing machines, three typewriters, and shoe soles from the goods that had been confiscated from the Jews, he acted on it only on 11 May 1944, after 11 days, and then he approved only the sewing machines.

During his interrogation the accused Ferenc Hullmann denied that he was the expert adviser on Jewish matters, but in contrast to this denial are all the petitions that were resolved by him which can be found in the files. The accused could not justify why he failed to act on time on the petitions advanced by the Jewish Council, doing so only after approximately eight to ten days and then by inscribing his decision: "To be disregarded."

The executor of László Endre's instructions in Máramaros County was the county deputy prefect, Dr. László Illinyi, who through his administrative subordinates resolved the complaints of all the Jews in the county, namely those of Drágomérfalva, Aknasugatag, Felsővisó, etc., and carried out their removal to the ghetto of Máramarossziget. The accused Dr. László Illinyi also did not respect the exemptions from internment as provided by the decrees in effect, and with respect to Máramaros County he performed the same work relating to the inventory and confiscation of Jewish goods as the mayor of Máramarossziget did for the county seat.

How the Jews were housed in the ghetto of Máramarossziget was shown above. It was also shown that the accused Dr. Lajos Tóth, the police chief of Máramarossziget, was appointed commander of the ghetto. Finally, it was shown that 50 gendarmerie students were brought from Miskolc and placed under the command of Colonel Sárváry to guard the ghetto. It was also shown above how the Jews were searched and interned in the ghetto and were tortured to confess where they had hidden their valuables, i.e., their money and jewelry.

The investigations on file, namely the depositions of the witnesses Dezső Polyonka, László Kővi, Ferenc Dávidovits, Ignác Vogel, Fáni Perl, Margit Rosenberg, Fülöp Ferenc Oblát, and others, show the guilt for all these maltreatments and tortures of the accused Dr. Lajos Tóth, the ghetto commander; József Konyuk, the deputy ghetto commander, who before then and even at the time was the fire chief of Máramarossziget. With respect to this latter accused, Ferenc Hullmann declared during his interrogation that whenever there was a question related to a measure to be taken against the Jews, József Konyuk received it with pleasure and carried it out conscientiously, engaging in a very intensive activity. Also guilty of these maltreatments and tortures are the accused János Fehér, commissioner at the Máramarossziget police; Colonel Zoltán Agy, commander of the legion of gendarmes at Máramarossziget; and Colonel Miklós Sárváry, commander of the Fourth Gendarmerie District in Máramaros.

During May 1944, the Jews Shmil Indig and Paises Indig succeeded in escaping from the Bárdfalva camp, from where they were taken to Máramarossziget and hid in the home of Nuțu Pasca in Barcánfalva, Máramaros County.

He took care of them for a while in exchange for some monetary compensation promised by the two Jews, but fearing the consequences of the racial laws he denounced them to the deputy mayor of the village, who reported it to the notary, who in turn reported it to the gendarmerie station, where a squad of gendarmes composed of Florea Tascan, János Biró, and György Varga was formed that went to the home of Nuțu Pasca to pick up the two Jews. Up to this time nothing abnormal with respect to the racial provisions of the time took place, but what emerges next are the crude procedures used by the three gendarmes. After finding the two Jews, the accused Florea Tascan subjected them to a search in the course of which he fired his weapon first in the chest of the victim Shmil Indig, who dropped dead on the spot, and the following moment in the chest of Paises Indig, who did not die immediately but began to writhe, wailing at the gendarme by saying: "You shot my brother, aren't you ashamed? Is this what your laws prescribe, for you to kill all Jews?" to which the gendarme Florea Tascan responded: "This is what Hitler's law prescribes."

Having been gravely wounded, Paises Indig requested water and the witness Péter Cora wanted to give him water and to bandage him, but he was stopped by the accused Florea Tascan; at the same time the other two accused, János Biró and György Varga, also pulled the trigger and put a bullet each into the victim, after which the victim Paises Indig died immediately.

This is established through the deposition of the witnesses Simon Jakabovits, Péter Cora, Maria Pasca, Nuțu Pasca, and others.

A similar case took place at Máramarossziget in April 1944 even before the establishment of the ghetto; the perpetrators are the accused Gusztáv Sarkadi, a barber from Máramarossziget, and István Bede, a sergeant in the Hungarian army. These two accused were drinking in Pertea's tavern in Máramarossziget and, having left for the streets, somewhat dazed by the drinks, they began to shout that "all the stinking Jews must be shot," "death to the Jews," and that they "wanted to see Jewish blood." It so happened that at the corner of Dorobanților Street and Unirea Square they met two Jewish children, one of whom was Boris Frenkel, 12 years of age; the accused Sarkadi, having noticed the Yellow Star on his chest, addressed him with the words "You are Jewish" and upon the boy's affirmative response the accused Gusztáv Sarkadi urged the accused István Bede to shoot him, which the accused István Bede did. The victim Boris Frenkel fell to the ground and died the following day.

This was proved by the deposition of witnesses József Mureşan, Fülöp Oblát, Lázár Grün, Imre Fényes, Lajos Mezősi, and Mrs. János Roman.

During this apocalyptic time for the coinhabiting Jewish nation, the prefect of Máramaros County was the accused László Szaplonczai, a member of the Imrédyist party.

His responsibility was the responsibility of all prefects at that time.

The Ghetto of Szilágysomlyó

The heads of the administrative and law enforcement authorities who participated at the Szatmárnémeti preparatory conference called by László Endre on 26 April 1944, and whose objective was the internment of the Jews into ghettos and their deportation to the camps in Germany were: Dr. András Gazda, deputy prefect of Szilágy County; Dr. János Sréter, mayor of Zilah; Dr. József Udvari, mayor of Szilágysomlyó; Lieutenant Colonel György Mariska, commander of the legion of gendarmes in Szilágy; Ferenc Elekes, police chief of Zilah; and István Pethes, police chief of Szilágysomlyó.

Immediately after the return of the above from the conference, the deputy prefect of the county, Dr. András Gazda, brought the county prefect, Baron János Jósika, up to date with respect to the instructions received from Under-Secretary of State László Endre for "cleansing the country of Jews."

Baron János Jósika, reacting normally considering that these measures not only failed to have a legal basis, but, on the contrary, were obviously illegal and immoral, submitted his resignation from the position of prefect, and two days later the accused Dr. László Szlávi was appointed prefect of Szilágy County. Immediately after his appointment, in collaboration with Deputy Prefect Dr. András Gazda, he called a meeting at the county prefect's office, which was attended by all district administrators in the county, the mayors of Zilah and Szilágysomlyó, the commander of the legion of gendarmes, and the police chiefs of Zilah and Szilágysomlyó. At this conference the above participants received instructions on the roundup of the Jews into the ghetto.

It was also at this conference that they decided to establish a single ghetto for the territory of Szilágy County, namely in Szilágysomlyó, into which they would crowd all the Jews from the county.

For this purpose the county deputy prefect went to Szilágysomlyó, where in agreement with this city's mayor, the accused Dr. József Udvari, and the police chief of Szilágysomlyó, István Pethes, as well as with those who accompanied him from Zilah, namely Lieutenant Colonel György Mariska and the chief physician of the county, Dr. Suchi, they selected the ghetto location in Szilágysomlyó. At first they selected a quarter that was mostly inhabited by Jews around Báthori Street along with the vacant areas around the synagogue, but later they changed their minds and definitively chose a brick factory, the Klein Brickyards of Somlyócsehi, a village situated five kilometers from Szilágysomlyó, as the ghetto site.

Also participating in the selection of the ghetto site were the accused Dr. Ferenc Molnár, the medical examiner of Szilágysomlyó; Dr. László Krasznai, chief administrator of Szilágysomlyó District; and István Kemecsey, an engineer and chief of technical services in Szilágysomlyó.

At Szilágysomlyó as everywhere else, the well-known squads were established for the roundup of the Jews, each squad consisting of a policeman, a security agent, an administrative official, two paramilitary people, and a representative of the two extreme rightist parties, the Imrédyist party and the Arrow Cross Party.

As in the other ghettos, here too the executive organs entrusted with the establishment of the ghetto included the leading officials of the municipality: Mayor Dr. János Sréter for the city of Zilah, Mayor Dr. József Udvari for the city of Szilágysomlyó, and finally, the accused Dr. András Gazda, the county deputy prefect, for Szilágy County as a whole. Each of these had their well-known roles, for the reasons cited above in connection with other ghettos. The officials involved in the roundup of the Jews from their homes and in their internment in the ghetto were the accused Ferenc Elekes, police chief of Zilah, with respect to the city of Zilah; the accused István Pethes, the local police chief, with respect to Szilágysomlyó; and finally the local questors and Lieutenant Colonel György Mariska, commander of the legion of gendarmes in Szilágy, with respect to the Jews in the other communities in the county.

The operations relating to the roundup of the Jews and their internment in the ghetto began in all of Szilágy County on the morning of 3 May 1944, when they were picked up in accordance with the norms that are known by now and in the same record time of 15 to 20 minutes, as measured by the squad leader who stood by with a watch in his hands.

In Zilah the roundup and searching of the Jews was completed by the evening of 5 May 1944, when they were taken to the railway station; they were held there overnight in a shed and entrained the following day in freight cars and taken to the ghetto in the Klein Brickyard in the vicinity of Szilágysomlyó.

In Szilágysomlyó the roundup of the Jews was conducted by the chief of the police, the accused István Pethes, having as squad leaders such members of the Arrow Cross Party as József Lázár, Ioan Anghea, Sándor Nagy, János Vida, Ádám Kerekes, and Sándor Farmati. These squad leaders employed the same brutalities used in other ghettos, picking up the Jews in the greatest hurry and permitting them to take along only up to 50 kilograms of baggage and food for 14 days.

After the Jews of Szilágysomlyó were concentrated in the Jewish school, they were ordered to form a convoy and were taken toward the ghetto in Somlyócsehi; they forced even the old, the children, and the sick to walk, hitting those who could not walk with the butts of their rifles.

The commander of the ghetto at the Somlyócsehi brickyard was the accused Dr. László Krasznai, the chief district administrator of Szilágysomlyó District.

This ghetto was completely unsuitable from the point of view of housing; the factory building had only one three-room apartment, which was reserved for the ghetto commander, and the Jewish population was crowded into the factory drying area and the two sheds without side walls. Obviously the 8,500 Jews assembled in this ghetto could not be accommodated in these sheds, so that most of them remained under the open sky, creating a scene like a cattle market, as was described by the witnesses Dr. Zoltán Bartha and engineer István Kemecsei. It is true that in the meantime 25 sheds without side walls were built, but aside from the fact that they were unsuitable because they were exposed to the wind, they were not enough so that even after their construction about 2,500 people remained in the open and had to improvise tents from the few items of clothing they had been permitted to take along.

The feeding of the Jews in the ghetto left much to be desired. The mayor's office became totally disinterested in this problem, and the ghetto commander, Dr. László Krasznai, subjected the Jews to starvation, giving them food just once a day, which consisted of an inedible potato or bean soup and 80 grams of bread. Cases were noted that in the evenings and mornings Jews collected bread crusts thrown into the garbage by the gendarmes. (Deposition of witnesses Rachel Adler and Ármin Feiger)

The Jews were not better off with potable water either. There were two wells, one of which was reserved for the gendarmes acting as guards; the other, which was infected with colibacilli, was left for the Jews, and approximately 80 percent of the Jews suffered from enterocolitis and diarrhea. (Deposition of witnesses Dr. Bernát Krausz, Károly Tóth, and Dr. József Benedek)

A petition by Jewish physicians addressed to the mayor's office in

Szilágysomyló by way of Dr. Ferenc Molnár, the ghetto physician, remained without result.

Instead of toilets two parallel ditches without dividing walls were dug, where the ghetto inhabitants were compelled to satisfy their needs in the greatest promiscuity, without regard to sex or age, which induced the ghetto commander Dr. László Krasznai and the accused József Lázár to amuse themselves at the expense of these demeaning scenes and to take pictures, which the accused József Lázár then exhibited in the window of his bookstore under the heading "This is the morality of the Jews in the ghetto." (Depositions of witnesses Dr. Bernát Krausz, Rachel Adler, Pál Weinberger, and Dezső Izsák)

The health care of those in the ghetto was also deplorable. Indeed, for all of these Jews a hospital of sorts was improvised, which was composed of three small rooms, one of which served for emergency cases, the second for ordinary patients, and the third for the mentally disturbed patients.

Pregnant women were forced to give birth under the open sky or in barracks without flooring, on the wet ground, and without any medical assistance.

But the peak of misery here, as in the other ghettos, was brought about by the mistreatment and tortures used for the uncovery of hidden valuables.

In this respect the accused Dr. László Krasznai did not fall behind any other ghetto commander. His deputies, the accused József Lázár, First Sergeant Sárközi, József Pethes, Ioan Anghea, and others were selected because they resembled and reflected the nature of the ghetto commander.

The torture methods varied, ranging from beatings over the soles to squeezing the testicles in males and introducing wood sticks into the vaginae in women. In their ingeniousness, the searchers went so far as to place burning papers between the toes of those being tortured and to burn their hairy parts with lighted candles. There were cases when Jews went mad in the wake of these tortures.

All of these inquisitional tortures were proved through the depositions of the witnesses Leopold Silberger, Pál Weinberger, Dezső Izsák, Adolf Goldberger, Rachel Adler, Dr. Bernát Krausz, Imre Grünbaum, Ármin Feiger, Mrs. Ferenc Csengeri, József Birta, and Dr. Zoltán Barta.

In addition to the members of the squads entrusted with the roundup of the Jews and the inventory of their goods, a special detachment of gendarmes brought from Budapest to guard the ghetto also took part in these abuses; this detachment was urged on in these mistreatments by the accused leaders of the ghetto and roundup squads.

In the ghetto of Szilágysomlyó the beatings and tortures were administered in several phases, namely:

The squads entrusted with the roundup of the Jews first of all engaged in body searches, and in the case of women even in vaginal searches, at the time they picked the people up from their homes. The second search was conducted at the concentration site in the Jewish school, and finally the third search was undertaken upon arrival in the ghetto and within the ghetto. All of these searches were carried out in the most inhumane manner, being accompanied by beatings and mistreatment.

Within the ghetto the life of the internees was unbearable. The ghetto commander behaved like a true satrap. He would punish—by hanging by the feet or by tying hand and foot and other corporal punishment—any Jew who in his view did not salute him properly when he went through the ghetto, did not stand at attention, dared to pray in accordance with his religious rites, or, finally, did not work as desired on certain assignments in the city such as for example sweeping streets, carrying lumber for the construction of barracks, etc. The accused Dr. László Krasznai lent himself to even more cruel acts. Organizing nocturnal feasts in his home and even in the ghetto, he brought in young Jewish women from the ghetto whom he raped and had the sexual intercourse photographed, as revealed by the witnesses Imre Grünbaum and Klára Grünbaum.

The depositions of the witnesses heard with respect to the establishment of the ghetto of Szilágysomlyó and to the living conditions of the Jews in this ghetto reveal other horrors as well; it is sufficient to note here that, as revealed by the depositions of the witnesses Leopold Silberger, Ármin Feiger, Dezső Izsák, Dr. József Benedek, and Dr. Bernát Krausz, because of the special conditions there, the Jews who reached Auschwitz from the ghetto of Szilágysomlyó were the most debilitated ones of all the deported Jews. Thus, because of this debilitation, which was a consequence of the inhumane living conditions in the ghetto of Szilágysomlyó, the Jews from this ghetto had the highest percentage of selections for gassing and thus for extermination.

Investigating the activity of each of the accused separately, it is found that the person responsible for supervising how the Jews lived in the Szilágysomlyó ghetto was the accused Dr. József Udvari, the mayor of Szilágysomlyó. His guilt is same as that of all the mayors of cities in which there were ghettos. Thus the poor housing, the selection of the ghetto site in a brickyard far from the city and without enough buildings for shelter, the lack of food supplies, the lack of potable water, and the confiscation of the Jews' goods are so many facts that substantiate his guilt.

The mayor of Zilah, the accused Dr. János Sréter, was also involved in these activities except for the housing and feeding of the ghetto. But this accused took anti-Jewish measures even before the establishment of the ghetto. Thus, under Decree No. 4092 of 25 April 1944, he forbade Jews to shop in the city market before 11 A.M.

What the accused Dr. János Sréter did in the city of Zilah, the accused Dr.

András Gazda, the deputy prefect of Szilágy County, did in the territory of Szilágy County.

Even before the establishment of the ghetto, this official took illegal measures by evacuating several Jewish families from their homes, forcing them to live compressed in the homes of other Jewish families, and gave the homes that had thus become available to inhabitants of Hungarian ethnic origin. This accused also brought about the internment of about 120 people of various nationalities who were suspected of anti-Fascist activity into the camps at Zilah and Püspökladány.

Throughout the four years of Horthy's rule, he engaged in evil activities, contributing to the forced dispatch of Romanians to Germany for work. He also contributed to the identification of all suspected Jews at recruitment centers to ensure their being recruited into special labor detachments. During the same period, he withdrew numerous licenses and prohibited numerous professionals to practice, thus contributing to the elimination of non-Hungarians from economic life.

During the establishment of the ghetto in Szilágy County, it was he who brought along and transmitted the orders received from László Endre at the Szatmárnémeti conference. It was he who, at a specially convened conference, instructed the other heads of authorities on how to proceed with the roundup of the Jews into the ghetto, and it was also he who went to the scene in Szilágysomlyó and contributed to the designation of the ghetto site under the conditions described above.

The accused Dr. András Gazda was also the direct executor, through his deputies—the district administrators of the various districts—of the measures relating to the roundup of the Jews in Szilágy County, except for the cities of Zilah and Szilágysomlyó, and for taking these Jews into the ghetto of Szilágysomlyó.

How the heads of the law enforcement organs and in general all members of the squads entrusted with the roundup of the Jews and their internment into the ghetto mistreated and tortured these victims was described above. It only remains to be pointed out who was guilty of this mistreatment.

The heads of the law enforcement authorities in Zilah were the chief of police, the accused Ferenc Elekes, and the commander of the legion of gendarmes in Szilágy, the accused Lieutenant Colonel György Mariska. In addition to their involvement in the roundup of the Jews on their way into the ghetto, these two individuals distinguished themselves even before this operation by the arrest of all persons suspected of anti-Fascist activities.

The same act of mistreatment was also engaged in by the accused István Pethes in his capacity as chief of police of Szilágycseh and by Dr. Sándor Horváth, the commander of the gendarmerie in the same city.

But the scourge of the ghetto of Szilágysomlyó was the accused Dr. László

Krasznai. It was described above how far this accused's inhumanity went. His cruelty was reflected in the manner in which he tried to impose exaggerated discipline in the ghetto and in the nocturnal orgies with young Jewish girls taken at night from the ghetto for the satisfaction of his perverse appetites.

The hangings from poles and the tying of victims hands and feet mostly took place in the presence of the accused Dr. László Krasznai, as was the case with old Sámuel Paszternec and Lázár Hersch.

He organized investigations and tortures for the discovery of hidden valuables in a room at the ghetto command station, an operation in which he was aided by First Sergeant Sárközi, József Lázár, Ioan Anghea, and First Sergeant László Petővári. Similar torture chambers also existed at the gendarmerie command post and the police station, where the accused Lieutenant Colonel György Mariska, Captain Sándor Horváth, János Vida, Ádám Kerekes, Sándor Nagy, Mihály Kovács, and Sándor Farmati operated.

Here is how the witness Éva Farkas described such a scene:

> After we had been interned ten days in the ghetto, Krasznai called my parents and asked them to tell him where they had hidden their valuables and jewelry. My parents refused. The following day they called me and took me to the torture chamber. I entered the room, a small room with an earth flooring, which was mixed with mud because of the water that was poured onto the people who fainted from the beatings. In that room I saw Krasznai, First Sergeant Sarkadi, and another gendarme. As I entered they asked me: "Do you declare or not?" and I answered: "I have nothing to declare." I removed my dress, then undressed myself, and then, in order not to soil myself with the mud, lay face down on a bench. They ordered me to lay down in the mud, then a gendarme took off my underpants, and then they hit me for half an hour on the soles of my feet. After that they threw me out. When I went out I could not walk and was taken to the ghetto on a stretcher. The next day around 11 A.M. Krasznai sent for me. I was again taken on a stretcher because I could not walk due to the beating I had received the previous day. There a gendarmerie captain ordered that the stretcher be taken away because he said that I would be able to walk on my feet. Krasznai asked me what relationship I had with police chief Pethes, and when I told him that I had nothing to do with him he had me checked. In the afternoon Dr. Molnár, assisted by Dr. Kráusz, visited me. They noted that I was a virgin. A few days later he called me again and told me to have love relations with him.

It is in the same vein that the witness Leopold Silberger stated:

> In the ghetto of Somlyócsehi we were interrogated to reveal where we had placed our wealth. Those who conducted the interrogations were three detectives from Kolozsvár, one of whom was Sárközi, the most brutal one and the chief beater, who mistreated us. During the interrogations we were beaten with a rubber truncheon by Sárközi on the palms of the hands and the soles of the feet, on the stomach and

testicles. Some were undressed and then beaten, and others were beaten with their clothes on. Others were beaten as follows: they were forced to put their fingers into a machine that they had, or into the opening by the hinges of a door; then they tightened the machine or closed the door and their fingers were injured.

With regard to the orgies of the accused Krasznai, here is what the witness Imre Grünbaum stated:

The accused Krasznai took the most beautiful girls from the ghetto and took them to a room in his apartment where there were several of his friends, among them Dr. Ferenc Molnár and the notary Kertész; after they got drunk they had great fun with the Jewish women and girls. I was the one who had to take the Jewish women and girls to this house. On several occasions I also took items that I collected in the ghetto from the Jews to this house—clothing, packages, valuables, money, and even gold. On several occasions, while they were amusing themselves inside, I was next to the carriage outside with a guard next to me until they were through, and then I took the girls and women back to the ghetto. Dr. Molnár, the ghetto physician, also participated in the fun. I heard the girls and women talk among themselves as I took them back in the carriage about what had been done to them. They complained that they were undressed stark naked, were poked fun at, and violated.

One could cite many other feats of this accused—for example, the inducement of Jewish physicians to poison three Jewish women who went mad in the ghetto or the violation of two Jewish women and the forcing of the Jewish physician Ödön Márguliesz to induce an abortion in one of them after she became pregnant—but all these acts will not change the measure of his punishment, which is sufficiently determined by the other acts already described. It is enough to note, in addition, the statement of the witness Bernát Kráusz, who said: "There was so much horror in the ghetto that the moment the accused Krasznai appeared the news spread like electricity and everyone said in horror: 'There comes Krasznai!' and tried to keep out of his path."

But in addition to the heads of the law enforcement authorities, a number of civilians of the city also contributed to the mistreatment and tortures—members of the extreme rightist parties who volunteered to become active in the roundup of the Jews and in their internment in the ghetto as well as in investigating them to make them confess where they had hidden their valuables.

One of these people is the accused József Lázár, who came from Trianon Hungary, and established himself in the city of Szilágysomlyó as a bookstore owner. He was a member of the Arrow Cross Party, and only this can explain why he cooperated in these deeds without holding any public position that would have obliged him to participate in the roundup of the Jews.

The accused József Lázár demonstrated his racial hatred of the Jews even before the establishment of the ghetto.

The witness Márton Steiner stated that in Szilágysomlyó, when the accused Lázár came onto the sidewalk the Jews who encountered him had to go to the other side of the street or he would harangue and mistreat them.

In his capacity as commander of premilitary units, he used the Jewish premilitary personnel for cleaning the Roman Catholic church whose guardian he was, and at this time he would poke fun at them and beat them in various ways.

During the establishment of the ghetto, he was involved in everything. He was a member of the squad for rounding up Jews, he personally searched Jews, confiscated their clothing, jewelry, and even food, and finally he participated personally in the tortures and mistreatments aimed at compelling the Jews to declare where they had hidden their valuables.

The same witness, Márton Steiner, stated before this Court Panel that the accused József Lázár confiscated the food of this witness's children and beat and mistreated both his children and his wife. The same was described about the accused by the witnesses Sándor Fischmann and Dr. Zoltán Bartha, and the witness Klára Grünbaum described the activity of the accused as follows:

> József Lázár came to the ghetto several times and performed atrocities. Thus, the day after we were taken into the ghetto József Lázár was not satisfied with the way I worked because I was not taken to work on the transportation of construction materials and, becoming angry with me, tied me to a pole and hit me with his foot so badly that because of these atrocities I fainted and could not get up for a week. Tying to the pole meant that my hands and feet were tied up, with my hands behind my back, and then I was hanged with a rope to the pole so that my feet could not reach the ground. József Lázár made the dentist Radu and the physician Dr. Markovics tie me up and after I fainted they poured water over me.

The witness Márton Steiner completely corroborated before this Court Panel the declaration he made during the investigation, a declaration which being more complete is reproduced below to illustrate one of the scenes in which the accused József Lázár participated. Here is the deposition made by the witness Márton Steiner during the investigation:

> The Jews who were interrogated were subjected to tortures which were also attended by the accused József Lázár; these interrogations were conducted in accordance with the instructions and suggestions made by him, and he incited the gendarmes to beat the Jews brought in for interrogation. The Jews were tortured and beaten personally by József Lázár, and others by gendarmes incited by his stating:
> "Don't have mercy on these pig Jews, and beat them so they will divulge the hiding places of their valuables." On this occasion they beat Mrs. Béla Schönberg, whom

they gave 100 strokes with a rubber truncheon over the soles so that she could not put her shoes on. When she tried to put her shoes on, blood gushed out from her feet passing through her shoes. In this same manner they beat Móric Goldglanz and his wife and daughter; on the latter two they tied the handcuffs so tightly that their hands turned black. Móric Goldglanz was beaten so severely over the soles that he was full of bruises and could walk only barefooted. In the course of the beatings the accused József Lázár said to him: "You stinking Jew, you still don't want to state where you hid your gold? I shall teach you a lesson so that you will not lie any longer."

With respect to the accused József Lázár's own initiative and his Fascist soul, here is what the witness Mrs. Ferenc Csengeri declared:

At the time of the searches at the Jewish school he took all my jewelry, all my food, and my children's good shoes and threatened that he would teach me a lesson, calling me, "You Jewish whore" and hitting me in the chest with his fist, and then he took the ring off his finger saying that he did not need the ring of a Jewish woman, but then he took my watch.

The accused József Lázár also took part in the searches for hidden valuables conducted in the homes of Jews in the presence of the Jews taken there for this very purpose; on these occasions the accused József Lázár maltreated many Jews on his own initiative.

Numerous are the cases of mistreatment committed by the accused József Lázár and numerous are the ways in which this mistreatment was committed; to enumerate them one would need a very large space and for this reason we believe it is sufficient to synthesize the activities of this accused in the words of the witness Dr. József Benedek, who said in his declaration before this Court Panel that "Whenever he could József Lázár got involved on his own initiative in beating or torturing someone either in the ghetto or outside the ghetto."

If one adds that this accused had no official position and thus could not even invoke the excuse of a public official who in some way carries out certain acts on the orders of a superior, it is easily understood that the responsibility of the accused József Lázár is well established.

His defense during the trial, that he was not in his right mind, had to be rejected by the People's Tribunal since one could conclude from the way in which he conducted himself during the trial that the accused merely simulated the change in his mental faculties.

On the other hand, the accused did not even attempt to prove that his mental faculties had been altered at the time he committed the infractions imputed to him, the only operative period for a determination of a lack of imputability and thus for an absence of penal responsibility.

The accused Quartermaster Miklós Sárközi, the gendarmerie commander of the gendarmerie post at Zsibó, and First Sergeant János Horváth, the commander of the gendarmerie section at Szilágynagyfalu, were also torturers like the above, whose deeds do not differ in any respect from those of the other investigators. Their activity within their territorial jurisdictions was described by the witnesses cited above.

Another series of torturers of Jews in Szilágysomlyó consisted of the accused János Vida, Ádám Kerekes, Mihály Kovács, Sándor Farmati, Ioan Anghea, Quartermaster László Petővári Petrik, Albert Szabó, and Irén Duha.

The special characteristics of each of these, in addition to the procedures common to all of them as well as to the other investigators, i.e., the personal stamp of each of these accused, can be seen from the following:

The accused János Vida is noted for the torturing of Béla Klermann; he put a red flag improvised from a rag into his hands and forced him to drink quantities of vinegar and water to make him confess where he had hidden his valuables. Because of the mistreatment, the victim Béla Klermann became sick and died during the transport to Auschwitz.

This maltreatment and mockery was committed by the accused János Vida in cooperation with the accused Ádám Kerekes; this latter also mistreated the Jew Ármin Feiger and handed him over to an SS soldier to continue the mistreatment.

Another specialty of the accused János Vida in collaboration with the accused Mihály Kovács was to take Jews from the ghetto and, following them on their bicycles, chase them toward the city at a run into their homes, where they investigated and tortured the Jews to make them reveal where they had hidden their valuables.

These deeds of the accused are also proved by the depositions of the witnesses Dezső Izsák, Ármin Feiger, and Pál Weinberger. [. . . these accused engaged] on their own initiative in maltreatments and searches for hidden valuables, as shown by the deposition of the witnesses cited below.

The accused Sándor Farmati, being in the premilitary unit and in this capacity being called to help in the roundup of the Jews into the ghetto, committed the same brutalities as the other accused but singled himself out by burning the armpits of Sámuel Moskovics, who was suspected of having hidden a barrel of vegetable oil. He used a candle to burn him.

His acts were proved by the depositions of witnesses Pál Weinberger, József Adler, Dezső Izsák, and others.

The accused Ioan Anghea, participating as a volunteer in the roundup of the Jews as a member of the Arrow Cross Party, attracted attention from the beginning for his great cruelty. Thus, when the Jews of Szilágysomlyó were assembled in the Jewish school waiting to be transported to the Klein Brickyard at Somlyócsehi and the accused József Lázár was mocking them during the searches by making them stand at attention facing the wall, the accused Ioan Anghea shot over the heads of these Jews to intimidate them.

Another characteristic deed of the accused Ioan Anghea was to compel the victim Dezső Rosenberg to enter the interior of a toilet, i.e., into the feces, and to look for the radio that he had hidden there.

The accused Ioan Anghea, having been alerted that the Jew Ignác Hirschfeld, who had escaped during the transport to Auschwitz and after several months in the woods had returned to Szilágysomlyó driven by hunger and misery, went and captured him and, instead of taking him to the hospital as the unfortunate Jew requested, took him to the police and handed him over.

All the deeds of this accused were abundantly proved by the depositions of the witnesses Mrs. Ferenc Csengeri, Chaim Weiss, Márton Steiner, Dezső Izsák, Rudolf Hirschfeld, Márton Hirschfeld, Mária Oltean, Mária Dobos, the widow Ludovika Dobos, Erzsébet Tokai, Katalin Hexan, and Erzsébet Takács née Borcs.

The accused Quartermaster László Petővári Petrik was the chief of the gendarmerie post from 1941 to 1944. This accused distinguished himself during the internment of the Jews into the ghetto when, escorting a convoy of Jews from several villages, he beat them and confiscated their most important goods; after taking them into the ghetto he took part together with First Sergeant Sárközi in torturing the Jews, beating, among others, Izidor [illegible] and Lajos Schreiber.

This accused already began his career as a torturer during his first year as chief of the gendarmerie post. His targets were Romanians and Jews. He persecuted the Romanians, forcing them to leave town for the slightest motives; for example he cruelly beat 15 young Romanians from Alsóbán, then those living at Valkó, then those in the village of Felsőszék whom he tried to send to Germany for labor, and similarly many other Romanians. Thus it is not surprising that when the occasion arose for him to take Jews from some communities within his jurisdiction into the ghetto he behaved so inhumanely.

Another one of the torturers is the accused Albert Szabó, a former official of the Szilágysomlyó district administrator's office. He was entrusted by the accused László Krasznai with the supervision of a group of 50 young Jews whose assignment was to gather wood for barracks. On this occasion he behaved in a completely inhumane manner toward these young people, starving them, forcing them to work beyond their strength, and beating as cruelly as possible. But his personal imprint, distinguishing him from the other beaters, is the ingenuity with which he introduced the custom of making these young Jews sing anti-Semitic songs on their way back from work at night.

Vaginal searches were not absent in the ghetto of Szilágysomlyó either, as already described above. But in this ghetto, in addition to the midwives entrusted with this procedure, the accused Irén Duha, who was an official in the Szilágysomlyó mayor's office and was sent into the ghetto only to issue receipts for the items confiscated from the Jews, got involved in this procedure on her own initiative and offered to search women and to perform vaginal searches. She did not conduct these searches in a civilized manner, but was as brutal as possible and had a special enthusiasm stemming from racial hatred.

The deposition of the witness Shulamit Adler about the activities of the accused Irén Duha is instructive. This witness stated that the accused Irén Duha was among those who performed searches, that she took her best clothes, and that when the witness begged her to leave her at least a sweater she received the reply: "You stinking Jews, you won't need it anyway where you are going." The same witness stated that the accused also performed vaginal searches, doing such a search on this witness herself.

That the accused Irén Duha indeed performed vaginal searches and did so in a brutal manner is also proved by the witness Éva Fazakas.

This is something that remains unexplained even today, more than two years after the ghettos were established, how an administrative official, whose normal good sense and modesty would have dictated that she concern herself only with the function that had been assigned to her, should at a given moment go beyond them and carry out functions that are repugnant even to a midwife. And if one also adds the circumstance that the accused was unmarried, her actions can indeed only be explained by the collective madness that engulfed those who were poisoned by the ideas of the demented man from Berchtesgaden.

The person who was supposed to supervise the health conditions in the ghetto of Szilágysomlyó was the medical examiner of the city of Szilágysomlyó, the accused Dr. Ferenc Molnár. Not only did this accused not protest when the ghetto site was selected at the Klein Brickyard at Somlyócsehi, half of whose terrain was marshland, and not take any measures to ensure that those interned in the ghetto would have enough potable water, but he showed total disinterest in everything that was happening in the ghetto and in particular to the health conditions there. The witness Dr. József Benedek, a Jewish physician, described in his deposition how this physician was disinterested in the sanitary conditions in the ghetto although he saw that a large proportion of the interned people had to sleep on the ground under the open sky, that the women had to give birth in a room without a proper floor, on straw, like cattle.

In the face of this deplorable situation, in the face of the infection of the water with colibacilli, and in the face of the 22 Jews who died in the ghetto as a consequence of these conditions, the accused Dr. Ferenc Molnár was satisfied with reporting that all was well in the ghetto. These reports on his visits to the ghetto on May 2, 4, 5, 6, 8, 12, 16 and 20, as well as on 5 June 1944, are attached to the file of this case.

The accused defended himself by stating that he could not do more because it was not up to him, and that he helped where he could, as for example through the inoculation of all the internees against typhoid, something that was not done in any other ghetto in Transylvania.

At first sight it might be thought that the accused Dr. Ferenc Molnár as a physician could not do more, since he did not have the materials to do so; but when the problem is viewed in more depth and the mind of the accused is examined in greater detail, as shown in the depositions of the witnesses Dr. József Benedek and Dr. Bernát Kráusz, it appears that the accused Dr. Ferenc Molnár did not wish to come to the aid of those interned in the ghetto even when he could have done so. Thus the witness Dr. József Benedek declared that no one could approach the accused to ask him for redress, as no one dared to do so because the accused was not on speaking terms with anyone, and the witness Dr. Bernát Kráusz reveals that, when his old mother-in-law was interned in the ghetto and he himself was at first exempted from this measure, having previously been friendly with the accused, he sent a small box of sugar for his sick mother-in-law through a friend, requesting him to ask the ghetto physician, i.e., the accused, to do him the favor of delivering it. The accused Dr. Ferenc Molnár refused this small service requested of him by a friend of a different race.

From this it can be deduced that the accused Dr. Ferenc Molnár refrained from doing a good deed even when he had the means to do so, and this being the case it is difficult to assume that he took all possible hygienic measures and thus bears no guilt whatever for the state of misery of the Jews in the ghetto of Szilágysomlyó.

A collaborator of the accused Dr. András Gazda was the chief county administrator, Dr. Béla Sámi. He accompanied his chief, Deputy Prefect Dr. András Gazda, to all the conferences that were held both at the prefect's office in Zilah and in the city of Szilágysomlyó.

It was he who requested the district administrators and mayors in the county to submit the total number of Jews so that he would know how to arrange the transports. This is shown by his Ordinance No. 7607 of 4 May 1944.

Following the deportation of the Jews, having received a number of petitions from Jews in labor service companies requesting to be allowed to convert to the Christian religion, the accused Dr. Béla Sámi issued Ordinance

No. 12145 of 29 June 1944, in which he ordered the rejection of all such petitions even before he registered them, and at the same time issued an order to have the petitioning Jews handed over to the police and the gendarmerie, which authorities in turn deported them to the extermination camps in Germany.

The justification for this Ordinance reads as follows:

> "By their mass conversion to Christianity, the Jews want only to accomplish a weakening of the racial measures in regard to themselves and their descendants, and to mislead the authorities."

Although the accused Dr. Béla Sámi denied during the interrogation that he was the expert adviser on Jewish affairs, it was he who issued a series of ordinances even before the establishment of the ghetto, such as the ordinances pertaining to the dissolution of all Jewish associations:

- An ordinance that bread should not be distributed to Jews at the official price, but rather at an arbitrary price set by the bakers.
- An ordinance of 19 April 1944, in which he requested the administrative authorities to expel from the territory of the county any Jews who did not belong there.
- An ordinance banning all books written by Jewish authors.
- An ordinance pertaining to the transfer of the medical offices of Jewish physicians to Christian physicians.
- Circulars and orders pertaining to the closing and inventorying of Jewish stores and their transfer to Fascist business associations.

The functions filled by the accused Dr. Béla Sámi for deputy prefect Dr. András Gazda were filled by the accused Dr. Dezső Dénes for the mayor of Zilah, the accused Dr. János Sréter.

The accused Dr. Dezső Dénes was a notary in the village of Kraszna, Szilágy County, from 9 September 1940 to March 1941, and served as secretary general of the mayor's office in Zilah from June 1943 to October 1944.

The activity of this accused as secretary general of the mayor's office in Zilah can be summarized as follows:

1. By Decision No. 4092 of 25 April 1944, he forbade Jews to shop in the market before 10 A.M., either in person or through intermediaries. He did this merely on hearing the suggestion of the head of the accounting bureau in the prefect's office, that in other cities Jews were forbidden to shop in the market.

   He collaborated in the deportation of the Jews, for which purpose the mayor's office urged the Jews to submit requests for the issuance of ration cards to all members of their families; the purpose of this was to gain knowledge as to how many there were, for reasons of deportation. He kept track of all the petitions received.

2. In May 1944 he prepared a list of 21 people—all Hungarian Fascists —to whom he distributed, free of charge, radio sets confiscated from Jews.

Under order No. 3797 of 17 April 1944, prepared and signed by the accused János Sréter, he provided for the closing of the shops of 10 Jews as early as 17 April 1944, by which time he no [longer felt obliged to apply] to the prefect's office for the closures.

3. By order No. 4797 of 29 April 1944, he advised that the closed shops of the Jews should be guarded and that nothing should be given to anyone without receiving money, and in his resolution No. 5546 of May 1944 he wrote, verbatim:

> I want to mention that I already took measures for the closing of Jewish shops on 16 April 1944, i.e., before the appearance of Decree No. 50.500/1944.K.K. on this matter.

By order No. 6955 of 22 April 1944, he informed the prefect that he had brought about the closing of the shops. (See list of closed shops No. 807/1944)

4. Through his approval on Document No. 5585 of 9 May 1944, he gave notice that he had handed over to the Financial Administration the animals that formerly belonged to the Jews.

5. On 22 April 1944, having received communication No. 2731 of 22 April 1944 of Army Corps IX, Kolozsvár, which requested that the apartments of the Jews to be evacuated should be handed over to military personnel, he noted on it that he had taken this into consideration, which reveals that he had knowledge about the deportation of the Jews.

But aside from these actions by the accused in 1943–44 as secretary general of the mayor's office in Zilah, the accused acted in an excessively racial manner from the first months of his appointment as notary of the village of Kraszna, Szilágy County. The military administration of Northern Transylvania— which lasted from 7 September 1940 to November 26 of the same year— prepared lists of Jews, who, according to the Fascist conception of this administration, were not of the village of Kraszna.

Instead of putting these lists into the wastepaper basket immediately after the end of the military administration, the accused Dr. Dezső Dénes took them into his study, used them, and issued Decision No. 2650 of 29 November 1940, by which he denied the right of 22 Jewish families to live in the village, ordering their expulsion within five days. He did this on the basis of Law No. IV of 1939, which had not yet been extended to Northern Transylvania.

Here is how the accused justified that decision: "Taking into consideration the state of war, the food situation of the population was serious, and what's more, mountable difficulties were often encountered with respect to the supply of essential items; thus the sharing of these small quantities of essential food with the lazy population [referring to the Jews] was not in agreement with the interests of the nation."

All those affected by these decisions of expulsion from the territory of Kraszna village submitted appeals, and some of them were even supported by the accused Dr. Dezső Dénes, who then created another source of income for himself through this.

Most of these appeals were upheld even by the Fascist authorities of the time, including Dr. András Gazda and the chief notary of the city, Dr. Béla Sámi.

If there were no other tests about the activity of the accused Dr. Dezső Dénes relating to the excessive application of anti-Jewish laws and measures except for these decisions relating to expulsions from the village of Kraszna, there would be enough to establish the criminal responsibility of this accused on the basis of the laws relating to war criminals, since on his own initiative he brought about the excessive execution of the completely illegal measures taken by the Hungarian military administration in the fall of 1940.

All of these war crimes and illegal acts were covered up by the well-disposed eyes of the then prefect of Szilágy County, Dr. László Szlávi, who was appointed to this position by the Fascist government of Döme Sztójay.

The responsibility of this prefect is similar to that of all other prefects, whose support of the establishment of the ghetto identified them as favoring this measure, unique in the history of mankind.

The Ghetto of Dés

At the meeting with Under-Secretary of State László Endre held in Szatmárnémeti on 26 April 1944, the following participated as representatives of Szamos County: Dr. János Schilling, county deputy prefect; Dr. Jenő Veress, mayor of the city of Dés; Dr. Lajos Tamási, mayor of the city of Szamosujvár; Dr. Gyula Sárosi, police chief of Dés; Ernő Berecki, police chief of Szamosujvár; and Major Pál Antalffy, commander of the legion of gendarmes in Szamos County.

The orders of László Endre were transmitted to the other heads of governmental authorities in Szamos County by the accused Dr. János Schilling, who called a meeting at the Szamos County prefect's office for 30 April 1944, attended by all the district administrators of the county, the mayors of Dés and Szamosujvár, the commander of the legion of gendarmes, and the city medical examiner Dr. Zsigmond Léhnár. Here the accused Dr. János Schilling issued all the necessary instructions, and they jointly agreed on the site of the ghetto—the cleared Bungur forest, which was three kilometers from Dés, and a brickyard in Szamosujvár.

In order that the Jews of Dés [not be alarmed about their fate] . . . in view of the measures that had been taken, this commission also started a rumor in the city to the effect that a section of the Bungur forest was being cleared and that barracks were being built for the accommodation of German refugees from the Ukraine.

In Dés as in the other cities, the squads were established, an announcement prohibiting the Jews from leaving their homes was issued, and in the morning of 3 May 1944 at about 5:00 A.M. these squads simultaneously and in a surprise manner descended on all Jewish homes.

The roundup of the Jews from their homes was carried out with the same brutality as elsewhere. Here too not enough time to get ready was given those to be rounded up. Here too no one was exempted from internment into the ghetto, and even persons who according to the decrees in effect were exempted from wearing the Yellow Star were picked up.

At the beginning all the Jews from the city were concentrated in three areas, where they were subjected to body searches; after they were stripped of all their valuables they were organized into columns and led to the ghetto site in the Bungur forest.

Here is how the witness Ana Schwartz described this operation:

I lived in the house of Miklós Bakay, where the Jews were assembled on 3–5 May 1944, and where they were subjected to searches. In the hallway the women were searched by the accused Mária Fekete, Mrs. Jakabffy, Mrs. Labó, and other *Nyilas* women I cannot remember. Entering the house I saw on the table a pile of jewelry and a list of the people from whom they had confiscated things. Ana Jakabffy was the chief of the women involved in the searches, and I saw a heap of confiscated money in front of her and a case next to her. The Jewesses Hédi Weisberger, Dina Hendler, and Olga Elefánt told us after they left the search room that their money that was hidden in their hair had been taken and they all cried, but I could not ask them why they cried because we were not permitted to talk with them.

On 4 May 1944 Mr. Bakay forbade the searching of women in his house and then they continued the searching of women in the garage. In another room of the garage they also searched men. Being close to the garage in a floor of Bakay's house, I heard shouts, wailing, and the sound of the sticks used in the beatings from the room where they searched the men. While cleaning the rooms after the searches ended, I saw about eight four-centimeter-thick sticks that had broken and been thrown on the floor. I saw the accused Mária Fekete with four golden women's watches. I was curious to see what kind of watches she had, but noticing my interest she covered them up with her sleeve. In the room in which the women were searched, I saw several pieces of clothing taken from the searched Jewish women. I know from Miss Olga Wolff, Miss Olga Hirsch, and Mrs. Klermann that the accused Mária Fekete and the other women in her group performed vaginal searches on the Jewish women.

The person who executed the order for the establishment of the ghetto in Dés was the mayor of the city, the accused Dr. Jenő Veress, and the person in charge of health services was the city medical examiner, Dr. Zsigmond Léhnár. . . .

Dr. István Takács, the government commissioner, was appointed commander of the ghetto.

Life in the ghetto was very bad. Housing was also unsuitable, and the food supply was defective. At the beginning those interned in the ghetto did not have drinking water either; after a while water was delivered in a firemen's tank-car, after the intervention of the then prefect, Count Béla Bethlen.[14]

Because of these miserable living conditions 25 Jews died, as did the newborn children.

The sanitary conditions were also miserable, but the accused Dr. Zsigmond Léhnár was not concerned with this.

Here is how the witness Dr. Dezső Steinfeld described this state of affairs:

> When they picked us up in our homes, special squads confiscated our money and all the jewelry, and sealed the apartments. When they took us from our apartments they did not allow us to take more than 25 kilograms of food per person and they interned us in three areas of the city where the *Nyilas* József Fekete, József Gecse, Jenő Takács, and József Lakadár searched us and beat us with sticks all over our bodies after we were undressed naked. They confiscated everything we had in our baggage except for two sets of underwear and food. After they interned us in the ghetto in the Bungur forest under inhumane conditions, without shelter, without food, without water, without toilets, and without bedding except dry leaves, we stayed there, 8,500 Jews, under absolutely inhumane conditions as a result of which many became ill and 25 Jews died, as did several suckling children whose undernourished mothers could no longer provide milk for them.
>
> To correct this miserable situation, I intervened personally with the city medical examiner Dr. Léhnár, who came into the ghetto daily, and I requested drugs for the sick and lumber for toilets since we had to use ordinary ditches in the middle of the ghetto without any dividing walls to hide them, but Dr. Léhnár refused categorically, saying that he had no time and that he did not care inasmuch as the Jews were being interned for extermination. When the first Jew died in the ghetto I requested Dr. Léhnár to identify a place where we could set up a cemetery. Then he selected

one for us; he pointed to a pit near a creek and told me that it would do and that we could put all the Jews into it.

After the internment of the Jews into the ghetto, there began the chase after the so-called hidden valuables. Those who did the searching were policemen as well as some members of the Arrow Cross Party in Dés.

As is revealed by the deposition of the witness Dezső Steinfeld, among the torturers were József Fekete, József Gecse, Jenő Takács, József Lakadár, and police officers Désaknai, Garamvölgyi, Somorlyai, and Kassay.

To show how these investigations took place and the antecedents of the ghetto's establishment, we shall cite from the deposition of the witness Dr. Manó Weinberger:

> Before the establishment of the ghetto, I heard from my former tenant Nagy, a police agent in Dés, that the establishment of the ghetto was left to the discretion of the local authorities. Having heard of this possibility and having been wounded twice during the 1914–1918 war and thus being exempted from wearing the distinctive star, I went to Mayor Veress and asked him for information relating to the establishment of the ghetto, begging him that in case it should be established he should exempt me from internment, and requested him to spare the city from the establishment of the ghetto, telling him that I would assume personal responsibility for the Jews in the city.
>
> When I talked with Mayor Veress about the site of the ghetto, reproaching him about its unsuitability—the lack of buildings, water, or sun in the forest—he told me that it was not his fault, that it was the accused Dr. Léhnár who had proposed the site.
>
> Having been interned only on the third day, I intervened with Mayor Veress to supply the ghetto with water but he answered that it was not possible for him and that the Jews should take the necessary measures; this left it without water for five days. After five days we worked out something; Izsák, the driver, brought us water with great difficulty at 2–3-day intervals, with each person receiving half a liter of water.
>
> Seven thousand, eight hundred sixty people were interned in the ghetto. The first measure was to cut off the hair of the men and to shorten it for women. On the eighth day, children came down with measles and I intervened with István Takács to bring in city medical examiner Léhnár to take measures for the health and the sanitary life of the ghetto. Coming into the ghetto, Dr. Léhnár ordered that ditches be dug to serve as toilets for the common use of the men and women. I intervened with Dr. Léhnár to permit the removal of the sick Jews to the city hospital of Dés, but he did not permit this and took no measures, making only promises. They searched Jews suspected of having hidden goods in a shed at the edge of the ghetto. One day around 6:00 A.M. I also was called by the Fascists and taken to this shed. As soon as I entered the shed, Désaknai asked me to get undressed to my skin and to lie on the ground on my stomach. After I did this, they twisted my hands behind my back

and then they bent my feet toward my back and tied them to my hands with belts and they stuffed my own socks in my mouth. While in this position a *Nyilas* whose name I do not know stepped on my back so that I would not be able to move and Désaknai began to beat me with an unbending rubber truncheon on the soles of the feet until I became unconscious. After a few minutes I felt cold water running down my head and then I came to, my hands and feet having been untied and the socks taken out of my mouth. Once I was on my feet Désaknai ordered me to dance the folk dance and make my head touch the ceiling of the shed, which was a half a meter above my head. With my swollen feet full of bruises I was compelled to dance the folk dance while Désaknai beat me with the rubber truncheon on my stomach and back. Having been given the order to get dressed, I was unable to put on my pants and boots because my feet were swollen. Then two *Nyilas* came who took me under their arms and after I was taken out of the shed I was thrown into a nearby stable on some straw. Because I did not declare where I had hidden certain things, while on the straw I saw that my sons Eric and Norbert Weinberger were also taken into the shed and I heard their shouts and moans. After they too left the shed unable to get dressed and put their shoes on, I was told that they were beaten over their hands and soles by police commissioner Désaknai to make them divulge the place and the persons with whom I had deposited certain things, and had been told that I had confessed to very few places and persons. After half an hour I saw a *Nyilas* take my wife into the shed and my two sons were taken to an adjacent room to see how their mother, my wife, was going to be tortured. At first she did not tell where we had hidden our valuables, but then they took her shoes off and laid her on the ground face down and beat her on her soles so hard that I heard her shouts and moans in the stable. After a few minutes Désaknai came to me and told me that I was a liar and that my wife had identified the persons with whom I had hidden things, and since I was afraid that they would torture me again I agreed that this was correct.

The responsibility of the accused Jenő Veress, the former mayor of Dés, is similar to that of the other mayors; he was the chief functionary of the municipality and was responsible for both the housing and the feeding of those interned in the ghetto. The objective acts described above and resulting from the depositions of the witnesses—depositions that were partially quoted—constitute the basis for the penal responsibility of the accused.

With respect to the principal collaborator of the city's mayor, i.e., the accused Dr. Zsigmond Léhnár, it is enough to mention that, as the witness Manó Weinberger related, the accused Jenő Veress himself informed him that the physician Dr. Léhnár had been the one who decided that the Bungur forest should become the ghetto site.

One also notes that the accused Dr. Zsigmond Léhnár did not see to it in advance that the ghetto of Dés be supplied with water, did not see to it that the barracks be sufficient, did not see to it that pregnant women be allowed to give birth in hospitals but allowed them to give birth in the forest on the wet ground in the barracks, causing the death of all the newborn, and finally it was proved that even the dead were buried on the edge of the ghetto near the trenches that served as latrines and neither the ghetto commander nor the ghetto physician permitted these dead to be buried in the cemetery and with the traditional rites.

As for the accused Dr. János Schilling, the former deputy prefect of Szamos County, it is true that it was proved that on 2 May 1944 he entered a hospital and that there was a rumor in the city that this hospitalization was only an excuse for him to avoid taking part in the roundup of the Jews into the ghetto.

It is no less true, however, that up to 2 May 1944 the accused János Schilling participated in all the preparations for the internment of the Jews into the ghetto, and in particular that he participated at the Szatmárnémeti conference and convened the preparatory conferences of Dés and issued the necessary instructions.

Even where the selection of the ghetto site is concerned, the accused Dr. János Schilling played a contributory role inasmuch as this selection and the preparations for clearing the forest as well as the start of construction of the barracks took place before the hospitalization of the accused.

But the accused János Schilling displayed a chauvinistic attitude throughout the time he served as deputy prefect. He was the one who rejected the appeal of the witness Ágoston Pál against the internment decision made by chief district administrator of Ilonda District. The decision of the accused Dr. János Schilling bears No. 11,934 of 18 October 1941 and can be found in folder No. 53 of the file.

As revealed by the deposition of witness Dr. Andrei Macovei, during the four years of Horthyite occupation the accused Dr. János Schilling raised innumerable difficulties to prevent the opening of Romanian-language schools.

It was also the accused Dr. János Schilling who issued a written order to the notary offices instructing them to prepare lists of workers to be deported to Germany. These lists were to include inhabitants who did not own property, those who had been convicted of a crime, and those who had not been called to military service.

This fact is established through the interrogation of the notary József Zolya, the former notary of the village of Felsőilosva in Szamos County.

It was noted above that among the torturers were the accused József Gecse, Mária Fekete, and József Lakadár. The other torturers were just like these, but these three accused are nevertheless distinguished from the other investigators by certain particularities.

Although he had no official position because he was not a public functionary, the accused József Gecse volunteered as a member of the Arrow Cross Party to participate in the roundup of the Jews into the ghetto and in searching them to discover hidden valuables.

Aside from beatings and tortures that were no different from those administered by other torturers, this accused was proved to have hit Dr. Samu Biró, a lawyer from Magyar-Lápos, all over the body with his rubber truncheon. The beating was so hard that this lawyer had to be carried by others to be put onto the train, but once he arrived at the station he died within five minutes.

Here is how the witness József Goldstein described the above case:

> When Dr. Samu Biró was searched I was next to him, as were three others whose names I do not recall. I, Dr. Biró, and Ármin Rosenfeld appeared before the accused József Gecse to be searched at the same time, having been undressed naked. He went through the pockets of our clothes, taking everything out and throwing all the found things in a heap. When I was searched, the accused Gecse hit me over the back with a rubber truncheon, and when I bent down to pick up my clothes he slapped me, and then I left to get dressed. While I was getting dressed, the accused searched Dr. Biró, and after he took some documents from his pocket I heard Dr. Biró protesting against their removal because he had worked a whole life for them. Then the accused József Gecse hit him with the rubber truncheon over his back, neck, and head, saying that he did not need any documents because he was going to his death. When Dr. Biró tried to get out, the accused hit him again over the right side of his head, above the ear as a result of which the victim fell down. I and Ármin Rosenberg rushed to Dr. Biró, lifted him and took him aside where we dressed him—without his shoes—and from there we took him to the freight car, a distance of 150 meters, and when we put him down we noted that he was dead. It was in the same manner that the accused József Gecse beat the Jew Klermann from Dés.

Another figure among the torturers in the ghetto of Dés was the accused Mária Fekete. She too volunteered for the odious work relating to the searching of the victims in the ghetto although she did not hold any official position, and she did not limit herself to body searches but also performed vaginal searches of women. Her activity, like her attitude, is explained by the fact that she was a member of the Arrow Cross Party, both she and her husband, the latter having been visited by Szálasi himself during his visit to Dés, as was admitted by the accused during her interrogation. This explains why the accused Mária Fekete performed vaginal searches with a stick, as was the case with Mrs. Náthán Ábrahám.

This is also what explains that when the accused Mária Fekete searched the victim Frida Elek for some fur and the victim protested that she did not have any furs, she shouted threateningly, screaming that the victim was lying and that she was a beast. (Deposition of witness Frida Elek)

During the searches, the accused Mária Fekete expropriated for herself numerous objects of value such as gold watches, wedding bands, clothes, rings, and other things.

The accused József Lakadár did not have any official function either, but being a member of the Arrow Cross Party he too volunteered and participated in all the operations relating to the roundup of Jews into the ghetto and to the search for hidden valuables.

In the territory of Szamos County there were also mistreatments and tortures during the internment of the Jews into the ghetto, as well as during the four years of Horthyite occupation in general.

Thus in the village of Retteg, Szamos County, the accused Sándor Oláh behaved in an inhumane manner with the victims who were interned in the ghetto, beating them during the searches, aiming especially at violating women. At the same time he also guided German soldiers who passed through Retteg to young Jewish girls for sexual relations. This was the case of the young Gitta Hárnik, who was only able to escape from them with great difficulty.

Here is how the witness Florentina Izsák described the behavior of the accused during the vaginal searches performed by the accused Rozália Jancsó:

> I too was searched by the accused Rozália Jancsó, both bodily and vaginally. The room where the women were searched had a broken window that was covered with a torn paper, and through this paper the gendarmes, the accused Sándor Oláh, and the other men who were in the adjacent room watched how the accused undressed and searched the women, making fun of us and directing various critical remarks at us. After I was undressed she laid me on a table and searched me vaginally and then in this position she ordered me to wait; she left, but after a few minutes she returned with the accused Sándor Oláh whom she brought to me in the room and then she left and while the door was still open she said: "Go inside and see what a good piece of meat there is for you; do with her what you want."
>
> When I saw the accused, I jumped off the table shouting that he should leave, but he hurried toward me and wanted to take me into his arms and throw me onto the table, but he did not succeed because of my categorical opposition. During my struggle with the accused I was caught in many parts of my body and in my struggles I hit my left hand against the table so that I feel the pain even today.

In his capacity as deputy commander of the platoon of Romanian premilitary personnel in the village, the accused also displayed a Fascist attitude toward the Romanian and Jewish premilitary men in Retteg.

The accused Rozália Jancsó, the communal midwife of Retteg, also behaved chauvinistically and displayed racial hatred.

Not only did she subject young girls of six and seven years of age and old women of 70 to 80 years to vaginal searches, but her specialty was her desire to come to the aid of the accused Sándor Oláh, by placing at his disposal young defenseless girls during the searches and urging him to take advantage of them in the search room itself. This was the case of the witness Florentina Izsák as revealed by her deposition cited above.

Here is how the witness Dora Stern described the activity of the accused Rozália Jancsó:

> In a room next door to the room where the men were searched the accused Rozália Jancsó undressed the women to their skin and performed vaginal searches without wearing gloves, even in little girls of 6 to 12 years of age; she also searched me vaginally as she did my 12-year old girl Julia Stern who had been ill for three weeks. The witness Julia Hirsch says that she too was searched vaginally in an extremely brutal and dirty manner, as was her 13-year old younger sister Eszter Hirsch who was crying, and even though she asked the accused to spare her she refused. After the search, her sister Eszter Hirsch became very ill so that when the selection was done at Auschwitz she was classified among the ill and was burned in the crematorium.

But the accused Rozália Jancsó not only had anti-Jewish drives that stemmed from abstract Fascist conceptions, she also had a desire for enrichment, confiscating for personal profit items such as jewelry, money, and clothes from those she subjected to searching.

The acts committed by the accused Sándor Oláh and Rozália Jancsó were fully established through the depositions of the witnesses Margit Moskovits, Magda Berkovics, Helén and Margit Mendelsohn, Gitta Hárnik, Berta Naiovits, Florentina Izsák, Dora Stern, Dora Bernstein, and Julia Hirsch.

The accused Ferenc Lakatos served as a notary in the village of Csicsó-Györgyfalva, Szamos County, from the fall of 1940 to the summer of 1944. During his term of office he did not miss a single opportunity to persecute Romanians, terrorizing them so as to induce as many Romanians as possible to leave the village and to emigrate to Romania.

The specialty of this accused with respect to the Romanian persecution was the spoliation and dispossession of the family members of those who escaped to Romania, doing everything possible to prevent these family members from using the real estate left behind by those who had escaped to Romania.

This was the case of Sofia Banabic, whose sons went to Romania and who was also entitled to use the house since she was the widow of the father of the two sons who had emigrated; nevertheless the accused Ferenc Lakatos prevented her from this in order to assign the house to Hungarian settlers who bore the title of *"vitéz"* (brave). The witness Sofia Banabic explained how this accused brought the settlers into the house, restricting her rights to live there, maintaining that the house belonged to the two sons who had left for Romania and that therefore the Hungarian state could dispose over the house. Moreover, Sofia Banabic was not the only one dispossessed of her house; there were a number of other persons with similar cases.

The accused Ferenc Lakatos behaved as a Fascist during the roundup of the Jews into the ghetto as well. An act that is particularly revealing is the case of Moshe Friedmann's mother, from the village of Csicsó-Györgyfalva; although she was freed from the ghetto and returned to the village, the accused Ferenc Lakatos did not allow her to live in the village and forced her to return to the ghetto. (Deposition of the witness Moshe Friedmann)

The accused Pál Antalffy, the commander of the legion of gendarmes in Dés, was the leader of the gendarmes involved in the roundup of the Jews in Szamos County. His responsibility is the same as that of the other commanders of law enforcement authorities.

In Szamosujvár a ghetto was established in the area of the brickyard, and the Jews who were concentrated in this ghetto were transferred after seven days to the ghetto of Kolozsvár, from where they were subsequently deported to Germany. Those who established the ghetto and carried out the roundup of the Jews and their searching were the accused Lajos Tamási, mayor of Szamosujvár; András Iványi, chief police commissioner of Szamosujvár; and Ernő Berecki, police chief of Szamosujvár. The methods used in the roundup and searching of the Jews did not differ in any way from the methods used in the other ghettos. The housing and feeding of the Jews did not differ either.

This being the case, the responsibility of these accused is also similar to that of the others.

The Beszterce Ghetto

In the city of Beszterce the ghetto was set up at the Stamboli farm approximately four kilometers from the city.

The roundup of the Jews began on the morning of 3 May and was brought to completion by selected squads.

The housing was in barracks and in pig sties, but a large part of the population remained under the open sky. There was no kitchen, nor wells, nor infirmaries.

To serve as latrines there were a number of ditches that had been dug in the center of the camp but which, not having been fenced in and camouflaged, were not used because of the peoples' sense of modesty. No sanitary measures were taken, just as no measures were taken for the hospitalization of the ill and of the women about to give birth.

The food situation was no better either. For cooking, bathtubs were brought in from Jewish homes, and water, in completely insufficient quantity, was brought in a tank car belonging to the mayor's office.

This was the condition in which the close to 8,000 Jews who were interned in this camp were kept.

The primary functionary of the municipality was Mayor Norbert Kuales; of the county it was Deputy Prefect László Smolenszki. After they returned from their conference with László Endre at Marosvásárhely, these two leading officials, together with the then prefect Béla Bethlen, selected the site of the ghetto as was shown above and began the preparatory work for the construction of the barracks, trying to distract public opinion by launching the rumor that they were planning a pig-raising farm at Stamboli. They threatened to take severe measures against the Jewish community, which began to become restless after a few days when reality began to seep in.

The heads of the law enforcement authorities were the accused Debreczeni, chief of the Beszterce police, for the city, and gendarmerie Lieutenant Colonel Pásztai, commander of the legion of gendarmes in Naszód, for the county.

It is not necessary to note in detail the brutal and hasty manner in which the Jews were rounded up and interned into the ghetto, any more than it is necessary to mention the brutalities to which the internees were subjected during the searches and during the investigations for the discovery of hidden valuables. It is sufficient to state that here too the methods, from all of these points of view, were painfully similar to the methods used in the other ghettos.

Their guilt is also similar; specifically, the former mayor of Beszterce Norbert Kuales and the former deputy prefect of Naszód County László Smolenszki are responsible in their capacity as chief officials of the municipality, their responsibility being similar to that of the other mayors and deputy prefects.

The participation in these crimes of the accused Debreczeni, chief of police in Beszterce, and Pásztai, commander of the legion of gendarmes in Naszód, is similar to that of the other police chiefs and commanders of gendarme legions, just as their responsibility is similar.

The similarities in their participation and in their responsibility are revealed by the events that took place and are proved by the witnesses who have been heard in connection with the ghetto in Beszterce, to whom the People's Tribunal referred, as well as by the official status of these accused during that time.

As was the case in the other ghettos, in the Beszterce ghetto also there were a number of people who, without any official position or direct connections with the ghetto, volunteered their services and committed war crimes and brutalities for which the People's Tribunal established their individual responsibility.

Among these were:

The accused Gusztáv Orendi, the Gestapo agent in Beszterce, supervised the roundup of the Jews and their internment into the ghetto on his motorcycle, and after the internment he visited the ghetto frequently, hitting and mistreating the internees. His mistreatments consisted, among other things, in preventing the internees from preparing their food, in forbidding water and food supplies, and finally in forbidding peasants to sell food in the ghetto.

The accused Heinrich Smolka, although not a public functionary and an older man, volunteered for service in the Beszterce police to help in the roundup and internment of the Jews. In addition to his services in the roundup of the Jews, he also set himself up as a supervisor in the ghetto, forbidding the relatives of the internees who came from the labor service companies to see their family members. (Case of the witness Izidor Jakab)

The witness Herman Maierovits related how he had personally seen the accused Heinrich Smolka ordering the turning back of water at the ghetto gate to prevent its being given to the Jews.

The witness Mendel Brach declared that the accused Heinrich Smolka had been entrusted with the supply of food to the ghetto but did not take care of it; on the contrary, he took over all the food and gave it to the state cooperative *(Futura)*. The same witness described how he had tried to intercede with the accused to bring water into the ghetto, and stated that the accused did not want to talk with Jews, not even those whom he knew from earlier times.

Aside from this involvement of the accused in the affairs of the ghetto, he also took part in the body searches on which occasion he confiscated items of value from those being searched and expropriated some of them.

The defense raised the point that the accused Kálmán Borbély could not be tried by the Court Panel of the People's Tribunal because the public prosecutor had already stipulated the Classification Judgment *(Ordonanţa de clasare)* now on file for the acts that had been investigated.

Considering that at the time the Classification Judgment was passed, the public prosecutor did not have the documentary materials, i.e., the sentence of the People's Tribunal of Budapest which reveals precisely the responsibility and complicity of the prefects with respect to the inhumane treatment of the Jews interned in the ghettos.

Considering that only from this judgment of the People's Tribunal of Budapest was it possible to ascertain that had the accused Kálmán Borbély reported in his capacity as prefect of Naszód County—and this was his obligation as prefect—that the Jews interned in the ghetto of Beszterce were being treated inhumanely by not being allowed the most primitive installations for the sick and being deprived of water and food, the Ministry of the Interior would have taken measures to improve the situation.

The accounts of the acts of the accused Debreczeni and Pásztai show without a doubt that the Jews interned in the ghetto of Beszterce were mistreated horribly to make them confess with whom and where they had hidden their valuables—acts of which the accused Kálmán Borbély was aware following his visit to the ghetto, as is also evident from his wife's memorandum on file.

Considering that as prefect the accused Kálmán Borbély was aware of everything that was happening in the ghetto, he knew that the accused Debreczeni and Pásztai mistreated the interned Jews to force them to declare their hidden jewelry, and did not report to the Ministry of the Interior nor take any measures to halt the beatings and inhumane treatment in the ghetto, this intentional omission of the accused encompasses all the elements of complicity in the crime stipulated in Article 2, Paragraph h of Law No. 312/1945.

The accused Kálmán Borbély obtained his position as prefect on 10 May 1944, when the government of Döme Sztójay was installed in Hungary on Hitler's order.

This General Döme Sztójay was Hitler's confidence man and in his service; it is known specifically that the accused Kálmán Borbély was aware of this fact; thus by accepting the position of prefect he completely identified himself with the goals of the government, having received this position at the time when the illegal measures were being taken for the internment of the Jews throughout Hungary, measures that the accused today detests and declares to be inhumane and illegal.

The position of prefect was a political position, so that when the accused, an outspoken member of the extreme rightist Imrédyist organization, accepted the position of prefect with pleasure despite the government's adoption of anti-Jewish measures, he collaborated with the Fascist regime not only politically but also economically; helping the German war machine with his orders and decisions and by taking restrictive economic measures, he identified himself totally with the Hitlerite regime, acts that are covered under Article 2, Paragraph o of Law No. 312/1945.

These are the proved facts with regard to the establishment of ghettos in Northern Transylvania, the internment of the Jews in these ghettos, and the treatment of the internees by the authorities at the time.

On 8 May 1944 Under-Secretary of State László Endre and Gendarmerie Lieutenant Colonel László Ferenczy called another meeting at Munkács, which was attended by the top officials of all counties in Northern Transylvania, where the participants were informed about the plans for the deportation trains, the deportation conditions, and the place to which the people would be deported.

Between 18 and 20 May 1944 Lieutenant Colonel László Ferenczy, representing and substituting for László Endre, also organized an administrative conference similar to that of Munkács in Kolozsvár. This conference was attended by the representatives of the civilian and military administration in Kolozsvár region, including the cities of Kolozsvár, Dés, and Beszterce, as well as in Székely Land, including Marosvásárhely and Szászrégen. At this conference Lieutenant Colonel László Ferenczy explained to the participants how the Jews would have to be put onto trains for their deportation to Germany.

The deportation of all the Jews from the ghettos of Transylvania was carried out in the most inhumane manner. In the heat of the end of May and early June 1944 they were loaded into freight cars, some 70 to 80 people to a car —men, women, and children, the young and the old, the healthy and the sick, all in a topsy-turvy manner.

Each freight car was supplied only with two buckets, one for water and the other for excrements. Before boarding the train all the Jews were subjected to another search to confiscate the last items they could perhaps have hidden. After boarding, the freight cars were locked with special chains and the passengers were no longer allowed into the stations to fetch needed water or to empty the dirty buckets. Even worse, the corpses of those who died during the transports were not removed from the freight cars till Auschwitz, which was the final stop.

Aside from these excesses that caused physical and psychic pain, the accompanying gendarmes tried throughout the trip to intimidate these people on their last voyage in any way possible.

This was how the deportation took place in the Székely Land. But this was also how the Jews were deported from Máramarossziget and Szilágysomlyó and Beszterce and in general from all the ghettos.

The trains with the unfortunate victims were directed to the railway station at Kassa and there handed over to German soldiers who directed them to the labor and extermination camps at Auschwitz and Birkenau.

And with this the first act in the tragedy of the Jews of Transylvania came to an end, with the following act to be carried out in the extermination camp by the masters of the disciples who carried out the first act.

During this time the heads of the Hungarian Fascist administration in Transylvania inspired newspaper articles such as the article published in the *Székely Szó* (Székler Word), No. 100 of 4 May 1944, and inspired by the prefect of Maros County, the accused Andor Joós, that stated:

The orders of the Ministry of the Interior with regard to the roundup of the Jews in the ghetto was carried out here with exemplary discipline and with that chivalrous tone that has always characterized the Hungarian nation. With one hand it destroyed the enemy and with the other it hurried to aid the fallen enemy. The evacuated Jews were placed in camps and care was taken that no complaints could be made with regard to sanitation and food supply.

During the trial of this group of war criminals by the People's Tribunal, the innocence of some of the accused was ascertained, and in the absence of evidence they were acquitted. These are:

The accused Melánia Szilárszki née Kosári and Irén Kosári were accused of having handed over to the German Gestapo of Nagyvárad at 14 Kapucinus Street, on their own initiative and intentionally, the two daughters (one 10 and the other 11 years of age) of the Jewish pharmacist Dr. Roth.

It was proved before this People's Tribunal that these two accused indeed took the two little girls to 14 Kapucinus Street in Nagyvárad, but the facts showed:

That the pharmacist Szilárszki, the husband of the first accused, indeed requested a labor service pharmacist for the management of his pharmacy at the Felix Spa;

That the pharmacist Dr. Roth indeed came to this pharmacy, bringing along his family consisting of his wife and the two little girls;

That on the very day of his arrival the pharmacist Dr. Roth appeared before the security organs with his documents for clearance, but that his documents apparently were not in order and he was therefore picked up and taken to Nagyvárad after working only one week in the pharmacy of the accused.

This being the case it cannot be assumed that the accused intended to denounce the family of the pharmacist Dr. Roth, considering that it was the very husband of the first accused who requested him from the Ministry when the family of the accused needed this pharmacist.

One can more easily believe that the accused, having seen that the pharmacist Roth and his wife had been picked up and taken to Nagyvárad, and being ignorant about their fate, thought it natural when the pharmacist's little girls returned from the beach and were frightened over the absence of their parents, to take these girls to Nagyvárad, where the pharmacist Roth had been taken, so that these two little girls should not remain separated from their parents.

Moreover it was proved that the pharmacist Dr. Roth had encountered some complications with his documents a few days after his arrival at Felix Spa, so that the accused could have easily thought that Dr. Roth would settle his difficulty this time as well and for this reason it would be better for the girls to be with their parents. That it was the accused who took them to Nagyvárad is explained by the fact that since they lived in Váradszőllős, a village situated west of Nagyvárad, they went to Nagyvárad every night after the pharmacy closed, and so as to take another train from there to Sălăuș.

A wiser and more rational person might presumably have decided that under the circumstances of those times it would have been much more prudent to keep the two little girls hidden and not to take them to Nagyvárad, on the assumption that the pharmacist Dr. Roth could perhaps not get out of his difficulty, in which case deportation would await all of them, but it is probable that the accused, as women, did not have this sound reasoning power.

At any rate, there is quite a distance from the tactical mistake made by the accused to attributing to them the intention to denounce and hand over these two little girls to the German Gestapo for extermination; the People's Tribunal took account of this and concluded that the accused Melánia Szilárszki and Irén Kosári did not intend to hand over the two little girls of the pharmacist Dr. Roth of Bratislava to the Gestapo and consequently acquitted them from the accusation against them.

The second accused for whom the People's Tribunal reached the conclusion that there was no evidence of guilt is the accused Kálmán Szabó, the chief district administrator of Szászrégen District. It was charged against this accused that when the witness Gidáli Mármor appeared before the accused with a letter written by the accused's brother-in-law and a medical certificate showing that the witness's father, Éliás Mármor, was a 75 percent invalid, the accused tore up the letter and locked the invalid's certificate in his desk drawer, shouting that he did not engage in favoritism for Jews.

The People's Tribunal was unable to give any weight to this deposition since the accused was the chief district administrator not of the district from which the war invalid Éliás Mármor had been picked up, but of a district where the Jews were not rounded up.[15]

Moreover, the People's Tribunal did not accept that the deportation of Éliás Mármor was due to the accused's withholding of the document in his office desk, since Gidáli Mármor, the invalid's son, could not know whether Kálmán Szabó had or had not forwarded the document to the screening commission.

Moreover, if what the witness Gidáli Mármor declared were true, namely that the accused had withheld the document in his office desk, the witness could have gone to the hospital that issued the certificate and have received a duplicate which he could have forwarded to the screening commission directly, without requesting the accused to do him a favor.

This being the case, the People's Tribunal decided to acquit the accused Kálmán Szabó in the absence of proof of guilt.

With respect to the accused István Szilágyi, the People's Tribunal also had to issue a decision of acquittal because the depositions of the witnesses that were heard did not show that he had perpetrated the acts of which he was accused.

The fact that as a businessman in the village of Retteg he caused dissatisfaction during the distribution of rationed food cannot be considered to fall within the framework of Law No. 312/1945; moreover, it is a well-known fact that in rural communities such as Retteg so many rationed goods could not be distributed at all or in sufficient quantity that the peasant inhabitants of the village probably held the mistaken belief that the accused possessed large quantities of these goods and did not want to distribute them. This is what explains the animosity shown toward him by so many people in the village who were eager to make depositions unfavorable to the accused concerning certain acts which according to the People's Tribunal do not constitute war crimes; the deeds with which the accused was charged and which do constitute war crimes were not proved.

The accused István Nagy was charged with acting as a denouncer of Romanians and Jews to the Hungarian counterintelligence organs.

Since all the witnesses who were heard on these matters had no direct and *propri sensibus* knowledge about whether the accused really made those denunciations and brought about the arrest and expulsion of several Romanians and Jews or their internment into camps, the People's Tribunal found that there was insufficient evidence to convict the accused on this point of the indictment.

With respect to the accusation that after the Jews had been interned into the ghetto, while walking through the woods he caught on his own initiative the Jews Zsigmond Vidor and Mendel Rutner, who had escaped from the ghetto and hid in the Bicul forest, and brought them tied up to the Szilágysomlyó police from where they were interned into the ghetto and deported to Auschwitz where Zsigmond Vidor died, the People's Tribunal took into consideration the deposition of the witness Teodor Gavra, which proved that the accused István Nagy had been stationed in Zilah throughout the month of May. The witness knew this because as a finance official he constantly had to see him to collect certain taxes.

This being the case, the People's Tribunal recognized that there was no proof about the guilt of the accused and consequently acquitted him of the charges against him.

As far as the accused István Komán is concerned, it was proved before this People's Tribunal that although this accused was the chief notary in the village of Borsa, because he was of Romanian ethnic origin he was nevertheless not considered trustworthy by the Horthyite regime, and all secret and confidential matters were transmitted by Kadicsfalvi, the chief district administrator of Felsővisó District, to the accused József Farkas, notary of the village of Borsa, who alone dealt with the question of the 34 Jews who were expelled and exterminated on the Balosina mountain.

An accusation was also brought against the accused István Komán that when some Jews petitioned in Budapest for saving their fellow nationals and the ministry issued a telegraphic order for the revocation of the expulsion, the accused István Komán did not want to follow up this telegraphic order for revocation although it was brought to his attention.

The People's Tribunal noted, however, that there was no proof of the telegraphic or telephonic order's having been brought to the attention of the accused István Komán, and that even if the accused István Komán had heard some rumor about the existence of such an order, as an official he could not have taken any measures without a specific order from his direct superior, chief district administrator Kadicsfalvi.

Moreover, it was also proved that the accused István Komán's family was in Felsővisó and that every Saturday he would leave the village of Borsa for Felsővisó to be with his family, and it was further proved that this telephonic order came on a Saturday, i.e., at a time when the accused István Komán probably was not even in Borsa.

This being the case and in consideration of the fact that the accused was not involved with Jewish questions, all Jewish matters being assigned directly to notary József Farkas who handled them alone—for which he was condemned among Group 6 before this Tribunal—the People's Tribunal concluded that there was no proof of guilt with respect to the charges against the accused István Komán and consequently acquitted him from the indictment against him.

IN LAW:

Considering the acts perpetrated by the accused shown above;
Considering the investigations presented for each of the accused both before the Court Panel and before the investigating offices, which were cited in the public sessions;
Considering that the acts of the accused Dr. László Gyapai, János Nadányi, Dr. László Csóka, Endre Boér, Dr. László Vásárhelyi, Dr. József Székely, Dr. Zsigmond Marton, Dr. Ferenc Májay, Colonel Géza Körmendi, General István Kozma, Dezső Gálfy, Dr. István Bonda, Dr. Ferenc Filó, Dr. Imre Schmidt, Dr. Mátyás Tóth, Ernő Gaáli, Dr. József Ábrahám, Gerő Szász, Dr. Andor Barabás, András Virányi, Dr. Jenő Veress, Lajos Tamási, Dr. András Gazda, Dr. János Sréter, Dr. József Udvari, Dr. Sándor Gyulafalvi Rednik,

László Smolenszki, and Norbert Kuales who in their respective capacities as mayors, deputy prefects and commanders of army groups and garrisons intentionally followed certain oral orders and written instructions issued by the two under-secretaries of state in the Hungarian Ministry of the Interior, László Endre and László Baky, and proceeded with the establishment of ghettos in the territory of Northern Transylvania, although according to Decree No. 1610/1944 M.E. the establishment of ghettos and the displacement of Jews from a locality with fewer than 10,000 people were optional with the top functionary of the municipality, committed the crime stipulated in Paragraph *m* of Article 2 of Law No. 312/1945 since they intentionally ordered the establishment of Jewish ghettos and through their intentional acts perpetrated in the knowledge of what would happen to the Jews, i.e., knowing that the Royal Hungarian government had decided on "cleansing the country of Jews," that is, on their deportation to Germany, these accused, in addition to committing the war crime stipulated in Paragraph *m* of Article 2 of the Law, also committed those crimes stipulated by Paragraph *o* of the same article inasmuch as through these acts, which they perpetrated themselves, they placed themselves intentionally in the service of Hitlerism and fascism, contributing to the realization of their political objectives which at the time also involved, among other things, the extermination of the Jewish people.

The act of the accused Major N. Schröder falls within the definition of war crimes stipulated in Paragraph *f* of Article 2 of Law No. 312/1945, since in his capacity as chief of the German Gestapo in Marosvásárhely he intentionally contributed as a perpetrator to the organization of the Jewish deportations to Germany for purposes of extermination. Retaining the acts with which he was charged in the indictment, the People's Tribunal changed the classification given in the indictment, considering that his act only presents the elements of the crime stipulated in Paragraph *f* of Article 2 of the Law.

The acts of the accused Dr. János Schilling fall within the definition of war crimes stipulated in Paragraphs *m, n,* and *o* of Article 2 of Law No. 312/1945 because he intentionally contributed as perpetrator to the establishment of the ghetto of Dés, he intentionally carried out in an excessive manner the political and racial provisions ordering that Romanians be forcefully sent for labor to Germany, and finally by these acts he also violated the provisions of Paragraph *o* of Article 2 of the Law, since by these acts of his own he placed himself in the service of Hitlerism and fascism, contributing to the realization of their political goals.

The acts of the accused Dr. Lajos Varga, Barnabás Endrődi, Dr. László Szlávi, Dr. László Illinyi, Dr. László Szaplonczai, Kálmán Borbély, Károly Rajnay (Reiner), and Andor Joós fall within the definition of complicity in war crimes stipulated in Paragraphs [illegible] and *m* of the Law since they intentionally aided and abetted both the top officials of the municipalities in the establishment of ghettos and the law enforcement organs in the tortures and mistreatments for finding hidden valuables; their aiding and abetting consists in the fact that in their capacity as prefects they willfully tolerated these measures. By these acts of complicity carried out willfully and with full knowledge, these accused also violated the provisions of Paragraph *o* of Article 2 inasmuch as they placed themselves in the service of Hitlerism and fascism, contributing by these acts of theirs to the realization of their political objectives.

The acts of Gendarmerie Major Pál Antalffy, Péter Czeisberger, Zoltán Osváth, Lajos Ormos, Ioan Anghea, József Lázár, and Ioan Vancea fall within the definition of war crimes stipulated in Paragraphs *n* and *o* of Article 2 of the Law since they intentionally participated as perpetrators in the mistreatment of the Jews in the ghetto to find hidden valuables, acts by which they placed themselves in the service of Hitlerism and fascism, contributing to the realization of their political objectives. These same accused are also guilty of complicity in the war crimes stipulated in Paragraph *m* of Article 2 of the Law inasmuch as they knowingly and willingly contributed as helpers to the establishment of the Jewish ghettos.

The acts of the accused N. Deményi, Dr. László Urbán, Tibor Paksi-Kiss, Dr. Géza Papp, Ferenc Menyhért, József Orosz, András Szentkuti, Dr. Pál Boldizsár, Dr. Sandor Ojtózi, Colonel Dr. János Papp, Colonel János Zalantai, Dr. Géza Bedő, Gendarmerie Captain Konya, First Sergeant Ferenc Sallós, János Dudás, Gendarmerie Lieutenant Kálmán Szentpáli, György Kugler (Füleki), Quartermaster Bányai, First Sergeant Balázs Biró, First Sergeant András Fehér, István Gősi, Irma Lovas, Dr. Géza Polánkai, Dr. Imre Németh, Ágoston Félegyházi Medgyesi, Dr. Gyula Petri, János Frater, Dr. Béla Rektor, István Garai, Dr. Endre Bodolai, Ferenc Sziklai, András Medgyesi, Dezső Büss, Gyula Őri, György Fekete, Sándor Ilonka, János Teveli, István Szőllősi, Géza Szabados, János Tóth, Mihály Juhász, Sándor Posgai, Gábor Keresztesi, István Felföldi, Imre Garai, Sándor Fehér, József Horváth, Mihály Szabó, Gendarme Megyeri, Gendarme Budai, Dr. Miklós Toperczel, Mrs. József Medgyesi née Erzsébet Mutza, the widow of János Kiss née Rozália Zeffer, Dr. Béla Sárközi, Károly Csegezi, Béla Ferenczi, Dr. István Vincze, Lieutenant Colonel Balla, Dr. Gyula Sárosi, István Takács, János Somorlyai, János Kassay, Albert Garamvölgyi, Miklós Désaknai, József Gecse, Mária Fekete, József Lakadár, Rozália Jancsó, Ernő Berecki, András Iványi, Dr. Jenő Nagy, Károly Balogh, József Orgoványi, Imre Vajai, István Bertalan, Ferenc Elekes, Lieutenant Colonel György Mariska, István Pethes, Dr. Sándor Horváth, Dr. László Krasznai, Quartermaster Miklós Sárközi, Quartermaster János Horváth, László Petővári Petrik, Irén Duha, Dr. Lajos

Tóth, János Fehér, Colonel Miklós Sárváry, Florea Tascan, János Biró, György Varga, Dr. Miklós Debreczeni, Gusztáv Orendi, Lieutenant Ernő Pásztai and Lieutenant Colonel Miklós Jakab fall within the definition of war crimes stipulated in Paragraphs *h* and *o* of Article 2 of Law No. 312/1945 since in their capacity as investigators they intentionally subjected those they investigated in matters of a political and racial nature to acts of violence, tortures, and other illegal methods of constraint, and by these deeds of their own they at the same time placed themselves in the service of Hitlerism and fascism, contributing thereby to the realization of their political objectives.

The acts of the accused Captain László Berentes fall within the definition of instigation to war crimes stipulated in Paragraph *h* of Article 2 of the Law, since he deliberately brought about the torturing and mistreatment for political and racial motives of a large number of workers in the Phönix factory in Nagybánya where the accused served as military commander.

The acts of the accused István Bede fall within the definition of war crimes stipulated in Paragraph *o* of Article 2 of the Law, since he intentionally perpetrated individual repression, killing a Jew for reasons of political and racial persecution, and the acts of the accused Gusztáv Sarkadi, who intentionally induced him to commit this infraction, fall within the definition of instigation to this crime.

The acts of the accused József Lax and Sándor Farmati fall within the definition of complicity in war crimes stipulated in Paragraph *h* of Article 2 of the Law, since they intentionally aided in the mistreatment of the Jews in the ghetto for the discovery of hidden valuables, mistreatments and tortures that were applied in the course of investigations conducted in matters of a political and racial nature.

The acts of the accused Sámuel Császár and Zoltán Horkai fall within the definition of war crimes stipulated in Paragraph *1* of Article 2 of the law since they intentionally and illicitly enriched themselves during their participation in the conduct of the war and during the implementation of the racial measures relating to the deportation of the Jews of Northern Transylvania, and at the same time they aided in the torturing and mistreatment of these Jews by the investigators seeking hidden valuables, acts by which they became accomplices in the commission of war crimes stipulated in Paragraph *h* of Article 2 of the Law.

The acts of the accused Sándor Oláh fall within the definition of war crimes stipulated in Paragraph *o* of Article 2 of the Law since he intentionally placed himself in the service of Hitlerism and fascism by his activities in the premilitary during the training of Romanian and Jewish premilitary youth as well as during the roundup and internment of the Jews in the ghetto, contributing by these deeds to the realization of the political goals of fascism.

The acts of the accused János Botos also fall within the definition of war crimes stipulated in Paragraph *o* of Article 2 of the Law, since through the newspaper article he published he placed himself in the service of fascism, contributing to the realization of its political objectives and intentionally influencing Hungarian public opinion not to sympathize with the Jews interned in the ghetto.

The acts of Dr. Victor Capesius fall within the definition of war crimes stipulated in Paragraphs *g, h,* and *o* of Article 2 of the Law, since at Auschwitz he intentionally contributed as a perpetrator to the investigation of the Jews deported there for the discovery of valuables they still had with them, and then intentionally subjected these Jews in the Auschwitz camp to inhuman treatment, placing himself through these acts in the service of Hitlerism and thus contributing to the realization of its political objectives.

The acts of the accused András Lakatos and Kázmér Taar fall within the definition of war crimes stipulated in Paragraph *n* of Article 2 of the Law since they intentionally carried out the political and racial laws and orders in an excessive manner and at the same time made themselves accomplices to the war crimes stipulated in Paragraph *m* of Article 2 of the Law, since through their acts they helped in the internment of the Jews into the ghetto.

The acts of the accused Dr. Ernő Pirkler, Dr. Zoltán Rogozi Papp, Dr. József Forgács, Irén Ujvári, Irma Enyedi, Vilmos Horák, Ilona Báthori, Dr. Ferenc Henner, Ernő Jávor, Dr. János Zsigmond, Lieutenant Colonel László Kiss, Major László Komáromi, Jenő Csordácsics, Pál Farkas, Dr. Gábor Szentiványi, Tivadar Lohr, Lajos Cser, József Vadász, Erzsébet Fekete, István Kerényi, János Vida, Ádám Kerekes, and Mihály Kovács fall within the definition of complicity in war crimes stipulated in Paragraph *m* of Article 2 of the Law since, through their advice and aid either as officials or as denouncers, they intentionally contributed to the establishment of Jewish ghettos in Transylvania.

The acts of the accused Ferenc Lakatos, Dr. Béla Sámi, and Dr. Dezső Dénes fall within the definition of war crimes stipulated in Paragraph *n* of Article 2 of the Law since they intentionally carried out in an excessive manner the laws arising from the state of war and orders of a political and racial nature.

The acts of the accused Heinrich Smolka and Ferenc Hullmann fall within the definition of complicity in the war crimes stipulated in Paragraphs *m* and *n* of Article 2 of the Law since they intentionally contributed to the establishment of Jewish ghettos and intentionally carried out in an excessive manner orders of a political and racial nature.

The acts of the accused Albert Szabó, Dr. Ferenc Molnár, and Dr. Zsigmond Léhnár fall within the definition of war crimes stipulated in Paragraph *g* of Article 2 of the Law since in their capacity as physicians or ghetto supervisors they provided treatment that was inhumane from the sanitary and other points of view to the Jews interned in the ghettos.

Considering that the People's Tribunal passed sentence in accordance with these specifications, weighing them in terms of the seriousness of the acts of each accused, and passing the most severe [specified] sentences without increasing them further where the actual framework of the infractions was established as well as for ideal cumulations of infractions, namely both for cumulations of infractions of common law and for cumulations of both common-law and political infractions;

Considering that for the accused Péter Czeisberger and József Lázár, Paragraph *a,* Section 1 of Article 157 of the Penal Code was applied in view of the objective seriousness of the act specified as an infraction of common law, smaller infractions being considered as an objective mitigating circumstance, and lowering the penalty from hard labor for life to hard labor for a limited time, and considering that Articles 121 and 123 of the Penal Code were applied only with respect to complicity in the war crimes stipulated by Paragraph *m* of Article 2 of Law No. 312/1945;

Considering that Article 157 was also applied to the accused gendarme Kálmán Szentpáli, Dr. István Vincze, and Lieutenant Colonel Balla, with the objective extenuating circumstance arising from the lesser seriousness of the infractions committed by these accused;

Considering that for the accused Ioan Vancea and Zoltán Osváth the objective attenuating circumstance in the sense shown above was found only with respect to infractions of common law, and the article pertaining to complicity was applied only for the determination of the penalty of simple detention;

Considering that for the accused Mrs. József Medgyesi née Erzsébet Mutza and György Kugler (Füleki) the objective attenuating circumstance based on the lesser seriousness of the committed infraction applied only with regard to the infractions of common law, without applying to the crime stipulated in Paragraph *o* of Article 2 of the Law;

Considering that the same holds for the accused Mrs. János Kiss née Rozália Zeffer and Mária Fekete;

Considering that for the accused Gusztáv Sarkadi also, attenuating circumstances were found based on the lesser seriousness of the infraction;

Considering that the same holds for the accused Dr. Zsigmond Léhnár and Albert Szabó also;

Considering that for the accused Rozália Jancsó and László Petővári Petrik, the mitigating circumstances based on the lesser seriousness of the committed infractions were applied only to the war crime stipulated in Paragraph *h* of Article 2 of the Law;

Considering that for the accused Ioan Anghea, the mitigating circumstances relating to the lesser seriousness of the infraction were also only applied to the infraction stipulated by Paragraph *h* of Article 2 of the Law;

Considering that for the accused Dr. Ferenc Molnár also, mitigating circumstances based on the lesser seriousness of the infraction committed by him were found;

Considering that for the accused Kálmán Borbély mitigating circumstances were also found to apply only to complicity in the crime stipulated by Paragraph *h* of Article 2, based on the fact that the infraction he committed was less serious;

Considering that for the accused József Lax and Sándor Farmati also, mitigating circumstances based on the consideration of the lesser seriousness of the acts committed by them were found, and for the accused Irma Duha mitigating circumstances were applied for the same reason but only with respect to the crime stipulated in Paragraph *h* of Article 2 of the Law;

Noting also the provisions of Section 1 of Article 25 of the Penal Code and Section 2 of Article 25 as well as Section 2 of Article 58 of the same law;

Noting also the provisions of Paragraph I, Section 2 of Article 4 of the Penal Procedure;

Noting also the provisions of Article 14 of Law No. 312/1945;

For these reasons

IT IS DECIDED IN THE NAME OF THE LAW

And we find the accused:

1. Dr. LÁSZLÓ GYAPAI, 44 years old, Hungarian citizen (formerly known by the family name of Leier), born in Győr, former mayor of the municipality of Nagyvárad (married to Mária Mayer), last residing at the Matten camp in Bavaria, current whereabouts unknown;
2. Dr. JÁNOS NADÁNYI, adult, Hungarian citizen, former deputy prefect of Bihar County, last residing in Napraforgó Street, Budapest, Hungary, current whereabouts unknown;
3. Dr. IMRE NÉMETH, adult, Hungarian citizen, former police commissioner at the Royal Hungarian Police at Nagyvárad, last residing at 12 Nádor Street, Budapest, current whereabouts unknown;
4. LAJOS CSER, 55 years old, Romanian citizen, married with two children, private office worker *(funcţionar particular)*, residing at 7 Gyulai Pál Street, Nagyvárad, under arrest;
5. ÁGOSTON FÉLEGYHÁZI MEDGYESI, Hungarian citizen, former gendarmerie lieutenant, last residing in Budapest, current whereabouts unknown;

România
Tribunalul Poporului Cluj
Completul de judecată
Dos. Nr. 8/1946

856

HOTĂRÂRE Nr. 8/1946
Proces verbal
Ședința publică dela 31 Mai 1946.

TRIBUNALUL POPORULUI,
Pentru motivele ce se vor vedea

ÎN NUMELE LEGII

Hotărește:

solară pe acuzații:

1./ Dr GYAPAY LADISLAU, de 44 ani, cetățean maghiar /anterior purtând numele de familie LEIER/ născ. în Győr, fost primar al Municipiului Oradea /căsătorit Mayer Maria/ ultimul domiciliu cunoscut în lagărul Matten Bavaria, azi cu domiciliu necunoscut.

2./ vitéz Dr. NADÁNYI IOAN major, cetățean maghiar, fost subprefect al județului Bihor, cu ultimul domiciliu în Budapesta str Napraforgó, Ungaria, azi cu domiciliul în loc necunoscut.

3./ Dr. NÉMETH ERIC, major, cetățean maghiar, fost comisar de poliție la poliția regală maghiară Oradea, cu ultimul domiciliu în Budapesta str Nador Nr.12 azi cu domiciliul în loc necunoscut.

4./ vitéz CSER LUDOVIC, de 55 ani, cetățean român, căsătorit cu 2 copii, funcționar particular, domiciliat în Oradea str Gyulai Pál Nr.7, aflat în stare de arest.

5./ FÉLEGYHÁZI HEGYESI ÁGOSTON, cetățean maghiar, fost locotenent de jandarmi, cu ultimul domiciliu în Budapesta, azi cu domiciliu în loc necunoscut.

6./ Dr. PETRY IULIU, cetățean român, fost notar public și locotenent de jandarmi în rezervă, cu ultimul domiciliu în Oradea azi cu domiciliul în loc necunoscut.

7./ FRÁTER IOAN, cetățean maghiar, fost locotenent de jandarmi cu ultimul domiciliu cunoscut în Berettyó-Újfalu - Ungaria, azi cu domiciliul în loc necunoscut.

8./ Dr. REKTOR BÉLA, major, cetățean maghiar, fost locotenent de jandarmi, cu ultimul domiciliu cunoscut în Nyíregyháza, Ungaria, azi cu domiciliul în loc necunoscut.

9./ GARAI ȘTEFAN, major, cetățean maghiar, fost căpitan de jandarmi, cu ultimul domiciliu în Ungaria, azi domiciliat în loc necunoscut.

10./ D. BOXKLAY E... major, cetățean maghiar, fost locotenent de jandarmi, cu ultimul domiciliu cunoscut în Ungaria, azi cu domiciliul în loc necunoscut.

11./ SZIKLAY FRANCISC, major, cetățean maghiar, plotonier major de jandarmi, fost agent jandarm la Budapesta, azi cu domiciliul în loc necunoscut.

12./ MENYHEI ANDREI, major, cetățean maghiar, plotonier major fost agent de jandarmi la Budapesta, azi cu domiciliul în loc necunoscut.

6. Dr. GYULA PETRI, Romanian citizen, former public notary and gendarmerie lieutenant, last residing in Nagyvárad, current whereabouts unknown;
7. JÁNOS FRATER, Hungarian citizen, former gendarmerie lieutenant, last known residence at Berettyóujfalu in Hungary, current whereabouts unknown;
8. Dr. BÉLA REKTOR, adult, Hungarian citizen, former gendarmerie lieutenant, last known residence in Nyíregyháza, current whereabouts unknown;
9. ISTVÁN GARAI, adult, Hungarian citizen, former gendarmerie captain, last residing in Hungary, current whereabouts unknown;
10. Dr. ENDRE BODOLAI, adult, Hungarian citizen, former gendarmerie lieutenant, last known residence in Hungary, current whereabouts unknown;
11. FERENC SZIKLAI, adult, Hungarian citizen, gendarmerie quartermaster, former gendarmerie agent in Budapest, current whereabouts unknown;
12. ANDRÁS MEDGYESI, adult, Hungarian citizen, Quartermaster and former gendarmerie agent in Budapest, current whereabouts unknown;
13. DEZSŐ BÜSS, adult, Hungarian citizen, gendarmerie agent with the Hungarian Railways, current whereabouts unknown;
14. GYULA ŐRI, adult, Hungarian citizen, Quartermaster, agent with the Hungarian Railways, current whereabouts unknown;
15. GYÖRGY FEKETE, adult, Hungarian citizen, Quartermaster in the section of special agents in Debrecen, current whereabouts unknown;
16. SÁNDOR ILONKA, adult, Hungarian citizen, Quartermaster in the section of special agents in Debrecen, current whereabouts unknown;
17. JÁNOS TEVELI, adult, Hungarian citizen, Quartermaster in the section of special agents in Dunántul (Transdanubia), current whereabouts unknown;
18. ISTVÁN SZŐLLŐSI, adult, Hungarian citizen, Quartermaster in the section of special agents in Dunántul, current whereabouts unknown;
19. GÉZA SZABADOS, adult, Hungarian citizen, Quartermaster in the section of special agents in Dunántul, current whereabouts unknown;
20. JÁNOS TÓTH, adult, Hungarian citizen, Quartermaster in the section of special agents in Dunántul, current whereabouts unknown;
21. MIHÁLY JUHÁSZ, adult, Hungarian citizen, Quartermaster in the battalion of the Gendarmerie School of Nagyvárad, current whereabouts unknown;
22. SÁNDOR POSGAI, adult, Hungarian citizen, Quartermaster in the

battalion of the Gendarmerie School of Nagyvárad, current whereabouts unknown;
23. GÁBOR KERESZTESI, adult, Hungarian citizen, Quartermaster in the battalion of the Gendarmerie School of Nagyvárad, current whereabouts unknown;
24. ISTVÁN FELFÖLDI, adult, Hungarian citizen, Quartermaster in the battalion of the Gendarmerie School of Nagyvárad, current whereabouts unknown;
25. IMRE GARAI, adult, Hungarian citizen, Quartermaster in the battalion of the Gendarmerie School of Nagyvárad, current whereabouts unknown;
26. SÁNDOR FEHÉR, adult, Hungarian citizen, Quartermaster in the battalion of the Gendarmerie School of Nagyvárad, current whereabouts unknown;
27. JÓZSEF HORVÁTH, adult, Hungarian citizen, Quartermaster in the battalion of the Gendarmerie School of Nagyvárad, current whereabouts unknown;
28. MIHÁLY SZABÓ, adult, Hungarian citizen, from the battalion of the Gendarmerie School of Nagyvárad with the rank of Quartermaster, originally from Szentes, Hungary, current whereabouts unknown;
29. MEGYERI, gendarme, adult, Hungarian citizen, from the battalion of the Gendarmerie School of Nagyvárad, current whereabouts unknown;
30. BUDAI, gendarme, Hungarian citizen, from the battalion of the Gendarmerie School of Nagyvárad, current whereabouts unknown;
31. Dr. MIKLÓS TOPERCZEL, adult, Hungarian citizen, police commissioner, former chief of the political section of the Hungarian State Police in Nagyvárad, current whereabouts unknown;
32. Mrs. JÓZSEF MEDGYESI née ERZSÉBET MUTZA, Romanian citizen, 35 years old, married, one child, midwife by profession, residing in Margitta, under arrest;
33. Mrs. JÁNOS KISS (widow) née ROZÁLIA ZEFFER, Romanian citizen, adult, midwife by profession, residing in Érmihályfalva, Bihar County, under arrest;
34. JÓZSEF VADÁSZ, 45 years old, Romanian citizen, electrician, residing in Nagyvárad, married with two children, under arrest;
35. Dr. LÁSZLÓ CSÓKA, Hungarian citizen, 48 years old, former mayor of the municipality of Szatmárnémeti, married with two children, under arrest;
36. Dr. ERNŐ PIRKLER, Romanian citizen, 65 years old, married with two children, secretary of the municipality of Szatmárnémeti, residing in Szatmárnémeti, under arrest;

JUDGMENT OF THE PEOPLE'S TRIBUNAL 205

37. Dr. ZOLTÁN ROGOZI PAPP, adult, Romanian citizen, former deputy mayor of the municipality of Szatmárnémeti, last residing in Szatmárnémeti, current whereabouts unknown;
38. Dr. BÉLA SÁRKÖZI, adult, Hungarian citizen, police officer, chief of the Alien Control Office in the former Royal Hungarian Police in Szatmárnémeti, current whereabouts unknown;
39. KÁROLY CSEGEZI, adult, Hungarian citizen, former police inspector in the Royal Hungarian Police of Szatmárnémeti, current whereabouts unknown;
40. N. DEMÉNYI, adult, Hungarian citizen, former Gendarmerie Lieutenant Colonel and commander of the legion of gendarmes in Szatmárnémeti, current whereabouts unknown;
41. BARNABÁS ENDRŐDI, Hungarian citizen, former prefect of Szatmár County and the municipality of Szatmárnémeti, former Lieutenant Colonel in the Hungarian army, last residing in Hungary, current whereabouts unknown;
42. ENDRE BOÉR, adult, Hungarian citizen, former deputy prefect of Szatmár County, current whereabouts unknown;
43. ERZSÉBET FEKETE, 43 years old, residing in Szatmárnémeti, Romanian citizen, married with no children, under arrest;
44. IOAN VANCEA, adult, married with two children, former police agent in the Royal Hungarian Police of Szatmárnémeti, under arrest;
45. ISTVÁN KERÉNYI, adult, Romanian citizen, former porter residing in Szatmárnémeti, current whereabouts unknown;
46. Dr. LÁSZLÓ VÁSÁRHELYI, adult, Hungarian citizen, former mayor of the municipality of Kolozsvár, last residing in Budapest, current whereabouts unknown;
47. Dr. LÁSZLÓ (FERENC) URBÁN, Hungarian citizen, former police officer in the Royal Hungarian Police of Kolozsvár, approximately 38 years old, originally from Komárom, last residing in Miskolc, current whereabouts unknown;
48. TIBOR PAKSI-KISS, Hungarian citizen, commander of Gendarmerie District IX of Kolozsvár, Gendarmerie Colonel in the Royal Hungarian Gendarmerie, last residing in Budapest, current whereabouts unknown;
49. Dr. JÓZSEF FORGÁCS, Hungarian citizen, former chief notary of Kolozs County, last residing in Kolozsvár, current whereabouts unknown;
50. Dr. GÉZA PAPP, Hungarian citizen, police commissioner in the Royal Hungarian Police at Kolozsvár, former member of the ghetto commission, last residing in Kolozsvár, current whereabouts unknown;

51. KÁZMÉR TAAR, Romanian citizen, 31 years old, former functionary in the mayor's office in the municipality of Kolozsvár, residing at 6 Memorandului Street, Kolozsvár, unmarried, without property, under arrest;
52. Dr. LAJOS VARGA, Romanian citizen, former prefect of the municipality of Kolozsvár, last residing in Kolozsvár, current whereabouts unknown;
53. SÁMUEL CSÁSZÁR, Hungarian citizen, former finance administrator in the Finance Administration of Kolozsvár, last residing in Budapest, current whereabouts unknown;
54. ZOLTÁN HORKAI, Hungarian citizen, former financial guard officer in the Finance Administration of Kolozs County, last residing in Budapest at 6 Fiume Street, current whereabouts unknown;
55. Dr. JÓZSEF SZÉKELY, Hungarian citizen, former mayor of the urban community of Bánffyhunyad, last residing in Bánffyhunyad, current whereabouts unknown;
56. FERENC MENYHÉRT, Hungarian citizen, former police officer in the Royal Hungarian State Police of Bánffyhunyad holding the rank of inspector, last residing in Bánffyhunyad, current whereabouts unknown;
57. Dr. JÓZSEF OROSZ, Hungarian citizen, former chief of the Royal Hungarian Police of Bánffyhunyad, last residing in Budapest, current whereabouts unknown;
58. ANDRÁS SZENTKUTI, Hungarian citizen, former secret agent in the Royal Hungarian State Police of Bánffyhunyad, last residing in Budapest, current whereabouts unknown;
59. Dr. PÁL BOLDIZSÁR, Hungarian citizen, former assistant notary (supply counselor) in the mayor's office in Bánffyhunyad, last residing in Budapest, current whereabouts unknown;
60. ANDRÁS LAKATOS, Hungarian citizen, former cashier functionary in the Royal Hungarian Police in Bánffyhunyad, last residing in Bánffyhunyad, current whereabouts unknown;
61. SÁNDOR OJTÓZI, Hungarian citizen, former commissioner in the Royal Hungarian Police in Bánffyhunyad, last residing in Bánffyhunyad, current whereabouts unknown;
62. Dr. VICTOR CAPESIUS, Romanian citizen, originally from Sighişoara, former representative of the I.G. Farbenindustrie, pharmacist by profession, last residing in Sighişoara, current whereabouts unknown;
63. JÁNOS BOTOS, Romanian citizen, 50 years old, journalist, former secretary of the Kolozsvár branch of the *Erdélyi párt* (Transylvanian

Party), residing in the village of Bărghiş, Târnava Mare County, under arrest;
64. IRÉN UJVÁRI, Romanian citizen, 33 years old, housewife, formerly residing at 3 March 6 Street in Kolozsvár, current whereabouts unknown;
65. IRMA ENYEDI, Romanian citizen, 40 years old, housewife, residing at 15 Árpád Street, Kolozsvár, under arrest;
66. VILMOS HORÁK, Romanian citizen, 40 years old, worker, married with no children, residing at 28 Iaşilor Street, Kolozsvár, under arrest;
67. ILONA BÁTHORI, Romanian citizen, 46 years old, housewife, residing at 16 Moldovei Street, Kolozsvár, under arrest;
68. ANDOR JOÓS, Hungarian citizen, former prefect of Maros County during the Sztójay government, current whereabouts unknown;
69. Dr. ZSIGMOND MARTON, Hungarian citizen, former deputy prefect of Maros County, current whereabouts unknown;
70. Dr. FERENC MÁJAY, Hungarian citizen, former mayor of the city of Marosvásárhely, 52 years old, Unitarian, born in Gălăţeni, Maros County, residing at 2 King Carol I Street in Marosvásárhely, married, under arrest;
71. Dr. FERENC HENNER, Hungarian citizen, former chief notary of the city of Marosvásárhely, current whereabouts unknown;
72. Dr. ERNŐ JÁVOR, Hungarian citizen, former notary in the prefect's office, Maros County, current whereabouts unknown;
73. Colonel JÁNOS PAPP, Hungarian citizen, former commander of the inspectorate of gendarmes for the four Székely counties, current whereabouts unknown;
74. Colonel JÁNOS ZALANTAI, Hungarian citizen, former commander of the Maros legion of gendarmes, current whereabouts unknown;
75. Dr. GÉZA BEDŐ, Hungarian citizen, former police officer in the Marosvásárhely police, current whereabouts unknown;
76. Colonel GÉZA KÖRMENDI, Hungarian citizen, former commander of the military administration in Marosvásárhely during the Sztójay government, current whereabouts unknown;
77. ISTVÁN KOZMA, Army Corps general, Hungarian citizen, former commander of the Marosvásárhely garrison, current whereabouts unknown;
78. Major SCHRÖDER, German citizen, former chief of the Gestapo section in Marosvásárhely during the occupation of Hungary by German troops, current whereabouts unknown;
79. Gendarmerie Captain KONYA, associated with the gendarmerie investigative unit, Hungarian citizen, current whereabouts unknown;

80. Gendarmerie Captain PINTÉR, associated with the gendarmerie investigative unit, Hungarian citizen, current whereabouts unknown;
81. FERENC SALLÓS, Quartermaster in the gendarmerie investigative unit, Hungarian citizen, current whereabouts unknown;
82. JÓZSEF LAX, Romanian citizen, 41 years old, Jewish, jeweler, residing in Marosvásárhely, under arrest;
83. DEZSŐ GÁLFY, Hungarian citizen, former prefect of Udvarhely County during the Sztójay government, current whereabouts unknown;
84. Dr. ISTVÁN BONDA, Hungarian citizen, former prefect of Udvarhely County, current whereabouts unknown;
85. Dr. FERENC FILÓ, Hungarian citizen, former mayor of Udvarhely, current whereabouts unknown;
86. Dr. JÁNOS ZSIGMOND, Hungarian citizen, former police chief of Udvarhely, current whereabouts unknown;
87. Lieutenant Colonel LÁSZLÓ KISS, Hungarian citizen, former commander of the Udvarhely legion of gendarmes, current whereabouts unknown;
88. Dr. IMRE SCHMIDT, 61 years old, Romanian citizen, former mayor of Szászrégen, Maros County, residing in Szászregen at 7 Vasile Alexandri Street, Roman Catholic, under arrest;
89. Major LÁSZLÓ KOMÁROMI, Hungarian citizen, former commander of the military administration of the city of Szászrégen, current whereabouts unknown;
90. JÁNOS DUDÁS, Hungarian citizen, former police chief of Szászrégen, current whereabouts unknown;
91. G. KÁLMÁN SZENTPÁLI, gendarmerie lieutenant, Hungarian citizen, former commander of the section of gendarmes, current whereabouts unknown;
92. JENŐ CSORDÁCSICS, Hungarian citizen, former counselor in the mayor's office of Szászrégen, current whereabouts unknown;
93. GYÖRGY KUGLER (FÜLEKI), 42 years old, Romanian citizen, Roman Catholic, born in Marosvécs, Maros County, residing in the village of I. G. Duca, Maros County, private functionary, under arrest;
94. PÁL BÁNYAI, major in the special investigative unit of the gendarmerie, Hungarian citizen, current whereabouts unknown;
95. BALÁZS BIRÓ, Quartermaster in the special investigative unit of the gendarmerie, Hungarian citizen, current whereabouts unknown;
96. ANDRÁS FEHÉR, first sergeant in the special investigative unit of the gendarmerie, Hungarian citizen, current whereabouts unknown;

JUDGMENT OF THE PEOPLE'S TRIBUNAL

97. ISTVÁN GŐSI, first sergeant in the special investigative unit of the gendarmerie, Hungarian citizen, current whereabouts unknown;
98. IRMA LOVAS, 35 years old, Romanian citizen, born in Szászrégen, midwife by profession, last residing in Szászrégen at 25 Proletarilor Street, current whereabouts unknown;
99. Dr. MÁTYÁS TÓTH, Hungarian citizen, former mayor of Gyergyószentmiklós, Csík County, current whereabouts unknown;
100. Dr. GÉZA POLÁNKAI, Hungarian citizen, former deputy police chief in Gyergyószentmiklós police, current whereabouts unknown;
101. BÉLA FERENCZI, Hungarian citizen, former detective in the Gyergyószentmiklós police, current whereabouts unknown;
102. ERNŐ GAÁLI, Hungarian citizen, former prefect of Csík County during the Sztójay government, current whereabouts unknown;
103. Dr. JÓZSEF ÁBRAHÁM, Hungarian citizen, former deputy prefect of Csík County, current whereabouts unknown;
104. GERŐ SZÁSZ, Hungarian citizen, former mayor of Csíkszereda, current whereabouts unknown;
105. PÁL FARKAS, Hungarian citizen, former police chief of Csíkszereda, current whereabouts unknown;
106. Dr. GÁBOR SZENTIVÁNYI, 58 years old, Romanian citizen, born in Sepsiszentgyörgy, former prefect of Háromszék, under arrest;
107. Dr. ANDOR BARABÁS, Hungarian citizen, former deputy prefect of Háromszék County, current whereabouts unknown;
108. ANDRÁS VIRÁNYI, Hungarian citizen, former mayor of Sepsiszentgyörgy, current whereabouts unknown;
109. Dr. ISTVÁN VINCZE, Hungarian citizen, former police chief of Sepsiszentgyörgy, current whereabouts unknown;
110. Lieutenant Colonel BALLA, former commander of the Háromszék legion of gendarmes, current whereabouts unknown;
111. TIVADAR LOHR, colonel, former commander of the Csík legion of gendarmes, current whereabouts unknown;
112. Dr. JÁNOS SCHILLING, 63 years of age, Romanian citizen, landlord, born and residing in the village of Naszoly, Szamos County, under arrest;
113. Dr. JENŐ VERESS, Hungarian citizen, former mayor of Dés, last residing in Dés, current whereabouts unknown;
114. Dr. ZSIGMOND LÉHNÁR, 56 years old, Romanian citizen, physician born and residing in Dés at 3 King Ferdinand Street, under arrest;

115. Dr. GYULA SÁROSI, Hungarian citizen, former police chief of Dés, last residing in Dés, current whereabouts unknown;
116. ISTVÁN TAKÁCS, Hungarian citizen, former policeman in the Dés police, last residing in Dés, current whereabouts unknown;
117. JÁNOS SOMORLYAI, Hungarian citizen, former security agent in the Dés police, last residing in Dés, current whereabouts unknown;
118. JÁNOS KASSAY, Hungarian citizen, former security agent in the Dés police, last residing in Dés, current whereabouts unknown;
119. ALBERT GARAMVÖLGYI, Hungarian citizen, former security agent in the Dés police, last residing in Dés, current whereabouts unknown;
120. MIKLÓS DÉSAKNAI, Hungarian citizen, former police security agent in Dés, last residing in Dés, current whereabouts unknown;
121. JÓZSEF GECSE, 35 years old, Romanian citizen, potter, born and residing in Dés at 9 Cărăușilor Street, under arrest;
122. MÁRIA FEKETE, 25 years old, Romanian citizen, housewife, born in Budapest, residing at 11 Caragiale Street in Dés, under arrest;
123. JÓZSEF LAKADÁR, Romanian citizen, formerly workman with the Romanian Railways in Dés, current whereabouts unknown;
124. SÁNDOR OLÁH, 21 years old, Romanian citizen, tailor, born in Pusztakamarás, residing in Kolozsvár at 4 Bem Street, under arrest;
125. ROZÁLIA JANCSÓ, 51 years old, Romanian citizen, midwife by profession, born in the village of Uri, Szamos County, residing in Retteg, Szamos County, under arrest;
126. PÁL ANTALFFY, Gendarmerie major, Hungarian citizen, active officer, former commander of the Dés legion of gendarmes, current whereabouts unknown;
127. ERNŐ BERECKI, Hungarian citizen, former police chief of Szamosujvár, last residing in Szamosujvár, Szamos County, current whereabouts unknown;
128. ANDRÁS IVÁNYI, Hungarian citizen, former police chief of Szamosujvár, current whereabouts unknown;
129. LAJOS TAMÁSI, Hungarian citizen, former mayor of Szamosujvár, last residing in Szamosujvár, current whereabouts unknown;
130. FERENC LAKATOS, 48 years old, Romanian citizen, notary by profession, born and residing in Retteg, Szamos County, under arrest;
131. SÁNDOR VAJAI, Romanian citizen, former chief notary of Nagybánya, born and residing in Nagybánya, current whereabouts unknown;
132. Dr. JENŐ NAGY, Hungarian citizen, former police chief of Nagybánya, current whereabouts unknown;

JUDGMENT OF THE PEOPLE'S TRIBUNAL

133. KÁROLY BALOGH, Romanian citizen, former official at the Phönix factory in Nagybánya, last residing in Nagybánya, current whereabouts unknown;
134. JÓZSEF HARACSEK, Romanian citizen, former president of the Baross Association of Nagybánya, last residing in Nagybánya, current whereabouts unknown;
135. LÁSZLÓ BERENTES, captain, Hungarian citizen, former commander in charge of the Phönix factory in Nagybánya, current whereabouts unknown;
136. JÓZSEF ORGOVÁNYI, 34 years old, Hungarian citizen, detective by profession, born in Hungary, under arrest;
137. IMRE VAJAI, Romanian citizen, former detective in the Nagybánya police, last residing in Nagybánya, current whereabouts unknown;
138. ISTVÁN BERTALAN, Hungarian citizen, former detective in the Nagybánya police, last residing in Nagybánya, current whereabouts unknown;
139. PÉTER CZEISBERGER, 41 years old, Romanian citizen, shoemaker, born in Kolozsvár, residing in Nagybánya, under arrest;
140. ZOLTÁN OSVÁTH, 45 years old, Romanian citizen, mason, born in Kolozsvár, residing in Nagybánya at 42 Malinovsky Street, under arrest;
141. LAJOS ORMOS, Romanian citizen, driver, last residing in Nagyvárad at the electric power station, current whereabouts unknown;
142. Dr. LÁSZLÓ SZLÁVI, Hungarian citizen, former prefect of Szilágy County, last residing in Zilah, current whereabouts unknown;
143. Dr. ANDRÁS GAZDA, Romanian citizen, former deputy prefect of Szilágy County, last residing in Zilah, current whereabouts unknown;
144. Dr. JÁNOS SRÉTER, Hungarian citizen, former mayor of Zilah, last residing in Zilah, current whereabouts unknown;
145. Dr. JÓZSEF UDVARI, Romanian citizen, former mayor of Szilágysomlyó, last residing in Szilágysomlyó, current whereabouts unknown;
146. FERENC ELEKES, Hungarian citizen, former police chief of Zilah, residing in Zilah, current whereabouts unknown;
147. GYÖRGY MARISKA, lieutenant colonel, Hungarian citizen, active gendarmerie officer, former commander of the Szilágy legion of gendarmes, current whereabouts unknown;
148. ISTVÁN PETHES, Hungarian citizen, former police chief of Szilágysomlyó, last residing in Szilágysomlyó, current whereabouts unknown;

149. Dr. SÁNDOR HORVÁTH, gendarmerie captain, active officer, former commander of the Szilágysomlyó legion of gendarmes, current whereabouts unknown;
150. Dr. LÁSZLÓ KRASZNAI, Hungarian citizen, former chief district administrator of the district of Szilágysomlyó, last residing in Szilágysomlyó, current whereabouts unknown;
151. JÓZSEF LÁZÁR, 46 years old, Romanian citizen, librarian, born and residing in Szilágysomlyó at 7–8 G. Pop de Băseşti Street, under arrest;
152. MIKLÓS SÁRKÖZI, quartermaster, Hungarian citizen, former chief of the unit of gendarmes in Zsibó, Szilágy County, last residing in Zsibó, current whereabouts unknown;
153. JÁNOS HORVÁTH, quartermaster, Hungarian citizen, former chief of the unit of gendarmes in Szilágynagyfalu, Szilágy County, last residing in Szilágynagyfalu, current whereabouts unknown;
154. JÁNOS VIDA, 55 years of age, government official, born and residing in Szilágysomlyó at 13 Cuza Vodă Street, married with five children, under arrest;
155. ÁDÁM KEREKES, Romanian citizen, last residing in Szilágysomlyó, former premilitary, current whereabouts unknown;
156. MIHÁLY KOVÁCS, 52 years old, retired, Romanian citizen, born in the village of Szilágyborzos, Szilágy County, residing in Szilágysomlyó, under arrest;
157. SÁNDOR FARMATI, 19 years old, Romanian citizen, businessman, born and residing in Szilágysomlyó, under arrest;
158. IOAN ANGHEA, 34 years old, radiophone operator, born in the village of Magyarcséke, Bihar County, residing in Szilágysomlyó at 15 Alba-Iulia Street, under arrest;
159. LÁSZLÓ PETŐVÁRI PETRIK, 81 years old, Czechoslovak citizen, ploughman, former gendarmerie first sergeant, born in Nagysáró, Bars County, residing in Kraszna, under arrest;
160. ALBERT SZABÓ, 48 years old, government official, born in Marosvásárhely, residing in Szilágysomlyó at 8 Eminescu Street, under arrest;
161. IRÉN DUHA, 26 years old, housewife, former government official, born and residing in Szilágysomlyó, under arrest;
162. Dr. FERENC MOLNÁR, 36 years old, Romanian citizen, physician, born in Szamosardó, Szilágy County, residing in Szilágycseh, under arrest;
163. Dr. BÉLA SÁMI, 58 years old, Romanian citizen, retired, born in Szilagybogos, Szilágy County, residing in Zilah at 24 Crişana Street, under arrest;

JUDGMENT OF THE PEOPLE'S TRIBUNAL

164. Dr. DEZSŐ DÉNES, 40 years of age, secretary of the mayor's office in Zilah, born in Szilágyfőkeresztur, Szilágy County, residing in Zilah, under arrest;
165. Dr. LÁSZLÓ ILLINYI, Hungarian citizen, former prefect of Máramaros County, last residing in Máramarossziget, current whereabouts unknown;
166. Dr. SÁNDOR GYULAFALVI REDNIK, Romanian citizen, former mayor of Máramarossziget, last residing in Máramarossziget, current whereabouts unknown;
167. FERENC HULLMANN, 53 years old, residing in Máramarossziget at 36 Averescu Street, Romanian citizen, public official, under arrest;
168. Dr. LAJOS TÓTH, Hungarian citizen, former police chief of Máramarossziget, last residing in Máramarossziget, current whereabouts unknown;
169. JÁNOS FEHÉR, Hungarian citizen, former commissioner in the Máramarossziget police, current whereabouts unknown;
170. Colonel MIKLÓS SÁRVÁRY, Hungarian citizen, former commander of the fourth gendarmerie district in Máramarossziget, current whereabouts unknown;
171. FLOREA TASCAN, Romanian, Soviet citizen, former gendarme with the gendarmerie post at Barcánfalva, Máramaros County, originally from the village of Apsa de Mijloc and son of the village midwife, current whereabouts unknown;
172. JÁNOS BIRÓ, Hungarian citizen, former gendarme at the gendarmerie post at Barcánfalva, Máramaros County, current whereabouts unknown;
173. GYÖRGY VARGA, Hungarian citizen, former gendarme at the gendarmerie post at Barcánfalva, Máramaros County, current whereabouts unknown;
174. GUSZTÁV SARKADI, 57 years old, barber, Romanian citizen, born and residing in Máramarossziget, under arrest;
175. ISTVÁN BEDE, Hungarian citizen, former soldier at the Máramarossziget garrison, current whereabouts unknown;
176. Dr. LÁSZLÓ SZAPLONCZAI, Hungarian citizen, former prefect of Máramaros County, formerly residing in Máramarossziget, current whereabouts unknown;
177. KÁLMÁN BORBÉLY, 63 years old, Romanian citizen, landowner, former prefect, born in Szentgothárd, Szamos County, residing in Kolozsvár at 4 Moise Nicoara Street, under arrest;
178. LÁSZLÓ SMOLENSZKI, Hungarian citizen, former deputy prefect of Naszód County, formerly residing in Beszterce, current whereabouts unknown;

179. Dr. NORBERT KUALES, Romanian citizen, lawyer, former mayor of Beszterce, last residing in Beszterce, current whereabouts unknown;
180. Dr. MIKLÓS DEBRECZENI, Hungarian citizen, former police chief of Beszterce, last residing in Beszterce, current whereabouts unknown;
181. HEINRICH SMOLKA, 58 years old, Romanian citizen, businessman, born in Szászrégen, residing in Beszterce at 10 King Ferdinand Street, under arrest;
182. GUSZTÁV ORENDI, Romanian citizen, businessman, originally from Beszterce, last residing in Beszterce, current whereabouts unknown;
183. ERNŐ PÁSZTAI, lieutenant colonel, Hungarian citizen, gendarmerie officer and former commander of the Beszterce legion of gendarmes, current whereabouts unknown;
184. MIKLÓS JAKAB, lieutenant colonel, Hungarian citizen, active officer, former chief of the counterintelligence agency in Beszterce, last residing in Beszterce, current whereabouts unknown;
185. KÁROLY RAJNAY (REINER), reserve brigadier general, 63 years old, former military commander of Nagyvárad and prefect of the city of Nagyvárad and Bihar County, Hungarian citizen, under arrest;

guilty of the disaster of the country brought about by the war crimes stipulated in Article 2 of Law No. 312/1945 relating to the pursuit and apprehension of those guilty of the disaster of the country and of war crimes, as published in the *Monitorul Oficial* (Official Gazette), No. 94, 24 April 1945, as follows:

The accused Dr. László Gyapai, János Nadányi, László Csóka, Endre Boér, Dr. László Vásárhelyi, Dr. József Székely, Dr. Zsigmond Marton, Dr. Ferenc Májay, Colonel Géza Körmendi, General István Kozma, Dezső Gálfy, Dr. István Bonda, Dr. Ferenc Filó, Dr. Imre Schmidt, Dr. Mátyás Tóth, Ernő Gaáli, Dr. József Ábrahám, Gerő Szász, Dr. Andor Barabás, András Virányi, Dr. Jenő Veress, Lajos Tamási, Dr. András Gazda, Dr. János Sréter, Dr. József Udvari, Dr. Sándor Gyulafalvi Rednik, László Smolenszki, and Norbert Kuales are found guilty of the crimes stipulated in Paragraphs *m* and *o* of Law No. 312/1945;

The accused Major N. Schröder is found guilty of the crime stipulated in Paragraph *f* of Article 2 of Law No. 312/1945;

The accused Dr. János Schilling is found guilty of the crimes stipulated in Paragraphs *m, n,* and *o* of Article 2 of Law No. 312/1945;

The accused Dr. Lajos Varga, Barnabás Endrődi, Dr. László Szlávi, Dr. László Illinyi, Dr. László Szaplonczai, Kálmán Borbély, Károly Rajnay

(Reiner), and Andor Joós are found guilty of complicity in the crimes stipulated in Paragraph *h* of Article 2 and of perpetrating the crime stipulated in Paragraph *o* of Article 2 of Law No. 312/1945;

The accused Gendarmerie Major Pál Antalffy, Péter Czeisberger, Zoltán Osváth, Lajos Ormos, Ioan Anghea, and József Lázár are found guilty of the crimes stipulated in Paragraphs *h* and *o* of Article 2 of the Law and for complicity in the crimes stipulated in Paragraph *m* of Article 2 of the Law; the accused Ioan Vancea is also found guilty of the same crimes.

The accused N. Deményi, Dr. László Urbán, Tibor Paksi-Kiss, Dr. Géza Papp, Ferenc Menyhért, Dr. József Orosz, András Szentkuti, Dr. Pál Boldizsár, Dr. Sándor Ojtózi, Colonel Dr. János Papp, Colonel János Zalantai, Dr. Géza Bedő, Gendarmerie Captain Konya, First Sergeant Ferenc Sallós, János Dudás, Gendarmerie Lieutenant Kálmán Szentpáli, György Kugler (Füleki), Quartermaster Bányai, First Sergeant Balázs Biró, First Sergeant András Fehér, István Gősi, Irma Lovas, Dr. Géza Polánkai, Dr. Imre Németh, Ágoston Félegyházi Medgyesi, Dr. Gyula Petri, János Frater, Dr. Béla Rektor, István Garai, Dr. Endre Bodolai, Ferenc Sziklai, András Medgyesi, Dezső Büss, Gyula Őri, György Fekete, Sándor Ilonka, János Teveli, István Szőllősi, Géza Szabados, János Tóth, Mihály Juhász, Sándor Posgai, Gábor Kereszresi, István Felföldi, Imre Garai, Sándor Fehér, József Horváth, Mihály Szabó, the gendarme Megyeri, the gendarme Budai, Dr. Miklós Toperczel, Mrs. József Medgyesi née Erzsébet Mutza, Mrs. János Kiss née Rozália Zeffer, Dr. Béla Sárközi, Károly Csegezi, Béla Ferenczi, Dr. István Vincze, Lieutenant Colonel Balla, Dr. Gyula Sárosi, István Takács, János Somorlyai, János Kassay, Albert Garamvölgyi, Miklós Désaknai, József Gecse, Mária Fekete, József Lakadár, Rozália Jancsó, Ernő Berecki, András Iványi, Dr. Jenő Nagy, Károly Balogh, József Orgoványi, Imre Vajai, István Bertalan, Ferenc Elekes, Lieutenant Colonel György Mariska, István Pethes, Dr. Sándor Horváth, Dr. László Krasznai, Quartermaster Miklós Sárközi, Quartermaster János Horváth, László Petővári Petrik, Irén Duha, Dr. Lajos Tóth, János Fehér, Colonel Miklós Sárváry, Florea Tascan, János Biró, György Varga, Dr. Miklós Debreczeni, Gusztáv Orendi, Lieutenant Ernő Pásztai, and Lieutenant Colonel Miklós Jakab are found guilty of the crimes stipulated in Paragraphs *h* and *o* of Article 2 of Law No. 312/1945.

The accused Captain László Berentes is found guilty of instigation to the war crime stipulated in Paragraph *h* of Article 2 of Law No. 312/1945.

The accused István Bede is found guilty of the crime stipulated in Paragraph *e* of Article 2 of Law No. 312/1945, and the accused Gusztáv Sarkadi of instigation to this crime.

The accused József Lax and Sándor Farmati are found guilty of complicity in the crime stipulated in Paragraph *h* of Article 2 of Law No. 312/1945.

The accused Sámuel Császár and Zoltán Horkai are found guilty of the crime stipulated in Paragraph *l* of Article 2 of the Law and of complicity in the crime stipulated in Paragraph *h* of Article 2 of Law No. 312/1945.

The accused Sándor Oláh is found guilty of the crime stipulated in Paragraph *o* of Article 2 of Law No. 312/1945, as is the accused János Botos.

The accused Victor Capesius is found guilty of the crimes stipulated in Paragraphs *g, h,* and *o* of Article 2 of Law No. 312/1945.

The accused András Lakatos and Kázmér Taar are found guilty of the crime stipulated in Paragraph *n* of Article 2 and of complicity in the crime stipulated in Paragraph *m* of Article 2 of Law No. 312/1945.

The accused Dr. Ernő Pirkler, Dr. Zoltán Rogozi Papp, Dr. József Forgács, Irén Ujvári, Irma Enyedi, Vilmos Horák, Ilona Báthori, Dr. Ferenc Henner, Ernő Jávor, Dr. János Zsigmond, Lieutenant Colonel László Kiss, Major László Komáromi, Jenő Csordácsics, Pál Farkas, Dr. Gábor Szentiványi, Tivadar Lohr, Lajos Cser, József Vadász, Erzsébet Fekete, István Kerényi, János Vida, Ádám Kerekes, and Mihály Kovács are found guilty of complicity in the war crime stipulated in Paragraph *m* of Article 2 of Law No. 312/1945.

The accused Ferenc Lakatos, Dr. Béla Sámi, and Dr. Dezső Dénes are found guilty of the war crime stipulated in Paragraph *n* of Article 2 of the Law, and the accused Heinrich Smolka and Ferenc Hullmann are found guilty of complicity in the war crimes stipulated in Paragraphs *m* and *n* of Article 2 of Law No. 312/1945.

The accused Albert Szabó, Dr. Ferenc Molnár, and Dr. Zsigmond Léhnár are found guilty of the war crimes stipulated in Paragraph *g* of Article 2 of Law No. 312/1945.

Further:

On the basis of Paragraph II of Article 3 of Law No. 312/1945, combined with Article 101 of the Penal Code, the accused Ágoston Félegyházi Medgyesi, N. Deményi, Dr. László Urbán, Tibor Paksi-Kiss, Dr. Victor Capesius, Colonel Dr. János Papp, Colonel N. Zalantai, Dr. Géza Bedő, Major Schröder, Gendarmerie Captain Konya, Gendarmerie Captain Pintér, Quartermaster Ferenc Sallós, Quartermaster Pál Bányai, Quartermaster Balázs Biró, First Sergeant András Fehér, First Sergeant István Gösi, Gendarmerie Major Pál Antalffy, Ferenc Elekes, Lieutenant Colonel György Mariska, István Pethes, Dr. Sándor Horváth, Dr. László Krasznai, Dr. Lajos Tóth, Colonel Miklós Sárváry, Florea Tascan, János Biró, György Varga, Lieutenant Colonel Ernő Pásztai, and Lieutenant Colonel Miklós Jakab are condemned to DEATH.

On the basis of Paragraph II of Article 3 of Law No. 312/1945, the accused István Bede is condemned to DEATH.

On the basis of Paragraph II of Article 3 of Law No. 312/1945, combined with Articles 101 and 102 of the Penal Code, the accused Dr. Gyula Petri, János Frater, Dr. Béla Rektor, István Garai, Dr. Endre Bodolai, István Sziklai, András Medgyesi, Dezső Büss, Gyula Őri, György Fekete, Sándor Ilonka, János Teveli, István Szőllősi, Géza Szabados, János Tóth, Mihály Juhász, Sándor Posgai, Gábor Keresztesi, István Felföldi, Imre Garai, Sándor Fehér, József Horváth, Mihály Szabó, the gendarme Megyeri, the gendarme Budai, Dr. Béla Sárközi, Károly Csegezi, Dr. Géza Papp, Sámuel Császár, Zoltán Horkai, Ferenc Menyhért, Dr. József Orosz, András Szentkuti, Dr. Pál Boldizsár, Sándor Ojtózi, János Dudás, Dr. Jenő Veress, Dr. Gyula Sárosi, István Takács, József Lakadár, Dr. Jenő Nagy, Károly Balla, Imre Vajai, István Bertalan, Lajos Ormos, Quartermaster Miklós Sárközi, Quartermaster János Horváth, Dr. László Illinyi, János Fehér, Dr. Miklós Debreczeni, and Gusztáv Orendi are condemned to HARD LABOR FOR LIFE.

On the basis of Paragraphs I and II of Article 3 of Law No. 312/1945 and applying Articles 101 and 102 of the Penal Code, the accused József Gecse and József Orgoványi are condemned to HARD LABOR FOR LIFE for the crime stipulated in Paragraph *h* of Article 2 of Law No. 312/1945, and to 20 years each of RIGOROUS DETENTION for the crime stipulated in Paragraph *o* of Article 2 of Law No. 312/1945, with the most severe sentence, i.e., HARD LABOR FOR LIFE, to be served.

On the basis of Paragraph II of Article 3 of Law No. 312/1945, the accused Captain László Berentes is condemned to HARD LABOR FOR LIFE.

On the basis of Paragraph II of Article 3 of Law No. 312/1945, combined with Articles 101 and 102 of the Penal Code and applying Article 157 of the Penal Code, the accused Dr. Imre Németh, Dr. Miklós Toperczel, Lajos Varga, Andor Joós, Major László Komáromi, Dr. Géza Polánkai, Béla Ferenczi, János Somorlyai, János Kassay, Albert Garamvölgyi, Miklós Désaknai, Ernő Berecki, András Iványi, Dr. László Szlávi, and Dr. László Szaplonczai are each condemned to 25 years of HARD LABOR.

On the basis of Paragraphs I and II of Article 3 in combination with Articles 101 and 102 and Articles 121 and 123 of the Penal Code and applying Paragraph *a* of Section 1 of Article 157 of the Penal Code, the accused Péter Czeisberger and József Lázár are each condemned to 25 years of HARD LABOR for the crime stipulated in Paragraph *h* of Article 2, 5 years of RIGOROUS DETENTION for the crime stipulated in Paragraph *o* of Article 2, and 5 years of SIMPLE DETENTION for complicity in the crime stipulated in Paragraph *m* of Article 2 of Law No. 312/1945, with the most severe sentence, i.e., 25 years of HARD LABOR, to be served.

On the basis of Paragraph II of Article 3 of Law No. 312/1945 in combination with Articles 101 and 102 of the Penal Code and applying Article 157 of the Penal Code, the accused Gendarmerie Lieutenant Kálmán Szentpáli, Dr.

István Vincze, and Lieutenant Colonel Balla are each condemned to 20 (twenty) years of HARD LABOR.

On the basis of Paragraphs I and II of Article 3 of Law No. 312/1945 in combination with Articles 101 and 102 of the Penal Code and Articles 121 and 123 of the Penal Code and applying Paragraph *a* of Section 1 of Article 157 of the Penal Code, the accused Ioan Vancea and Zoltán Osváth are each condemned to 20 (twenty) years of HARD LABOR for the crime stipulated in Paragraph *h* of Article 2, 5 (five) years of RIGOROUS DETENTION for the crime stipulated in Paragraph *o* of Article 2, and 5 (five) years each of HARD DETENTION for complicity in the crime stipulated in Paragraph *m* of Article 2 of Law No. 312/1945, with the most severe sentence, i.e., 20 (twenty) years of HARD LABOR for each accused, to be served.

On the basis of Paragraphs I and II of Article 3 of Law No. 312/1945 in combination with Articles 101 and 102 of the Penal Code and applying Paragraph *a*, Section 1, of Article 157 of the Penal Code, the accused Mrs. József Medgyesi née Erzsébet Mutza and György Kugler (Füleki) are each condemned to 15 (fifteen) years of HARD LABOR for the crime stipulated in Paragraph *h* of Article 2 and 5 (five) years of HEAVY DETENTION for the crime stipulated in Paragraph *o* of Article 2 of Law No. 312/1945, with the most severe sentence, i.e., 15 (fifteen) years of HARD LABOR each, to be served.

On the basis of the same texts of laws, the accused Mrs. János Kiss née Rozália Zeffer, Irma Lovas, and Mária Fekete are each condemned to 10 (ten) years of HARD LABOR for the crime stipulated in Paragraph *h* of Article 2 and 5 (five) years of HEAVY DETENTION for the crime stipulated in Paragraph *o* of Article 2, with the most severe sentence, i.e., 10 (ten) years of HARD LABOR for each of the accused, to be served.

On the basis of Paragraphs I, II and V of Article 3 of Law No. 312/1945 in combination with Articles 101 and 102 and Articles 121 and 123 of the Penal Code, and applying Article 31 of the Penal Code, the accused Károly Rajnay (Reiner) is condemned to 20 (twenty) years of HARD PRISON *(Temniță grea)* for complicity in the crime stipulated by Paragraph *h* of Article 2 of Law No. 312/1945, 10 (ten) years of SIMPLE DETENTION for complicity in the crime stipulated by Paragraph *m* of Article 2, and 10 (ten) years of HEAVY DETENTION for perpetrating the crime stipulated in Paragraph *o* of Article 2 of Law No. 312/1945, and is to serve 20 (twenty) years of HARD PRISON, being the most severe sentence.

On the basis of Paragraph II of Article 3 of Law No. 312/1945 and applying Article 157, the accused Gusztáv Sarkadi is condemned to 20 (twenty) years of HARD PRISON.

On the basis of Paragraph II of Article 3 of Law No. 312/1945 applying Paragraph *a*, Section 1, of Article 157 of the Penal Code, the accused Dr.

Zsigmond Léhnár is condemned to 15 (fifteen) years of HARD PRISON and the accused Albert Szabó is condemned to 3 years of HARD PRISON for the crime stipulated in Paragraph *g* of Article 2 of Law No. 312/1945.

On the basis of Paragraphs I and II of Article 3 of Law No. 312/1945 and applying Paragraph *a,* Section 1, of Article 157 of the Penal Code, the accused Rozália Jancsó and László Petővári Petrik are each condemned to 10 years of HARD PRISON for the crime stipulated in Paragraph *h* of Article 2 and 3 years of RIGOROUS DETENTION for the crime stipulated in Paragraph *o* of Article 2, with each of them to serve the most severe sentence, i.e., 10 years of HARD PRISON.

On the basis of Paragraphs I and II of Article 3 and applying Articles 101, 102, 121, and 123 as well as Paragraph *a,* Section 1, of Article 157 of the Penal Code, the accused Ioan Anghea is condemned to 10 years of HARD PRISON for the crime stipulated in Paragraph *h* of Article 2, 3 years of RIGOROUS DETENTION for the crime stipulated in Paragraph *o* of Article 2, and 3 years of SIMPLE DETENTION for complicity in the crime stipulated in Paragraph *m* of Article 2 of the Law, and is to serve 10 years of HARD DETENTION, being the most severe sentence.

On the basis of Paragraph II of Article 3 of Law No. 312/1945 and applying Article 157 of the Penal Code, the accused Dr. Ferenc Molnár is condemned to 5 years of HARD PRISON.

On the basis of Paragraphs I and II of Article 3 of Law No. 312/1945 combined with Articles 101, 102, 121, and 123 of the Penal Code, and applying Paragraph *a,* Section 1, of Article 157 of the Penal Code, the accused Kálmán Borbély is condemned to 5 years of HARD PRISON for complicity in the crime stipulated in Paragraph *h* of Article 2, 3 years of RIGOROUS DETENTION for the crime stipulated in Paragraph *o* of Article 2, and 3 years of SIMPLE DETENTION for complicity in the crime stipulated by Paragraph *m* of Article 2 of Law No. 312/1945, and is to serve the most severe sentence of 5 years of HARD PRISON.

On the basis of Paragraph II of Article 3 of Law No. 312/1945 combined with Articles 121 and 123 of the Penal Code and applying Article 157 of the Penal Code, the accused József Lax and Sándor Farmati are each condemned to 3 years of HARD PRISON.

On the basis of Paragraphs I and II of Article 3 in combination with Articles 101, 102, and Paragraph *a* of Section 1 of Article 157 of the Penal Code, the accused Irén Duha is sentenced to 3 years of HARD PRISON for the crime stipulated in Paragraph *h* of Article 2 and 3 years of RIGOROUS DETENTION for the crime stipulated in Paragraph *o* of Article 2 of Law No. 312/1945, and is to serve the most severe sentence, i.e., 3 years of HARD PRISON.

On the basis of Paragraph I of Article 3 and applying Article 101 of the

Penal Code, the accused János Schilling is condemned to 10 years of RIGOROUS DETENTION for the crime stipulated in Paragraph *n* of Article 2, 5 years of RIGOROUS DETENTION for the crime stipulated in Paragraph *m* of Article 2, and 3 (three) years of RIGOROUS DETENTION for the crime stipulated in Paragraph *o* of Article 2, and the accused Dr. Ferenc Májay is condemned to 10 (ten) years of RIGOROUS DETENTION for the crime stipulated in Paragraph *m* of Article 2 and 8 (eight) years of RIGOROUS DETENTION for the crime stipulated in Paragraph *o* of Article 2, and the accused Imre Schmidt and Dr. Mátyás Tóth are each condemned to 10 (ten) years of HARD DETENTION for the crime stipulated in Paragraph *m* of Article 2 and 3 (three) years of RIGOROUS DETENTION for the crime stipulated in Paragraph *o* of Article 2 of Law No. 312/1945, with all of the accused to serve the most severe sentence, i.e., 10 (ten) years each of RIGOROUS DETENTION.

On the basis of Paragraph I of Article 3 in combination with Articles 101, 121, and 123 of the Penal Code, the accused Kázmér Taar is condemned to 10 (ten) years of RIGOROUS DETENTION for the crime stipulated in Paragraph *n* of Article 2 and 5 (five) years of SIMPLE DETENTION for complicity in the crime stipulated in Paragraph *m* of Article 2 of Law No. 312/1945, and is to serve the most severe sentence, i.e., 10 (ten) years of RIGOROUS DETENTION.

On the basis of the same texts of law, the accused Ferenc Lakatos is condemned to 3 (three) years of RIGOROUS DETENTION for the crime stipulated in Paragraph *n* of Article 2 and 3 (three) years of SIMPLE DETENTION for complicity in the crime stipulated in Paragraph *m* of Article 2 of Law No. 312/1945, and is to serve the most severe sentence, i.e., 3 (three) years of RIGOROUS DETENTION.

On the basis of Paragraph I of Article 3 of Law No. 312/1945, the accused Sándor Oláh is condemned to 3 (three) years of RIGOROUS DETENTION.

On the basis of Paragraph I of Article 3 of Law No. 312/1945 and applying Article 101 of the Penal Code, the accused Dr. László Gyapai, János Nadányi, Dr. Zoltán Rogozi Papp, Barnabás Endrődi, Endre Boér, Dr. László Vásárhelyi, Dr. József Székely, Dr. Zsigmond Marton, Colonel Géza Körmendi, István Kozma, Dr. András Gazda, Dr. János Sréter, Dr. József Udvari, Dr. Sándor Gyulafalvi Rednik, László Smolenszki, and Dr. Norbert Kuales are condemned to HARD DETENTION FOR LIFE, and the accused András Lakatos, Dr. István Bonda, Dr. Ferenc Filó, Dr. József Ábrahám, Gerő Szász, András Virányi, Dr. Andor Barabás, and Lajos Tamási to 20 (twenty) years each of HARD DETENTION.

On the basis of Paragraph I of Article 3 combined with Article 101 of the Penal Code, the accused Dr. László Csóka is condemned to HARD DETEN-

TION FOR LIFE for the crime stipulated in Paragraph *m* of Article 2 and to 20 (twenty) years of HARD DETENTION for the crime stipulated in Paragraph *o* of Article 2 of Law No. 312/1945, and is to serve the most severe sentence, i.e., HARD DETENTION FOR LIFE.

On the basis of Paragraph I of Article 3 of Law No. 312/1945, the accused Béla Sámi and Dezső Dénes are condemned to 10 (ten) years each of HARD DETENTION.

On the basis of Paragraph I of Article 3 of Law No. 312/1945 combined with Paragraph V of this Article and with Articles 121 and 123 of the Penal Code, the accused Erzsébet Fekete, István Kerényi, Dr. József Forgács, Irén Ujvári, Dr. Ferenc Henner, Ernő Jávor, Dezső Gálfy, Dr. János Zsigmond, Lieutenant Colonel László Kiss, Ernő Gaáli, Pál Farkas, Tivadar Lohr, Sándor Vajai, and József Haracsek are condemned to 12 (twelve) years each of SIMPLE DETENTION.

On the basis of the same texts of law, the accused Dr. Ernő Pirkler, Vilmos Horák, Ilona Báthori, Jenő Csordácsics and Ádám Kerekes are condemned to 10 (ten) years each of SIMPLE DETENTION, and the accused Irma Enyedi to 8 (eight) years of SIMPLE DETENTION.

On the basis of the same texts of law, the accused Lajos Cser, József Vadász, Dr. Gábor Szentiványi, János Vida, and Mihály Kovács are condemned to 5 (five) years each of SIMPLE DETENTION.

On the basis of Paragraphs I and V of Article 3 of Law No. 312/1945 combined with Articles 101, 121, and 123 of the Penal Code, the accused Ferenc Hullmann and Heinrich Smolka are condemned to 5 (five) years each of SIMPLE DETENTION for complicity in the crime stipulated in Paragraph *m* of Article 2 and to 3 (three) years each of SIMPLE DETENTION for complicity in the crime stipulated in Paragraph *n* of Article 2 of Law No. 312/1945, and both are to serve the most severe sentence, i.e., 5 (five) years each of SIMPLE DETENTION.

On the basis of Paragraph I of Article 3 of Law No. 312/1945, the accused János Botos is condemned to 15 (fifteen) years of HARD DETENTION.

For all the condemned under arrest, the time spent under preventive arrest since the issuance of the arrest order is counted as time already served under the sentence.

Also, on the basis of the last paragraph of Article 3 of Law No. 312/1945 in combination with Section 1 of Article 25 of the Penal Code, the accused József Lax, Sándor Farmati, Albert Szabó, Irén Duha, Dr. Ferenc Molnár, and Dr. Kálmán Borbély are each condemned to LOSS OF CIVIL RIGHTS for 3 (three) years.

On the basis of the last paragraph of Article 3 of Law No. 312/1945 combined with Section 1 of Article 25 of the Penal Code, the accused who were condemned to political penalties from rigorous detention to hard detention for life are also each condemned to 10 (ten) years each of LOSS OF CIVIC RIGHTS, except for the accused Sándor Oláh and Ferenc Lakatos who are condemned only to 3 (three) years each of LOSS OF CIVIL RIGHTS.

On the basis of the last paragraph of Article 3 of Law No. 312/1945 combined with Section 2 of Article 25 of the Penal Code, all the other accused who were condemned to correctional political penalties are also condemned to 5 (five) years of CORRECTIONAL INTERDICTION, by the suspension of the rights stipulated in Section 2 of Article 58 of the Penal Code.

At the same time, on the basis of the last paragraph of Article 3 of Law No. 312/1945, all the property of the accused who were condemned is to be confiscated for the benefit of the Romanian state as indemnification.

On the basis of Paragraph I, Section 2, of Article 4 of the Penal Procedure, the following accused are acquitted:

1. Melánia Szilárszki née Kosári, Romanian citizen, housewife, residing in Vadul Crişului, currently under arrest, and
2. Irén Kosári, Romanian citizen, 55 years old, housewife, residing in Nagyvárad, currently under arrest, of the indictment brought against them for war crimes stipulated in Paragraph *h* of Article 2 of Law No. 312/1945;
3. Kálmán Szabó, Romanian citizen, former district administrator of Szászrégen District in Maros County, residing in Szászrégen, currently under arrest, of his indictment for the war crime stipulated in Paragraphs *h* and *m* of Article 2 of Law No. 312/1945;
4. István Szilágyi, 40 years old, Romanian citizen, born in Beszterce, residing in Beszterce, currently under arrest, of his indictment for the war crime stipulated in Paragraphs *f, i,* and *o* of Article 2 of Law No. 312/1945;
5. István Nagy, 49 years old, Romanian citizen, builder, born and residing in Szilágysomlyó, currently under arrest, of his indictment for the war crime stipulated in Paragraphs *f, n,* and *o* of Article 2 of Law No. 312/1945; and
6. István Komán, Romanian citizen, chief notary of the village of Borsa, currently under arrest, of his indictment for the war crime stipulated in Paragraphs *f, h, m, n,* and *o* of Article 2 of Law No. 312/1945.

It is ordered that they be immediately set free.

On the basis of Paragraph I, Section 2, of Article 4 of the Penal Procedure, the following accused are acquitted:

Dr. László Gyapai, János Nadányi, László Csóka, János Boér, Dr. László Vásárhelyi, Dr. Zsigmond Marton, Dr. Ferenc Májay, Colonel Géza Körmendi, General István Kozma, Dezső Gálfy, Dr. István Bonda, Dr. Ferenc Filó, Dr. Imre Schmidt, Dr. Mátyás Tóth, Ernő Gaáli, Dr. József Ábrahám, Gerő Szász, Dr. Andor Barabás, András Virányi, Jenő Veress, Lajos Tamási, Dr. János Sréter, Dr. József Udvari, Dr. Sándor Gyulafalyi Rednik, László Smolenszki, and Norbert Kuales of the accusations stipulated by Paragraphs *f, h,* and *n* of Article 2 and punishable under Article 3 of Law No. 312/ 1945. . . .

On the basis of Paragraph I, Section 2, of Article 4 of the Penal Procedure, the following accused are acquitted:

Major Johann Schröder of the accusations stipulated by Paragraphs *h, m, n,* and *o* of Article 2 and punishable under Article 3 of Law No. 312/1945;

The accused Major Pál Antalffy, Dr. Lajos Varga, Barnabás Endrődi, Dr. László Szlávi, Dr. László Illinyi, László Szaplonczai, and Dr. Kálmán Borbély of the accusations stipulated by Paragraphs *f* and *n* of Article 2 and punishable under Article 3 of Law No. 312/1945;

The accused N. Deményi, Colonel János Papp, Géza Bedő, Géza Polánkai, Lieutenant Colonel Balla, Lieutenant Colonel György Mariska, Colonel Sárváry, Lieutenant Colonel Miklós Jakab, and Colonel János Zalantai of the accusations stipulated by Paragraphs *f, m,* and *n* of Article 2 and punishable under Article 3 of Law No. 312/1945;

The accused László Urbán, Dr. Géza Papp, György Kugler, Imre Németh, Dr. Ágoston Félegyházi Medgyesi, Dr. Gyula Petri, János Frater, Dr. Béla Rektor, István Garai, István Bodolai, Dr. Miklós Toperczel, Dr. Béla Sárközi, Károly Csegezi, Dr. Gyula Sárosi, István Takács, József Gecse, József Lakadár, Ferenc Elekes, István Pethes, Dr. Sándor Horváth, Dr. László Krasznai, Dr. Lajos Tóth, Dr. Miklós Debreczeni, and Gusztáv Orendi of the accusations stipulated by Paragraphs *g* and *l* of Article 2 and punishable under Article 3 of Law No. 312/1945;

The accused János Dudás, Kálmán Szentpáli and József Orgoványi of the accusations stipulated in Paragraph *f* of Article 2 and punishable under Article 3 of the Law;

The accused Ernő Berecki, András Iványi, Dr. Jenő Nagy, and Károly Balogh of the accusations stipulated by Paragraphs *g, l, m,* and *n* of Article 2 and punishable under Article 3 of the Law;

The accused László Berentes of the accusations stipulated by Paragraphs *f* and *o* of Article 2, and the accused Sándor Farmati of the accusations stipulated by Paragraphs *g, l,* and *o* of Article 2 of the Law;

The accused Ernő Pirkler, Dr. Ferenc Henner, Ernő Jávor, Lieutenant Colonel László Kiss, Major László Komáromi, Dr. Jenő Csordácsics, Dr. Pál Farkas, and Dr. Gábor Szentiványi of the accusations stipulated by Paragraphs *f, n,* and *o* of Article 2 and punishable under Article 3 of the Law;

The accused Irén Ujvári, Irma Enyedi, Vilmos Horák, Ilona Báthori, József

Vadász, and Erzsébet Fekete of the accusations stipulated by Paragraph *h* of Article 2 and punishable under Article 3 of the Law;

The accused János Vida, Ádám Kerekes, and Mihály Szabó of the accusations stipulated by Paragraphs *g, h,* and *l* of Article 2 and punishable under Article 3 of the Law;

The accused Béla Sámi of the accusation stipulated by Paragraphs *m* and *o* of Article 2 and punishable under Article 3 of the Law;

The accused Dr. Dezső Dénes of the accusations stipulated by Paragraphs *f, h, m,* and *o* of Article 2 and punishable under Article 3 of the Law.

The trial of the accused Dr. Ferenc Szász, Ödön Inczedi-Joksmann, and István Rosner is separated; they are to be tried subsequently.

The present judgment is to be carried out by the Prosecuting Magistracy *(Parchet)* attached to the Tribunal of Kolozsvár, on the basis of Article 14 of Law No. 312/1945.

The right to appeal is declared in force immediately after the passing of the sentences.

Issued and the sentences delivered in a public session of the People's Tribunal, Court Panel Kolozsvár, today 31 May 1946.[16]

PRESIDENT
(signed) Dr. Matei Nicolae

ASSESSOR
(signed) Dr. Nerva Hărăguş

PEOPLE'S JUDGES
(signed) Augustin Meseşan
Gheorghe Dan
Alexandru Gligorin
Victor Taflan
Pavel Bojan
Mihai Covaci
Ştefan Belovai

COURT RECORDER
(signed) Gavril Stanca

Notes

1. For text see *Monitorul Oficial* (Official Gazette), Bucharest, Part I, No. 94 (24 April 1945). 3362–364. For its English translation, see Appendix 2.

2. For the text of Decree No. 1.610/1944.M.E. of the "Royal Hungarian Ministry Concerning the Regulation of Certain Questions Relating to the Determination of the Jews' Apartments and Living Quarters," see *Budapesti Közlöny. Hivatalos Lap* (Gazette of Budapest. Official Journal), Budapest, No. 95 (28 April 1944). 2–3.

3. Reference is to Order No. 6163 of 7 April 1944 issued under the signature of Under Secretary of State László Baky. For its text in English translation, see Randolph L. Braham, *The Politics*

- 171 -

prevăzută de art. 2 petele g,h,l și pedepsite de art.3. din lege.

Pe acuzatul Cluj Bela de sub acuza prevăzută de art. 2 literele m,o și pedepsite de art.3. din lege.

Pe acuzatul Dr.Dénes Desideriu de sub acuzele prevăzute de art.2. literele f,h,m,o.și pedepsite de art.3. din lege.

Disjunge procesul în ceiace privește pe acuzații Dr.Balan Trasie,Incze M Joana născ.Bdön și Rosner Iosif n, urmând ca să fie judecați ulterior.

Prezenta hotărâre se va executa de încheotul de pe lângă Tribunalul Cluj în baza art. 14 din legea Nr.312/1945.

Cu drept de recurs declarat imediat după pronunțare.

Dată și pronunțată în ședința publică a Tribunalului Poporului Completul de Judecată Cluj, azi 31 Mai 1946.

PREȘEDINTE,   ASESOR,

of Genocide. The Holocaust in Hungary (New York: Columbia University Press, 1981), pp. 529–31.

4. For details on the Kamenets-Podolsk massacres of August 1941, see ibid., pp. 199–207.

5. For details relating to the massacres committed by Hungarian troops in and around Ujvidék *(Novi Sad)* in January–February 1942, see ibid., pp. 207–15.

6. A search of the 1942 *Congressional Record* revealed no such Resolution by either House of the U.S. Congress. In the House of Representatives Congressman Samuel Dickstein of New York spoke twice about the massacre of the Jews in Nazi-dominated Europe. His remarks of 20 July 1942 and 15 December 1942 are reproduced in *Appendix to the Congressional Record,* vol. 88, part 10 (Washington: U.S. Government Printing Office, 1942), pp. A2839–42, and A4331–32.

7. In the U.S. Senate, the persecution of Jews in Nazi-dominated Europe was the focus of New York Senator James M. Mead's remarks on 21 July 1942 and 11 December 1942. For text see Ibid, vol. 88, part 9, pp. A2867–68 and A4263.

8. The declaration of the United States, Great Britain, and the USSR of 2 November 1943, in contrast to their declaration of 17 December 1942, did not identify the Jews as the special target of the Nazis' fury. For further details on these declarations, see Braham, *The Politics of Genocide,* pp. 1098–99 and 1119.

9. For the text of Decree No. 1.240/1944.M.E. of the Royal Hungarian Ministry Concerning the Marking of the Jews for Purposes of Their Differentiation, see *Budapesti Közlöny,* No. 73 (31 March 1944): 3.

10. See Appendix 4. The original of the document is in the possession of this author.

11. See Appendix 5. The original of the document is in the possession of this author.

12. Tried in absentia in Kolozsvár, Dr. Victor Capesius was also one of the chief defendants in the "Auschwitz Trial" of Frankfurt (December 1963–August 1965). In Frankfurt he was condemned to nine years' imprisonment, but on 20 February 1969 the *Bundesgerichtshof* of Karlsruhe, while upholding the lower court's decision, ordered that the time Capesius had spent in internment after the war be counted as part of his sentence and he was freed shortly thereafter. For further details see Braham, *The Politics of Genocide,* p. 1172. See also Jenő Lévai, "The War Crimes Trials Relating to Hungary" in: *Hungarian-Jewish Studies,* Vol. 3., ed. Randolph L. Braham (New York: World Federation of Hungarian Jews, 1973), pp. 274–78, and Bernd Naumann, *Auschwitz. A Report on the Proceedings Against Robert Karl Ludwig Mulka and Others Before the Court at Frankfurt* (New York: Praeger, 1966), 433 p.

13. The original Romanian typewritten minutes of the trial erroneously referred to "eight" instead of three days.

14. Until late in April 1944, Count Béla Bethlen served as prefect of both Szolnok-Doboka and Beszterce-Naszód counties. When the pro-Sztójay prefects were appointed that month, the position of prefect in Beszterce-Naszód County was assumed by Kálmán Borbély.

15. This author is not aware of any district in Hungarian-held Northern Transylvania from which the Jews were not rounded up and deported.

16. The sentences, harsh as they appeared in May 1946, were practically nullified within a few years under a new policy calculated to bring about a restructuring of Romanian society. Under Decree No. 72 of the Ministry of the Interior, dated 23 March 1950 (*Colecție de Legi, Decrete, Hotărîri și Deciziuni;* Collection of Laws, Decrees, Resolutions and Decisions) (Bucharest: Editura de Stat, Vol. 28, 1950, pp. 76–79) the inmates who "demonstrated good behavior, performed their tasks conscientiously, and proved that they became fit for social cohabitation during their imprisonment" became eligible for immediate release irrespective of the severity of their original sentence. Among those released in the wake of this decree was, for example, József Gecse, the sadist of the ghetto of Dés, one of the three among those under arrest who were condemned to life imprisonment.

III APPENDIXES

Appendix 1: Reference List of Selected Geographic Name Changes

Hungarian	Romanian
Aknasugatag	Ocna Şugatag
Alőr	Vrîul de Jos
Alsobán	Bănişor
Alsórona	Rona de Jos
Alsóvalkó	Vâlcăul de Jos
Alsóvisó	Vişeul de Jos
Aranyosmeggyes	Mediaşul Aurit
Aranyszentmiklós	Sînnicoara
Avasujváros	Negreşti
Bánffyhunyad	Huedin
Barcánfalva	Bărsana
Bárdfalva	Berbeşti
Batiz	Botiz
Beszterce	Bistriţa
Bethlen	Beclean
Bikszád	Bixad
Borgóprund	Prundul Bărgăului
Bőd	Beudin
Borsa	Borşa
Budfalva	Budeşti

Coptelke	Pădureni
Csíkszereda	Miercurea Ciuc
Csícsógyörgyfalva	Ciceu Giurgeşti
Dengeleg	Livada
Derzse	Dîrja
Dés	Dej
Desenfalva	Deseşti
Devecser	Diviciorii
Drágomérfalva	Drăgomireşti
Élesd	Aleşd
Erdőd	Ardud
Érmihalyfalva	Valea lui Mihai
Farkasrev	Vad
Feketelak	Lacu
Felőr	Vrîul de Sus
Felsőilosva	Tîrlăşua
Felsőrona	Rona de Sus
Felsőszék	Sag (Sîg)
Felsővisó	Vişeul de Sus
Glod	Glod
Gyergyószentmiklós	Gheorgheni
Gyulafalva	Giuleşti
Gyulafehérvár	Alba-Iulia
Halmi	Halmeu
Havasmező	Poieni de Sub Munte
Hidalmás	Hida
Hosszumező	Câmpulung la Tisa
Iklód	Iclod
Izakonyha	Cuhea
Izaszacsal	Săcel
Jod	Jeud
Kápolnokmonostor	Popalnic Mănăştur
Karácsonyfalva	Crăciuneşti
Kecsed	Ghiciud or Miceştii de Cîmpie
Kékes	Chiochiş
Kérő	Băiţa
Kiskalota	Călăţele

Kissármás	Sărmăşel
Kolozsvár	Cluj or Cluj-Napoca
Kracsfalva	Crăceşti
Kraszna	Crasna
Leordina	Leordina
Lozsárd	Lajerd
Magyarcséke	Ceica
Magyarlápos	Tîrgul Lăpuşului
Majszin	Moisei
Mányik	Manic
Máramarossziget	Sighet or Sighetul Marmaţiei
Margitta	Mărghita
Marosvásárhely	Tîrgu-Mureş
Marosvécs	Brîncoveneşti
Mezőtelegd	Tiliagd
Nagybánya	Baia Mare
Nagybocskó	Bocicoiul Mare
Nagyilonda	Ileanda Mare
Nagykároly	Carei Mari
Nagysomkut	Şomcuta Mare
Nagyszalonta	Salonta Mare
Nagysármás	Sărmaş
Nagyvárad	Oradea Mare
Nánfalva	Năneşti
Naszód	Năsăud
Naszoly	Nasăl
Ördöngösfűzes	Fizeşul Gherlii
Pujon	Pui
Pusztakamarás	Cămăraşi
Remetefalva	Remeţi
Retteg	Reteag
Ronaszék	Costiui
Rozália	Rozavelea
Ruszkova	Ruscova
Sajófalva	Şieu
Segesvár	Sighişoara
Sárköz	Livada

Sepsiszentgyörgy	Sfîntu Gheorghe
Somlyócsehi	Cehei
Szák	Sac
Szamosardó	Arduzel
Szamosfalva	Someşeni
Szamosujvár	Gherla
Szaplonca	Sapanta
Szászrégen	Reghin
Szatmárnémeti	Satu Mare
Székelyhid	Secuieni
Székelyudvarhely	Odorhei
Szelistye	Sălişte
Szentgothárd	Sucutard
Szentmárton	Sînartin
Szerbfalva	Sârb
Szilágybogos	Boghiş
Szilágyborzos	Bozieş
Szilágyfőkeresztur	Cristur
Szilágynagyfalu	Nusfalău
Szilágysomlyó	Şimleul Silvaniei
Szlatina	Slatina
Szurdok	Strâmtura

Udvarhely *see* Székelyudvarhely

Váncsfalva	Onceşti
Váradszőllős	Sălăuş
Veresegyháza	Strugureni

Appendix 2: Number of Jews Deported from the Major Entrainment Centers in Northern Transylvania by Transport and Date of Entrainment

1944

May 16: Máramarossziget	3,007	May 30: Nagyvárad	3,187
May 17: Ökörmező	3,052	May 30: Szatmárnémeti	3,300
May 18: Máramarossziget	3,248	May 31: Kolozsvár	3,270
May 19: Felsővisó	3,032	May 31: Nagybánya	3,073
May 19: Szatmárnémeti	3,006	May 31: Szilágysomlyó	3,106
May 20: Máramarossziget	3,104	June 1: Nagyvárad	3,059
May 21: Felsővisó	3,013	June 1: Szatmárnémeti	2,615
May 22: Máramarossziget	3,490	June 2: Beszterce	3,106
May 22: Szatmárnémeti	3,300	June 2: Kolozsvár	3,100
May 23: Felsővisó	3,028	June 3: Nagyvárad	2,972
May 23: Nagyvárad	3,110	June 3: Szilágysomlyó	3,161
May 25: Nagyvárad	3,145	June 4: Szászrégen	3,149
May 25: Kolozsvár	3,130	June 5: Nagyvárad	2,527
May 25: Aknaszlatina	3,317	June 5: Nagybánya	2,844
May 25: Felsővisó	3,006	June 6: Dés	3,160
May 26: Szatmárnémeti	3,336	June 6: Beszterce	2,875
May 27: Marosvásárhely	3,183	June 6: Szilágysomlyó	1,584
May 28: Dés	3,150	June 8: Dés	1,364
May 28: Nagyvárad	3,227	June 8: Kolozsvár	1,784
May 29: Kolozsvár	3,417	June 8: Marosvásárhely	1,163
May 29: Szatmárnémeti	3,306	June 9: Kolozsvár	1,447
May 29: Nagyvárad	3,166	June 27: Nagyvárad	2,819
May 30: Marosvásárhely	3,203	Total	131,641

Based on data collected by the Hungarian military command at the Kassa railway station through which the transports from Northern Transylvania as from many other parts of Hungary were directed to Auschwitz.

Appendix 3: Law No. 312 of the Romanian Ministry of Justice dated 21 April 1945

Michael I,

By the grace of God and the will of the nation, King of Romania.

To all those present and in the future, health:

With respect to report No. 36,965 of 11 April 1945 of our Minister Secretary of State in the Ministry of Justice;

In view also of Minutes No. 666 of 1945 of the Council of Ministers;

On the basis of the provisions of High Royal Decree No. 1626 of 31 August 1945, published in the *Monitorul Oficial* (Official Gazette), No. 202 of 2 September 1944;

We have decreed and are decreeing:

DECREE LAW

for the Pursuit and Punishment of Those Guilty for the Country's Disaster or of War Crimes

Article 1.—Guilty for the country's disaster are those who:

(a) Militating for Hitlerism or fascism and having effective political responsibility, permitted the entry of the German armies into the country's territory;

(b) After 6 September 1940 militated for the preparation or implementation of the above orally or in writing or by any other means.

Article 2.—Guilty for the country's disaster through the commission of war crimes are those who:

(a) Decided on the declaration or the continuation of the war against the Union of Soviet Socialist Republics and the United Nations;

(b) Failed to respect the international rules relating to the conduct of war;

(c) Subjected prisoners of war and hostages to inhumane treatment;

(d) Ordered or perpetrated acts of terror, cruelty or oppression on the population of the territories in which the war was fought;

(e) Ordered or perpetrated collective or individual repressions against the civilian population for purposes of political persecution or for racial motives;

(f) Ordered or organized excessive labor or the displacement and transports of people for the purpose of their extermination;

(g) As commanders, directors, supervisors, and guards of prisons, camps for prisoners or political internees, and compulsory labor camps and companies, subjected those under their power to inhumane treatment;

(h) As judicial police officers or investigators of whatever title for questions of political or racial nature, committed acts of violence, tortures, or other illegal means of compulsion;

(i) As prosecutors or civilian or military judges, intentionally helped in or perpretrated acts of terror or violence;

(j) Left the nation's territory to place themselves in the service of Hitlerism or fascism, and attacked the country in writing, orally, or by any other means;

(k) Illicitly or forcibly acquired for themselves private or political goods from the areas in which the war was fought;

(l) Acquired wealth illicitly by their participation in the conduct of the war in whatever capacity, or by profiting from their connections with such persons or from the laws and measures of Hitlerite, legionnaire, or racial character;

(m) Ordered or initiated the establishment of ghettos, internment camps, or deportations for reasons of political or racial persecution;

(n) Ordered the issuance of unjust laws or measures of a Hitlerite, legionnaire, or racial nature, or intentionally practiced excessive execution of the laws derived from the state of war or of provisions of a political or racial character;

(o) Placed themselves in the service of Hitlerism or fascism and contributed through their own acts to the realization of their political goals or the enslavement of the economic life of the country, to the detriment of the interest of the Romanian people.

Article 3.—Those guilty of the acts stipulated in Article 1 and Paragraphs (m)–(o) of Article 2 will be punished by hard detention for life, or by hard detention for 5 to 20 years or by rigorous detention for 3 to 20 years.

Those guilty of the acts stipulated in Paragraphs (a)–(j) of Article 2 will be punished by death or hard labor for life.

Those guilty of the acts stipulated in Paragraphs (a)–(j) of Article 2 will be punished by hard labor for life, or hard labor for a determined period of 5 to 25 years, or hard imprisonment for 3 to 20 years.

The instigators and coperpretrators of those guilty of acts stipulated in the present Law will be punished by the same penalties.

The accomplices, supporters, and concealers of those guilty for the acts stipulated in the present Law will be punished by a penalty that is one degree lower than that provided for the principal perpetrator.

In addition to these penalties, sentences will also be passed relating to the loss of civil rights and the confiscation of property as indemnification for the benefit of the state.

Article 4.—The Minister of Justice will appoint a number of public prosecutors entrusted with the investigation and questioning of those indicted for committing the acts stipulated in the present Law, as well as their instigators, co-authors, accomplices, supporters and concealers.

One of the public prosecutors will be assigned to be the chief of the public prosecutors.

The public prosecutors will be selected from among adult Romanian citizens regardless of sex, and may be selected also from public functionaries.

Their appointment will take place through a High Royal Decree upon the proposal of the Minister of Justice.

The investigation and interrogation organs will operate under the Ministry of Justice with headquarters in Bucharest, and if necessary in the cities of residence of the Courts of Appeals as well.

Article 5.—The public prosecutors will investigate all cases referred by the Council of Ministers.

They may also proceed on their own or upon transmittals for investigation by the presidency of the Council of Ministers.

They are empowered to take any needed measures to safeguard the goods of the accused and other physical or juridical persons, measures that will remain in effect until the trial. The public prosecutors may lift these safeguarding measures in full or in part.

Article 6.—The public prosecutors are empowered to undertake any investigation and to collect any evidence, and to use the rights and powers granted by the Code of Penal Procedure to the Public Minister and the Judge of Instruction.

They may be assisted by magistrates, court recorders, and lawyers as well as by specialists in the financial area and experts and officials who will be appointed or delegated by the Ministry of Justice.

The public prosecutors are empowered to request the execution of their decisions by both the organs of the judiciary and executive organs of whatever nature. They are empowered to request the assistance under whatever circumstances of the organs of law enforcement. They are also empowered to search for, requisition, and collect evidence, and any and all documents from private individuals or any and all civilian or military authorities, including secret documents.

All public officials are obliged to assist the public prosecutors, under penalty of the provisions of Article 243 of the Penal Code for public officials who do not respect this obligation.

The military courts and the garrison commands are obliged to place military personnel in the active army cadre at the disposal of the public prosecutors. For officers with the rank of captain and higher, the prior authorization of the Minister of War must be requested.

Article 7.—Arrest orders will be issued by the Council of Ministers, or the public prosecutors with the concurrence of the chief prosecutor.

Ordered arrests are not subject to confirmation.

The public prosecutors are only empowered to order the freeing of persons arrested by them with the concurrence of the chief prosecutor.

The Council of Ministers may order the freeing of arrested persons in all cases.

Article 8.—Following the investigations, the public prosecutors will prepare the indictment which will be submitted to the Council of Ministers for approval.

The Council of Ministers will decide on the instruction of the court for the trial of the case.

The documents of the public prosecutors and the Council of Ministers may not be attacked in any way.

Article 9.—When a case is sent to trial, all the property of the accused is sequestered; the sequestering comes into force through publication in the *Monitorul Oficial* of the provision of the indictment.

The extinguishing of incrimination through the death of the accused subsequent to the start of the investigation does not prevent the taking of the measures stipulated in Article 5 nor the sequestration of property, and the investigation and trial will be pursued against the heirs for the confiscation of property for the benefit of the state as indemnification.

Article 10.—The acts stipulated by the present Law will be adjudicated by the People's Tribunal.

Article 11.—The People's Tribunal is composed of:

(a) Judges appointed by the Minister of Justice from among magistrates;

(b) People's judges, Romanian adult citizens, men or women, elected from among the seven political groupings which determine the composition of the government of democratic concentration.

Each of these groupings will designate five members who will appear on the list of people's judges.

If a grouping does not designate its members within 15 days from the publication of the present Law, the list will consist only of the persons designated by the other groupings.

Lists of people's judges will be established in each of the residence cities of the Courts of Appeals.

Article 12.—The Minister of Justice will establish one or several court panels of the People's Tribunal as required.

The court panel will consist of nine members, of which two will be appointed magistrates and seven people's judges.

The people's judges on the court panels will be selected by lot by the Minister of Justice, one each from the list of five judges that was submitted by each grouping separately. If one of the groupings did not submit a list, the selection by lot will be from among the members designated by the other groupings.

The court panel will be presided over by the appointed magistrate with higher rank or with seniority in the same rank.

In case one of the magistrates is prevented from participating in the trial, he will be replaced by another magistrate by the Minister of Justice.

In case one of the people's judges is prevented from participating in the trial, he will be replaced by another person chosen by lot from the list submitted by the members of the grouping to which the absent judge belongs, and in the absence of members designated by that grouping drawn by lot from members designated by the other groupings.

Prior to taking up their function, the people's judges drawn by lot will take before the Minister of Justice the oath that is prescribed for the judiciary corps.

The appointed magistrates and the people's judges drawn by lot cannot be challenged.

Article 13.—The court panels will operate in Bucharest.

The Minister of Justice may also establish court panels in the cities of residence of the other Courts of Appeals. In this case, these panels will be competent to try offenders who committed their deeds in the area of jurisdiction of the particular Court of Appeals.

Offenders who committed their acts outside the borders of the country will be tried by the People's Tribunal of Bucharest.

Instigators, co-authors, accomplices, supporters and concealers will be judged by the same instances.

Article 14.—The president opens the session, orders the calling of the parties and witnesses, establishes the identity of the accused, and orders the reading of the indictment. Next he proceeds with the interrogation of the accused and the testimony of the witnesses, after which he calls upon the public prosecutor and the defense, giving the last word to the defense. The president declares the proceedings closed, after which the tribunal issues its decision.

Minutes of the proceedings will be summary.

The decision will be substantiated and may only be appealed to the High Court of Appeal and Justice *(Înalta Curte de Casație și Justiție)* on the grounds of improper composition of the court or faulty application of the penalty.

The appeal is made orally before the court of adjudication and will be adjudicated within three days from receipt of the files. The reasons for the appeal will be submitted and developed in written memoranda submitted up to the adjudication date.

An appeal suspends execution of the penalty only in the case of a death sentence.

The decision will be implemented by the prosecutors of the County Tribunal in the seat of the court that passed the judgment.

Article 15.—The provisions of the Code of Penal Procedure relating to judgment and execution in criminal matters are applicable before the People's Tribunal whenever they are not contrary to the provisions of the present Law.

Article 16.—Any and all legal acts of whatever nature pertaining to the property of persons condemned on the basis of the present law that were entered into after 23 August 1944 are null and void in law, and the goods forming part of their wealth will be subject to confiscation as specified by the court.

Goods or rights belonging to the wife or descendants of a condemned person which were acquired after 6 September 1940 are subjected to the same provisions except for goods acquired by inheritance.

Article 17.—Persons who in any manner hide or aid in the flight of those referred to by the present Law as well as persons who hide their property will be punished by the People's Tribunal with correctional imprisonment of three to five years.

Article 18.—The provisions of Law Number 50 relating to the pursuit and punishment of war criminals and profiteers and Law Number 51 relating to the pursuit and punishment of persons guilty for the country's disaster, published in the *Monitorul Oficial* of 21 January 1945, as well as any other contrary provisions are and remain abrogated.

The documents relating to investigation and instruction, as well as the arrest orders, issued on the basis of those Laws remain in effect until the publication of the present Decree Law.

The investigation and trial of persons guilty for the country's disaster or of war crimes may be continued on the basis of the present Decree Law until 1 September 1945.

Issued in Bucharest on 21 April 1945.

Michael

Minister of Justice
L. Pătrăşcanu

et. 11.

Jegyzőkönyv

felveve a budapesti Népügyészségen 1945. december 17-én dr. Gyapai László, dr. Csuka László, dr. Vásárhelyi László ellen háborus büncselekmények miatt folyamatban lévő bünügyben.

A fenti bünügyben tanuként kihallgatandó dr. Endre Laszlo kihallgatásánal a romániai néptörvényszék kolozsvári tagozatának közvádlója, dr. Pollák Endre megjelenik.

Jelenvannak:

Dr. Gyarmathy Istvan népügyész
Dr. Pollák Endre
közvádló

dr. Endre László
tanu

Timár Georgina jkv. vezető

Dr. Endre László szül. 1895.január 1-én Abonyban, rk. vallásu, nős, volt államtitkár, anyja: Gullner Irma, bpesti Marku u.27. lakos, erdektelen tanu a törvenyes figyelmeztetés után a következőket adja elő:

Emlékezetem szerint 1944.év április hó utolsó napjaiban nagyobb szabásu értekezletet tartottam Szatmárnémetiben. Erre az értekezletre meghivást kaptak az északerdélyi közigazgatás törvényhatóságainak vezetői: alispán, főispán, polg.mester, csendőr kerületi parancsnokok és rendőrkapitányok. És emlékezetem szerint magasabb katonai parancsnokok is. Az értekezlet tárgya a zsidók gettóba, illetve táborba szállitása. Gettőnek tekintettük az összeköltöztetésnek ezt a módját, amikor a zsidókat emberi lakás céljaira épitett lakásokban zsufolták össze, mig tábornak a nagyobb befogadó képességü, gyári, vagy gazdasági épületet, vagy külön e célra deszkából épitett barakkok összességét.

A kárpátaljai gyakorlattal nem lévén megelégedve a szatmári értekezleten nyomatékosan felhivtam a vezetők figyelmét arra, gondoskodjanak arról, hogy mindenki tisztességes emberi elhelyezésben részesüljön, hogy az öregeknek külön aggokházát létesitsenek, terhesanyáknak szülőotthont, kórházat és külön járványkorházat. Ajánlottam, hogy gyárépületet ezek között téglagyárat, vagy nagyobb gazdasági épületeket vegyenek igénybe. Szigoruan figyelmeztettem a közegeket arra, hogy a zsidó javaknak összeszedésével kapcsolatban mindenféle visszaéléstől tartózkodnajak, mert ezt a legsulyosabb hazaárulásnak tekintem. Ugyanigy minősitettem az embertelen bánásmódot is. Arra is kitértem, hogy a táborban, illetve a Gettóben lévő személyek élelmezéséről az illető törvényhatóság köteles gondoskodni és hogy erre a célra a közellátási miniszter ur megfelelő intezkedéseket hozott, illetve felhatalmazást adott a tartalékkészletek felhatalmazására. Ilyen természetü kritérium nem volt. A törvényhatóság első tisztviselőjének hatáskörébe állt annak elhatározása, hogy a közbiztonsági szervekkel és a németekkel egyetértésben gettót, vagy tábort fognak felállitani. Nincs tudomásom arról, és nem emlékszem rá, hogy olyan intézkedést hoztam volna, hogy Gettóbizottságokat kell felállitani. Szatmáron a katonai intézkedés vonalán kiadott rendelet alapján jártam el.-

Velem volt a szatmári értekezleten Takács Albert miniszteri titkárom, Szanik Géza aszódi főszolgabiró, később Bereg vm. főispánja, dr. Rozsnyai Béla közjóléti felügyelő székesfehérvári, dr. Simon Ákos fővárosi tisztiorvos, dr. Tardi Sándor főorvos, a Közellátási minisztérium kiküldötte.

Emlékezetem szerint a szatmári értekezlet után kiszálltunk Mateszalkára és ott megtekintettük a zsidók elhelyezését. Szatmárnémeti után Marosvásárhelyre mentem ahol a főispánnal, alispánnal, polgármesterrel tartottam rövid félórás beszélgetést.

Marosvásárhelyen több időt töltöttem. Az utasitások azonosak
voltak, mint a Szatmárnemetiek. Ez után Sepsziszentgyörgyön voltam, ott dr. Szentiványi Gábor főispánnal és az alispánnal tárgyaltam, akikkel megtekintettem laktanyát, vagy katonai barakktábort. Innen Kolozsvárra mentem ott Veres Lajos altábornagyal,
Vásárhelyi polgármesterrel, Hollósi rendőrségi tábornokkal tárgyaltam s nem emlékszem rá, hogy helyszini vizsgálatot tartottam
volna.Nem tartózkodtam hoszabb ideig fél óránál. Kolozsvárról
Nagyvaradra mentem. Emlékezetem szerint Gyapai polgármesterrel
Nadányi alispánnal tárgyaltam mások személyére nem is tudok emlékezni, nem tudom mennyi időt töltöttem, de nem volt szükség
soha beszelgetésre, mert a vezetők részt vettek, vagy a szatmár
nemeti, vagy a nyiregyházi értekezleten, legalább is meghivót
kaptak. Nem emlékszem rá, hogy megtekintettem volna a Gettóra
kijelölt helyet. Nem tudok róla, hogy 1944.május 8-án Munkácson
értekezlet lett volna, melyre meghivták az északerdélyi közigazgatás képviselőit is, s mélyen közölték, hogy megkezdődik a
zsidók elszállitása Kassán keresztül egy Lengyelországi táborba. Az elszallitásokra az intézkedéseket a németek adták meg,
én ebbe nem is szóltam bele. A magyar szerveknek csak annyi
feladata volt, hogy gondoskodni kellett tartalék élelmiszerkészletről és ivóvizről az ellátásnál. A csendőrségi utasitásokat
tudomásom szerint Ferenci László csendőrezredes,-aki a németek
mellé volt beosztva adta ki,-mint összekötő. Igaz, hogy nekem
régi tervem volt a zsidóknak a kitelepitése ezt meg is irtam
többször, de nekem nem volt tudomásom arról, hogy az 1944.májusában gettókba és táborokba tömöritett Magyarországi zsidókat
hová viszik és ott mi történik velük. Illetve határozott választ kaptam a nemetektől, oly értelemben,hogy ezeket munkára
viszik s a családtagokat pedig azert viszik velük,hogy jobban
tudjanak dolgozni.Bár kifejezetten nem volt róla szó, de az én

utasitásaimból következett, hogy a betegeket, akik nem szállithatók, vagy akiknek az utazás ártalmas, illetve életveszélyes, azokat nem kell elszállitani. Tudok róla, hogy az elszállitással kapcsolatban élelmezési és szállitási költség megtéritési igényeik voltak. Erről nekem Eichmann akkor tett emlitést, amikor a szállitás először került szóba, de hogy ők tovább kivel tárgyaltak arról tovább nem tudok. Az én tudomásom szerint az elszallitások május közepén kezdődtek, addig nem történt elszállitást, azt hogy külföldre, illetve Németországba fogják vinni a zsidókat azt tudtam, de hogy megsemmisitő lágerokba viszik őket, arról egyáltalán nem tudtam.

Annak sem tudom okát adni, hogy a Kárpátaljai Felvidéki es északerdélyi zsidókat miert szállitottak Auszschnitzba, a Duna- Tiszaközi, Dunántuli és más Magyarországi zsidókat Ausztriába és a budapestieket pedig egyáltalán nem szállitották el.

Nekem vasut technikai okokkal magyarázták, hogy az első kategoriát Kassa felé viszik ki Magyarországról és ez előttem érthető is volt. Azt is természetesnek találtam, hogy nyugatra viszik a többieket, azt pedig pontosan tudom, hogy a pesti zsidóságot azért nem szállitották el, hogy a kormányzó közbelépett.

Nincsen tudomásom arról, hogy zsidók tárgyalásokat folytattak volna a gestapoval, akár az egész Magyarországi zsidóság, akar bizonyos zart számu zsidók megmentése érdekében. Csak annyit hallottam, hogy bizonyos semleges államok a vöröskereszttel karöltve állampolgárságot nyujtanak s igy próbalnak bizonyos személyeket a rendelkezések alól kivonni. Arról hogy Kasztel Rezső, Brant Joel és mások közvetlen a gestapo vezetőivel tárgyaltak pénz ellenében való mentésitésekről, erről nekem nincs tudomásom s arról sem tudok, hogy ezeket az embereket e miatt őrizetbe vették volna magyar hatóságok.

- 5 -

Azt tudom, hogy 1944.julius 7-én Jaross Andor belügyminiszter lemondott es hogy már ezt megelőzően engem felmentettek a zsidóügyek intezese alól. Az én felmentésem után ezeket az intézkedéseket a Belügyminisztetiumban Szilagyi László miniszteri tanacsos, csendőrsegi vonalon pedig Ferenci László csendőr alezredes intézte. Azt, hogy a zsidók egy részét megsemmisitő taborokba vitték s ott gázzal megölték őket csak ez év nyarán tudtam meg, addig semmit nem is hallottam ezekről. Ezt is amerikaiaktol tudtam meg.

Más előadni valom nincs.
Felolvasás után hh. aláiratott.

Kmf.

népügyész.

közvadló   jkvvezető.   tanu.

J e g y z ő k ö n y v

felvéve a Budapesti Népügyészségen 1945. december 18-án
dr. Gyapai Laszló, dr. Csuka László, dr. Vásárhelyi László
ellen haborus büncselekmények miatt folyamatban lévő bünügyben.

Fenti ügyben tanuként kihallgatandó Baky László. A kihallgatásnál a romániai néptörvényszék kolozsvári tagozatának közvádlója dr. Pollák Endre megjelenik.

J e l e n v a n n a k :

Dr. Gyarmathy István népügyész
dr. Pollák Endre közvádló
Tisár Georgina jkv.vezető

Baky László tanu

Tanu: Baky László szül. 1898. szeptember 13. Budapesten,
ref.vallásu, nős, volt államtitkár anyja: Ács Margit, bpesti
lakos Marko u.27. érdektelen tanu a törv. figyelmeztetés után
a következőket adja elő:

1944. március 24-én lettem államtitkár a Sztójai kormányban
s ezt az állásomat ugyanez év. aug. 27-ig tartottam meg; amikor
is állásomból felmentettek. Mint államtitkár a csendőrség és
rendőrségi osztály felügyeletével voltam megbizva. A gettózás
nem tartozott a hatáskörömbe ezt Endre László intézte. Való az,
hogy 1944. apr. 7-én egy rendeletet kiadmányoztam /e rendeletnek
az eredetije elfekszik a bpesti Népbiróságnál folyamatban lévő
háborus és népellenes bünügyem iratainál./ Ennek tartalmára részletesen nem emlékszem, mert nem az én munkám volt, de ezt tudom
hogy a hadműveleti területen lévő zsidó lakosság koncentrálására
vonatkozott. A rendeletet Endre László fogalmazta az ő kézjegyével
is van ellátva, de azért kellett nekem kiadmányozni ,mert abban
az időben még nem jelent meg az ő államtitkári kinevezése .

- 2 -

Tudomásom szerint Magyarországon a zsidók összeszedését a csendőrség és rendőrség hajtotta végre. Az e tárgyban kiadott alaprendelkezések szerint hozzám legfeljebb csak jelentések futottak be arról, hogy hová milyen mennyiségü csendőr, vagy rendőr létszámra van szükség. A rendeletek végrehajtás során több izben megtörtént, hogy az érdekeltek panasszal kerestek meg, azért, mert a végrehajtó szervek a csillagrendelet hatálya alá nem eső személyeket is begettozta. Ilyen esetekben intézkedtem hogy tartsák be a törvényes rendelkezéseket.

Nincs tudomásom arról, hogy olyan rendelkezés ment volna ki, amely szerint a rendőrség mellőzhető, mint megbizhatatlan és igy helyette a csendőrség használandó fel. Utólag hallottam és jelentés is jött be erről, hogy Endre László államtitkár, aki Kárpátalján és Erdélyben a Belügyminiszter különös felhatalmazása alapján egy körutat tett, hozott ilyen természetü intézkedéseket és egyes rendőrkapitányságok vezetőit fel is váltotta. Később én ezen ügyekben vizsgálatot rendeltem el és felmentett rendőrvezetőket állásukba visszahelyeztem. A helyszinen a csendőrség a legmagasabb csendőrtiszt rendelkezése alatt állott és ez volt felelős azért, hogy a kiadott rendeleteket hogyan hajtják végre. Nem tudok arról, hogy olyan rendelet ment volna felülről a csendőrparancsnokoknak, hogy a Gettóba zárt zsidókat kinozni, ütni, vagy verni kell. Ellenkezőleg szóban és irásban személyesen utasitottam a csendőrparancsnokokat, hogy minden durvaságtól és kegyetlenkedéstől tartozkodni kell és ezért a parancsnokok személyében teszem felelőssé. Nagyobb centrumokban a csendő rosztályparancsnok volt a legmagasabb rangu tiszt. Ezeknek parancsnoka volt a csendőrparancsnok.

Csendőr kegyetlenkedésekről több bántalmazási panasz érkezett be hozzám ezeket én kivizsgálásra a csendőrosztálynak kiadtam megbeszélést is tartottam Faragó altábornaggyal a csendőrség főparancsnokával és Szegeden és Siófon személyesen is eljártam és nyomatékosan figyelmeztettem a csendőrparancsnokokat felelősségükre. Faragó altábornagy közölte is velem, hogy a beérkezett panaszok alapján 8-10 esetben hadbirósági marasztaló itéletet is hoztak. Egyetlen olyan jelentés nem jött be hozzám, hogy a bántalmazások következtében valaki életét vesztette volna. Az érték kutatásokra vonatkozóan sem adtam ki semmifele külön utasitast.

Nem adtam utasitat a csendőrségnek a berakásban való közreműködésre sem. Ha a csendőrség mégis valahogy ezt a munkát elvégezte ugy a parancsnok felelős érte. Nem volt törvényes az az intézkedés, hogy a csendőrparancsnok a németek rendelkezését végrehajtja, mert csak a felettes hatósága, vagy az Összekötő tiszt Ferenczi csendőralezredes adhatott érvényes utasitást.

Az én tudomásom szerint a szállitást képtelen betegekre az elszállitási utasitás nem vonatkozhatott. Ha ilyen személyeket mégis elszállitottak ugy ezért szerintem a helybeli parancsnok a felelős. Hozzám nem fordultak ilyen panasszal hogy szállitásképtelen betegeket elvisznek, de ha ilyen panasz befutott volna ugy azonnal intézkedtem volna a felelősségrevonás irányában is.

Később tudtam meg az elszállitás körülményeit, valamint azt hogy vagononként egy később 2 vödör vizet adtak be. Ezért az intézkedésért az elszállitásnál közreműködő szervek afelelelősek, mert ilyen intézkedést, vagy utasitást én nem adtam ki.

Én egyetlen esetben sem voltam jelen gettóba való összeszedésnél, vagy szállitmány összeállitásnál. Geske ezredes a német gestapo egyik parancsnoka május végén, vagy junius elején közölte velem, hogy a Hain Péterék szervezete nekik egy bizalmi zsidó megbizottjukat letartóztatta s kérte, hogy intézkedjek ennek szabadlábrahelyezése iránt. Én azonnal intézkedtem az illetőt szabadlabra is helyezték, de kiderült, hogy félholtra verték és valutahiányok is voltak. Tudomásom szerint a gestapó ezen bizalmi embere utján Törökország felé valami hadifogolycsere üzletről tárgyalt. Annak idején ezért az eljárásért Hain Pétert igazolásra szólitottam fel s ez volt egyik oka annak, hogy csoportját német közbelépés elenére is feloszlatta.

A fenti ügyre vonatkozóan Hain Péter és társai bővebb felvilágositást kell hogy adjon.

Tudok arról, hogy a deportálással kapcsolatban a németek minden egyes elszállitott személy után szállitási költséget és 1 évi élelmezési költséget igényeltek. Hogy a valóságban a magyar kormány fizetett-e és mennyit azt nem tudom. Egyéb előadni valóm ninc..

A jegyzőkönyv felolvasás hh. után aláiratott.

Kmf.

népügyész.
közvádló
jkv.vezető
tanu.

Selected Bibliography

Bibliographical Guides

Randolph L. Braham, comp. *The Hungarian Jewish Catastrophe. A Selected and Annotated Bibliography.* New York: YIVO-Institute for Jewish Research, 1962, 86 p.
Arthúr Geyer, comp. *A magyarországi fasizmus zsidóüldözésének bibliográfiája, 1945–1958* (The Bibliography of the Jewish Persecutions by Fascism in Hungary, 1945–1958). Budapest: Magyar Izraeliták Országos Képviselete, 1958, 167 p.

Comprehensive Works

Randolph L. Braham. *The Politics of Genocide. The Holocaust in Hungary.* New York: Columbia University Press, 1981, 2 vols. (1269 p.)

General Works

Daniel Csatári. *Dans la tourmente. Les relations hungaro-roumaines de 1940 à 1945.* Budapest: Akadémiai Kiadó, 1974, 418 p.
G. Zaharia and L. Vajda, eds. *The Anti-Fascist Resistance in the North-East of Transylvania. (September 1940–October 1944).* Bucharest: Editura Academiei Republicii Socialiste România, 1979, 240 p.

Memorial Volumes

Michael Bar-On (Deutsch), ed. *Szamosujvár, Iklód és környeke* (Szamosujvár, Iklód, and Environs). Tel Aviv: Izsák Efrájim és Fia, 1971, 90+190 p.
Mózes Carmilly-Weinberger, ed. *A kolozsvári zsidóság emlékkönyve* (The Memorial Book of Kolozsvár's Jewry). New York: The Editor, 1970, 313+147 pp.
Béla Katona. *Várad a viharban* (Várad in the Storm). Nagyvárad: Tealah Korháztámogató Egyesület, 1946, 363 p.
Alexander Leitner. *Die Tragödie der Juden in Nagyvárad.* Jerusalem: Yad Vashem, Archives JM/2686. (Manuscript)
Jicchak Perri (Friedmann) ed. *Prakim be'toldot ha'yehudim be'Transylvania b'et hekadasha. Korot yehudei Marosvásárhely ve'hasviva* (Chapters from the History of the Jews of Transylvania in Modern Times. History of the Jews of Marosvásárhely and Environs). Tel Aviv: Bet Lohamei Hagetaot, 1977, 2 vols. (311+287+41 p.)
Dezsö Schön et al, eds. *A tegnap városa. A nagyváradi zsidóság emlékkönyve* (The City of Yesterday. The Memorial Book of the Jews of Nagyvárad). Tel Aviv: Lahav for the A Nagyváradról Elszármazottak Egyesülete Izraelben, 1981, 446 p.

Yehuda Schwarz, ed. *Toldot ha'kehilot b'Transylvania* (History of the Communities of Transylvania). Tel Aviv: Ha'aguda Yad le'Kehilot Transylvania, 1976, 294 p.
Zoltán Singer, ed. *Volt egyszer egy Dés . . . Bethlen, Magyarlápos, Retteg, Nagyilonda és környéke* (There Was Once Upon a Time a Dés . . . Bethlen, Magyarlápos, Retteg, Nagyilonda and Environs). Tel Aviv: A Dés és Vidékéről Elszármazottak Landsmannschaftja, n.d., 2 vols. (284+683 p.)
Naftali Stern, ed. *Baia Mare. Nagybánya és vidéke mártirjainak emlékkönyve* (The Memorial Book of the Martyrs of Nagybánya and Environs). B'nei B'rak: The Editor, 1979, 245+164 p. (Mimeographed)
Sh. Zimroni and Y. Schwartz, eds. *Zikkaron netsah le'kehila ha'kedosha Kolozhvar-Klauzenburg asher nehreva ba'shoa* (Everlasting Memorial to the Martyred Community of Kolozsvár Which Perished in the Holocaust). Tel Aviv: Former Residents of Kolozsvár in Israel, 1968, 118 p. (Mimeographed)

Articles

Livia Bitton. "The Zionist Movement in Transylvania." In Carmilly-Weinberger, ed., *A kolozsvári zsidóság emlékkönyve,* pp. 277–85.
Mózes Carmilly-Weinberger. "Jewish Education in Transylvania in the Days of the Holocaust." In *A kolozsvári zsidóság emlékkönyve,* pp. 269–76.
———. Zsidók Erdélyben (Jews in Transylvania). In *A kolozsvári zsidóság emlékkönyve,* pp. 7–28, 263–68.
Hans Holzträger. "Ghettoisierung und Deportation der jüdischen Bevölkerung Nordsiebenbürgens April bis Juni 1944." In *Siebenbürgisches Jahrbuch, 1979.* Munich, 1979, pp. 57–68.
Kálmán Káhán. "Az erdélyi zsidó sajtó története" (The History of the Transylvanian Jewish Press). In Carmilly-Weinberger, ed., *A kolozsvári zsidóság emlékkönyve,* pp. 185–202.
Ernő Ligeti. "Erdély zsidósága" (Transylvania's Jewry). In *Ararát. Magyar zsidó évkönyv az 1941. évre* (Ararát. Hungarian-Jewish Yearbook for 1941), ed. Aladár Komlós. Budapest: Országos Izr. Leányárvaház, 1941, pp. 81–88.
Yehuda Marton "Transylvania." In *Encyclopaedia Judaica.* Jerusalem, 1971, Vol. 15, pp. 1342–46.
Béla Vágó. "The Destruction of the Jews of Transylvania." In: *Hungarian-Jewish Studies,* Vol. I, ed. Randolph L. Braham. New York: World Federation of Hungarian Jews, 1966, pp. 171–221.

Name Index

Abel, Edmund (Ödön), 27
Ábrahám, József (Iosif, Dr.), 40, 57, 156, 195, 209, 214, 220, 223
Abraham, Mrs. Náthán, 184
Ábrahám, Samu, 37
Abromeit, Franz, 20, 32
Adler, Rachel, 165
Ágai, Andor, 29
Ágoston, Pál, 183
Agy, Zoltán, 40, 157, 158, 161
Ajtay, Gábor, 14
Albert, Lázár, 29
Amiras, Aladár, 58
Anghea, Ioan (János Angya), 30, 57, 58, 60, 164, 165, 168, 172, 173, 197, 200–201, 212, 215, 219
Antal, István, 31
Antalffy, Pál (Paul), 27, 28, 57, 178, 187, 197, 210, 215, 216, 223
Áron, József, 90

Bajor, Gen., 108
Bak, Jenő, 119
Bakay, Miklós, 28, 179
Baky, László, 16, 61, 62, 69, 73, 85, 196
Balázs, Imre, 97, 98
Balla (Loc. Col.), 40, 57, 156, 197, 200, 209, 215, 217, 218, 223
Balogh, Károly (Carol; Kornel), 32, 57, 116, 211, 215, 223
Bányai, Pál (Pavel), 39, 57, 154, 197, 208, 215, 216
Barabás, Andor (Andrei; András, Dr.), 40, 57, 156, 195, 209, 214, 220, 223
Barcsay, Károly, 49
Báthori, Ilona, (Elena), 56, 58, 62, 135–137, 199, 207, 216, 221, 223
Bauer, Ágnes, 101
Bede, István (Ştefan), 57, 161, 162, 198, 213, 215, 216
Bedő, Géza (Dr.), 37, 38, 56, 143, 145, 147, 197, 207, 215, 216, 223
Begosi, Sándor, 59
Belovai, Ştefan, 55, 224
Belteki, Sándor, 151
Bene, Imre, 97, 98
Benedek, József, 164, 166, 171, 175
Benedek, László, 114
Berecki, Ernő (Ernest), 27, 57, 178, 187, 197, 210, 215, 217, 223
Berentes, László (Vasile), 32, 57, 117, 119, 198, 211, 215, 217, 223
Berger, Julia, 115
Berkovits, Berta, 100
Bertalan, István (Ştefan), 32, 57, 119, 197, 211, 215, 217

Bethlen, Béla, 27, 44, 180, 188
Bethlen, Gábor, 3
Biró, Balázs, 39, 57, 154, 197, 208, 215, 216
Biró, János (Ioan), 57, 161, 198, 213, 215, 216
Biró, Samu, 29, 184
Blazsek, Alfred, 58
Bocskor, Loránt, 38, 147
Bodolai, Endre (Bodolay), 35, 56, 90, 197, 203, 215, 217, 223
Boér, Endre (vitéz), 31, 56, 101, 112, 115, 121, 195, 205, 214, 220, 222
Bojan, Pavel, 55, 224
Boldizsár, Pál (Paul, Dr.), 25, 56, 137, 138, 197, 206, 215, 217
Bonda, István (Ştefan, Dr.), 38, 56, 150, 195, 208, 214, 220, 223
Bonyhai, István, 62, 131, 132, 133
Borbély, Kálmán (Coloman), 33, 57, 58, 59, 64, 189–190, 196, 201, 213, 214, 219, 221, 223
Borgida, József, 31, 102, 103, 107, 108
Borkay, Ernő, 134, 135
Botos, István, 58
Botos, János (Ioan), 56, 58, 59, 62, 139–140, 199, 206, 216, 221
Brach, Mendel, 189
Budai (Gendarme), 35, 56, 91, 197, 204, 215, 217
Buia, Ilona, 92
Büss, Dezső (Desideriu Bus), 35, 56, 90, 197, 203, 215, 217

Capesius, Victor (Kapezius, N.), 56, 140–141, 199, 206, 216
Cetăţeanu, Juliu, 118
Charap, Béla, 148
Ciano, Galeazzo, 8
Cora, Péter, 161
Covaci, Mihai, 56, 224
Criveanu, Teodor, 59
Csáky, István, 7
Császár, Sámuel (Samuilă; zegemi), 56, 198, 206, 216, 217
Csegezi, Károly (Carol Czegényi), 31, 56, 101, 103, 108, 197, 205, 215, 217, 223
Csengeri, Mrs. Ferenc, 165, 171, 173
Csengeri, Mayer, 37
Cser, Lajos (Ludovic, vitéz), 33, 56, 58, 60, 80, 91, 199, 201, 216, 221
Csóka, László (Ladislau, Dr.), 31, 32, 56, 58, 61, 77, 78, 101, 102, 104–106, 107, 195, 204, 214, 220–221, 222
Csordácsics, Jenő (Egon), 39, 57, 151, 152, 199, 208, 216, 221, 223
Csurka, Péter, 90
Czeisberger, Péter (Petru Csisperger), 32, 57, 58, 60, 120–121, 197, 200, 211, 215, 217

In the documents of the People's Tribunal, including the Judgment reproduced in this volume, the names (especially first names) of many of the Hungarian defendants are misspelled or rendered in their Romanian version. In this book, the defendants are identified by their original names as they appear in the 3 June 1946 issue of *Igazság* (Truth) of Kolozsvár (Cluj). This index records all the names and titles by which a particular defendant is identified.

NAME INDEX

Dan, Gheorghe, 55, 224
Dannecker, Theodor, 35, 36
Danzig, Hillel, 27, 41
Danzig, Samu, 41
Danzinger, Olga, 60
Darvas, Mór, 37
Dávid, Oszkár, 97, 98
Debreczeni, Miklós (N., Dr.), 33, 57, 188, 190, 198, 214, 215, 217, 223
Delmann, Endre, 103
Deményi, N. (Demeny, vitéz), 31, 56, 101, 103, 108, 197, 205, 215, 216, 223
Dénes, Dezső (Desideriu, Dr.), 30, 57, 58, 59, 64, 176–178, 199, 213, 216, 221, 224
Désaknai, Miklós (N.), 28, 57, 181, 182, 197, 210, 215, 217
Deutsch, Ernő, 31
Deutsch, Ignác, 90
Deutsch, Margit, 127
Dudás, János (Ioan), 38, 39, 57, 151, 152, 153, 154, 197, 208, 215, 217, 223
Duha, Irén (Irina), 30, 57, 58, 60, 172, 197, 212, 215, 219, 221
Dunca, E., 59

Eichmann, Adolf, 16
Elek, Frida, 184
Elekes, Ferenc (Francisc), 29, 30, 57, 162, 163, 167, 197, 211, 215, 216, 223
Elekes, Miksa, 146
Endre, László, 16, 18, 22, 23, 32, 36, 42, 43, 61, 62, 65, 69, 71, 85, 142, 157, 190
Endrődi, Barnabás (vitéz), 32, 56, 121–123, 196, 205, 214, 220, 223
Engelberg, Oszkár, 29
Enyedi, Irma (Irina), 56, 58, 62, 131–133, 199, 207, 216, 221, 223

Fábián, Julia, 134
Faraghó, Gábor, 43
Farkas, Ana, 136
Farkas, Éva, 168
Farkas, József, 195
Farkas, Pál (Pavel), 40, 57, 156, 199, 209, 216, 221, 223
Farmati, Sándor (Alexandru), 30, 57, 58, 60, 164, 168, 172, 198, 201, 212, 215, 219, 221, 223
Fehér, András (Fejér), 39, 57, 154, 197, 208, 215, 216
Fehér, Endre, 88
Fehér, János (Ioan), 57, 161, 198, 213, 215, 217
Fehér, Sándor (Alexandru), 35, 56, 91, 197, 204, 215, 217
Fekete, Erzsébet (Elisabeta), 56, 58, 60, 109–110, 199, 205, 216, 221, 224
Fekete, György (Gheorghe, vitéz), 35, 56, 90, 197, 203, 215, 217
Fekete, József, 122
Fekete, József, 28, 180, 181
Fekete, Mária (Margareta; Margit), 28, 57, 58, 59, 60, 179, 180, 183, 184–185, 197, 200, 210, 215, 218
Félegyházi Medgyesi, Ágoston, 35, 56, 87, 90, 197, 201, 215, 216, 223,
Felföldi, István (Ştefan), 35, 56, 91, 197, 204, 215, 217
Felszner, Samu, 127
Fenichel, József, 26
Fenyves, Ármin, 31
Ferenczi, Béla, 39, 57, 153, 154, 155, 197, 209, 215, 217
Ferenczy, László, 17, 18, 20, 24, 30, 32, 43, 63, 126, 190, 191
Filipaş, Lajos, 117, 118
Filipescu, Richard, 58
Filó, Ferenc (Francisc, Dr.), 38, 57, 150, 195, 208, 214, 220, 223
Fischer, József, 6, 26, 27
Fischer, Margit, 138
Fischer, Tivadar, 6
Fischmann, Sándor, 170
Forgács, József (Iosif, Dr.), 56, 125, 199, 205, 216, 221
Frankovics, Sándor, 128
Frater, János (Ioan), 56, 87, 90, 197, 203, 215, 217, 223
Freud, Wilhelm, 111
Friedmann, Moshe, 187
Friedmann, Sándor, 112
Friedmann, Sarolta, 115

Gaáli, Ernő (Ernest; Gálli, vitéz), 40, 57, 156, 195, 209, 214, 221, 223
Gál, István, 149
Gálfy, Dezső (Desideriu Galfi), 38, 56, 150, 195, 208, 214, 221, 223
Garai, Imre (Emeric), 35, 56, 91, 197, 204, 215, 217
Garai, István (Ştefan Garay), 35, 56, 90, 197, 203, 215, 217, 223
Garamvölgyi, Albert (Adalbert; Béla), 28, 57, 181, 197, 210, 215, 217
Gárdos, Aladár, 145, 148
Gazda, Ákos, 113, 115, 116
Gazda, András (Andrei; Andor, Dr.), 29, 30, 57, 162, 163, 167, 175, 178, 195, 211, 214, 220
Gecse, József (Iosif), 28, 57, 58, 60, 180, 181, 183, 184, 197, 210, 215, 217, 223
Geller, Mihály, 125, 128
Gellért, Béla, 114, 117
Gergely, Gyula, 32, 113
Gerő, Sándor, 176
Glasner, Akiba, 26
Gligorin, Alexandru, 55, 224
Glück, Icu, 60, 100
Goldberger, Margit, 115
Goldfinger, Mrs. Tibor, 111
Goldstein, Ernő, 37
Goldstein, József, 184
Gősi, István (Ştefan), 39, 57, 154, 197, 209, 215, 216
Gottlieb, László, 114

Grosz, Samu, 104
Grünbaum, Imre, 169
Grünbaum, Klára, 170
Grünfeld, Aranka, 100
Grünfeld, Hermann, 90
Grünfeld, Ilona, 100
Gurkovski, Aliz, 129
Guttmann, Mrs. Manó, 89
Gyapai, László (Ladislau; Gyapay, Dr.), 21, 23, 33, 34, 56, 73, 79–84, 85, 94, 195, 201, 214, 220, 222
Gyenge, László, 58
Gyulafalvi Rednik, Sándor (Alexandru, Dr.), 40, 41, 57, 157, 158, 159, 195, 213, 214, 220, 223

Hăgăduş, Nerva, 55, 224
Hain, Péter, 35
Haracsek, József (Iosif Horacsek), 32, 57, 113, 116, 211, 221
Hárnik, Gitta, 185, 186
Haus, Márton, 144
Heller, Miklós, 90
Helmer, József, 37
Henner, Ferenc (Francisc; Hennel, Dr.), 38, 56, 144, 145, 199, 207, 216, 221, 223
Hermann, Dezső, 26
Hermann, László, 155
Herskovits, Sarolta, 100
Hevesi, Miklós, 124, 127
Hitler, Adolf, 7
Hollóssy-Kuthy, Lajos, 23, 24, 25
Horák, Vilmos (Vilhelm), 56, 58, 59, 60, 133–135, 199, 207, 216, 221, 223
Horkai, Zoltán, 56, 198, 206, 216, 217
Horthy, Miklós, 7
Horváth, Ádám, 37, 144
Horváth, János (Ioan), 57, 172, 197, 212, 215, 217
Horváth, József (Iosif), 35, 56, 91, 197, 204, 215, 217
Horváth, Sándor (Alexandru, Dr.), 30, 57, 167, 168, 197, 212, 215, 216, 223
Hullmann, Ferenc (Francisc), 41, 57, 58, 59, 64, 159–160, 161, 199, 213, 216, 221

Illinyi, László (Vasile, Dr.), 40, 57, 157, 159, 160, 196, 213, 214, 217, 223
Ilonka, Sándor (Alexandru), 35, 56, 90, 197, 203, 215, 217
Inczedi-Joksmann, Ödön, 56, 58, 59, 60, 75, 224
Indig, Paises, 161
Indig, Shmil, 161
Iványi, András (Andrei; Andor), 27, 57, 187, 210, 215, 217, 223
Izsák, Dezső, 172, 173
Izsák, Florentina, 185, 186

Jakab, Izidor, 189
Jakab, Lajos, 79, 80
Jakab, Miklós, 57, 189, 214, 215, 216, 223
Jakobovics, Lajos, 31
Jakobovits, Mór, 41

Jancsó, Rozália, 28, 57, 58, 60, 185–186, 197, 200, 210, 215, 219
Jaross, Andor, 16, 35, 69, 94
Jávor, Ernő (Ernest, vitéz, Dr.), 38, 56, 145, 199, 207, 216, 221, 223
Joós, Andor, 38, 56, 145, 150, 153, 207, 215, 217
Jósika, János, 29, 162
Joszovits, Lipót, 41
Józan, Miklós, 24
Juhász, Mihály (Mihail), 35, 56, 91, 197, 203, 215, 217

Kadicsfalvi, 195
Kala, Gusztáv, 98
Kállay, Miklós, 16
Kassay, János (Ioan; Kassai), 28, 57, 181, 210, 215, 217
Kasztner, Rezső (Rudolph), 26
Katona, Béla, 82
Keledy, Tibor, 45
Kemecsey, István, 30, 163
Kerekes, Ádám, 30, 57, 164, 168, 172, 199, 212, 216, 221, 224
Kerényi, István (Ştefan), 56, 111, 199, 205, 216, 221
Keresztesi, Gábor (Gavril), 35, 56, 91, 197, 204, 215, 217
Kertész, Jenő, 27
Keszner, Jenő, 41
Király, Jenő, 129, 140
Kiss, Mrs. János (Ioan) née Rozália Zeffer, 56, 58, 60, 100–101, 197, 200, 204, 215, 218
Kiss, László (Vasile, Loc.-Col.), 38, 57, 150, 199, 208, 216, 221, 223
Klein, Adolf, 120–121
Klein, Gyula, 26
Kocsibár, Endre, 121
Komán, István (Ştefan), 57, 59, 60, 64, 194, 195, 222
Komáromi, László (Ladislau, Maj.), 39, 57, 63, 151, 152, 153, 154, 199, 208, 216, 217, 223
Konya, (Gendarme, Capt.), 38, 56, 148, 197, 207, 215, 216
Konyuk, József, 41, 160, 161
Koréh, Ferenc, 13
Körmendi, Géza (Gheza; Körmendy, Col., vitéz), 37, 56, 145, 195, 207, 214, 220, 222–223
Kőrösi, Zoltán, 130, 131
Kos, Julia, 129
Kosári, Irén (Coşariu, Irina), 56, 58, 61, 192, 193, 222
Kovács, Dénes, 35
Kovács, István, 123, 124
Kovács, László, 144, 147
Kovács, Mihály (Mihail), 30, 57, 58, 60, 168, 172, 199, 212, 216, 221
Kovács-Nagy, István, 34
Kőváry, Tibor, 31
Kőves, Sándor, 27
Kozma, István (Ştefan, vitéz), 37, 56, 145, 195, 207, 214, 220, 223

NAME INDEX

Krämer, Lajos, 28
Krasznai, László (Vasile; Krasznay, Dr.), 30, 57, 163, 164, 165, 166, 167–168, 169, 173, 197, 212, 215, 216, 223
Kraus, Gábor, 144
Krausz, Bernát, 165, 166, 175
Krausz, Ferenc, 41
Krausz, Margit, 129
Krausz, Márton, 148, 149
Kretz, József, 121
Kristóffy, József, 44
Kuales, Norbert (Dr.), 33, 57, 188, 196, 214, 220, 223
Kugler, György (Gheorghe zis Füleki), 39, 57, 58, 60, 153, 197, 200, 208, 215, 218, 223
Kupfer, Miksa, 90

Lakadár, József (Iosif), 28, 57, 180, 181, 183, 185, 197, 210, 215, 217, 223
Lakatos, András (Andrei; Andor), 25, 56, 137, 138, 199, 206, 216, 220
Lakatos, Ferenc (Francisc), 57, 58, 60, 186–187, 199, 210, 216, 220, 222
Lakli, Mrs. Antal, 111
László, Ferenc, 138
Lax, József (Iosif), 38, 56, 58, 59, 63, 148–150, 198, 201, 208, 215, 219, 221
Lázár, József (Iosif), 30, 57, 58, 60, 164, 165, 168, 169–171, 173, 197, 200, 212, 215, 217
Lázárovics, Margit, 114
Léb, Zsigmond, 26, 27
Lebovits, Leopold, 104
Léderer, Dezső, 37
Lefkovits, Edmond, 111
Lehnár, Zsigmond (Sigismund; Léhner, Dr.), 28, 57, 58, 59, 63, 179, 180, 181, 182, 199, 200, 209, 216, 219
Lembel, Lajos, 121
Lévi, Zoltán, 118
Lidenthal, Adela, 61, 111
Liptai, Dezső, 37
Lohr, Tivadar (Loór Teodor), 40, 57, 157, 199, 209, 216, 221
Lőrincz, Sándor, 34
Lovas, Irma (Lovász), 39, 57, 154, 197, 209, 215, 218
Lupu, Zsiga, 155
Lustig, David, 112

Magyar, Tivadar, 121
Macovei, Andrei, 183
Májay, Ferenc (Francisc, Dr.), 37, 38, 56, 58, 62–63, 71, 74, 77, 142, 144–147, 150, 195, 207, 214, 220, 222
Marguliesz, Ödön, 169
Mariska, György (Gheorghe), 29, 30, 57, 162, 163, 167, 168, 197, 211, 215, 216, 223
Mármor, Gidáli, 193
Marton, Áron, 24
Marton, Ernő, 6, 26
Marton, Lajos, 27

Marton, Zsigmond (Dr.), 38, 56, 145, 147, 195, 207, 214, 220, 222
Matei, Nicolae, 55, 224
Medgyesi, András (Andrei; Andor Megyesi), 35, 56, 90, 197, 203, 215, 217
Medgyesi, Mrs. József (Iosif) neé Erzsébet (Elisabeta) Mutza, 56, 58, 59, 60, 99–100, 197, 200, 204, 215, 218
Meggyesi, Lajos, 18, 20
Megyeri (Gendarme), 35, 56, 91, 197, 204, 215, 217
Mendelsohn, Helén, 186
Mendelsohn, Margit, 186
Menyhért, Ferenc (Francisc; Menyhárt), 25, 56, 137, 138, 197, 206, 215, 217
Meseşan, Augustin, 55, 224
Metzen, Samuel, 34
Mikó, Prefect, 150
Molnár, Ferenc (Francisc, Dr.), 30, 57, 58, 59, 63–64, 163, 165, 175, 199, 201, 212, 216, 219, 221
Molnár, Izidor, 129
Morariu, Ghiran, 56
Moskovits, József, 26
Müller, Sándor, 130
Mureşan, József, 162
Mutza, Erzsébet: see Medgyesi, Mrs. József

Nadányi, János (Ioan, vitéz, Dr.), 23, 33, 34, 56, 84, 85, 195, 201, 214, 220, 222
Nagy, György, 58
Nagy, István (Ştefan), 57, 58, 60, 159, 194, 222
Nagy, Jenő (Eugen, Dr.), 18, 20, 31, 32, 57, 101, 113, 114, 115–116, 210, 215, 217, 223
Nagy, Julianna, 125
Nagy, Rozália, 80
Nagy, Sándor, 30, 164, 168
Nemecz, Alois, 59
Német, Zoltán, 59
Németh, Imre (Emeric), 34, 56, 84, 85, 197, 201, 215, 217, 223
Neumann, Mrs. László, 154
Niptai, Dezső, 143
Nussbaum, Béla, 79, 88
Nyirő, József, 13

Oblát, Fülöp, 162
Ojtózi, Sándor (Alex; Elek), 25, 56, 137, 197, 206, 215, 217
Oláh, Sándor (Alexandru), 28, 57, 58, 60, 185, 198, 210, 216, 220, 222
Oraş, Vasile, 97
Ordentlich, Ferenc, 29
Őrendi, Gusztáv (Gustav), 33, 57, 189, 198, 214, 215, 217, 223
Orgoványi, József (Iosif), 32, 57, 58, 60, 114, 115, 116–119, 211, 215, 217, 223
Őri, Gyula (Iuliu), 35, 56, 90, 197, 203, 215, 217
Örményi, 39, 155
Ormos, Lajos (Ludovic), 57, 197, 211, 215, 217
Orosz, József (Iosif, Dr.), 25, 56, 137, 138, 197, 206, 215, 217
Osváth, René, 34

Osváth, Zoltán, 32, 57, 58, 60, 197, 200, 211, 215, 218

Paksi-Kiss, Tibor (Tiberiu; Paksy), 22, 25, 33, 38, 56, 123, 125–126, 197, 205, 215, 216
Palkovics, Izidor, 115
Paláti, István, 158, 159
Paneth, József, 29
Papp, Géza (Gheza, Dr.), 25, 56, 126, 128, 197, 205, 215, 217, 223
Papp, János (Ioan, Col., Dr.), 37, 56, 145, 197, 207, 215, 216, 223
Pásztai, Ernő (Pásztapi, Ernest; Pásztóhi), 33, 57, 59, 188, 190, 198, 214, 215, 216
Patos, Mária, 101
Paul, Andrei, 56. See also Endre Pollák.
Perl, Fáni, 158
Péterffy, Jenő, 22, 33, 34, 35, 65, 81, 84, 85, 86–87, 90, 126
Pethes, István (Ştefan), 29, 30, 57, 162, 163, 164, 165, 167, 197, 211, 215, 216, 223
Petővári Petrik, László (Vasile), 30, 57, 58, 60, 168, 172, 173, 197, 200, 212, 215, 219
Petri, Gyula (Iuliu, Dr.), 35, 56, 86, 90, 197, 203, 215, 217, 223
Pfeffermann, Jenő, 31
Pintér (Gendarme, Capt.), 38, 56, 148, 208, 216
Pirkler, Ernő (Ernest, Dr.), 31, 56, 58, 61, 101, 106, 107, 108, 199, 204, 216, 221, 223
Polánkai, Géza (Plonkay Gheza; Polonsky, Dr.), 39, 57, 155, 197, 209, 215, 217, 223
Pollák, Endre, 45
Pollák, Lujza, 100
Pop, Liviu, 117
Pop, Simion, 56
Popovici, Nicolae, 96
Posgai, Sándor (Alexandru; Pozsgai), 35, 56, 91, 197, 203–204, 215, 217
Preisler, Mrs. Abraham, 100
Princz, József, 104
Puţovan, János, 60, 91, 92

Rajnay (Reiner), Károly (Carol, vitéz), 34, 35, 57, 58, 64–65, 92–97, 196, 214, 218
Răpeanu, Grigore, 56
Reiter, Imre, 104
Rektor, Béla (Dr.), 35, 56, 87, 90, 197, 203, 215, 217, 223
Réti, György, 148
Reviczky, Imre, 15
Ribbentrop, Joachim von, 8
Ricsóy-Uhlarik, Béla, 17, 44
Rogozi Papp, Zoltán (Dr.), 31, 56, 101, 106, 108, 199, 205, 216, 220
Rosenberg, Sámuel, 31
Rosenfeld, Ármin, 184
Rosenberg, Margit, 158
Rosenfeld, Móric, 116
Rosner, István, 32, 57, 59, 60, 113, 115, 224
Roth, Dr. 192, 193
Roth, Piroska, 118

Rothbart, Zoltán, 90
Rozsnyai, Béla, 18
Rutner, Mendel, 194

Salamon, Árpád, 131, 132, 133
Salamon, Ernő, 131, 132, 133
Salamon, Heinrich, 104
Sallós, Ferenc (Francisc), 38, 56, 148, 197, 208, 215, 216
Sámi, Béla (Sámy, Dr.), 30, 57, 58, 64, 175–176, 178, 199, 212, 216, 221, 224
Sary, István, 58
Sarkadi, Gusztáv (Augustin), 57, 58, 61, 161, 162, 200, 213, 215, 218
Sárkány, László, 31
Sárközi, Béla (Dr.), 31, 56, 101, 103, 108, 197, 205, 215, 217, 223
Sárközi, Miklós (N.), 30, 57, 165, 168, 172, 197, 212, 215, 217
Sárosi, Gyula (Iuliu, Dr.), 27, 57, 178, 197, 210, 215, 217, 223
Sárvári, Col. 40, 41
Sárváry, Miklós (N., Col.), 57, 157, 161, 198, 213, 215, 216, 223
Sáska, Kálmán, 121
Schilling, János (Ioan, Dr.), 27, 28, 29, 57, 58, 63, 178, 179, 183, 196, 209, 214, 220
Schmack, Ferenc, 98
Schmidt, Imre (Emeric, Dr.), 38, 57, 58, 63, 151, 152, 153, 154, 195, 208, 214, 220, 223
Schmuck, Irma, 153–154, 155
Schmuck, Sándor, 153, 154
Schönhaus, Miksa, 133–134, 135
Schreiber, Endre, 125
Schröder (Maj.), 38, 56, 145, 196, 207, 214, 216, 223
Schwartz, Ana, 179
Schwartz, Ernő, 87
Schwartz, Hermann, 109, 110
Schwartz, Jenő, 109, 110
Schwartz, Lázár, 146
Schwartz, Zoltán, 31
Schwechter, Jenő, 150
Schwimmer, Jenő, 37
Sebestyén, Endre, 135
Sedlacek, Rudolf, 26
Silberger, Leopold, 168–169
Simon, Ákos, 18
Singer, Ernő, 37
Singer, Zoltán, 29
Smolenszki, László (Ladislau; Szmolenszki), 33, 57, 188, 196, 213, 214, 220, 223
Smolka, Heinrich (Henric), 33, 57, 58, 61, 189, 199, 214, 216, 221
Socol, Aurel, 59
Somorlyai, János (Ioan, Zomorjai), 28, 57, 181, 197, 210, 215, 217
Spitz, Béla, 104
Spitzer, Arthúr, 90
Sréter, János (Ioan, Schréter, Dr.), 29, 57, 162, 163, 166, 176, 177, 195, 211, 214, 220, 223

NAME INDEX

Stanca, Gavril, 56, 224
Steier, Blanka, 144
Steiner, Márton, 170
Steinfeld, Dezső, 180–181
Stern, Dora, 186
Stössel, Ernő, 130, 131
Stroschneider, 25
Suchi, Dr., 30, 163
Szabados, Géza (Gheza), 35, 56, 91, 197, 203, 215, 217
Szabó, Albert (Adalbert; Béla), 30, 57, 58, 60, 172, 173, 199, 200, 212, 219, 221
Szabó, János, 95
Szabó, Kálmán (Coloman), 57, 58, 60, 193, 222
Szabó, Mihály (Mihail), 35, 56, 91, 197, 204, 215, 217, 224
Szanik, Géza, 18
Szaplonczai, László (Vasile, Dr.), 41, 57, 162, 196, 213, 214, 217, 223
Szász, Ferenc, 25, 56, 59, 60, 137, 224
Szász, Gerő, 40, 57, 156, 195, 209, 214, 220, 223
Szatmári, János, 58
Székely, József (Iosif, Dr.), 25, 56, 137, 138, 195, 206, 214, 220
Szentiványi, Gábor (Gavril, Dr.), 22, 39–40, 57, 58, 63, 75, 156, 199, 209, 216, 221, 223
Szentkuti, András (Andrei; Andor), 25, 56, 137, 138, 197, 206, 215, 217
Szentmiklósy, László, 98, 99
Szentpáli G., Kálmán, 39, 57, 151, 154, 197, 200, 208, 215, 217, 223
Sziklai, Ferenc (Francisc), 35, 56, 90, 197, 203, 215, 217
Szilágyi, István (Ştefan), 57, 58, 60, 194, 222
Szilárszki, Melánia neé Kosári (Coşaru), 56, 58, 61, 192, 193, 222
Szinetár, Ávrám, 117
Szlávi, László (Vasile; Szlávy, Dr.), 30, 57, 162, 178, 196, 211, 214, 217, 223
Szófer, Manón, 37
Szőllősi, István (Ştefan), 35, 56, 91, 197, 203, 215, 217
Sztójay, Döme, 16, 69, 190
Sztojka, Laszló, 13, 28

Taar, Kázmér (Cazmir; Tarr), 25, 56, 58, 61, 129–130, 199, 206, 216, 220
Taflan, Victor, 56, 224
Takács, Albert, 18
Takács, István (Emil; Ştefan), 57, 197, 210, 215, 217, 223
Takács, Jenő, 28, 180, 181
Talos, Mátyás, 37, 144
Tamás, Károly, 32, 113
Tamási, Lajos (Ludovic), 27, 57, 178, 187, 195, 210, 214, 220, 223
Tanner, Olga, 62, 135, 136
Tapasztó, 35, 91
Tardi, Sándor, 18
Tascan, Florea, 57, 161, 198, 213, 215, 216
Teleki, Pál, 7

Teveli, János (Ioan), 35, 56, 91, 197, 203, 215, 217
Toperczel, Miklós (Toperczer; N. Dr.), 35, 56, 91, 197, 204, 215, 217, 223
Tóth, János (Ioan), 56, 197, 203, 215, 217
Tóth, József, 35, 91
Tóth, Lajos (Ludovic, Dr.), 40, 41, 57, 157, 158, 160, 197–180, 213, 215, 216, 223
Tóth, Mátyás (Matei, Dr.), 39, 57, 155, 195, 209, 214, 220, 223
Trainin, A., 67
Turi, Kálmán, 97

Udvari, József (Iosif, Dr.), 29, 57, 162, 163, 166, 195, 211, 214, 220, 223
Ujvári, Irén (Irina), 56, 130–131, 199, 207, 216, 221, 223
Urbán, László (Ladislau, Francisc, Dr.), 25, 56, 123, 126, 127, 197, 205, 215, 216, 223

Vadász, József (Iosif), 56, 58, 60, 97–99, 199, 204, 216, 221, 223–224
Vaida, Felician, 58
Vajai, Imre (Emeric), 32, 57, 119, 211, 215, 217
Vajai, Sándor (Alexandru; Vajay), 32, 57, 113, 210, 221
Vajda, István, 34
Valkó, Erzsébet, 99, 100
Vancea, Ioan, 56, 58, 61, 110–112, 197, 200, 205, 215, 218
Vancea, József, 144
Váradi, 35
Varga, György (Gheorghe), 57, 161, 198, 213, 215, 216
Varga, Lajos (Ludovic, Dr.), 56, 196, 206, 214, 217, 223
Várhelyi, Tibor, 18, 20, 32, 113, 115
Vásárhelyi, János, 24
Vásárhelyi, László (Ladislau, Dr.), 23, 56, 123, 124–126, 195, 205, 214, 220, 222
Vékas, Jenő, 28
Veres, Lajos, 23
Veress, Jenő (Eugen, dr.), 27, 28, 57, 178, 180, 181, 182, 195, 209, 214, 217, 223
Vida, János (Ioan), 30, 57, 58, 60, 164, 168, 172, 199, 212, 216, 221
Vidor, Zsigmond, 194
Vincze, István (Ştefan, Dr.), 40, 57, 156, 197, 200, 209, 215, 218
Vinkler, Lajos, 31
Virányi, András (Andrei), 40, 57, 156, 195, 209, 214, 220, 223
Vogel, Ignátz, 41

Weinberger, Manó, 29, 181–182
Weinberger, Margit, 101
Weinberger, Mózes, 26
Weinberger, Pál, 165, 172
Weinberger, Samu, 29
Weisz, Manó, 90

Weisz, Miklós, 111
Weisz, Sándor, 27
Wennholz, 34
Werner, László, 158
Werth, Henrik, 7, 43
Wilhelm, Velemin, 115
Wisliceny, Dieter, 26

Xantorpol, Constantin, 59

Zalantai, János (Ioan, Col.), 37, 56, 145, 197, 207, 215, 216, 223
Zathúreczky, Gyula, 13
Zeffer, Rozália see Kiss, Mrs. János
Zolya, József, 183
Zsigmond, János (Ioan, Dr.), 38, 57, 150, 199, 208, 216, 221

Geographic and Subject Index

Aknasugatag, 41, 51, 160
Alien Jews, drive against, 14–15
Alőr, 47, 51
Alsóbán, 173
Alsó-Ilosva, 47
Alsóróna, 42
Alsóvalkó: see Valkó
Alsóvisó, 11, 42
Anti-Jewish measures, 12–16, 69, 105–106, 159–160, 176–177
Anti-Semitism, 65–66
Apa, 31
Apanagyfalu, 47
Aranyosmeggyes, 11, 31
Aranyszentmiklós, 27
Aszupatak, 131–133
Attitudes toward Jews
  Christians, 23–24, 32
  Church leaders, 24
  Romanians, 24
  U.S., 67–68
Auschwitz, 140–141, 191
Avasfelsőfalu, 31
Avaslekence, 31
Avasujváros, 31
Awareness of the Final Solution, 23

Bánffyhunyad, 11, 25, 51, 137–138
Barcánfalva, 11, 41
Bárdfalva, 11, 41, 51
Baross Association, 32, 116
Batiz, 31
Beltek, 31
Beregszász, 23
Bergenye, 50
Bessarabia, 6, 7, 8
Beszterce, 11, 21, 22, 33, 51, 187–190, 191
Beszterce-Naszód County, 8, 11, 13, 18, 33, 188
Bethlen, 11, 28, 47, 51
Bihar County, 11, 12, 18, 33, 34, 35, 79, 84
Biharnagybajom, 51
Biharpüspöki, 49

Bikszád, 31
Böd, 27
Bor, 15
Borpatak, 32, 113
Borsa, 11, 42, 51, 194
Botiza, 42
Bözödujfalu, 37
Brickyards, ghettos in, 25, 30, 37, 38, 39, 143–144, 151, 164
Bukovina, Northern, 6, 7, 8
Buza, 27

Carpatho-Ruthenia, 7, 17, 35, 40
Confiscations and expropriations, 20, 22, 26, 27, 35, 38, 41, 81, 82, 87–90, 158, 185
Congress of 1868–69, 5
Coptelke, 27
Csárda, 51
Csicsó-Györgyfalva, 29, 186–187
Csík County, 8, 11, 13, 18, 36, 39, 40, 141, 152, 156
Csíkszereda, 11, 40, 156–157

Demography and statistics, 10–12
Dengeleg, 27
Denunciations, 32, 97–99, 109–112, 130–137, 161
Deportation
  Planning, 17–18
  Transports, 27, 29, 30, 32–33, 36, 38
Derzse, 27
Derecske, 51
Dés, 11, 20, 21, 22, 27–29, 51, 178–187, 191, 196
Desenfalva, 41
Devecser, 27
Diószeg, 49
Domokos, 47
Drágomérfalva, 11, 41, 160

Eichmann-*Sonderkommando*, 16, 17, 36
Élesd, 34, 49, 84
Ellenzék, 13

The geographic names of the communities in Northern Transylvania are rendered in their Hungarian version. For their Romanian equivalents, see Appendix 1.

GEOGRAPHIC AND SUBJECT INDEX

Erdélyi Helikon, 13
Erdőd, 31
Erdőszentgyörgy, 11, 50
Érmihályfalva, 11, 34, 51, 84, 100

Farkasrev, 41
Feketelak, 27
Felőr, 47
Felsőbánya, 20
Felsőróna, 42
Felsőszék, 173
Felsővisó, 11, 41, 42, 51, 160
Felvidék, 7
Fugyivásárhely, 49

Galgó, 47
Gendarmerie, role of, 17–18, 28, 30, 39, 43, 73, 86, 126–127, 148
Ghettoization
  Announcements, text of, 22, 73–74, 101
  Conferences, 18, 20, 71, 72
  Decree, 16, 70, 71
  Drive, 17, 20–23, 28, 30, 31, 33–34, 38, 70–71, 80, 163–164, 190–192
  Role of the SS, 25, 32, 36, 38, 40
German occupation, 16–18
Glód, 42
Goga-Cuza era, 6
Gyergyói Lapok, 13
Gyergyószentmiklós, 11, 13, 39, 155
Gyergyótölgyes, 11
Gyulafalva, 41
Gyulafehérvár, 3, 4

Halmi, 51
Háromszék County, 8, 11, 13, 18, 36, 39, 141, 156
Havasmező, 42, 51
Hidalmás, 11, 51
Hiding, 36
Hitel, 13
Hosszumező, 42
Hungarian army *(Honvéd),* involvement of, 37
Hungarian Party *(Magyar Párt),* 6
Huta, 31
Hygiene and health problems, 82, 164–165

Iklód, 27, 51
Indictment, summary of, 56–59
Informers, 148–150. *See also* Denunciations
Iron Guard *(Garda de Fier),* 6
Ispánmező, 47
Izakonyha, 42
Izaszacsal, 42

Jewish Councils, 16, 26, 27, 29, 31, 34, 37, 41
Jewish Party *(Partidul Evreesc),* 6
Jews in Transylvania, history of, 3–5
Jod, 11, 42
Judenrat: see Jewish Council

Kacs, 31
Kaczkó, 47
Kamenets-Podolsk, 15
Kápolnokmonostor, 20, 32, 113
Karácsonyfalva, 42
Kassa, 24
Kasztner transport, 26–27
Katolikus Status, 13
Kecsed, 27
Kékes, 27
Kenyérmező, 23
KEOKH, 14, 15
Kérő, 27
Kiskalota, 51
Kissármás, 51
Kolozs County, 8, 11, 12, 18, 25, 137
Kolozsvár, 4, 10, 11, 12, 14, 18, 21, 22, 23, 24–27, 43, 51, 123–141, 191
Kosály, 47
Kracsfalva, 41
Kraszna, 30, 51, 176, 177, 178

Labor service, 15–16
Leordina, 42
Lozsárd, 27

Magyarlápos, 11, 28, 47, 51
Magyarnemecse, 11
Majszin, 11, 42
Mányik, 27
Máramaros County, 11, 14, 40, 42, 51, 157, 160
Máramarossziget, 10, 11, 21, 23, 40–42, 51, 157–162, 191
Margitta, 11, 34, 51, 84, 99, 100
Maros-Torda County, 8, 11, 18, 36–39, 141, 143, 150, 152
Marosvásárhely, 10, 11, 12, 13, 18, 21, 22, 36, 37–38, 51, 141, 143–150, 196
Massacres
  Kamenets-Podolsk, 15
  Újvidék, 65
  USSR, 66–67
Matéfalva, 27
Mezőbánd, 50
Mezőtelegd, 49, 51
Midwives, role in searches, 99–101, 154, 185–186
Mikeháza, 47
Mócs, 51
Moldavia, 6
Munkács, 23, 40, 43, 190

Nagybánya, 11, 15, 18, 20, 21, 32–33, 51, 101, 113–123
Nagybárod, 49
Nagybocskó, 42
Nagyilonda, 28, 47, 51
Nagykároly, 10, 11, 31, 51, 101, 112–113
Nagysármás, 51
Nagysomkut, 11, 20, 32, 51, 113
Nagyszalonta, 11, 49, 51, 84

Nagyvárad, 10, 11, 12, 14, 20, 21, 22, 23, 33–36, 51, 60, 79–101, 126, 192–193
Nánfalva, 41
Naszód, 11, 51, 188
Naszóly, 27
Náznánfalva, 51
Numerus Clausus law, 13–14
Nyárádszereda, 50

Ökörmező, 42
Óradna, 11
Ördöngösfüzes, 27

Petrova, 11, 42
Parajd, 50
Pásztortüz, 13
People's tribunal
  Composition of, 55–56
  Establishment of, ix
People's Tribunal of Budapest, findings of, 69, 72
Political activism, 6
Public officials, responsibility of, 76–79
Pujon, 27

Remetefalva, 42
Retteg, 28, 47, 51, 185–186
Righteous gentiles, 15
Rónaszék, 42
Rozália, 11, 42
Ruszkova, 42

Sabbatarians, 37
Sajófalva, 42
Sarkod, 31
Sárközujlak, 11
Second Vienna Award, 7–10
Segesvár, 140
Sepsiszentgyörgy, 11, 13, 21, 36, 39–40, 51, 141, 155–157
Siebenbürgische Deutsche Zeitung, 13
Socioeconomic structure, 6
Somkerék, 47
Somlyócsehi, 30, 164–165
Survivors, statements of, 87–90, 102–104, 107, 108, 114, 115, 119–121, 123–125, 127–131, 138, 146, 148, 151–154, 168–171, 179–182, 184–186
Szalárd, 49
Szalonta: *see* Nagyszalonta
Szamos County: *see* Szolnok-Doboka County
Szamoskend, 27
Szamoskrassó, 31
Szamosujvár, 11, 20, 21, 27, 28, 51, 187
Szamosvölgye, 13
Szaplonca, 11, 42, 51
Szászrégen, 11, 21, 22, 36, 38–39, 51, 141, 150–155, 193
Szatmár County, 11, 12, 18, 31, 32
Szatmárhegy, 31
Szatmárnémeti, 10, 11, 12, 20, 21, 22, 31–32, 51, 101–112

Szék, 27
Székely Border Guard *(Székely Határőr)*, 37
Székely Land, 12, 36–37, 141–142, 191
Székely Nép, 13
Székely Szó, 13
Székelyhid, 11, 34, 49, 84
Székelykeresztur, 50
Székelyudvarhely, 11, 37, 38, 50
Szelistye, 11, 42
Szentgothárd, 27
Szentmárton, 27
Szerbfalva, 41
Szilágy County, 8, 11, 13, 18, 29, 30, 162, 163, 167
Szilágycseh, 11, 51, 167
Szilágynagyfalu, 172
Szilágysomlyó, 11, 20, 21, 29–30, 51, 162–178, 191, 194
Szinérváralja, 11, 31
Szlatina, 42
Szöcs, 47
Szolnok-Doboka County, 8, 11, 13, 18, 27, 47, 178, 185
Szőnyü, 121
Szováta, 50
Szurdok, 41

Tasnád, 11, 30
Terep, 31
Tiszakarácsonyfalva, 11
Tortures, 26, 31, 32, 34, 35, 38, 75, 81, 87–90, 103, 104, 114, 116, 119–121, 123–125, 127–131, 148, 153, 165. *See also* Survivors, statements of.
Transylvanian Jewish National League *(Erdélyi Zsidó Nemzeti Szövetség)*, 6

Udvarhely County, 11, 13, 18, 36, 37, 38, 141, 143
Új Kelet, 12
Ukraine, 15
Ungvár, 23
United Nations, declarations of, 68
Upper Province: *see* Felvidék

Valkó, 173
Vámfalu, 31
Váncsfalva, 41
Veresegyháza, 27
Visóoroszi, 11

Wallachia, 6
War Criminals
  Defense position of, 59–65
  Dismissal of charges against, 192–195
  Sentencing of, ix–x, 195–224

Yellow badge, 16, 77

Zilah, 11, 29, 30, 163–164, 166, 176, 177
Zionism, 6
Zsibó, 30